French: A Linguistic Introduction

French is used on every continent, spoken not only in France but also in Belgium, Switzerland, North America, the Caribbean, Polynesia and Africa. This is a comprehensive and accessible guide to the structure of French, suitable for those with little prior knowledge of linguistics or of the French language. It clearly introduces the language's history, phonetics (pronunciation), phonology (sound system), morpho-syntax (how words and sentences are formed), pragmatics (how speakers express meaning), and lexicology (the study of word composition and derivation) – with each chapter showing how these aspects are subject to regional and social variation. English translations are provided for all examples, and the book contains an extensive bilingual glossary of linguistic terms, and numerous exercises and essay questions in every chapter. *French: A Linguistic Introduction* will be welcomed by advanced language learners, and by linguists studying the structure of this important language.

ZSUZSANNA FAGYAL is Assistant Professor of French Linguistics at the University of Illinois, Urbana-Champaign, specializing in phonetics, phonology, and the sociolinguistics of contemporary Parisian French. She is the author of numerous conference papers and journal articles on sound change and variation in contemporary spoken French.

DOUGLAS KIBBEE is Professor of French Linguistics at the University of Illinois, Urbana-Champaign, whose research and teaching focuses on the history of French language, language and the law, and the history of linguistic theories. He is the author of four monographs and edited volumes on sixteenth-century studies of French grammar, language legislation, and most recently a translation of folk tales from Côte d'Ivoire.

FRED JENKINS is Associate Professor Emeritus of French Linguistics at the University of Illinois, Urbana-Champaign, and for eighteen years was Executive Director of the American Association of Teachers of French. His research has dealt with many different areas of contemporary French, and since his retirement he has remained actively involved in working with his colleagues in French and linguistics.

Linguistic Introductions available from Cambridge University Press

YARON MATRAS *Romani: A Linguistic Introduction*
NEIL G. JACOBS *Yiddish: A Linguistic Introduction*
MILTON AZEVEDO *Portuguese: A Linguistic Introduction*
ANTONIO LOPRIENO *Ancient Egyptian: A Linguistic Introduction*
CHAO FEN SUN *Chinese: A Linguistic Introduction*
PAUL CUBBERLEY *Russian: A Linguistic Introduction*
JOSE IGNACIO HUALDE, ANTXON OLARREA, ANNA MARÍA
  ESCOBAR *Introducción a la lingüística hispánica*
ZSUZSANNA FAGYAL, DOUGLAS KIBBEE AND FRED JENKINS
  French: A Linguistic Introduction

French

A Linguistic Introduction

Zsuzsanna Fagyal
Douglas Kibbee
Fred Jenkins

CAMBRIDGE
UNIVERSITY PRESS

CAMBRIDGE UNIVERSITY PRESS
Cambridge, New York, Melbourne, Madrid, Cape Town, Singapore, São Paulo

Cambridge University Press
The Edinburgh Building, Cambridge CB2 2RU, UK

Published in the United States of America by Cambridge University Press, New York

www.cambridge.org
Information on this title: www.cambridge.org/9780521528962

First published 2006

Printed in the United Kingdom at the University Press, Cambridge

A catalogue record for this publication is available from the British Library

Library of Congress Cataloguing in Publication data
Fagyal, Zsuzsanna, 1966–
French: a linguistic introduction / Zsuzsanna Fagyal, Douglas Kibbee, Fred Jenkins.
     p.   cm.
Includes bibliographical references and index.
ISBN-13: 978-0-521-82144-5 (hardback)
ISBN-10: 0-521-82144-4 (hardback)
ISBN-13: 978-0-521-52896-2 (pbk.)
ISBN-10: 0-521-52896-8 (pbk.)
1. French language.   2. Linguistics.   I. Kibbee, Douglas, 1949–
II. Jenkins, Fred, 1930–   III. Title.

PC2073.F34   2006
440 – dc22   2006013836

ISBN-13 978-0-521-82144-5 hardback
ISBN-10 0-521-82144-4 hardback

ISBN-13 978-0-521-52896-2 paperback
ISBN-10 0-521-52896-8 paperback

Contents

Contents

Figures

Tables

Preface

This book makes the perhaps audacious presumption that it is possible to write an accessible, and yet state-of-the art, introduction to the structure of French for a motivated public of non-specialists.

As instructors in the French linguistics program of the University of Illinois at Urbana-Champaign, we have long been confronted with the need for teaching graduate students of French and linguistics a highly technical literature about the structure of French, and simultaneously having to make ourselves understood by undergraduate students who, although having a sound knowledge of French, are not specializing in linguistics. Thus, upon an inquiry from Kate Brett from Cambridge University Press about writing such a book, we set out to combine our lectures notes, newspaper clippings, various technical and non-technical readings, and writing into a single book to be used to teach basic concepts of linguistic analysis through a panoramic tour of the defining characteristics of the French language.

As one of the volumes published in the *Linguistic Introduction* series of Cambridge University Press, this book provides a linguistic, i.e. relatively technical, overview of several fields of French linguistics. Its novelty resides in its pluralistic approach to French and its presentation of domains of linguistic analyses, e.g. pragmatics, that are rarely, if ever, discussed in similar works.

Chapter 1, *Defining the object of study*, lays out the concept of language and linguistics which we advocate and teach in our classes, namely that French is plural and multiform. Therefore a presentation of its structural characteristics must encompass a wide variety of features, ranging from highly standardized written forms to peculiarities of spoken regional and social dialects. Thus, we chose not to have a separate chapter dedicated to sociolinguistics. We examine the structure of French by definition 'from within' its social, geographic, and individual variation, discussing the degree of variability of each aspect of the language virtually everywhere in the following five chapters of the book.

Chapter 2 provides an overview of the sounds of French from both a physical and a structural point of view, which explains the double heading *Phonetics and phonology*. Chapter 3, *Topics in morphology and syntax*, aims to accomplish a similar goal with respect to word formation and sentence structure: building on insights and issues in inflectional morphology it analyzes the ways and means in which the word-size 'building blocks' of language can be assembled in various syntactic structures.

Chapter 4, *Lexicology and derivational morphology*, combines analyses in derivational morphology, including word games such as *verlan*, along with presentations of contact-induced borrowings, and state intervention in vocabulary. Chapter 5, *Pragmatics*, examines how speakers and listeners 'make meaning' with words and utterances in context in French, by introducing concepts such as reference, implicature, and politeness. Chapter 6, *Historical perspectives*, intentionally put at the end of the volume, is destined to provide the preceding analyses with a historical context. It shows continuity and rupture between well-known characteristics of the language, while also revealing new aspects of its history, such as proper name formation and use.

We could never have written this book without the unfailing support and patience of Kate Brett, Helen Barton, Alison Powell, Adrian Stenton and Caroline Murray at Cambridge University Press, and the help with proofreading and comments from our colleagues Peter Golato (UIUC), Noël Nguyen (Université de Provence, Aix-en-Provence), Elisabeth Delais-Roussarie (Université de Paris VII, Aix-en-Provence), and our current graduate student, Elizabeth Blount. We also thank our former graduate students Samira Hassa (Rockford College, IL), Viviane Ruellot (Western Michigan University), and Frédérique Grimm (Colorado State University) and our colleague Jeffrey Chamberlain (George Mason University) for having tested the usefulness of manuscript versions of this book in their undergraduate and graduate teaching. But most of all, we would like to thank our undergraduate students who agreed to learn from earlier versions of these pages, told us to translate all French examples and quotes to English, to pick examples 'from real life', and overall to show French as it works in all its forms and manifestations around the world. We can only hope that these 'long lecture notes', as technical as they still might appear to them, will ease them into the fascinating world of French linguistic variation and change as we have learned to see and appreciate it.

Note to the reader

Throughout the book we have used *italics* to show example words and phrases. Glosses or translation equivalents are shown in 'single quotes'. Technical terms which appears in the Glossary are shown in **bold**. "Double quotes" are used for direct quotations from sources.

Zsuzsanna Fagyal-Le Mentec
Douglas Kibbee
Fred Jenkins

French Department
University of Illinois at Urbana-Champaign
Les Etats-Unis d'Amérique

1 Defining the object of study

1.1 French is plural

What 'French' means seems intuitive: French is the language that French people learn in their childhood and that non-French people can acquire from them when learning French as a second language. A more specific definition going beyond this practical description and suitable for the purposes of this introduction to the structural properties of 'French', however, ends up either too restrictive or outright circular.

If, for instance, we stick to a geographic approach to 'the French language' by saying that it is the language spoken in France, we obviously leave out places like Belgium, Canada, Louisiana, and Switzerland, all of which have substantial French-speaking populations, as well as many other languages spoken within French borders. A definition based on speakers' social characteristics would not score any better. The educated elite in Montreal speak a different type of French than do educated people in Paris, and the same is presumably true for farmers in France, Nova Scotia, Switzerland, and other francophone countries and regions in the world. If one would try to pin down what unites varieties of French by simultaneously looking into social and dialectal differences, then the French spoken by diplomats at the United Nations and by a sizeable population of countries in Sub-Saharan Africa would fall out of our categories as well, since these varieties neither represent a single dialect, nor a single social group or **community of practice**. Choosing one spoken **genre** or **contextual style** over another as the defining structural criterion for 'the French language' would again be too restrictive: any advanced speaker of French as a foreign language would agree that the French read in grammar books or heard on the evening news is not necessarily the type of French encountered in other contexts in or outside the metropolitan area. Thus our intuitions tell us that dialect, social group, and situational context all play a role in what variety of French we speak and hear, but that enlarging the scope of the definition to include all these sources would also lead to a dead end: saying that irrespective of geographic, social, and contextual differences, French is the language spoken, written, and understood by speakers who speak French would amount to stating the obvious: French is the language of those who speak French!

Another solution, in fact the most widely adopted, is to call 'French' every variety of the language that native speakers would perceive and accept as 'French'. While this seems sufficiently open-ended to encompass a wide range of spoken and written varieties, we must bear in mind that it reflects an external point of view. It reflects the point of view of teachers, politicians, social workers, researchers in linguistics, and many other observers of linguistic practices, and as such it can differ from what people living the same linguistic reality 'on the ground' would call their own language. What we, external observers, would qualify as 'Belgian' or 'southern' French can be commonly perceived as *liégeois* or *marseillais* by speakers who speak that local variety, even if the speakers would otherwise also agree to classify their own speech as a 'dialect' or 'variety' of French (see also section 1.4.1). Such discrepancies between global and local, external and internal perceptions, and labels of different 'tongues' are far from being in agreement, and therefore far from making it possible to come up with a single definition of the object of study that this book sets out to explore.

'French' in this book will be used as a shorthand to a complex linguistic reality 'on the ground', even though we adopt an external point of view when describing the many aspects of its structure. We will attempt to provide the reader with a glimpse into the rich world of dialectal, social, and situational variation in French together, and often in contrast, with the 'standard'.

The linguistic standard called *français standard* or *français de référence* 'standard French' has been in the making since the Middle Ages. It was codified in the sixteenth and seventeenth centuries, and encouraged by the centralized nation-state at least since the founding of the Académie Française in 1635. But many other varieties of French have continued to flourish. We will consider these varieties as an organic part of 'French', knowing that it is only through the understanding of all their structural features and forms, variable or not, that one can comprehend what French means to all its speakers around the world.

We will be focusing on native, i.e. not French as a second language, varieties and, as a guiding thread, northern varieties of French spoken in France (henceforth, Metropolitan French). These geographical varieties or **dialects** can be historically tied to northern 'Gallo-Romance' (see Chapter 6) and have been undergoing constant change since the Middle Ages. One particular northern Gallo-Romance variety, itself a blend or **koiné** of many local varieties (see Lodge 2004), has spread through annexation, conquest, and colonization first to other parts of France, and then to many regions around the world. Thus what we, from an external point of view, will be calling 'French' is a foreign language for millions of language learners around the world, and a **heritage language** for many descendants of former colonists or emigrants who now learn French as a foreign or second language, e.g. in Louisiana or the predominantly anglophone areas of Canada. The standardized and codified variety referred to as 'standard French' has become the official language in former French colonies around the world, such as the West African countries of Senegal, Mali, and Côte d'Ivoire. Some varieties of French originated through colonization and immigration, especially in the New World, and then blended with other local and immigrant languages to give rise to entirely new and sometimes subsequently standardized language forms, as in the case of Haitian **Creole**, now the official language of Haiti. Varieties that did not achieve the status of a 'standard' nonetheless continue to show strong affiliation with French, their **lexifier language**: many of the structural properties of **French-based Creoles** (see section 1.3) are attested in other varieties of French, underscoring the assumption that despite prolonged contact with languages from Africa, creoles can be considered "legitimate offsprings of their lexifiers" (see Mufwene 2001:85).

Just like English words that refer to objects and persons that are inherently 'more than one' and that are not grammatically marked for plural (e.g. *luggage, family*), French is an essentially plural concept expressed in singular form. It is simultaneously a historical, geographic, and social construct that, in addition, shows situational-stylistic and individual variation. The problem, of course, is what to say about 'the' structure of French in light of this rich array of variation. What is common to all these varieties? What unites all these ways of speaking and writing? In trying to answer this question, we will first propose labeling these different, more or less easily distinguishable, types or varieties of French. Such a method is well known from studies of the history of French. What historians call northern Gallo-Romance was formed from Latin through countless small steps and changes over centuries, and yet historians refer to the chronological order of the formation of this group of varieties in terms of discrete periods, such as 'Old', 'Middle', and 'Modern' French (see Chapter 6). Throughout this book, we will apply a similar 'labeling technique' to geographic and social variation in the language. As we proceed, we will note that geographic diversity gave rise to many labels, such as northern and southern Metropolitan French, Canadian, Québécois, Cajun, Belgian, and Swiss French, all of which are commonly used in discussions and treatises about French. The French used in various social-stylistic settings will be called *français standard* 'standard French', *français familier* 'casual French', *français populaire* (working-class French), and *français vulgaire* ('vulgar French') depending on stylistic and social characteristics of the uses of the language in real-life situations. Although no more than convenient shorthand to a complex linguistic reality, these labels will be helpful in focusing on certain aspects of language use, e.g. **register**, genre, social group, etc.

1) Explain the analogy between the English words *luggage* and *information* and the pluralistic definition of 'French' advocated above.
2) Give a definition of the terms *community of practice*, *koiné*, and *lexifier language*.

1.2   Prescriptivism and the idea of 'standard' French

The pluralistic conception of French in this book contrasts sharply with a more monolithic view – often depicted in essays and treatises on French – which posits the 'standard' language as the only publicly acceptable language variety. According to this 'ideology of the standard', as linguists propose to call it (see Milroy & Milroy 1985), standard French is the indivisible *trésor* 'treasury' or *patrimoine* 'heritage' of the French nation that should be preserved by all the people. While the cohesive force of a common language is not to be doubted, we will see that the above concept of standard French presupposes an imaginary, ethnically, and socially homogeneous group of speakers. National identity in France is so closely tied to this concept of French viewed as a mutually shared and 'cherished' standard language that one can probably go so far as to declare with Posner (1997:48) that being French is "not a question of genetics but of cultural allegiance". In simple terms, cultural allegiance means that as long as people abide by their obligation to use standard French, they are considered 'good citizens' of the country (see below). The roots of such a view reach far back in the history of the country, and leads us to the discussion of linguistic **prescriptivism**.

Prescriptivism can be broadly defined as an authoritative way of expressing views about the language. One expression of linguistic prescriptivism has always been mockery: from at least the twelfth century, speakers and writers felt that they would be the object of ridicule if they strayed from the language of Ile-de-France, the region around Paris, home to the ruling social elite surrounding the French king. By the end of the thirteenth century the long arm of royal power, centered in Paris, extended the use of the king's dialect to other parts of the country. The Hundred Years War (1337–1453) encouraged the development of a sense of nation, of 'us' (the French) against 'them' (the English); with that came a sense of Frenchness which extended beyond the local manors and provinces in the king's possession. At the same time, the law, especially in northern France, was essentially a local law, expressed through an oral tradition called *coutumes* 'customs'. In the fifteenth century the kings made several changes to the legal system that increased the sense of a central power, and with that the sense of a commonly shared language. First, new parliaments (law courts) were established throughout the southern half of the country. Following their establishment, oral legal codes were to be written down and approved by the Parliament of Paris. This process took more than a century to spread throughout France. As a third step, starting cautiously but increasing in scope and authority, a series of royal *ordonnances* 'royal decrees' required that French be the language of the courts. This process culminated in the Ordonnances de Villers-Cotterêts (1539), which decreed that all legal activity in the country be conducted in *"langage maternel françois"* 'the maternal French language', an ambiguous phrase interpreted by the courts in an unambiguous manner: the king's French. Although French law was not entirely unified until the French Revolution, the principle of a central legal authority, expressed in a single language, the language of the legal community in Paris, was set. This had lasting implications for the formation of a 'standard' form of written and oral expression in what later became the modern French nation-state.

It was, nonetheless, hard to talk about a 'standard' language in times when there existed no grammars, i.e. books laying out rules defining what language variety should be shared by all speakers. In the later Middle Ages some grammatical descriptions of French were written in England, but the first French grammar appeared only in 1531. It was written by Jacques Dubois, a medical doctor from Picardy. The next grammar was written by Louis Meigret (1550), a lawyer from Lyon. The provincial origins of these authors were transparent in the linguistic forms (sounds, words, and expressions) that they prescribed, so their books were not accepted as defining a standard for all, especially not for the Parisian elite. It was not until the seventeenth century that linguistic forms considered as 'standard' received a meticulous description, for instance in dictionaries written by Nicot (1530–1600), Richelet (1631–1698), and Furetière (1619–1688), as well as the dictionary of the Académie Française, published in 1694. Grammars by Maupas (1600–1625), Oudin (1595–1653), Irson (1650–1700), and Régnier-Desmarais (1632–1713) represent the same intent to provide a thorough documentation of the standard. Commentaries on the French language by Malherbe (1555–1628), Vaugelas (1585–1650), and others, sometimes in agreement with the grammarians, sometimes not, completed this work. Written documentation of a shared linguistic standard had the advantage of facilitating communication in a linguistically diverse country. But the work of some authors spreading the newly forming standard quickly went beyond concerns of mutual intelligibility. Many of them, especially commentators (*remarqueurs)* like Vaugelas, advocated what some linguists call a 'supernorm' (Garmadi 1981:65), i.e. linguistic forms selected because they matched "the esthetic or socio-cultural ideals of social groups holding prestige and power in society". Thus besides its indispensible communicative functions, 'standard French' is also a social phenomenon reflecting the most 'valued' ways of speaking and writing the language. Thus there was nothing inherently better or 'more correct' in the way of pronouncing certain words in Gallo-Romance varieties of Metropolian French rather than as advocated by the sixteenth-century grammarians Dubois or Meigret. What made the 'linguistic ways and means' of these grammarians less desirable for many is that they did not reflect the use of the language by those groups of the social elite that were posited as models to emulate for all other social groups of French society.

As the linguistic norm, roughly the king's and the royal court's French, was not yet the focal point of education, the production of grammars, dictionaries, and commentaries initially had limited impact. The goal of the educational system, controlled by the Church until the late eighteenth century, was not to propagate the ways in which the urban social elite was speaking and writing in Paris, but to teach students the Latin that made religious texts accessible to them. At the end of the seventeenth and through the eighteenth century, numerous reformers of the educational system proposed that the study of French, together with the disciplines of modern science, be given a more prominent place in the curriculum. Major change in education would not occur until the Revolution, when the newly formed Committee on Public Instruction stated that mastery of the national language would be the most important goal of education, and launched a contest to select the one elementary grammar book to be used in every school. The norms of French were consequently enforced through national examinations such as the *baccalauréat* and the *aggrégation*, both established in 1808, and through the fittingly named *écoles normales* 'normal schools' (teacher training colleges). In these schools, teachers learned to speak and teach the officially-supported standard variety of French. This centralized, universal teacher education was enforced through school inspection: regular visits to schools by civil servants whose role was to ensure that the goals of the national elementary education system were being met.

It was, however, not until elementary education became free, mandatory, and delivered by the French nation-state in the 1880s that the linguistic variety set as 'the standard' was to reach almost every young person in the country. Bilingualism and **diglossia**, that is, equal or asymmetric competence in at least two languages, was therefore common until that point. Students spoke one language, often referred to as *patois*, a derogatory label for local dialect, and did their best to speak the 'national standard' at school. The penalties for not using standard French at school were often severe, ranging from physical punishment to mockery and public humiliation. Occasionally, literary texts preserve the memory of such painful encounters with the standard. The first day in school of the main character, Philomène, born in a mountainous region in south-west France in the novel *Les cailloux bleus* of Christian Signol (1984) is depicted in the following excerpt:

Elle s'approcha du poêle de fonte situé au fond de la classe, entre deux meubles aux étagères chargées de livres, en ouvrit la porte, glissa les bûches dans le four après avoir attisé les braises.
– *"Quo rounflo" – dit-elle en revenant s'asseoir.*
  La mère [religieuse] se retourna brusquement et son visage prit un air sévère.
– *Ici, Philomène, il est interdit de parler patois. On apprend et on parle le français qui est la langue de notre pays. Tu comprends?*
– *Oui, murmura Philomène, tandis que les larmes lui montaient aux yeux à l'idée d'apprendre une langue qu'elle parlait à peine.*

'She went up to the cast iron stove which stood at the back of the classroom between two heavy bookcases stuffed with books. She opened the door, and slipped the logs on the fire after reviving the dying embers.
– "Quo rounflo" – she said as she returned to her seat.
  The nun turned sharply and glowered.
– "Here, Philomène, speaking *patois* is forbidden. One learns and one speaks French, the language of our country. Do you understand?"
– "Yes", murmured Philomène, as her eyes filled with tears at the thought of learning a language that she hardly understood.' [All translations by the authors of this book.]

Prescriptive attitudes and educational methods were exported and other varieties of French (e.g. Canadian, Cajun) and French-based Creoles were likewise scorned.

But in spite of all the efforts to eradicate regional variation over the course of several centuries, French has remained plural. This is especially true if variation in French is considered globally. Although some studies suggest that most northern dialects of Metropolitan French are losing their local dialectal characteristics and switching, or as linguists say "leveling in the direction of the standard" (see Armstrong 2001), there is still ample evidence of geographic and social variation. In fact the leveling of different language varieties does not necessarily preclude variation; on the contrary, it can also be fueled by linguistic variation. Out of a large pool of variable features in French new standards are forming, as a region like Quebec has already created its own local norms, and the issue of a *norme pluricentrique* 'multi-centric norm' of French has come up in countries such as Belgium and Switzerland (Pöll 2001, Singy 1996).

---

1) List the major historical events in the formation of a linguistic standard in French, and elaborate on the communicative and social functions of 'standard French'.
2) Why are grammar books written and what are they used for? What happens to languages for which we do not have grammar books? Do you know of any such cases?
3) Give a definition of the terms *prescriptivism*, *diglossia*, *patois*.

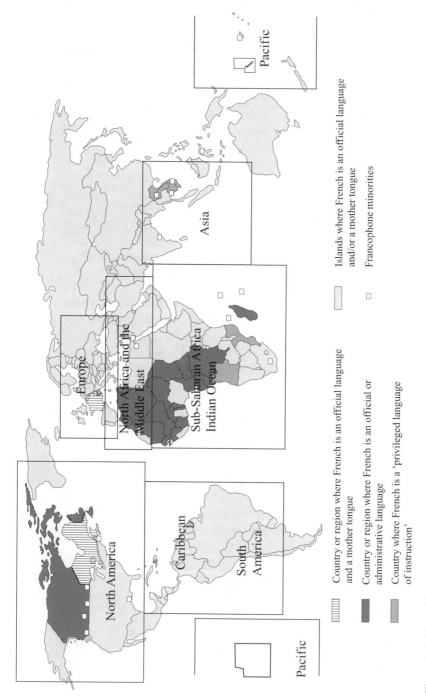

Figure 1.1 Map of francophone countries

Country or region where French is an official language and a mother tongue

Country or region where French is an official or administrative language

Country where French is a 'privileged language of instruction'

Islands where French is an official language and/or a mother tongue

Francophone minorities

North America

Caribbean

South America

Pacific

Europe

North Africa and the Middle East

Sub-Saharan Africa Indian Ocean

Asia

Pacific

1.3   Francophonie

The idea of multiple standards brings us to the topic of French around the world.
The French language has spread beyond France and Europe through conquests
and colonization; it is today an international **vehicular language** or *lingua
franca*.

French is spoken natively by an estimated 80 million people in the world. It
is ranked eleventh among the most widely spoken languages according to the
Summer Institute of Linguistics *Ethnologue* Survey (Grimes 1996). The number of French-speaking people is closer to 169 million, if so-called secondary
speakers, or people who are not born as native speakers but use French as their
regular or primary means of communication, are also counted. As opposed to
natively spoken languages like Mandarin Chinese that are concentrated in a single geographical location, French as an official native language is spoken on five
different continents: Europe (44% of French speakers), the Americas (7.6%),
Africa (46.3%), Asia (1.8%), and Oceania (0.3%). The largest number of native
francophone speakers, about 71 million, lives in Europe, and most of them are
in France. Approximately 45% of Belgians and 20% of the Swiss are also native
speakers of French. In the Americas, the largest francophone community is in
Quebec, Canada, representing about 5.9 million speakers (Canadian Census
2001). The rest of the francophone communities in the Americas are three of
the DOMs (*Départements d'Outre Mer* 'Overseas Departments'): the islands
of Guadeloupe, Martinique, and French Guyana in the Caribbean. The state of
Louisiana in the United States counted about 200,000 speakers of French in
2000 (US Census), and roughly 23% of the population spoke French on the
island of Haiti in 1997 (estimate of the Agence de la Francophonie).

The largest francophone population in Africa is concentrated in the western
Sub-Saharan regions of the continent, with French as an official or administrative language in more than ten different countries from Mauritania and Senegal
to Gabon and the Congo (see Figure 1.1). In the Indian Ocean, the islands of
Madagascar, Seychelles, and Mauritius stand out as the largest francophone
communities, with about 23% of the local population (18.4 million people).
In North Africa, French has the status of a 'privileged' foreign language, and
several decades after decolonization it remains the dominant language of higher
education for roughly 33 million people. About 57% of the inhabitants of Alge-
ria (French colony 1848–1962), 41% of Moroccans, and 64% of Tunisians
(under French Protectorate 1912–1956 and 1881–1955, respectively) can speak
French. The largest francophone community in the Middle East is in Lebanon
(under French mandate 1920–1941), totalling about 1.5 million speakers. In
Asia, Vietnam and Cambodia have roughly 375,000 francophones.

The worldwide influence of the language today is supported through the
actions of the *Organisation Internationale de la Francophonie*, which was

founded in the 1980s and which aims to unite and coordinate the actions of French-speaking countries around the world. The word *francophonie* was first proposed by the geographer Onésime Reclus (1837–1916), a patriot and fervent advocate of French colonial rule who wished to promote in his writings the more humanistic aspects of colonialism, namely the cultural, linguistic, and demographic ties between France and its colonies. Author of numerous books on French colonial Africa and Asia, in his book *Un grand destin commence* 'The start of a great destiny', published in 1917, Reclus argued for the need to reinforce what he called the "ties of solidarity" between the French colonists and the indigenous populations through the common use of standard French. He saw the spread of the standard language as capable of transcending ethnic and racial lines and making the people belong to a single entity: *la langue fait le peuple* (*lingua gentem facit*) 'language makes the people', he argued. The central role of language in reinforcing historical ties between francophone countries served as a founding principle for the movement of *francophonie* later in the twentieth century. Forty-eight countries and two provinces in Canada are permanent members of the *Organisation Internationale de la Francophonie*, which also includes four associated countries: Albania, Andorra, Greece, and Macedonia. French is at least a minor language spoken in all states, but the major language of only some of its permanent member states. Ten additional countries from Eastern Europe are invited observers at its summits that are held every two years in one of the member states: Armenia, Austria, Croatia, Georgia, Hungary, Lithuania, Poland, the Czech Republic, Slovakia, and Slovenia. The *Organisation Internationale de la Francophonie* promotes and supervises scientific, economical, and international legal cooperation between its permanent and associated member states.

---

1) List at least three countries or regions where French is spoken natively in Europe, Asia, and the Americas.
2) What is *francophonie* and where does the concept come from?
3) What languages, besides French, are used as *lingua francas* in the world today? Is it true that a *lingua franca* should be easy to learn for foreigners? Explain.

1.4   Variation 'omnibus'

1.4.1   Geographical variation

Geographical variation in languages is typically analyzed in terms of **dialects**. A dialect is a variant of a language spoken in a certain, usually large, geographic location. Smaller areas within a given dialect have sub-dialects, sharing some common characteristics but also differing in specific ways from other surrounding language varieties. The most common illustrations of dialectal and sub-dialectal differences in a given language are provided by atlases. The well-known *Atlas linguistique de la France* by Gilliéron and Edmont (1902–1920), for instance, records variations within the lexicon and the pronunciation of people who lived in francophone regions of Europe (France, Belgium, and Switzerland) at the end of the nineteenth and the beginning of the twentieth centuries (see section 4.9.1). The idea behind such a practice is to identify **isoglosses**, i.e. boundaries delimiting localities in which certain features of vocabulary and speech are used.

Isoglosses do not always – one might even say rarely – coincide with political boundaries. This is because the history of the migrations and military conquests that shaped political boundaries does not necessarily pattern together with language change and variation. Isoglosses can cross administrative borders: e.g. French-speaking communities in Belgium and Switzerland, obviously, do not belong to France. But isoglosses can also 'fit in' with existing administrative borders, which is the case of the main isogloss, the imaginary line drawn from Bordeaux to Grenoble in France (see Figure 1.2), which separates the two principal groups of medieval Gallo-Romance dialects of *langues d'Oc* and *langues d'Oïl* (see Chapter 6). The very names of these two dialect groups refer to the way in which the word 'yes' was pronounced in northern (*oïl*) and southern (*oc*) Gallo-Romance. These two areas can be further broken down into several sub-dialects delimited by smaller isoglosses. The *langues d'Oc* region in southern France, for instance, includes numerous local rural dialects such as *limousin*, *auvergnat*, *gascon*, different varieties of *occitan*, and *provençal*. Some of these sub-dialects played an important political role in the history of the French, and most of them still exert an important influence on the structure of the French spoken in these areas. The technical term for a local language variety that influences a language brought into the community through migrations or conquest is **substratum**. The variety that is brought in is called a **superstratum** (see Chapter 6).

Two other concepts are helpful in the analysis of geographic variation in French: *français régional* 'regional French' and, as already mentioned, *patois*. While the first term is a neutral label for regionally based varieties of a language, the second has a definite derogatory flavour. The word *patois* was handed down to us from the prescriptivist tradition that long considered regional varieties as "localized spoken varieties which are believed to have developed among the peasantry in the post-medieval period and which lack historical authenticity and homogeneity ('purity')" (Lodge 2004:8). However, since prescriptive attitudes mostly aimed to preserve the 'purity' of the literary language, there has been a considerable body of written literature in various *patois* throughout French history (see Chapter 6). The concept of *patois*, with its negative connotation of

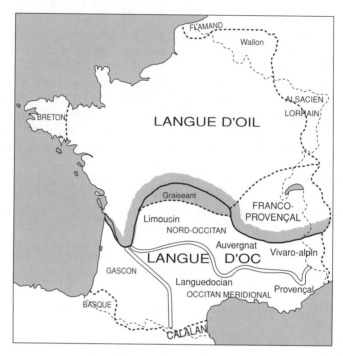

Figure 1.2   Map of France with the isogloss separating the *Oc* and *Oïl* dialects

'inferior linguistic variety', seems so deeply rooted in the collective conscious-
ness of French speakers that it is common to find speakers of French in France
today who refer to local tongues (*parlers*) spoken in their families (e.g. Occitan
and Normand), as *patois*.

   Although a wide variety of labels refer to geographic variation in French,
one must bear in mind at all times that these labels are no more than a shorthand for a complex sociolinguistic reality, combining elements of geographic
location and symbolic belonging (see section 1.1). Let us take for instance the
case of 'Belgian French' (*français de Belgique*). It is a label that indisputably
attributes 'French' to a single country: Belgium. And yet, everybody agrees that
Belgium cannot be equated with French, since it comprises at least two other
regions inhabited by predominantly German and Flemish speakers. Understood as French spoken 'somewhere' in Belgium, the label becomes imprecise,
because it does not designate specifically what Hambye and Francard (2004)
call the *Communauté Wallonie-Bruxelles*, i.e. the French-speaking communities living in the region called *Wallonie* and the Belgian capital Brussels. But
'Belgian French' is not a symbolic entity, either, since members of this

community do not see themselves as speaking some kind of a unified variety that could be referred to in such a way:

En effet, les références identitaires des francophones de Belgique semblent à ce point éclatées (les individus se définissant tantôt comme belges, tantôt comme wallons, francophones, liégeois, gaumais, etc.) qu'elles peuvent difficilement permettre aux Wallons et aux Bruxellois de se sentir liés de façon privilégiée à un groupe d'appartenance unique. (Hambye and Francard 2004:54)

'Indeed, references to the identity of Belgian francophones seem so scattered (individuals define themselves alternatively as Belgian, Walloon, francophone, *Liégeois*, and *Gaumais*) that they hardly allow the Wallons and Bruxellois to feel they belong, in some privileged way, to a unified community.'

This discussion thus brings us back to a 'definition' of our object of study: French. When addressing geographic variation, we will concentrate on the structural properties of the linguistic variety spoken in a given region, thus expressions like 'Belgian French' and 'French spoken in Belgium' will refer to certain 'ways' of speaking (see section 2.2.1.3) or of selecting words (see section 5.9.1) in French by people living in the country known as Belgium. In other words varieties of French will be situated in or with certain communities rather than equated with them.

---

1) What are the consequences, in modern sociolinguistics, of the ways in which the word for 'yes' was pronounced in ancient Gaul?
2) Give examples of isoglosses matching and not matching existing political boundaries from non-francophone countries.

1.4.2   Social variation

Social variation is typically cast in terms of **sociolects**: these are language varieties spoken and/or written by a certain social stratum, i.e. a social group, a social class, or a **subculture**. But the notion of sociolect is often closely intertwined with that of a dialect. As mentioned earlier, *patois* used to refer to the tongue of the 'unsophisticated peasantry' besides having the primary meaning of a regional sub-dialect. The expression 'Parisian French' (*le français de Paris* or *français parisien*) is also perceived by members of francophone communities outside of France simultaneously as a geographic and a social entity: it is the dialect spoken in the capital of France, but since the capital of France has long been the symbolic center of *francophonie*, Parisian French is also synonymous with the everyday language of the francophone social and cultural elite. Such perceptions of the language derive from linguistic insecurity, and can be typical not just of France, but also of other centralized nation-states.

Other common labels and concepts referring to social variation in French are *français familier* and *français populaire*. The first refers to the informal way of speaking of educated people, while the second is seen as typical of the uneducated masses. Although, presumably, uneducated masses live in the countryside as well as in cities, for reasons that have to do with the formation of the standard language in France (see section 1.2 and Chapter 6), *français populaire* has largely been attributed to the Parisian working classes. Both *français familier* and *français populaire* are part of a speaker's **vernacular** or everyday language, as in one of its specific senses, the term *vernacular* in linguistics means the way in which speakers speak in an unrehearsed manner (also 'casual speech', Labov 2001:570).

Few would disagree, on the other hand, that the way in which people speak 'every day' also varies according to the situation in which they express themselves (buying a watch or talking to a superior), the medium of expression that they use (reading or writing), and the degree of practice that they have in discussing a given topic. All these sources of variation are grouped under the term **register**, or (sometimes) **style**. In the following pages, when we refer to formal vs. informal or casual ways of speaking and writing, it is this type of social-situational variation that we will have in mind; we recognize, however, that these sources of variation cannot be easily disentangled from each other without significant loss of meaning.

Another, crucially important, dimension of socio-stylistic variation is the question of 'standard' French, as we explained it in section 1.2. Most treatises of French linguistics consider 'standard' French their main object of study, and treat 'variable features' of the language on the side, typically grouped together in a subsection under the heading of 'sociolinguistics'. This book takes a radically different approach by treating all sources of variation as an organic part of speakers' mental grammars. In our view, separating some features of the language and positing them as 'variable', while holding that others form a so-called 'core' of the language that can be considered 'invariable', is very likely inaccurate: as we will see, variation in the structure of the language is in every part of the grammar, and is responsible for the dynamic processes that mold and change the language.

Geographic and socio-stylistic variation in pronunciation, one of the most commonly perceived variable domains in French and other languages, will be evidenced by examples in Chapter 2. Contrary to widespread beliefs, morphosyntax is also not immune to variation either, as *ne* dropping, the variable order of clitics in negative imperatives, and a typically 'Canadian way' of floating the quantifier *tout* will demonstrate in Chapter 3. The lexicon is widely recognized as the most variable aspect of a language, and Chapter 4 will report on this fact with abundant examples of words belonging to regional varieties, social groups, and particular speech situations and registers. Much less studied to date is variation in pragmatics, which will be exemplified in Chapter 5, among others, with the variable meaning of the expression *par exemple* 'for instance' in Canadian vs. Metropolitan French.

Each of these linguistic phenomena has a history as old as Gaul. The chapter on the history of French (Chapter 6) attempts to show the relationship between dominant forms and regional variation throughout the history of the language; thus it is an approach centered around the concept of 'variation', as well. Gallo-Romance developed through the loss of one centralizing model (Classical Latin). A new centralizing model slowly took its place, culminating in Classical French and its centralizing successors (the language of the *écoles de la République* 'public schools of the Republic' and the various national examinations). More recently, though, the tight strictures on that concept have been gradually loosened, starting with the French Revolution, and a century later the *tolérances officielles* 'official leeway' on national exams (1901), and most recently by more generous grading of orthographic 'errors' (1990).

1) What type of phenomena should be considered as social variation in French? Give examples.
2) Adolescents are often said to have 'subcultures', and can use language in ways that differ from adults' language use. What, in your opinion, is implied by such a term, e.g. why can't we say that adolescents speak a dialect or a sociolect?

1.5 Looking ahead

In this book, when we look at the relationship between larger norms and local norms, it is with the idea that there is still much more to be done in revealing French as an inherently plural linguistic entity. Much dialectal literature and many non-literary regional texts from earlier periods of French have not yet been studied linguistically. Much spoken and written information has yet to be collected and analyzed on variable pronunciation, syntactic, and lexical features, and probably even more needs to be done examining uses of these features in specific discourse contexts. By doing such work in the future, a different picture of contemporary and historical changes in French is likely to emerge; this book is merely a first attempt undertaken in this direction.

French: A Linguistic Introduction seeks to emphasize 'variation within varieties'. Its focus on diversity opens the door for future research, as the relationship between the standard(s) in each community and usage within those communities offers rich material for further study. From the various sections of the book, we hope, it will become obvious that linguistic variation in French-speaking communities is widespread, effectively underscoring the idea of *francophonie* 'a francophone world'. Although the influence of the undisputable center of this francophone 'world', namely France, together with the 'standard' it sets in matters of linguistic practices, remains strong, individual 'actors' (i.e. countries and regions) continue to possess their own distinctive geographical and socio-stylistic 'ways' of speaking and writing French – in the plural. The future will tell us whether increasing regional (supranational) integration in Europe and around the world will render them not only united under the umbrella of *francophonie*, but also more forthcoming and vocal about their local norms and differences.

2 Phonetics and phonology

2.1 Preliminaries

2.1.1 Sounds, spelling, and the IPA

Phonetics and phonology are related areas of the study of the sounds of languages. The phonetics concentrates on the physical properties of sounds, i.e. how speech sounds are articulated ('articulatory phonetics'), how these articulations are manifested in the acoustic waveform ('acoustic phonetics'), and how acoustic information is perceived and processed to form mental representations of sounds in the brain ('auditory phonetics', psycholinguistics). The phonetic sciences are also involved in documenting the sounds of the world's languages (e.g. Grimes and Pittaran1996, Maddieson 1984), collecting information about **endangered languages** (e.g. Gordon 2003), lending expertise to forensic investigators on speaker identity and language identification ('forensic phonetics', e.g. Byrne and Faulkes 2004), and collaborating with paleo-anthropologists on issues such as the anatomical capacity of the Neanderthal to produce intelligible speech (e.g. Lieberman and Crelin 1971, Boë et al. 2002).

Systematic studies of the sound systems of languages go back to the earliest studies of Sanskrit in ancient India. In Western scientific thought, largely under the influence of **structuralism** in the late nineteenth and early twentieth century, the study of the physical properties of speech sounds ('phonetics') became separated from – although remained associated with – studies of the function of speech sounds within and across languages. This latter approach received the name of 'phonology' from the association of the Greek words *phone* 'voice/sound' and *logos* 'speech/voice'. These early functional approaches to the sound systems of languages were motivated by the observation that even though the speech signal is continuous rather than discrete, languages are based on a limited number of sounds capable of expressing an infinite number of lexical meanings. In this chapter for instance we will retain nineteen vowels, twenty-three consonants and three **glides**, also called **semi-vowels** or **semi-consonants**, for French, while keeping in mind that their total combinations make up several hundred thousand different words. Thus, as functionalist approaches in phonology rightly assumed (see e.g. Trubetzkoy 1939), there is a finite set of sounds forming the sound inventory of each language (see the concept of **phoneme** in section 2.1.4). But how do we find out what these sounds are and how can we refer to them without ambiguity?

At a first glance, the answer seems unproblematic for French, as this language has an alphabetical writing system where letters are meant to represent sounds. Thus, we could conceivably take the first letter of the word *pont* 'bridge' and assume that it also refers to the sound |p| in words such as *épée* 'sword', *remplacer* 'replace', and *rampe* 'slope'. Or we could select the first letter of the word *dur* 'hard' and the last letter of the word *papa* 'dad', and expect that both represent in other contexts the same sound they exemplify in our selections.

By generalizing this method of mapping letters onto sounds, however, we would quickly run into contradictions. We would discover for instance that the letter *p* does not correspond to the sound /p/ at the beginning of the word *photo* 'picture', and it does not correspond to any sound at all in *beaucoup* 'many' and *sculpture* 'sculpture'. The letter *d* would turn out to be silent in *pied* 'foot' and *(il) comprend* '(he) understands', and it would have a pronunciation other than we would have predicted in the expression *vend-il* 'does he sell'. Using other letters to represent sounds unequivocally would lead to similar problems. The letter *a*, for instance, would be a good choice for representing the second sound in *pape* 'pope' and *bar* 'bar', but it does not correspond to an /a/ sound when it is followed by *i*, such as in words like *mais* 'but' and *clair* 'clear'. However, when the letter *i* following the letter *a* is written with two dots (called *tréma*), as in *maïs* 'corn' and *naïf* 'naive', then *a* reverts to the pronunciation it has in *pape* 'pope'. But using letter sequences rather than individual letters to represent the sounds of French would still not give us unequivocal representations of sounds. Although it is true that the frequent pronunciation of the *ai* letter sequence is the one we find in *mais* 'but' and *clair* 'clear', the same sequence in *faisan* 'pheasant' cues yet another sound, which is the same as *oeu* in *moeurs* 'morals' and *coeur* 'heart'. Therefore one is forced to conclude that the alphabet in French does not provide an unambiguous symbolic representation for the sounds of the language: one letter or letter sequence can correspond to different sounds, and a particular sound can be cued by different letters or letter sequences.

A closer inspection reveals that such a lack of one-to-one correspondence between spelling and pronunciation also characterizes English. According to a famous statement by G. B. Shaw, spelling in English is so arbitrary that the word *fish* could equally well be spelled *ghoti*, i.e. *gh* corresponding to the sound /f/ as in the word *enough*, *o* signalling the sound /ɪ/ as in the word *women*, and *ti* standing for the sound /ʃ/ as in *mention*. Shaw's witty remark confirms a pattern common in both English and French: spelling represents a late medieval, early modern pronunciation, quite distant from contemporary pronunciations of these languages. The writing system of today's standard written French was adopted during the sixteenth and seventeenth centuries, and despite numerous attempts at reforming it (see Catach 2001 on spelling reforms), it has been preserved virtually unchanged ever since. The gap between the written and the spoken forms of the language in French and in many other languages renders spelling largely inadequate to represent speech sounds. The need to unambiguously refer to speech sounds necessitated a better alternative, and led to the foundation of the International Phonetic Alphabet or IPA.

> Does the mismatch between spelling and sounds also hold for languages other than English and French? How about Spanish?

2.1.2 Phonetic symbols

The IPA, regularly up-dated by the International Phonetic Association since its foundation in the nineteenth century (see Ladefoged 1999), uses letters of the Roman and Greek alphabets, adding special signs and characters modifying these letters. Each IPA symbol is meant to refer to only one sound, and aims at representing the same sound across languages. IPA symbols are divided in three groups that reflect major differences between speech sounds: vowels, consonants, and glides (semi-vowels or semi-consonants).

Vowels are articulated with no major closure or stricture in the vocal tract when the air is expelled freely through the oral cavity (oral vowels) or both the oral and the nasal cavities (nasal vowels). Different vowels arise as the sound generated at the larynx by the vibrating vocal folds is 'filtered' through the oral and nasal cavities, whose size and shape are actively modified most importantly by the tongue and the lips. Table 2.1 shows the inventory of oral vowels common to most varieties of French, with the exception of /ɪ/, /ʏ/, and /ʊ/ that are used only in the French spoken in Canada and Louisiana, and /ɑ/ which, besides its widespread use in Canadian French, is now heard only in the rural areas of France, Belgium, and Switzerland.

> Use the symbols to transcribe the following words [(Symbols for f, t, and l are /f/, /t/, and /l/)]: peau 'skin', peu 'little/small', pie 'magpie', fée 'fairy', fête 'party', and loup 'wolf'.

Among the four nasal vowel symbols shown in Table 2.2, /œ̃/ no longer seems to characterize northern Metropolitan French, but it is used in southern varieties, as well as in French spoken in Quebec (see section 2.2.2).

Table 2.1 *IPA symbols for oral vowels in French*

i	si	/si/	'if'	u	sous	/su/	'under'
e	ses	/se/	'his, her'	o	saut	/so/	'jump'
ɛ	serre	/sɛʁ/	'greenhouse'	ɔ	pote	/pɔt/	'buddy'
y	su	/sy/	'known'	a	patte	/pat/	'paw'
ø	ceux	/sø/	'these'	ɑ	pâte	/pɑt/	'pasta'
œ	soeur	/sœʁ/	'sister'				
ɪ	pile	/pɪl/*	'pile'	ə	ce	/sə/	'this'
ʏ	pull	/pʏl/*	'pullover'				
ʊ	poule	/pʊl/*	'hen'				

*in certain dialects of French only

Table 2.2 *IPA symbols for nasal vowels in French*

ɛ̃	fin	/fɛ̃/	'end'
ɔ̃	(ils) font	/fɔ̃/	(they) 'do'
ɑ̃	faon	/fɑ̃/	'fawn'
œ̃	parfum	/paʁfœ̃/*	'perfume'

*in certain dialects of French only

Numerous other symbols are used to transcribe fine-grained characteristics of sounds. Such signs are called diacritics, and are placed above or below the symbol that they modify. In the following discussion about the sounds of French we will concentrate only on a few fine-grained details, and therefore use few diacritics. One of them will be the tilde /˜/, placed on top of vowel symbols to mark a nasal sound, another the colon /:/, placed after a phonetic symbol to indicate that the sound has to be lengthened (see section 2.3.5). Unlike English, French nasality is not just a metaphor for a particular way of speaking: the nasal vowel /ɔ̃/ in the word *bon* /bɔ̃/ 'good' for instance distinguishes the masculine form of the adjective from its feminine counterpart *bonne* /bɔn/ or any other word containing the sequence 'b + vowel' (*beau* /bo/ 'pretty', *ban* /bɑ̃/ 'proclamation', and *boeufs* /bø/ 'oxen'). No such distinctions exist in English.

Some words like *enfin* /ɑ̃fɛ̃/ 'finally' and *enfant* /ɑ̃fɑ̃/ 'child' contain two nasal vowels. Find more examples like these and transcribe them phonetically. For additional consonant symbols, refer to Table 2.3.

Table 2.3 *IPA symbols for consonants in French*

p	*poux*	/pu/	'lice'	f	*fou*	/fu/	'mad'
t	*tout*	/tu/	'all'	s	*sou*	/su/	'cent'
k	*coup*	/ku/	'knock'	ʃ	*choux*	/ʃu/	'cabbage'
b	*boue*	/bu/	'mud'	v	*vous*	/vu/	'you (pl.)
d	*doux*	/du/	'tender'	z	*zoo*	/zo/	'zoo'
g	*goût*	/gu/	'taste'	ʒ	*joue*	/ʒu/	'(he) plays'
l	*loup*	/lu/	'wolf'	R	*roue*	/Ru/	'wheel'
m	*mou*	/mu/	'soft'	ʁ	*cour*	/kuʁ/	'court'
n	*nous*	/nu/	'we/us'	χ	*heureux*	/øχø/	'happy'
ɲ	*bagne*	/baɲ/	'labor'	r	(cover symbol for the last three)		
ŋ	*parking*	/paʁkiŋ/	'parking'				
ts	*petit*	/pətsɪ/*	'little'	dz	*dûr*	/dzʏʁ/*	'hard'

*in certain dialects of French only

Table 2.4 *IPA symbols for glides in French*

j	*nier*	/nje/	'to deny'
ɥ	*nuée*	/nɥe/	'cloud'
w	*nouer*	/nwe/	'to tie'

Consonants, from the Latin *consonantes* 'sounding together', are commonly defined as sounds that cannot be pronounced alone, but have to be 'sounded with' a vowel. The reason for this 'dependency' is the articulatory characteristics of consonants: they are formed by creating some kind of an obstruction in the way of the air stream, which is released or discontinued at the **onset** of a following vowel. As opposed to vowels, consonants are not **syllabic** in French. This means that they cannot form the center of a syllable, as consonants like /r/ and /l/ do for instance a language like Czech (*vlk* /vl̩k/ 'wolf').

Table 2.3 lists twenty-three symbols for consonants in French. Among diacritics used to modify these symbols are: /ˬ/ for voicing, /ˬ/ for devoicing, /ʲ/ for palatalization, and /:/ for lengthening. The use of these symbols will be exemplified later in various sections of this chapter.

Simply stated, glides (semi-vowels or semi-consonants) are articulated like vowels but behave in many respects like consonants (see section 2.2.3). Different varieties of French can have up to three glides: /j/, /ɥ/, and /w/ (Table 2.4). As their spelling indicates, glides maintain close connections with the vowels /i/, /y/, and /u/ (see section 2.2.3).

Use the preceding symbols to transcribe phonetically the following words: *porte* 'door', *marée* 'tide', *gagner* 'to win', *gong* 'gong', *biais* 'bias', *billet* 'ticket'.

2.1.3   Phonetic values of letters and letter sequences

As determined earlier, there is no one-to-one correspondence between letters and sounds in French, but if there were no correspondence at all, it would be impossible for native speakers to read words and names unknown to them!

In reality, letters of the French alphabet do have so-called phonetic values, i.e. sounds that systematically correspond to them, but these values vary widely from one context to another. We can identify, for instance, the primary phonetic value of a letter or a letter sequence, which is its most frequent pronunciation, but that value will change depending on the surrounding consonants and vowels. Let us consider, for instance, the letter *g*. In words like *gardien* /gaʁdjɛ̃/ 'guard' and *gomme* /gɔm/ 'eraser', *g* has the phonetic value of /g/. This is, however, not true in words like *gibier* /ʒibje/ 'prey' and *manger* /mɑ̃ʒe/ 'to eat' where *g* is pronounced /ʒ/. Because of its higher relative frequency as a pronunciation of *g* (Tranel 1987), the primary phonetic value of *g* is /g/, while /ʒ/ corresponds to its positional or secondary phonetic value when *g* is followed by *i, e, é, è* or *ê*. The letter *g* has a null phonetic value, i.e. it is silent, in *rang* /ʁɑ̃/ 'rank', and has an auxiliary phonetic value when it is part of the *gn* letter sequence, pronounced /ɲ/ in *montagne* /mɔ̃taɲ/ 'mountain' or *agneau* /aɲo/ 'lamb'. It is beyond the scope of this chapter to examine the phonetic values of each orthographic symbol, not to mention all their possible combinations.

1) Find words in which the sound /k/ is in word-initial, word-internal, and word-final positions. What spelling sequences do you encounter?
2) Explain why a silent *e* has to be inserted in the spelling of the verb form *nous mangeons* 'we eat'.

2.1.4   Phonemes, minimal pairs, and allophones

Many words change their meaning when one sound in them is replaced by another sound. Replacing the vowel /o/ with other vowels in a monosyllabic word after /o/ can lead to many words with different meanings: *saut* /so/ 'jump', *sous* /su/ 'under', *ses* /se/ 'his/her', and *ceux* /sø/ (Table 2.1). Similar chains of lexical contrast can be obtained by replacing the consonants in monosyllabic words before /u/ (Table 2.3) or glides before /e/ (Table 2.4). The segments or phonemes that contrast in these environments are **distinctive**, i.e. they make a word contrast in meaning with another word while keeping the rest of the phonetic environment the same. Words that form such contrasts are called **minimal pairs**, because they represent a necessary and sufficient 'minimal' contrast between two phonemes of a language.

Besides sounds that have so-called 'phonemic', i.e. lexical meaning-bearing, status in the language, there are also sounds that are **contextual variants** of other sounds, and which are called **allophones**. According to the structuralist tradition (see section 2.1.1), the former are usually indicated between slashes, while the latter are put in square brackets. Often times, however, since distinctions between allophones and phonemes are not as clear-cut as one might think (see e.g. mid vowels in section 2.2.1.3), phonetic symbols will appear in slashes throughout this chapter.

The 'phonemic view' of the sounds of languages goes back many centuries, but became dominant in the Western scholarly tradition only in the twentieth century. Since then, several other ways of thinking about sounds has emerged, one of which considers speech sounds not as more or less distinct, meaning-bearing elements, but as a series of universal articulatory gestures timed and grouped differently in different languages and dialects (Browman and Goldstein 1986). The nature of phonological representations, i.e. the way(s) in which sounds are represented in the brain, remains a hotly debated topic today.

Find the missing word of the minimal pair and transcribe it phonetically:
(a) *marée* /maʀe/ 'tide' — _____ 'cross out', ('to bar') (b) *rire* /ʀiʀ/ 'to laugh' – __ 'shot', (c) *bien* /bjɛ̃/ 'good' – __ 'nothing'.

2.2   Vowels and glides

2.2.1   Oral vowels

Vowels are formed with no major obstacles in the vocal tract (see Figure 2.1). They are formed by several moving speech organs, the so-called articulators, that 'shape the mouth' into different resonance cavities giving a characteristic 'color' (acoustic quality) for each vowel. The size and shape of the vocal tract is varied primarily by positioning the tongue and the lips. Besides the vibration of the vocal folds placed in the larynx, which creates **voicing** (most vowels are **voiced**), the raising and lowering of the **velum** (**soft palate** or **uvula**) is responsible for the closing and opening of the nasal passage, and thus creating

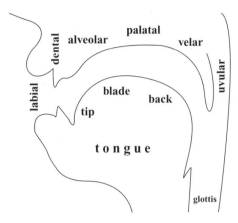

Figure 2.1 Principal places of articulation

a difference between oral and nasal vowels. The tongue, the lips, the glottis, and the velum are referred to as active (moving) articulators.

Although tongue movements, which can be more or less fronted or retracted, raised or lowered, are essentially continuous, and therefore hard to assign to a single location, phoneticians assume that the highest point of the tongue body during the articulation of a vowel is sufficient to characterize the sound in two dimensions: tongue 'height' or the degree of raising or lowering of the tongue (*aperture* in French terminology) and tongue 'fronting' or 'backing', i.e. the degree with which the tongue is advanced or retracted within the oral cavity. Vowels are routinely represented along these two dimensions of the tongue movements on a diagram called a **vowel quadrilateral** (see Figure 2.2). On such a diagram, the vertical axis shows the tongue 'height', while the horizontal axis depicts tongue 'fronting'. Going from the top to the bottom of the quadrilateral corresponds to the progressive lowering of the tongue, which results in gradually more open vowels. The vowels /i/, /y/, and /u/, placed at the top, are called **closed vowels**, the vowels /a/ and /ɑ/ at the bottom of the quadrilateral are **open vowels**. Vowels placed in between these two series are referred to as **mid vowels**: /e/, /ø/ and /o/, are 'closed' (*mi-fermées*), /ɛ/, /œ/, and /ɔ/ are 'open' (*mi-ouvertes*). The two series are sometimes referred to as **tense** and lax. Going from left to right on the quadrilateral, on the other hand, traces the trajectory of the tongue movements from a position close to the teeth, called 'front', to a position in the back of the throat, called 'back'. Thus /i/, /e/, and /ɛ/ are 'front' vowels, while /u/, /o/, /ɔ/, and /ɑ/ are 'back' vowels. In northern Metropolitan varieties of French the open vowel /a/ is 'front' rather than 'central' (see section 2.1.5).

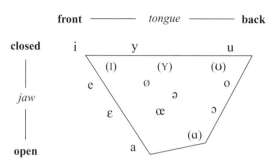

Figure 2.2 Oral vowels of French

The rounding of the lips, the third primary dimension of vowel articulation, also plays an important role in French. Backing and lowering of the tongue body are always accompanied by some degree of rounding, as front vowels are usually unrounded and back vowels are usually rounded (see Ladefoged and Maddieson 1996:292). This does not mean, however, that there are no front rounded and back unrounded vowels, since the actions of the lips can also be dissociated from the movements of the tongue, and give rise to a series of vowels contrasting in lip position only. Most varieties of French, for instance, have a series of front rounded vowels. Within this series, /y/ is the least and /œ/ is the most open vowel (Figure 2.2). The height of the tongue in these vowels is, to a large extent, comparable to that of their front unrounded and back rounded counterparts. Another dimension of the position of the lips is **protrusion**, i.e. the projection of the upper and lower lips forward so as to form a 'tunnel', and thus lengthen the vocal tract. Protrusion has an impact on the size of the front resonance cavity, and therefore resonance frequencies, allowing additional vowel contrasts in front vowels (e.g. /y/ vs. /i/). Protrusion does not play a role in /i/, /e/, and /ɛ/, but it is crucial in /u/. The vowel /ə/, placed in the middle of the quadrilateral, is called **schwa** (see section 2.4.3). The three vowels left out of this presentation take us to the next section.

---

1) Which vowel is defined as a 'closed front rounded oral' vowel?
2) Describe the vowel /o/ in terms of the position of the tongue and the lips.

2.2.1.1 Laxing

The vowels /ɪ/, /ʏ/, and /ʊ/ are part of the closed vowel series. Together with /i/, /y/, and /u/, they are often referred to as **high vowels**, because the tongue-body is elevated close to the roof of the mouth during their articulation. The vowels /ɪ/, /ʏ/, and /ʊ/, however, have a slightly more open and less fronted articulation than /i/, /y/, and /u/. This modification, accompanied by a shortening of the duration of these vowels, is referred to as **laxing**. 'Lax' intuitively evokes some kind of 'relaxation', such as less muscular tension and less extreme movements of the articulators in lax than in tense vowels (see Trask 1996). Thus 'laxing' of muscular tension would result in slightly shorter duration in vowels, and explain why lax vowels occupy more central positions on the quadrilateral than tense vowels (see /ɪ/ vs. /i/ in Figure 2.2). Minimal pairs such as *beet–bit* and *lead–lid* in English involve the same kind of distinction.

The laxing of high vowels, *relâchement des voyelles fermées*, is one of the most marked pronunciation features of the French spoken in Canada and Louisiana. It seems to be a geographically widespread and a socially neutral phenomenon, thus typical to all Canadian French speakers regardless of where they live and to what social category they belong (PHONO 1998). The two series of closed vowels are positional variants of each other: the lax series, /ɪ/, /ʏ/, /ʊ/ only appear in **closed syllables** (syllables that end with a consonant), while the tense series, /i/, /y/, /u/ appear in **open syllables** (syllables that end with a vowel). Examples in (1) and (2) illustrate words from both series.

(1)   *pile* /pɪl/ 'pile'   (2)   *pie* /pi/ 'magpie'
        lutte /lʏt/ 'wrestling'   *lu* /ly/ 'read' (past participle.)
        doute /dʊt/ 'doubt'   *doux* /du/ 'smooth'

For laxing to apply, however, two additional conditions have to be fulfilled: the consonant closing the syllable cannot be /v/, /z/, /ʒ/, or /ʁ/ and the syllable has to be a **stressed** syllable. Since primary stress in most varieties of French is invariably located on the final full (non-schwa) syllable of a word (see section 2.5.1), the laxing of /y/ and /i/ is optional in the first and second (unstressed) syllables of the word *multiplier* /mʏltɪplije/ 'multiply', but it is mandatory in the primary stressed, final syllable of the word *multitude* /myltitʏd/ 'multiplicity'.

Circle all vowels that would be pronounced as lax vowels in Canadian French in the following sentence: *Cette lustre me paraît trop petite, il me dit.* 'This chandelier seems too small to me, he tells me.'

2.2.1.2   Devoicing

The actions of the fourth active articulator, the glottis, are manifest through the vibration of the vocal folds, and result in voicing. Voicing characterizes every oral and nasal vowel in French, but high vowels can become devoiced, i.e. pronounced with no vocal fold vibrations during the entire or the final part of their articulation. When devoiced, vowels sound as if they were whispered or outright omitted from speech.

One variety in which this phenomenon occurs is Parisian French where high and mid front vowels at the end of utterances can entirely or partially lose voicing throughout their articulation. This way of ending an utterance or a speaker's turn in conversation can be accompanied by a hissing sound added to the devoiced vowel: *Merci‿ch!*, *Oui‿ch!* (Fónagy 1989). Devoicing primarily affects the vowels /i/ and /y/, but it also 'spills over' to the mid-front vowels /e/ and /ɛ/ (Fagyal and Moisset 1999, Smith 2003). Whether or not they are followed by a consonant, only vowels at the end of a major prosodic unit, such as an utterance or a turn, can be devoiced:

(3)   *Je suis sure que tu l'as déjà entendue‿ch.*
        'I am sure you've already heard it.'

Canadian French also exhibits devoicing of high vowels, but the conditioning factors are different from devoicing in northern Metropolitan French. Similar to laxing, devoicing or *désonorisation* only affects high vowels in unstressed, i.e. non final, prosodic position between two voiceless consonants. The five-syllable word *université* 'university', for instance, is pronounced /y n i v ɛ ʁ s i̥ t e/, with the **penultimate** /i/ devoiced, i.e. sounding as if it had been deleted. Devoicing in Canadian French is widespread geographically and socially (PHONO 1998).

To sum up, high vowels have a tendency to 'weaken' their articulatory characteristics in certain contexts either by laxing, i.e. becoming shorter, less open, and more central, or by devoicing, i.e. weakening their laryngeal gesture (voicing). The overall weakening of articulatory gestures seems like a good explanation for devoicing in Canadian French where the laryngeal gesture appears to be absent or incomplete during the articulation of longer stretches of consecutive, unstressed voiceless sounds (e.g. /ʁ s i̥ t / in *université*). The same interpretation, however, is much more difficult to defend with respect to Parisian French, where devoicing affects vowels in phrase-final, primary stressed positions (see section 2.5.1).

---

1) What is 'relaxed' during the articulation of 'lax' vowels?
2) Why would the devoicing of high vowels mean 'weakening' of articulatory gestures?

2.2.1.3 Mid vowels

Mid vowels are probably the most variable of French vowels. This might be due to the fact that there is only a slight difference between the two series of vowels in terms of tongue height: although speakers vary to a great extent in their realizations of mid-vowels, /ɛ/, /œ/, and /ɔ/, the so-called 'half-open' (*mi-ouvertes*) vowels, are somewhat more lowered and retracted towards the back of the oral cavity than /e/, /ø/, and /o/, their 'half-closed' (*mi-fermées*) counterparts. Apart from a few contexts in which these vowels still exhibit phonemic contrast in some varieties of French (see e.g. Table 2.5), the two series can be regarded as positional variants of each other. Similar to the two high vowel series in Canadian French, mid vowels have also been analyzed in terms of a tense–lax distinction (Scullen 1997).

The general rule that captures the positional variation of mid vowels is called *la loi de position* 'the law of position', translated as **open/closed syllable adjustment** in English (Casagrande 1984:213). This rule states that mid vowels in closed syllables have to be open, and in open syllables they have to be closed. Rephrasing this in terms of a tense–lax distinction would amount to saying that mid vowels undergo laxing in closed syllables, and tensing in open syllables. This rule or constraint is manifest in different ways in different varieties of French. It applies with virtually no exception in southern varieties of Metropolitan French where vowels in the two series are strict allophones, leaving room for no phonemic oppositions: closed mid vowels only appear in open syllables (*fait* /fe/ 'fact', *peu* /pø/ 'little/few', *chaud* /ʃo/ 'hot'), and open mid vowels are only appropriate in closed syllables (*fête* /fɛt/ 'party', *peur* /pœʁ/ 'fear', *chose* /ʃɔz/ 'thing'). Thus none of the phonemic distinctions listed in Table 2.5 applies in the southern Metropolitan varieties.

There are many exceptions to **open/closed syllable adjustment** in northern Metropolitan varieties, however. The half-closed vowel /e/ cannot appear in closed syllables; the mid-open /ɛ/, on the other hand, can appear in open syllables where it is supposed to contrast with /e/ in minimal pairs such as *prêt* /pʁɛ/ 'loan' vs. *pré* /pʁe/ 'meadow', and *taie* /tɛ/ 'pillow case' vs. *thé* /te/ 'tea', as well as in the conditional vs. future verb endings (*je mettrais* /mɛtʁɛ/ 'I would put' vs. *je mettrai* /mɛtʁe/ 'I will put'). But in many young Parisian speakers' speech this distinction seems to be weakening, and /ɛ/ appears to be reliably maintained only in the vicinity of the uvular **fricative** /ʁ/, as well as in frequent lexical items (Landick 1995). The /e/–/ɛ/ opposition in word-final open syllables is stable in most areas of francophone Switzerland (Singy 1996:56).

According to the predictions of the *loi de position*, /œ/ and /ɔ/should also be excluded from open syllables in word-final positions. This is indeed the case in the French spoken in northern areas of France where words such as *feu* /fø/ 'fire' and *beau* /bo/ 'pretty' contain a half-closed vowel. But in the French spoken in Belgium and Switzerland, the /o/–/ɔ/ opposition is still contrastive word-finally. Spelling is often a good indicator: when the vowel is spelled with a complex letter sequence, a diphthong in Old French, the half-closed vowel is preferred: *peau* /po/ 'skin', *l'eau* /lo/ 'water'. When the vowel, originally a monophthong, is spelled *o*, then the mid vowel is half-open: *pot* /pɔ/ 'jar', *lot* /lɔ/ 'share'.

Table 2.5 *Mid vowels in closed (CVC) and open (CV) syllables in northern Metropolitan French*

V	CVC		CV	
	Spelling	Minimal pairs	Spelling	Minimal pairs
/e/	–	–	**-é** *l'été* **-er** *regarder* **-ez** *regardez* **-e** *les*	/ɛ/ – /e/ *(il) était – été* *baie – Bé* *fait – fée* *marais – marée* *paix – Pé*
/ɛ/	**-è** *la mère* **-ê** *la bête* **-aî** *le maître* **-ai** *le maire* **-e** *la messe* **-ei** *seize*	/ɛ/ – /ɛː/ *belle – (il) bêle* *mettre – maître*	**-et** *le sommet* **-êt** *le prêt* **-ais** *le palais* **-ait** *le lait* **-aie** *la baie* **-aix** *la paix* **-aye** *La Haye*	*prêt – pré* *taie – thé*
/ø/	**w-final /z/ forces /ø/**: *la chanteuse*	/ø/ – /œ/ *veule – (ils) veulent* *(il) jeûne – jeune*	**-eu** *le feu* **-eux** *sérieux* **-e** *Mange-le̲*	–
/œ/	**-eu** *la veuve* **-oeu** *le coeur* **-e** *le parlement* **w-final /z/ forces /o/**: *la chose, la rose*		–	
/o/	**-ô** *Rhône, le gône* **-eau** *le heaume* **-au** *le royaume* **-one** *le polygone* **-ome** *l'atome* **-ose** *l'arthrose*	/o/ – /ɔ/ *saule – sol* *Paule – Paul* *heaume – homme* *(il) saute – sotte*	**-o** *la moto* **-eau** *beau* **-au** *le haut* **-ot** *le mot, sot*	–
/ɔ/	**-o** *le corps* **-osse** *la bosse*		–	

The same is true in varieties of Belgian French (Blampain 1997). The vowels /ø/ and /o/, inappropriate in closed syllables according to the *loi de position*, are nonetheless the preferred realization before /z/ in the northern varieties of Metropolitan French. This results in half-closed pronunciations of mid vowels in words such as *chose* /ʃoz/ 'thing', *rose* /ʀoz/ 'rose', and *chanteuse* /ʃɑ̃tøz/ 'singer', which are typically pronounced half-open in the south.

The distribution of mid vowels is even more variable in word-internal position. A possible way to predict vowel height word-internally is **vowel harmony**, a type of vowel-to-vowel **assimilation** which, in French, makes all non-word-final mid vowels in open syllables assimilate in height to the final, primary stressed vowel of the word. For instance, the first vowel in the words *chocolat* 'chocolate' and *choral* 'choir' is likely to be half-open in anticipation of the /a/ in the final syllable. Also, /o/ in *grossir* 'put on weight' tends to be half-closed because of the closed final vowel /i/. Unstressed vowels harmonize in tongue height with the vowel of the primary stressed syllable in morphologically derived contexts, as well. This means that despite the fact that in base words such as *gros* /gʁo/ 'huge' the half-closed vowel /o/ is preferred, the vowel of the base will tend to be open if the vowel in the following suffix is open or half-open, as in *grossesse* /gʁɔsɛs/ 'pregnancy'. However, individual variations cannot be ruled out. For instance, the recommended pronunciation by the dictionary *Le Petit Robert* (1989) for *o* in *grossesse* (see above) is /o/ and not /ɔ/, and recent studies have shown that vowel harmony appears to be stronger in northern than in southern varieties of Metropolitan French (see e.g. Fagyal et al. 2002, Nguyen and Fagyal in press), and also depends on the individual speaker (see e.g. Landick 2004).

---

1) Give examples of minimal pairs involving mid vowels. In what variety of French would these examples not hold?
2) Guess the geographical origin of the speakers pronouncing the following words in the way specified in the phonetic transcriptions: a) /ɔtɔ/ *auto* 'car', b) /dɑ̃søz/ *danseuse* 'female dancer', c) /tɛ/ *taie* 'pillow case'.

2.2.1.4 Diphthongs

Canadian French has vowels reaching two different target positions during their articulation. Such vowels are called **diphthongs**. Mid vowels prominently figure among diphthongized vowels in Canadian French. The vowel /ɛ/ in *neige* 'snow' and *mère* 'mother' for instance sounds as /ɛ/ followed by a short /ı/-or /j/-like sound, also called a front 'upglide': /neˈɜ/ and /mɛˈʁ/. Similarly, /o/ sounds /o^u/ in words like *cause* 'reason' /ko^{u}z/ and *chose* /ʃo^{u}z/ 'thing', and /ɔ/ becomes a diphthong when followed by a so-called lengthening consonant (see section 2.3.5) as in *fort* /fɔ^{u}ʁ/ 'strong'. Diphthongization, however, is not limited to mid vowels. Apart from a few exceptions, all vowels may diphthongize "given the appropriate circumstances" (Walker 1984:61). These 'circumstances' or conditioning environments are: closed syllable, strong prosodic position, and/or a lengthening consonant following the vowel. Vowels preceding the final, stressed syllables of major prosodic units (see sections 2.4.2 and 2.5.1) are also known to have extensive lengthening in Canadian French which, as opposed to lengthening in Metropolitan varieties, favors diphthongization. Even high vowels, intrinsically the shortest of all vowels, can develop a glide and sound like diphthongs when followed by a lengthening consonant: *pire* /piʲʁ/ 'worse', *juge* /ʒyᵕʒ/ 'judge', *tour* /tuʷʁ/ 'tower' (Walker 1984:61). The vowels /e/, /a/, and the schwa (/ə/), on the other hand, resist diphthongization.

There seems to be, however, a lack of general agreement about the phonetic nature of diphthongs in Canadian French, as suggested by a vast array of different phonetic symbols used to describe these vowels. The diphthongized front mid vowel in *neige* 'snow', *mère* 'mother', and *rêve* 'dream' for instance is variably transcribed as /ɛ¹/ (Tranel 1987:40), /ɛj/ (Walker 1984:61), or /ᵃɛ/ (Martin 2002:87).

2.2.1.5 Open vowels
Traditionally in Metropolitan varieties of French the vowel /a/ is considered a front rather than a central vowel, while /ɑ/ is always listed as a back vowel. Relatively rare in the speech of young Parisian speakers, the back open vowel does not appear in the latest update of IPA symbols recommended for French (Ladefoged 1999).

Support for the traditional analysis of /a/ as a front vowel (see Coveney 2001:76) is supported by data from different sociolects. Descendants of the Parisian aristocracy still pronounced /a/ reminiscent of /æ/, i.e. more fronted and raised than a central vowel in the early 1970s (Mettas 1979), and this tendency was also attested in the speech of middle-class Parisian speakers at that time (Lennig 1978). With /a/ as a front vowel, the French vowel system could be analyzed as showing a relatively rare four-way contrast in tongue height in both the front and the back dimensions of the vowel space. In reality, however, in many varieties of the French spoken in Paris and most parts of Belgium, /ɑ/ is now merged with /a/, and the mid vowel pairs also show **merger**, i.e. loss of distinction resulting in a single sound in some contexts (see section 2.1.3). This reduces possible phonological oppositions to a more common three-way contrast.

In varieties where the /a/–/ɑ/ contrast still exists, possible minimal pairs are: *patte* /pat/ 'paw' vs. *pâte* /pɑt/ 'pasta', and *tache* /taʃ/ 'stain' vs. *tâche* /tɑʃ/ 'task'. The back open /ɑ/ primarily characterizes Swiss French and rural varieties of French spoken in France where, besides the minimal pairs in the closed syllables identified above, /a/ also appears in relatively frequent words in open syllables, such as the negative particle *pas* /pɑ/. It is also a frequently used allophone in Canadian French. Due to the general lowering and backing, i.e. a counter-clockwise shift, in the articulation of vowels in open stressed syllables in Canadian French, /ɑ/ has a less open realization (reminiscent of /ɔ/ or /o/) in many Canadian French speakers' speech (Walker 1984:76). Among the two back vowels, only /ɑ/ seems to have a tendency to diphthongize, and words like *pâte* 'pasta' tend to develop a back upglide: /pɑ^wt/.

> Transcribe the following sentences using two phonetic symbols for *a*: *Voilà le pâté de foie gras! L'âne a mal à la patte.* What variety of French does your transcription illustrate?

2.2.2   Nasal vowels

2.2.2.1   What is nasalization?

Nasal sounds are produced by the flow of air entering the nasal cavity through the lowering of the velum, a muscular flap that closes off the nasal passage, and the simultaneous exhalation of the air through both the oral and nasal cavities. The lowered position of the velum corresponds, in general, to the resting position of the articulators. It allows for easier breathing through the nose, which is why in speech the velum is lowered during pauses and breath intake. The velum, however, is closed off during swallowing and the articulation of most speech sounds which tend to be articulated in the oral cavity. Languages therefore primarily have oral rather than nasal sounds, and if a language has only a few consonants, nasal vowels and consonants are not among the first to be selected. Nasality is regarded as secondary articulation.

French is one of the few languages of the world in which nasal vowels are involved in phonemic distinctions. This is, however, a relatively recent phenomenon in the history of the language, since nasal vowels were 'contextually' nasalized in Old French. **Contextual nasalization** is a widespread phenomenon in languages, affecting oral vowels followed by a nasal consonant. In English, the vowel /ɪ/ followed by /n/ in words like *pink* and *bin* is slightly nasalized because the velum is lowered early in anticipation of the nasal consonant, resulting in a weak nasal airflow throughout some portion of the vowel. Similarly in Old French, vowels like /i/ in *vingt* 'twenty' had allophonic status: their nasality depended on their proximity to a nasal consonant. According to one scenario, over the course of several centuries, nasal consonants in word-final position, or when followed by another consonant in the same syllable, weakened, and the preceding nasalized vowels came to be pronounced with greater nasal airflow throughout their duration. At the end, the nasal consonants were no longer audible, while the vowels became fully nasal, and assumed a lexically distinctive role (e.g. *bas* 'low' /ba/ vs. *ban* 'ban' /bɑ̃/).

2.2.2.2 Northern Metropolitan French

French, all varieties taken together, can have four nasal phonemes: two in the front (/ɛ̃/ and /œ̃/) and two in the back (/ɑ̃/ and /ɔ̃/). The two front nasal vowels are mainly distinguished from each other in terms of rounding: /œ̃/ is more rounded than /ɛ̃/. The back nasal vowels differ principally in tongue height: /ɑ̃/ is more open and less rounded than /ɔ̃/ (Bothorel et al. 1986). In northern Metropolitan varieties, a vowel can be oral as /ɔ/ in *bonne* /bɔn/ 'good' (fem.), nasalized as in *bonnet* /bɔnɛ/ 'hat', or fully nasal as in *bon* /bɔ̃/ 'good' (masc.). Only two of these phonetic distinctions, namely the oral vs. nasal contrast, ensuring maximum distinction between the vowels, are used phonemically (Cohn 1990). In conveying gender distinctions in French, for instance, each nasal vowel alternates with a sequence of an oral vowel and a nasal consonant: /ɛ̃/ alternates with /ɛn/ or /in/ (*citoyen* vs. *citoyenne* 'citizen', *voisin* vs. *voisine* 'neighbor'), /ɑ̃/ with /an/ (*paysan* vs. *paysanne* 'farmer'), and /ɔ̃/ with /ɔn/ (*Breton* vs. *Bretonne* 'Breton'). A diminishing number of northern Metropolitan French speakers still have the front rounded vowel /œ̃/ contrasting with /yn/ (*chacun* vs. *chacune* 'each').

But the nasal vowel system is changing. The long-predicted merger of /ɛ̃/ and /œ̃/ (Malécot and Lindsay 1976), distinguishing relatively few minimal pairs, has come to completion in many young speakers' speech. As a result, words such as *brin* /bʁɛ̃/ 'sprig' and *brun* /bʁœ̃/ 'brown' no longer sound different in the speech of most Parisian speakers, and are pronounced with an unrounded and slightly open front nasal vowel. Such open articulations of /ɛ̃/ have been attested in northern speakers' speech since the early 1980s (Maddieson 1984:251), and seem to have become the trend over the past few decades, with /ɛ̃/ now 'impeding' on the vowel space formerly occupied by the open nasal vowel /ɑ̃/. Evidence that /ɛ̃/ had started to be articulated as an open nasal vowel comes from frequent misunderstandings between minimal pairs such as *vin* /vɛ̃/ 'wine' vs. *vent* /vɑ̃/ 'wind', and *maman* /mamɑ̃/ 'mother' vs. ma main /mamɛ̃/ 'my hand' (Fónagy 1989, Malderez 1991), and has been confirmed by recent perceptual experiments (see e.g. Montagu 2004). The vowel /ɑ̃/, 'pushed' by /ɛ̃/, also started 'moving' in the direction of /ɔ̃/. As a result, /ɔ̃/ is becoming a more closed /õ/-like vowel (Hansen 2001). This counter-clockwise 'chain reaction' in the articulation of vowels is called a **chain shift**. When the shift is initiated by a vowel that is moving towards another vowel at one extremity of the 'chain', the movement of all the vowels is called a **push shift** (pattern (a) in Figure 2.3).

While mergers entail the loss of phonemic distinctions (merged vowels can no longer encode meaning distinctions between words), vowel shifts tend to preserve lexical distinctions: although the vowels alter their original qualities, they remain phonetically different from each other (Table 2.6).

Table 2.6 *Three-way opposition of nasal vowels in northern Metropolitan French*

ɛ̃			ɑ̃			ɔ̃		
bain	/bɛ̃/	'bath'	*ban*	/bɑ̃/	'ban'	*bon*	/bɔ̃/	'form'
faim	/fɛ̃/	'hunger'	*faon*	/fɑ̃/	'fawn'	(ils) *font*	/fɔ̃/	'(they) do'
teint	/tɛ̃/	'complexion'	*temps*	/tɑ̃/	'time'	*ton*	/tɔ̃/	'tone'
vin	/vɛ̃/	'wind'	*vent*	/vɑ̃/	'wind'	(ils) *vont*	/vɔ̃/	'(they) go'

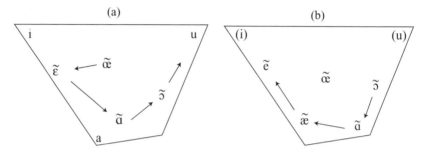

Figure 2.3 Counter-clockwise (a) and clockwise (b) shift of nasal vowels in Parisian (a) and Canadian French (b)

2.2.2.3 *Southern French and French in North America*

There are also considerable geographical differences in the nasal vowel system of French. One of the most important features of southern varieties is the replacement of full nasal vowels by a sequence of a nasalized vowel followed by an audible consonantal element called a **nasal appendix** (Léon and Carton 1983). For instance, the open nasal vowel /ɑ̃/ is partially nasalized and followed by a pronounced nasal consonant, yielding /aãn/. Probably due to the influence of closed nasal vowels in *Provençal*, an important substrat language in the South of France, /ɛ̃/ and /ɔ̃/, besides being partially nasalized (sounding more like /eɛ̃/ and /oɔ̃/), also have a much less open quality. The word *instinct* 'instinct' is better transcribed as /eɛ̃stɛ̃ŋ/, and the word *pont* 'bridge' sounds more like /pũŋ/.

The phonemic inventory of nasal vowels in Canadian French is similar to that of southern varieties of Metropolitan French, in that it uses the complete set of four nasal vowels: /ɛ̃/ and /œ̃/ in the front, /ɔ̃/ and /ɑ̃/ in the back. The actual pronunciation of these vowels, however, again sets off the Canadian system from European varieties of French in a characteristic manner. Nasals being inherently long vocalic segments, they tend to diphthongize in closed syllables in stressed position (see section 2.1.4). Thus, as opposed to the vowels in *bain* /bɛ̃/ 'bath' and *faim* /fɛ̃/ 'hunger', vowels in *quinze* /kɛ̃ᶦz/ 'fifteen' and *simple* /sɛ̃ᶦpl/ 'simple' can have a short up-glide. The phonetic quality of Canadian French nasal vowels also shows a general tendency towards fronting and rising, i.e. the opposite of the northern Metropolitan French pattern (pattern (b) in Figure 2.3). This clockwise shift of nasals in Canadian French makes /ɛ̃/ sound more like /ẽ/, /ɑ̃/ more like /æ̃/, but also /ɔ̃/ more like /ũ/, with the last responsible for many misunderstandings between speakers of European and Canadian French.

In Haitian Creole (Valdman and Iskrova 2003), Cajun French (Papen and Rottet 1997), and in French-lexifier Creoles in general, contextual nasalization affects high vowels, but there is no convincing evidence for the phonemic status of nasality in these varieties.

2.2.2.4 *On the phonological status of nasal vowels*

French nasal phonemes, on the other hand, are of particular interest in borrowings. Long-term contact between languages usually results in the borrowing of new words in which sound segments absent in the borrowing language become 'nativized', i.e. adapted to the phonological system of the language. Borrowed words can sometimes 'gain' or 'lose' sounds or syllables as they become part of the lexicon of the borrowing language. If its sounds do not get lost or 'eroded' in the process, they usually tend to be adapted or replaced by corresponding single sounds from the borrowing language. The interesting fact about nasal vowels is that they systematically appear as two segments: an oral vowel followed by a nasal consonant. Some adaptations of this type are shown in three African languages in (4). This phenomenon, called 'unpacking' of nasal vowels, has virtually no exception in a corpus of several thousands of French borrowings in typologically different languages (Paradis and Prunet 2000).

(4)   *ingénieur* /ɛ̃ʒenjœʁ/ → /ɛnʒenjœʁ/ 'engineer' (Fula)
       comptant /kɔ̃tɑ/   → /kunṭa/   'cash'   (Moroccan Arabic)
       balance /balɑ̃s/   → /balansi/   'scale'   (Lingala)

Thus nasal vowels seem to be 'underlyingly biphonemic', i.e. inherently composed of two segments. This is also supported by examples in (5) showing that nasal vowels are 'unpacked' before another vowel in standard French. In southern Metropolitan French varieties, on the other hand, where nasal vowels are pronounced as sequence of nasalized vowel followed by a nasal consonant or 'appendix' (see section 2.2.2.3), this biphonemic status is more transparent.

As for the borrowing of nasals into French, the case of the suffix *-ing*, frequent in many borrowings from English, will be discussed in section 2.3.2.

(5)

intolérant	/ɛ̃toleʁɑ̃/	'intolerant'	vs.	*inadéquat*	/inadekwa/	'inadequate'
parfum	/paʁfœ̃/	'perfume'	vs.	*parfumer*	/paʁfyme/	'to perfume'
bon	/bɔ̃/	'good'(masc.)	vs.	*bonne*	/bɔn/	'good' (fem.)

---

1) How many nasal vowels does a typical Parisian speaker have? Give examples.
2) What do borrowings from French in other languages reveal about nasal vowels in French?
3) Transcribe phonetically the word *paon* 'peacock' as pronounced in Parisian French, Quebec French, and southern Metropolitan French. When does the word become nearly homophonous with other words, such as *pain* 'bread'and *pont* 'bridge'?

2.2.3   Glides

2.2.3.1   What are glides?

As mentioned in the introductory parts of this chapter (see section 2.1.2 and Table 2.4), glides (/j/, /ɥ/, and /w/), also called semi-vowels or semi-consonants, are vowel-like segments that 'behave' like consonants. Thus these sounds can be thought of as an 'intermediate category' between the two main groups of sounds that characterize human speech. In simple terms, glides are articulated like vowels, i.e. without major obstruction or stricture in the vocal tract, but their 'behavior' with respect to other sounds of the language makes them more similar to consonants. They are 'phonetically', i.e. as far as their physical properties are concerned, similar to closed vowels, namely /i/, /y/, and /u/. In fact, each glide has its closed vowel counterpart: /i/–/j/, /y/–/ɥ/, and /u/–/w/. Each pair has nearly identical tongue-body positions and degree of rounding without creating an obstruction to the airflow in the oral cavity. Because of this articulatory similarity with closed vowels, glides are also referred to as semi-vowels in English phonetic terminology, while *semi-voyelle* is the preferred technical term in French.

As also mentioned, different varieties of French can have up to three glides: the non-rounded palatal front glide /j/, the rounded labiopalatal front glide /ɥ/, and the rounded labiovelar back glide /w/ (for these terms of articulation, see section 2.3.2). While northern and southern varieties of Metropolitan French have three glides, in the French spoken in Belgium /ɥ/ is often replaced by /w/.

Cajun French, as well as French-based Creoles lack /ɥ/, or both /ɥ/ and /w/, but usually have /j/.

Gliding is a highly variable phonological process in French. One source of variation concerns the actual presence or absence of gliding in certain contexts, while others seem to depend on the speaker.

2.2.3.2   The general process of gliding

Gliding occurs when the closed vowels /i/, /y/, and /u/ preceded by a single consonant or a group of consonants that contains no /l/ or /ʁ/ (called liquids, see section 2.3) are followed by another vowel in the same word. Three examples are *pied* /pje/ 'foot', *puits* /pɥi/ 'well', and *Louis* /lwi/.

Thus one can say that closed vowels /i/, /y/, and /u/ in these contexts, i.e. essentially before another vowel in the same syllable, take on a more conso-nantal character and become glides. As a consequence, they are articulated somewhat faster and with a slightly narrower stricture than the corresponding closed vowels usually are. Unlike vowels, however, glides are **approximant**-type articulations. This means that they lack what phoneticians call a 'stable phase', i.e. a portion of the sound throughout which its quality remains the same.

The inherently transitional nature of glides has important consequences for their behavior. The most important one is that they cannot form the nucleus of a syllable, i.e. they are not syllabic (see also section 2.1.2). It is this loss of syllabic status that renders the otherwise vowel-like glides 'consonantal', and explains the label 'semi-consonant'. There is, however, more to the behavior of glides than the simple statement that they 'behave like consonants'. The existence of alternations such as *abbé* /abe/ 'abbot' – *abeille* /abɛj/ 'bee' – *abbaye* /abei/ 'abbey', for instance suggests that there are near-minimal pairs involving glides (see also Walker 2001:103), and therefore in some cases glides should be considered phonemes rather than allophones (see discussion of these terms in section 2.1.4).

2.2.3.3   The front and back rounded glides /ɥ/ and /w/

The front and back rounded glides /ɥ/ and /w/ occur mainly in word-internal positions. Among the few words in which they occupy a word-initial position are *huit* /ɥit/ 'eight', *huile* /ɥil/ 'oil', *watt* /wat/ 'watt' and *ouate* /wat/ 'cotton', but there are no instances of word-final /ɥ/ or /w/.

Gliding of /y/ to /ɥ/ and of /u/ to /w/ is generally blocked after obstruent-liquid clusters (**OL cluster**), i.e. groups of consonants whose first element is either a **stop** or a fricative, and the second is either /l/ or /ʁ/. Blocking gliding results in **hiatus**. In such cases, shown in (6), the closed vowel /i/, /y/, or /u/ does not 'glide' to /j/, /ɥ/, and /w/ as we have seen for instance in *pied* /pje/

'foot', *puits* /pɥi/ 'well', and *Louis* /lwi/. Instead, the closed vowel retains its full vocalic characteristics, and with the following vowel it is is pronounced as two independent syllable nuclei: e.g. ***truand*** /tʁyã/ 'crook' in (6).

But things are even more complex than this, because examples in (7) shows that gliding after OL clusters also depends on the type of the vowel that follows /i/, /y/, or /u/. As an example, gliding of /y/ to /ɥ/ is not blocked when /y/ is followed by /i/ as in *truite* 'trout' in (7), but it is blocked when /y/ is followed by a non-high vowel such as in words like *truand* 'crook' and *cruel* 'cruel' (6). But the same generalization does not necessarily hold for the gliding of /u/ to /w/: the vowel /u/ glides to /w/ before /i/ as in *Louis* in (8), but not before /ɛ/ as in *brouette* 'wheel-barrow' in (6). On the other hand, a contradictory example appears to be the possible phonemic distinction that many native speakers suggest can arise when /u/ glides to /w/ before /a/ in words such as *(il) troua* 'he punch-holed' in (6) vs. *trois* 'three' in (7). Thus it would appear that it is difficult to capture variation in the gliding of /y/ and /u/ to /ɥ/ and /w/ with just a handful of generalizations.

(6)   *truand* /tʁyã/ 'crook'   (7)   *truite* /tʁɥit/ 'cross'
       cruel /kʁyɛl/ 'cruel'   *Louis* /lwi/ 'Louis'
       brouette /bʁuɛt/ 'wheel-barrow'   *croix* /kʁwa/ 'cross'
       (il) troua /tʁua/ 'he punch-holed'   *trois* /tʁwa/ 'three'

2.2.3.4   *The palatal glide* /j/

The glide /j/ in French can occur as a single word-initial segment in *yoga* /joga/ and *hier* /jɛʁ/ 'yesterday' or as a segment following another word-initial consonant like in *tiède* /tjɛd/ 'lukewarm' and *pied* /pje/ 'foot'. It can also appear as a single segment word-finally: *travail* /tʁavaj/ 'work', *paye* /pɛj/ 'paycheck'.

As in the case of /ɥ/ and /w/ (see section 2.2.3.3), the gliding of /i/ to /j/ is subject to special considerations after OL clusters: following a group of consonants that contains either /l/ or /ʁ/, gliding is either blocked (/i/ does not glide to /j/) or it is partial, i.e. /i/ glides to /j/ but /i/ is also preserved. For example the word *brioche* can be pronounced either /bʁijɔʃ/ or /bʁiɔʃ/, *plier* 'to fold' might sound like /plije/ or /plie/, and *trier* 'to sort out' can be /tʁije/ or /tʁie/. Although there is full gliding of /i/ to /j/ after OL clusters as in /buklje/ for *(que vous) boucliez* 'you buckle up (subjunctive)' (see Tranel 1987:121), a word-initial OL cluster followed by a palatal glide seems almost impossible to articulate.

Potential phonemic distinctions involving /j/ arise in a few pairs of words. In one case, /j/ alternates with hiatus, i.e. the absence of /j/: *biais* /biɛ/ 'bias' vs. *billet* /bijɛ/ 'ticket' and *balai* /balɛ/ 'broom' vs. *(il) balaie* /balɛj/ '(he) sweeps'. In English, the word pair *East* /i:st/ vs. *yeast* /ji:st/ is reminiscent of such oppositions. In other cases, the alternation is between /i/ and /j/: *pays* /pɛi/ 'country' vs. *paye* /pɛj/ 'paycheck' and *abbaye* /abɛi/ 'abbey' vs. *abeille* /abɛj/ 'bee'. Whether or not the existence of such minimal pairs renders the palatal glide a phoneme rather than an allophone of /i/ is still a matter of debate (see also section 2.2.3.2).

The palatal glide /j/ is often inserted as a transitional segment between two vowels or vocalic segments of different tongue height to avoid hiatus: between /e/ and /ɔ̃/ in *crayon* /kʁejɔ̃/ 'pencil', and between /i/ and /e/ in *ennuyer* /ɑ̃nɥije/ 'bother'. Apart from the expression *il y a* 'there is', customarily pronounced as /ija/ or even /ja/, gliding is thought to stop at the word boundary. In reality, colloquial speech styles abound in examples of gliding across word boundaries, thus *si elle* /siɛl/ 'if she' can be heard *ciel* /sjɛl/ 'sky', and *tu as* 'you have' can sound like (*il*) *tua* /tɥa/ '(he) killed'.

---

1) Why are the terms 'semi-vowel' and 'semi-consonant' legitimate syn-onyms for 'glide'?
2) Give examples of all three glides in word-initial, word-medial, and word-final positions. What is the most preferred position of each?

2.3   Consonants

2.3.1   *Phonation types*

Consonants are formed by creating a closure or a constriction in the way of the air stream at a particular place in the vocal tract. Depending on where and how this constriction is formed, and what kind of airflow is used, consonants are classified in terms of (1) place of articulation, (2) manner of articulation, and (3) phonation type. French uses what is called **voicing** to articulate voiced consonants. During this phonation type, the vocal folds are held close together, as shown in position 1 in Figure 2.4.

Another phonation type used in producing French consonants is the absence of vocal fold vibrations. It is most often achieved by opening the glottis widely enough to set the folds too far apart to vibrate, while letting the air escape through the opening. Consonants produced with no vocal fold vibrations are called **voiceless** consonants. Vocal fold positions for voiced and voiceless consonants are distinct from positions of inhaling during speech and deep sleep (positions 2 and 3 in Figure 2.4) during which the glottis is wide open, and from whispering (position 4 in Figure 2.4) when there is a small opening between the folds, otherwise held tightly together.

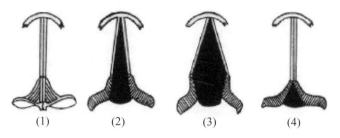

(1)   (2)   (3)   (4)

Figure 2.4 Vocal fold positions (vertical lines) and opening of the glottis (dark area between vertical lines) in different phonation types (1 – phonation, 2 – inhalation, 3 – inhalation, 4 – whispering), following Léon (1992:54)

2.3.2   Places of articulation

Places of articulation are target locations within the vocal tract at which articulatory gestures are aimed to be executed. Places of articulation typical of French consonants are shown in Figure 2.1 and Table 2.7. Their descriptions rely on three parameters: the speech organ that moves, and the direction and the timing of its movement.

Table 2.7 shows a simplified classification of places of articulation. The term 'labio-dental' refers to the joint contribution of the (lower) lips and the (upper) teeth, 'labial' means 'articulated with the lips', and 'bilabial' refers to the lips coming together to form the closure characteristic to /m/, /p/, and /b/. In other cases, the exact part of the active articulator needs to be specified. The 'alveo-dental' place of articulation, for instance, is the target region of a large number of consonants that can be further distinguished from each other by naming the part of the tongue involved in their production. Thus the consonant /n/, formed with the tip of the tongue, called the 'apex', is defined as apico-alveo-dental, while /s/, articulated with the tongue blade or 'lamina', is called lamino-alveo-dental.

The consonants /ʃ/, /ʒ/, /tʃ/, and /dʒ/ are 'palato-alveolar', which might seem confusing at first since 'alveolar' and 'palatal' are two separate regions of the hard palate (see Figure 2.1). But the label is correct in that the articulation of these consonants generally extends over a larger zone, encompassing both the post-alveolar and the palatal regions. The consonants /ʃ/ and /ʒ/, articulated with the tongue dorsum ('back' of the tongue), are dorso-palato-alveolar. Since they also involve considerable lip rounding, they are referred to as 'labialized'. The consonants /tʃ/ and /dʒ/ involve the precise timing of several gestures (see section 2.3.3).

The palatal consonant /ɲ/ is a dorso-palatal sound, which is sometimes split into two distinct articulatory gestures: an /n/ and an immediately following palatal glide /j/. Thus /ɲ/ in a word like *agneau* 'lamb' can sound like either /aɲo/ or /anjo/, depending on the speaker.

Table 2.7 *French consonants by place (horizontally) and manner (vertically) of articulation*

		bilabial	labio-dental	alveo-dental	palato-alveolar	palatal	velar	uvular
stops	nasal	m		n		ɲ	ŋ	
	oral voiceless	p		t			k	
	oral voiced	b		d			g	
fricatives	voiceless		f	s	ʃ			χ
	voiced		v	z	ʒ			ʁ
Affricates	voiceless			ts	tʃ			
	voiced			dz	dʒ			
trill				r				ʀ
approximants	lateral			l				
	central						ɥ	

The place of articulation referred to as **velar** is usually exemplified by three sounds, one of which, /ŋ/, is thought to exist only in English loanwords like *camping*, *parking*, and *jogging*. Although some had predicted the nativization of /ŋ/ by /ɛ̃/, following the model of words such as *shampooing* /ʃɑ̃pwɛ̃/ 'shampoo' (Walter 1983), the velar nasal seems alive and well in the Parisian French vernacular today (Walter 2002). In long-term borrowings, such as *parking* and *camping*, the *-ing* suffix is also often pronounced /ing/, which could be a case of nativization through 'nasal unpacking' (see section 2.2.2). The velar consonants /k/ and /g/ in French are 'velar' when they are followed by back vowels, i.e. the tongue root is retracted towards the back in anticipation of the upcoming vowel. When /k/ and /g/ are followed by a front vowel, however, the tongue body is raised towards the front of the palate in anticipation of the vowel, resulting in the **palatalization**, i.e. a slight shift towards the palatal region, of the articulation of the consonant and the vowel. Palatalized velar consonants have been attested for instance in lower-class varieties of Parisian French (Gadet 1992). In Parisian blue-collar workers' speech it is still possible to hear /k/ and /g/ palatalized to the extent to which the consonants seem to modify their places of articulation: e.g. *paquet* 'package' pronounced /patʲɛ/ rather than /pakɛ/, and *guitare* 'guitar' sounding like /dʲitaʁ/ rather than /gitaʁ/. The uvular region, the target place of articulation of most allophones of /ʁ/, is discussed in section 3.2.3.

---

1) Define the place of articulation of the following consonants: /b/, /f/, /ɲ/, and /ʁ/.
2) Identify what consonant's place of articulation is 'apico-alveo-dental'.

2.3.3   *Manners of articulation*

The way in which consonants are articulated at different locations in the vocal tract is called manner of articulation. Consonants in French can be nasals or orals, voiced or voiceless, and can be further divided into **stops**, **fricatives**, **affricates**, **trills**, and **approximants**. Each manner involves some kind of obstruction in the oral cavity which, placed on a continuum, can be of four general types: (1) complete closure (stops), with active and passive articulators touching so that no air can escape through the oral cavity; (2) 'stricture' or partial closure (fricatives and trills), when the articulators are held in close approximation to each other, i.e. close enough to produce audible friction, but with the air still escaping orally; (3) a combination of closure and stricture (affricates); or (4) virtually no closure (approximants), i.e. the articulators are placed in open approximation, too far from each other to produce audible friction. The term **obstruent** refers to consonants with relatively tight closure, such as stops and fricatives, while the terms **liquid** and **continuant** evoke consonants that let the outgoing air pass through or around the obstruction created in the oral cavity.

2.3.3.1 Stops and fricatives

Stops are the only consonants that occur in every language. A stop in French can be oral or nasal, voiced or voiceless, and can involve a minimum of four places of articulation (see Table 2.7). The production of stops involves three phases: closing, holding, and releasing. First a closure is created at some place in the oral cavity. Then, once the closure is in place, pressure in the oral cavity builds up during the hold phase until the closure and the air held behind it are abruptly released. Stops made by pushing air out through the vocal tract are called **plosives**. The release of the stop and the onset of voicing in the next vowel are timed variably in different languages, giving rise to different types of stop consonants. Phoneticians use a measure called **voice onset time** (VOT) to quantify this timing. English voiceless stops (/p/, /t/, /k/) in word-initial position have relatively longer VOTs then their French counterparts, which means that voicing starts relatively late after the stop release in English, while it starts almost instantaneously in French. A later start in voicing following the stop, coupled with a wider opening of the glottis (vocal folds set further apart) in English results in **aspiration**, i.e. a puff of outward air following the release of voiceless stops. Unlike in English, in French all voiceless stops are unaspirated.

Nasal stops (/m/, /n/, /ɲ/, /ŋ/) involve the momentary blockage of the oral cavity while the velum is lowered, letting the air out through the nasal passage. Thus nasal stops, contrary to oral stops, are maintainable articulations, and can be used for instance in humming a tune or marking audible hesitation in conversation. All nasal segments in French are voiced.

Fricatives, produced through the partial closure of the oral cavity, can be the result of two separate articulatory mechanisms: (1) a turbulent air stream generated at the constriction itself; or (2) a jet of air formed at some place in the oral cavity striking the teeth. The first type characterizes the non-**sibilant** fricatives /f/ and /v/. These two consonants are formed by pushing the air through a narrow labio-dental stricture created by the upper lips and the retracted lower lips raised below the upper teeth. The second type of fricatives, /s/, /z/, /ʃ/, and /ʒ/, are called **sibilants**. The alveolar sibilants or *sifflantes*, /s/ and /z/, are formed by the outward air striking a constriction set against the alveolar ridge, while the palato-alveolar sibilants or *chuintantes*, /ʃ/ and /ʒ/, are produced by the same air mechanism hitting against a constriction set further back in the oral cavity. These two types of fricative, however, are also distinguished by other fine movements: the shape of the tongue tuck behind the teeth is hollow for /s/ and /z/, while it is raised or 'domed' for /ʃ/ and /ʒ/. The lips are stretched for the former, but protruded and rounded for the latter. Seemingly unimportant details, these shapes and positions must be set and timed perfectly to obtain the desired fricative. These similarities and yet very precise differences between fricatives are what motivate tongue twisters such as *Les chaussettes de l'archiduchesse, sont-elles sèches, archi-sèches?*, exploiting alternating sequences of sibilants (Coveney 2001:47).

---

1) A particular way of pronouncing a consonant in *une tasse de thé* 'a cup of tea' makes native English speakers of French instantly recognizable. What is it?
2) Humming a tune can be done by using a nasal but not an oral stop consonant. Why?

2.3.3.2 Affricates

Affricates (/ts/, /dz/, /tʃ/, /dʒ/) are stop consonants whose release contains a prolonged period of friction. The process, and result of the process, during which stop consonants acquire a friction-like noise in their release is referred to as **assibilation**. Affricates are a manner of articulation intermediate between a stop consonant and a sequence of stop and fricative consonants. Traditionally the category of affricates is reserved for consonants whose place of articulation is 'adjusted', i.e. moved forward or backward, when passing from the stop to fricative phase (Ladefoged and Maddieson 1996:90). For instance, /tʃ/, the most common affricate in the world, which also exists in loanwords in French (e.g. *tchatcher* /tʃatʃe/ 'to blabber'), involves the movement of the blade of the tongue from an alveolar (/t/) to more of a palatal (/ʃ/) place of articulation. Its voiced counterpart /dʒ/, also common in English loanwords in French (*jeans* /dʒins/, *jet* /dʒɛt/ 'airplane'), involves the same type of movement coupled with voicing.

Assibilation is most commonly associated with the consonantal systems of Canadian French (Walker 1984:91–92) and Cajun French (Papen and Rottet 1997). In these varieties, assibilation is understood as an assimilatory process (see section 2.3.4) during which the apico-alveolar stops /t/ and /d/ acquire some friction in their release before a high front vowel or a front glide within the word, and become affricates: /tˢ/ and /dᶻ/ (Table 2.8). Depending on the speaker, assibilation can extend to larger phrases, e.g. *avant-hier* /avãtsjɛʁ/ 'day before yesterday', *parfait idiot* /paʁfɛtsidjo/ 'perfect idiot'.

Working-class Parisian French in contact with immigrant languages seems to have recently developed assibilation of word-initial alveolar stops before closed, open, and nasal vowels (Armstrong and Jamin 2002:133). Thus /k/ in *qui* 'who' and /t/ and /d/ in *tu dis* 'you say' are not only palatalized (see the *paquet* and *guitare* examples in 2.3.2), but also assibilated, yielding *qui* /tʃi/ and *tu dis* /tʃydzi/. This would represent a new development in the phonological system

Table 2.8 *Contexts of assibilation in three varieties of French*

word	Pronunciation		meaning
	Canadian and Cajun French	Middle-class varieties of Metropolitan French	
petit	pətˢɪ	pətɪ	'small'
dur	dᶻʏʁ	dyʁ	'hard'
soutien	sutˢjɛ̃	sutjɛ̃	'support'
Indien	ɛ̃dᶻjɛ̃	ɛ̃djɛ̃	'Indian'

of a variety (working-class Parisian French) known to have palatalization, but not assibilation. Considering all varieties of French, however, our conclusions should be modified: assibilation is 'familiar' to the sound system of French; that is in French in the plural (see our definition of 'French' in section 1.1), as it represents an important feature of several varieties of French spoken in the North America.

Palatalization and assibilation have much in common from both articulatory and diachronic points of view. A comparison between palatalized stops in Belgian French and assibilated stops in Quebec French (Corneau 2000) reveals that the main difference between the two types of stop, both arising before front vowels, seems to be the length of the period of friction following the release. When the period of friction is relatively short, the stop is perceived as palatalized, i.e. anticipating the lingual position of the upcoming front vowel, as is the case in Belgian French. When, however, the period of friction is relatively long, the stop is perceived as assibilated, as in Quebec French. As we have discussed above, this change in the length, and probably the intensity, of the friction period encodes important geographic variation in French. But it also replicates a sound change well-known from the history of the language: in the second century, /k/ became palatalized, then by the end of the seventh century, it had changed its place of articulation to alveolar stop and assibilated to /tʃ/, to finally loose its closure phase entirely in the thirteenth century and become a sibilant /ʃ/ (*cantare* /kantare/ (Latin) < *chanter* /ʃɑ̃te/ 'to sing').

---

1) Explain the difference between palatalization and assibilation. Note that both involve a specific way of pronouncing a stop consonant before certain vowels.
2) How would the stop consonants in the words *patiner* 'to skate' and *ridicule* 'ridiculous' be pronounced in Paris and in Montreal today and in the early 1950s? Explain your answers.

2.3.3.3 Trills and approximants

Although the latest revision of the IPA (Ladefoged 1999) gives only one allo-phone, /ʁ/, for 'r-like' sounds or **rhotics** for French, all varieties and styles of French taken together, there are many more allophones worth mentioning. Varieties of French can have: apical (/r/) and uvular (/ʀ/) trills, uvular fricatives (/ʁ/) typical of consonant clusters (e.g *train* /tʁɛ̃/ 'train', *après* /apʁɛ/ 'then'), and less frequently also velar approximants (/ɰ/) and voiced uvular fricatives (/χ/), often substitute for uvular trills in intervocalic position.

Trills arise from the vibration of one speech organ against another under special aerodynamic conditions. The apical /r/ or *r roulé* 'rolled r' is articulated by the tongue tip or apex moved close enough to the alveolar region of the palate, so that when the airflow passes through the small opening between the two, a repeated closing and opening of the flow of air could occur. The uvular trill /ʀ/ involves the same type of mechanism, except that the constriction occurs between the uvula and the back of the tongue or tongue dorsum. There is no explicit muscular control involved in the production of either trill: the size of the opening and the strength of the airflow should be sufficient to make the tongue tip vibrate, and allow several **taps** against a given region of the hard palate. Multiple taps of the active articulator against the passive articulator result in the repetitive cycles of vibration called trilling. In rural areas of France and in some parts of francophone Canada the *r roulé* can still be heard, although younger generations seem to be massively shifting to uvular allophones (/ʀ/ and /ʁ/) called *r grasseyé* even in parts of Quebec, e.g. Montreal, where the apical trill was the predominant pattern until the early 1950s (Sankoff et al. 2001). Apical /r/ is also characteristic in Cajun French, and it is largely replaced by the approximant /w/ in most French-based Creoles of the Caribbean.

Rhotics ('r-like' sounds) are very sensitive to their immediate phonetic envi-ronment. Before back vowels they tend to be uvular, while before front vowels they tend to be articulated as velar allophones (CALLIOPE 1989:114). They can also become velar approximants before front and back vowels in words like *heureux* /øɰø/ 'happy' or *Paris* /paɰi/. As its name indicates, the velar approximant /ɰ/ is an 'r'-like sound that is formed by the open approximation of the closure between the tongue dorsum and the velum, with no actual con-tact between the two. Velar allophones have also been attested in intervocalic position in Belgian French (Demolin 2001), and shown before front vowels in so-called 'standard' French (Bothorel et al. 1986, see Coveney 2001:60).

French has other approximants, as well. The glides /w/, /ɥ/, and /j/ (see section 2.2.3) are prominent members of this category, since their articulation involves an uninterrupted airflow passing through a wide stricture placed in its way. Another type of approximant is the alveo-dental lateral approximant /l/. This is the only type of 'l' pronounced in modern French, and it does not seem to be currently subject to much geographical or social variation. This, however, has not always been the case. A labialized velar, so-called 'dark', transcribed /ł/, similar to the sound English speakers pronounce in words like *listen* and *look* existed in Early Old French, but it vocalized before consonants into /u/ around the eleventh century. Spelling is still a good indicator of this early change from Latin in words such as: *aube* /ob/ 'dawn' < 'alba', *chevaux* /ʃəvo/ 'horses' < caballos, and *mieux* /mjø/ 'better' < melius. Old French also had had a palatal *l* (transcribed with the IPA symbol /ʎ/), for instance in *fille* /fij/ 'girl', for which the spelling sequence *lh* is still a reliable indicator in Occitan. This sound gave way to the palatal glide /j/ in lower-class Parisian French around in the thirteenth century, and in upper-class pronunciation in the early eighteenth century. According to Bourciez and Bourciez (1978:189), the palatal *l* was maintained in Languedoc, Gascony, and the French-speaking areas of Switzerland until the twentieth century.

---

1) How many different types of 'r-like' sounds are there if all varieties of French are considered? Give examples.
2) The French spoken in Montreal seems to be trading off its traditional *'r roulé'* /r/ sounds for *'r grasseyé'* (/ʀ/ and /ʁ/). What could be some of the reasons for this change?

2.3.4   Assimilatory processes

Speech sounds are not stand-alone units like letters on a piece of paper. Immediately adjacent speech segments, and even longer stretches of sounds, are formed by articulatory gestures that can interact and overlap in both anticipatory ('look-ahead') and perseverative ('carry-over') fashions. Such context-dependent interactions of gestures are known as **coarticulation**. When, in a sequence of adjacent sounds, the leftmost segment anticipates the articulatory properties of the rightmost segment, it is a case of 'anticipatory' coarticulation. Examples of this type include **vowel harmony** (2.1.3), **nasalization** (2.2.2.1), and **palatalization** (2.3.2.2 and 2.3.3.2). When coarticulatory influence goes in the other direction, i.e. the rightmost segment shows the influence of the preceding sound, it is called 'perseverative' or 'carry-over' coarticulation.

2.3.4.1   Voicing assimilation

Voicing assimilation is a particular type of coarticulation between laryngeal gestures of adjacent consonants. In simple terms, in a group of consonants, certain constraints are stronger than others and impose their sonority (voicing or lack of it) on the others. The most important point is that each consonant in the group has to have the same pattern of voicing, i.e. 'agree' in voicing. Which consonant assimilates to which, however, depends on the position of the consonants within the cluster and the position of the cluster in the word.

In French, voiceless obstruents (stops and fricatives, see section 2.3.3.1) that are the least sonorous of all consonants form the leftmost segment of a word-initial cluster. The least frequent cluster-initial segments are /ʃ/, /f/, and /v/, which appear in just a small set of proper names, loanwords, and onomatopoeic expressions: e.g. *schtrumpf* /ʃtʁumpf/ 'name of a Belgian cartoon character', *vlan!* /vlã/ 'Bang!', and *FLE* /flø/ 'français langue étrangère'. The leftmost spot in word-initial and word-final consonant clusters is usually filled by the voiceless sibilant /s/ before obstruents (*sport*, *style*, *ski*, and *liste* 'list', *risque* 'risk'), nasals (*snob*, *smash*) and liquids (*slave*, *slogan*), mostly loanwords from English. In a few cases, cluster-initial /s/ becomes /z/ via regressive assimilation to another obstruent (*sbire* /zbiʁ/ 'henchman', *svelte* /zvɛlt/).

In a group of any voiceless consonant and a voiced **sonorant** (i.e. /l/, /ʀ/, or a glide) word-initially and word-finally, the second segment is subjected to the influence of the first, and gets devoiced. **Devoicing** in this case is perseverative: e.g. *pli* /pl̥i/ 'fold', *tri* /tʁi/ 'selection', *communisme* /komynism̥/ 'communism', and *ample* /ãpl̥/ 'wide'. The devoicing of liquids word-finally contributes to their frequent **elision** in colloquial speech: e.g. *simple* /sɛ̃pl̥/ 'simple' becomes /sɛ̃p/, *quatre* /katʁ/ 'four' is simplified to /kat/. When sonorants are the leftmost segment of a consonant cluster and are followed by a voiceless consonant word-finally, the vocal folds open up during the articulation of the sonorant, 'anticipating' the lack of voicing in the following consonant. This is called regressive assimilation by voicing: e.g. *bourse* /buʁ̥s/ 'fellowship' and *carte* /kaʁ̥t/ 'map'.

Word-internally and across word boundaries, even after the deletion of a schwa vowel (see section below), regressive assimilation between obstruents is the rule in French: a voiced obstruent devoices in contact with a following voiceless obstruent (e.g. *absent* /apsã/ 'missing', *coup de coude* /kutkud/ 'nudge'), and vice versa (e.g. *anecdote* /anɛgdɔt/ 'story', *s(e)cond* /zgɔ̃/ 'second'). However, according to Rialland (1994), there seems to be no regressive assimilation by voicing across word-boundaries where assimilation could provoke loss of grammatical or lexical information. For example in *il va t(e) gronder* 'he will scold you' the /t/ of *te* does not undergo voicing in contact with the following /g/ (Rialland 1994), and in expressions like *Bac de science* 'Bachelor of science' speakers would tend to avoid pronouncing the word *Bac* with a word-final /g/ in order to avoid any confusion with *bague* /bag/ 'ring'. This might, however, be speaker-dependent rather than a rule in contemporary Parisian French, and in expressions such as *bec de gaz* 'gas burner' others signaled the existence of regressive assimilation (see Dell 1973) despite possible interference with *bègue* 'stutterer'.

2.3.4.2 Place assimilation

Anticipatory coarticulation frequently leads to a change in the place of articulation in English, while this type of assimilation is thought to be non-existent in French. It is true that there seems to be no regressive assimilation by place of articulation in groups of consonants as a result of the deletion of a schwa. To put it more simply, this means that for instance the /d/ in *médecin* 'doctor', although it devoices to /t/ and is pronounced /metsɛ̃/, does not become a dental sound like /s/ in contact with this consonant. Similarly, /n/ does not become velar /ŋ/ like the final consonant of 'parking' before /k/ in *mannequin* /mankɛ̃/ 'dummy', and /t/ is not transformed into a voiceless labial consonant (/p/) when it is followed by /b/ in *porte-bonheur* /pɔʁdbɔnœʁ/ 'bringer of good luck' after the schwa (word-medial and spelled *e* in each word) falls out. And yet French is not 'immune' to assimilation of place of articulation.

After schwa deletion in northern Metropolitan French, sibilant + sibilant fricative sequences do show anticipatory assimilation of place. For instance in *quinze juin* 'June fifteen' and *dimanche soir* 'Sunday evening' the two adjacent fricatives form a '**homorganic** consonant cluster' (group of consonants having the same place of articulation) when the schwa is deleted: /kɛ̃ʒ:ɥɛ̃/, /dimɑ̃s:waʁ/ (Léon and Carton 1983, Gadet 1992). Another case of such assimilation is the palatalization of velar consonants in working-class Parisian French (see section 2.3.2).

2.3.4.3 Other assimilatory processes

Allophones of |r|, pronounced as **geminates** at morpheme and word boundaries, are primarily affected by a third type of assimilation between consonants: assimilation of manner of articulation (see section 2.3.5). Besides the cases of lingual coarticulation discussed so far, labial and velo-pharyngeal coarticulations are also important in French. Labial coarticulation usually involves the anticipation of lip movements several consonants or vowels before the labial segment. In the phrase *sinistre structure* /sinistʁəstʁyktyʁ/ 'disastrous structure', for instance, the protrusion of the first /y/ vowel in *structure* is anticipated as early as the first /s/ of the preceding /stʁ/ in the /stʁəstʁ/ sequence (Benguerel and Cowan 1974).

---

1) List ways in which consonants in a group exert an influence on each other in French.
2) Who is called a /lɛʒbɔt/? Why is 'ch' realized as /ʒ/ in this expression?
3) In English, assimilation by place of articulation between consonants is frequent. What should we predict, for instance, between *s* and *sh* in *He loves shelves*?

2.3.5   Lengthening

Lengthening seems intuitive: 'making longer'. However, from a phonetic stand-point, 'how' a speech sound is lengthened can be crucial! Lengthening of a sound implies that the tongue body position of a vowel or the closure (stricture) of a consonant is held for a longer duration than that of adjacent speech sounds. In French, this contrast between shorter vs. longer segments is important for encoding meaning differences with vowels and consonants. Except for a few cases and in a diminishing number of varieties, however, the length of a sound is only marginally involved in encoding phonemic distinctions.

Everything else being equal, vowels have measurably longer duration before voiced than before voiceless consonants. The vowel /ɔ/ before /d/ in *mode* /mɔd/ 'mode' is slightly longer than it is before /t/ in *motte* /mɔt/ 'turf'. This subtle difference is due to universal constraints in speech production. Nasal vowels are also inherently longer than their oral counterparts, because lowering the velum during the articulation of the vowel is a gesture that necessitates additional time to be executed (see section 2.2.2). Diphthongs are also inherently longer than monophthongs for similar reasons: reaching two targets during the articulation of the syllable nucleus necessitates more time than reaching only one (see section 2.2.1.4).

A case of vowel lengthening typical of Metropolitan and Canadian varieties of French is the case of so-called **lengthening consonants**. Any vowel in the primary stressed syllable of a lexical word and a prosodic phrase (see section 2.4.2) that is not a schwa, and that is followed by /v/, /z/, /ʒ/, or /ʁ/ is lengthened. The conditions listed in the previous statement have to be fulfilled simultaneously or lengthening does not occur. Thus, the vowel /a/ in the first syllable of the word *marqueur* /maʁkœːʁ/ 'marker', although part of a closed syllable in a lexical word and followed by a lengthening consonant, is not lengthened because it is not in the primary stressed (final) syllable of the word/phrase. The vowel /œ/, on the other hand, which is in the final syllable of the same word, is lengthened for the same reasons. Restricting 'lengthening' to open-class items excludes prepositions and pronouns such as *par* 'via', *pour* 'for', *notre* 'our', and *votre* 'your', which are usually unaccented function words, and are not lengthened.

The half-closed mid vowels /o/ and /ø/ in closed syllables and under primary stress are also presumed to be longer than their half-open counterparts /ɔ/ and /œ/ in the same context. This could be an indication of 'tensing' (see section 2.1.3). Thus in northern Metropolitan French /o/ and /ɔ/ in *(il) saute* /sot/ '(he) jumps' and *sotte* /sɔt/ 'silly', as well as /ø/ and /œ/ in *jeûne* /ʒøn/ 'to fast' and *jeune* /ʒœn/ 'young', might not only be opposed in vowel quality but also in length. Length distinctions between 'tense' and 'lax' mid vowels play an important role in Canadian French (see section 2.2.1.1).

A diminishing number of speakers in rural areas of France, but a large number of speakers in Canada (Walker 1984:27) and Switzerland (Knecht and Rubattel 1984:75) still have phonemic opposition between short and long /ɛ:/ in a small number of minimal pairs: e.g. *maître* /mɛ:tʁ/ 'master' vs. *mettre* /mɛtʁ/ 'to put', *(il) bêle* /bɛ:l/ 'to bleat' vs. *belle* /bɛl/ 'pretty (fem.)' based on the longer duration of /ɛ/ in the first vs. the second word of each pair. This type of phonemic opposition, however, seems to no longer exist in Parisian French (Landick 1995).

2.3.6   Geminates

Long consonants, called **geminates**, also exist in French. Spelling is far from being a good indicator, however, since consonants spelled 'double' usually correspond to a single sound. Thus /p/ in *appliquer* 'apply' and /t/ in *lettre* 'letter' are not pronounced longer than /p/ in *épée* 'sword' and /t/ in *bâton* 'stick'. Geminate consonants frequently arise when identical consonants 'meet' at a word boundary. Such cases involve for instance pronouns and clitics before a conjugated verb (*il l'a vu* /il:avy/ 'he has seen it') or words within a larger phrase (*grande dame* /ɡʁɑ̃d:am/ 'great lady').

Gemination does not generally happen at morpheme boundaries, although there is at least one noticeable exception: double *rr* is pronounced a geminate between the verb stem and the following future and present conditional endings in *courir* 'to run' (*courra* /kuχ:a/ '(he) will run', *courrait* /kuχ:ɛ/ '(he) would run') and *mourir* 'to die' (*mourra* /muχ:a/ '(he) will die', *mourrait* /muχ:ɛ/ '(he) would die'). Although transcriptions often indicate a trill (/ʁ:/) in such contexts, the difficulty of maintaining a trill over an extended time makes it likely that the actual realization involves an approximant (/χ:/) not a trill. In *pouvoir* 'to be able to', on the other hand, *rr* is pronounced with a single consonant in both the future tense (*(il) pourra* '(he) can') and the present conditional (*(il) pourrait* '(he) could'). The likely explanation for gemination in *courir* and *mourir* is that in these verbs the stem ends in /ʁ/, while in *pouvoir* it does not. Gemination in the former case allows a phonological opposition between the present conditional (*(il) courrait* /kuχ:ɛ/ 'he would run', *(il) mourrait* /muχ:ɛ/ 'he would die') and the imperfect verb form (*(il) courait* /kuʁɛ/ 'he was running', *(il) mourait* /muʁɛ/ 'he was dying').

The double consonant letters in e.g. *irresponsable* 'irresponsible', *illisible* 'illegible', *grammaire* 'grammar', and *sommet* 'peak' are sometimes pronounced as geminates. They are thought to be **spelling pronunciation**: educated speakers might pronounce geminates where they see double consonants in writing (Yaguello 1991).

1) What phenomena exemplify the pronunciation of the words *observer* and *médecin*? The singer Edith Piaf was famous for her multiple uvular trills in sequences like *je ne regrette rien* . . . 'I don't regret anything'. Why is such an ability remarkable?

2) In adjectives such as *immense* 'huge' and *immonde* 'foul', 'unclean', French speakers can produce geminate consonants. Why would they do that if there were no geminates in French?

2.4   Beyond the segment

2.4.1   From phonemes to syllables

Adjacent sounds are articulated in such a way as to form with one another larger structures in speech. As a consequence, the articulatory characteristics of individual speech segments are modified to conform to rules and constraints applying to larger structures. We have seen that non-word-final mid vowels assimilate in height to the final stressed vowel of the word (vowel harmony, see section 2.1.3), oral vowels become nasalized in contact with nasal consonants (contextual nasalization, see section 2.2.2.), and consonants in a cluster pick up the voicing characteristics of consonants that precede or follow (voicing assimilation, see section 2.3.4). Humans can perceive and use such characteristics of speech segments to speed up the processing of spoken language (Martin and Bunell 1981).

2.4.1.1   The internal structure of syllables

Syllables, the smallest structures composed of individual sounds, are crucially important units of speech production and perception. They are typically larger than a phone and smaller than or equal to a word. Syllables are the operating units in language games like *verlan* (see section 4.9.2), in children's first 'words', and in slips of the tongue, i.e. saying *David Bear's Bear* instead of *David Blair's Bear* by anticipating an upcoming syllable (*Bear*) instead of the actual syllable to be pronounced (*Blair*). The way in which vowels and consonants come together to form syllables is also not random: syllables have their own internal structure. Figure 2.5 shows simplified representations of several types of syllable, each corresponding to one word.

In CV, V, VC, and CVC syllables (see Figure 2.5) there is one segment filling each or some of the slots defining the internal structure of the syllable. This structure is universally composed of an onset and a **rhyme**, with the latter further subdivided into a **nucleus** and a **coda**. Most varieties of French also allow more complex structures at each of these locations. When onsets, nuclei, and

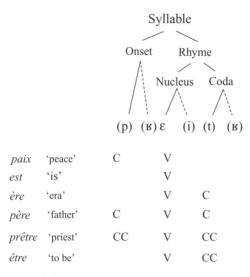

paix	'peace'	C	V	
est	'is'		V	
ère	'era'		V	C
père	'father'	C	V	C
prêtre	'priest'	CC	V	CC
être	'to be'		V	CC

Figure 2.5 Simple and branching syllable structures in French

codas contain more than one segment, they are called complex or 'branching'. Branching onsets and codas can have up to three consonants in most varieties of French, e.g. *strident* /stʁidɑ̃/ 'shrill', *astre* /astʁ/ 'star'. Branching nuclei are typical of diphthongs (see section 2.1.4) and according to some phonological analyses (Tranel 1987) of the word-initial glide /w/ followed by a vowel in words such as *oiseau* /wazo/ 'bird' and *watt* /wat/.

General knowledge about the internal structure of syllables, however, does not help determining where a syllable starts and where it ends in the speech flow. This is because, although some syllabification rules are universal, many differ from one language to another. Here is an overview of these rules.

As shown in the sequence /bɛlɛ/, underlined in (8) below, speakers of French would tend to link the consonant surrounded by two vowels to the vowel on the right. This tendency is so strong that it applies across word-boundaries, i.e. across *bel* and *example* in (8), and only stops at the end of phrase units (speech units larger than the individual word). Called **forward syllabification** or ***enchaînement* 'linking'** (see section 2.4.4), this is an important characteristic of syllabification in French, as opposed to English which would tend to leave an intervocalic consonant such as /l/ in /bɛlɛ/ in the coda (the last consonantal slot) of the preceding syllable, rather than syllabifying it in the onset (the first consonantal slot) of the next syllable. The forward syllabification of intervocalic consonants can be considered 'rule number 1 of syllabification' in French.

(8)   *un bel exemple* /ɛ̃|bɛ|lɛ|gzɑ̃pl̥/ 'a nice example'

When there is a group of consonants between two vowels, i.e. in intervocalic consonant clusters, the syllable boundary is determined by the joint contribution of two principles: the **Maximal Onset Principle** and the **Sonority Hierarchy**. The former is a constraint maximizing the size of the onset rather than that of the coda. For instance, when the group /kstʁ/ before and after /ɛ/ in *extraire* 'extract' is to be divided between the preceding and the following vowels, the cut maximizing the onset of the following syllable (/ɛk|stʁɛ/) rather than the coda of the preceding syllable (/ɛks|tʁɛ/) will be preferred (see a similar example below). Sonority hierarchy, on the other hand, is a relative scale of sounds based on their inherent loudness. Its applications are discussed in the next section.

2.4.1.2   Distributing segments in syllables

There is general agreement that vowels are on the very top of the sonority scale. This has to do with vowels' general articulatory characteristics: they are articulated with unobstructed airflow radiating a larger amount of energy than other sounds. Thus, the most sonorous vowel is the open vowel /a/, and the least sonorous ones are the closed vowels (/i/, /y/, /u/, etc.). The second most sonorous segments are glides (/j/, /ɥ/, and /w/) and liquids (/l/ and voiced allophones of /ʁ/). The least sonorous segments are voiceless fricatives such as /s/ and /f/.

The sonority scale, together with the maximum onset principle in French, allows us to predict with some certainty in which part of the syllable each segment should be placed.

As one might have expected, the most sonorous segments, vowels, are placed in the 'middle', i.e. in the nucleus of the syllable. Consonants in syllable onsets are always aligned in increasing levels of sonority: the least sonorous ones (the voiceless fricatives /s/, /f/, and /ʃ/) should be the leftmost segments, while sonorants (/l/, /ʁ/, and glides) should be the nearest to the vocalic nucleus (see also section 2.3.4). With these rules, we are able to explain why some sequences, such as an invented sequence like *msam*, cannot be parsed into a single syllable. Going left-to-right, one can observe that according to the sonority hierarchy, the order of consonants in the onset of *msam* should be /s/ + /m/ and not /m/ + /s/. The vowel /a/ in the nucleus of the syllable satisfies the sonority hierarchy, and since consonants cannot form a branching nucleus with the vowel, /m/ was correctly parsed into the coda.

When there is more than one consonant in the coda, the coda should show decreasing order of sonority: glides should be the leftmost segments, i.e. the closest to the nucleus with the vowel, while voiceless stops and fricatives should be situated at the rightmost edge of the coda.

Besides these factors, the tendency in French to maximize the size of onsets rather than of codas means that French prefers to put the largest number of segments at the beginning rather than at the end of a syllable. Thus in a sequence like *extra* /ɛkstʁa/, the voiceless fricative /s/ is assigned to the onset of the second syllable rather than forming a branching coda with /k/ in the preceding syllable. Sonority hierarchy and the maximal onset principle are rules number 2 and number 3 of syllabification in French.

Another even more straightforward way of thinking about the syllabification of consonant clusters in French is to ask the question of whether a given sequence can appear in the onset of an existing one-syllable word (Valdman 1993). As far as the /kstʁ/ cluster in *extraordinaire* 'extraordinary' is concerned, for instance, there are many words starting with /stʁ/, but none with /kstʁ/. Consequently, the syllable boundary should separate /k/ from /s/. This 'vocabulary test', so to speak, is more difficult to apply to clusters that are infrequent word-initially. Although the cluster /gz/ appears in only a few words and proper names in French, it seems to be a legitimate word-initial onset e.g. in words like *xylophone* /gzilofɔn/ 'xylophone', *Xérès* /gzeʁɛs/ 'brand name of a vinegar', and *Xantia* /gzɑ̃tja/ 'model of a car'.

---

1) Represent graphically the internal structure of the syllable *brusque* /bʁysk/ 'sudden'.
2) Syllabify the following series of vowels and consonants: *la construction d'une piste de course* /lakɔ̃stʁyksjɔ̃ ‖ dynpistədəkuʁs/ 'the construction of a running trail'.
3) Why are word boundaries not marked in a phonetic transcription in French?

2.4.2   From syllables to phrases

In speech, as in writing, segments form structures in which smaller units become part of larger units superimposed on them. Adjacent syllables form words, words cluster in small phrases, and small phrases are grouped into large phrases set off from other large phrases. In each case, it is supposed that a given group of speech segments is exhaustively contained in the next largest constituent of which it is a part. This hierarchical organization of speech units that are exhaustively contained in each other received the name of **strict layer hypothesis** (Selkirk 1986). The series of 'groups' or constituents 'built' in this way is referred to as **prosodic hierarchy** (see Figure 2.6).

The idea of such a hierarchy is that the continuous flow of speech is processed and mentally represented by the hearer in hierarchically arranged chunks called 'the prosodic constituents of the grammar'. These constituents, it is hypothesized, are 'audible' in speech since they are 'signaled' by subtle acoustic modifications (e.g. harmony, assimilation, nasalization, etc.) at the lowest levels of processing, which is typically the level of the syllable. Changes in intonation and rhythm on the other hand would signal boundaries of higher-level constituents

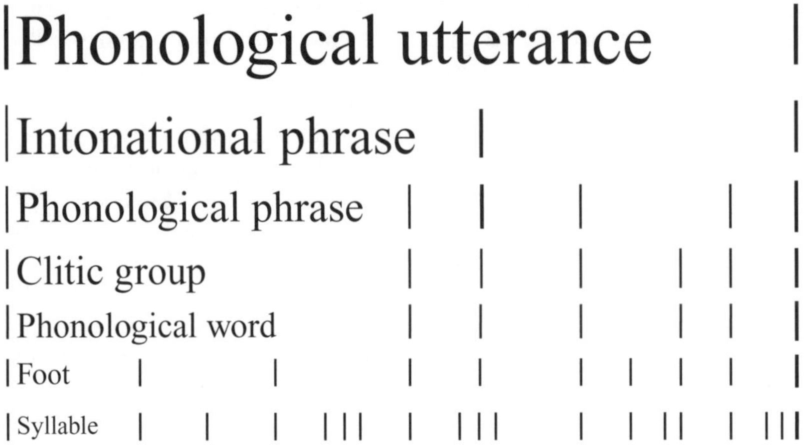

|Phonological utterance |

|Intonational phrase | |

	Phonological phrase					
|Clitic group						
|Phonological word						
|Foot								
|Syllable			||	|||		||	|||

Figure 2.6 A model of the hierarchy of the prosodic constituents (following Nespor and Vogel 1986)

in the hierarchy. According to the model presented here, prosodic constituents might or might not overlap with syntactic and morphological constituents (see Chapter 3). Each unit of the hierarchy, however, should be necessary for the formulation of at least one phonological rule (Selkirk 1986, Nespor and Vogel 1986, Delais-Roussarie 2000).

2.4.2.1   The foot
The prosodic unit above the syllable, the foot, is well known from poetry since ancient times. Syllables can be parsed into different patterns based on the alternation of metrically (from 'meter' in poetry) strong (σ) and weak (ω) syllables. Two-syllable foot types, such as **trochee** and **iamb**, are composed of one strong and one weak syllable. The strong syllable is at the left edge in trochees, and at the right edge in iambs: e.g. *'permit* (noun) vs. *per'mit* (verb)). The metrical foot is also an operating prosodic unit in French. The tendency of northern Metropolitan varieties to have phrase-final stress is sometimes referred to as iambic, thus favoring a weak-strong foot pattern. It is often contrasted with the trochaic, strong-weak, rhythmic preferences of southern Metropolitan varieties (Léon and Carton 1983). The foot has been found a relevant lower-level prosodic domain in several varieties of French (Selkirk 1978, Coquillon et al. 2000, Montreuil 2002).

2.4.2.2   The phonological word
The phonological word (PhW) is the lowest unit in which interactions between phonological and morphological information in the grammar can be observed;

in syllables and metrical feet only purely phonological rules are 'at work' (following Nespor and Vogel 1986). The domain of the PhW would be, for instance, a compound word or a single word with all its affixes (see Chapter 3). In French, the association of the prefix *in-* followed by the adjectives *possible* (*impossible*) or *né* (*inné*) would qualify for such a domain through assimilation of place of articulation between the adjacent consonants of the prefix and the adjective (see also section 2.3.4).

Another phonological process that takes place at the PhW level in French is 'open/closed syllable adjustment', also known as *la loi de position*. As we have seen in section 2.1.3, when we discussed the behavior of mid vowels, closed syllable adjustment (*la loi de position*) requires the front mid vowel /ɛ/ in a word like *pierre* /pjɛʀ/ 'stone' to be half-open, since the syllable is closed, having a coda consonant. When this word appears in a larger phrase, e.g. *pierre identique* 'identical stone', this would contradict rule number 1 of syllabification, requiring intervocalic consonants to be syllabified with the following vowel! In other words /ʀ/ should be syllabified with /i/ across the word boundary: /pjɛ|ʀi|dɑ̃|tik/.

Thus the question is: how do we obtain a half-open vowel /ɛ/ in *pierre* when, due to obligatory forward resyllabification, it is an open syllable, and therefore the vowel /e/ is expected? The solution suggested by some is to model open/closed syllable adjustment (*la loi de position*) at the PhW level and forward resyllabification at a higher prosodic level. This way, adjustment rules at a lower level of the prosodic hierarchy would apply 'first' and the syllabification rule second (for alternative explanations see section 2.4.4).

2.4.2.3   The clitic group

The clitic group (ClG), in models that recognize its existence as a unit separate from the phonological phrase, is hierarchically superior to the PhW. Following Nespor and Vogel's (1986) model, the ClG is the 'lowest' prosodic constituent in the hierarchy to take syntactic information into account.

In French, ClGs are verb phrases preceded or followed by clitics, e.g. *Je les ai vus* 'I saw them' or *Regardez-les!* 'Look at them!' Clitics are not autonomous words, but obligatorily need a verb to be their lexical head (see section 3.6.2). From a phonological point of view, on the other hand, they seem to 'behave' similarly to pronouns (*nous*, *vous*) and determiners, and processes like **liaison** also apply to them (*Je les‿ai vus* 'I saw them') just as automatically as they do to pronouns (*Nous‿avons vu ces films* 'We saw these movies'). Thus it would seem that the accentual and metrical properties of clitics and pronouns can be captured in a unifying way in French, which also entails that ClGs might not show any particular 'phonological behavior', setting them aside from other other phonological phrases, such as verbs with no clitics or noun phrases. In other words, there are reasons to believe that ClGs in French are not an independent prosodic constituent (see e.g. Delais-Roussarie 2001).

2.4.2.4 The phonological phrase

The phonological phrase (PhP) is also motivated on the grounds that it is necessary for modeling a phonological process. One such process in French is **liaison**, the forward syllabification of a word-final consonant to the first vowel of the following word (see also section 2.4.4). Since liaison only applies in some syntactic contexts, its modeling should necessarily take sentence structure into account. But 'explaining' liaison from a purely syntactic point of view has also been difficult. As we will see in Chapter 3, syntactic rules are blind to the fact that nouns and adjectives that belong to the same larger syntactic phrase may or may not have liaison: e.g. liaison is obligatory in *de bons_amis* 'good friends', but is frequenty omitted in *des amis/incroyables* 'incredible friends'. As we will see in section 2.4.4, the analyses of various examples of liaison will suggest that liaison is the result of interactions between several components of the grammar, and is also motivated by non-linguistic factors.

2.4.2.5 At the top of the hierarchy

The prosodic constituents occupying the highest levels of the prosodic hierarchy are the intonational phrase (IP) and the phonological utterance (PU). One can say in general that the higher the level, the more general and complex the nature of its definition becomes (Nespor and Vogel 1986:187). The IP is not syntactically attached to the sentence but makes use of syntactic information, for instance to know where it can be inserted in a larger utterance. This is the case for instance with short sentences that are added as side comments to a main sentence: *J'ai tout fini, dit Pierre, et il est parti pour le week-end* 'I am done with everything, Peter said, and he left for the week-end.' The phrase *dit Pierre* 'Peter said' forms an autonomous prosodic unit that could be inserted only at certain locations in the utterance (see e.g. Espinal 1991, Fagyal 2002). In traditional models of prosodic hierarchy, the IP is claimed to be defined on the basis of intonational and rhythmic constraints, e.g. major pitch rises and falls, tempo, and the overall length of the phrase (see section 2.5).

The PU, which consists of one or more IPs, does not simply correspond to a sentence-long syntactic structure. Like the other constituents of the prosodic hierarchy, the PU has a syntactic structure, but it is also defined on factors related to utterance meaning and discourse context. However, similarly to lower-level constituents, the PU is also a phonological domain in French. The gemination of identical consonants at adjacent prosodic boundaries, for instance, applies in all constituents dominated by it, but it is stopped only at PU boundaries (9a–e).

(9)	a)	*il mourra*	/muʁːa/	'he will die'	PhW
	b)	*il l'a lu*	/ilːaly/	'he read it'	ClG
	c)	*grande dame*	/gʁɑ̃dːam/	'great lady'	PhP
	d)	*La bonne, nous l'avons vue.*	/labɔnːulavɔ̃vy/	'The servant, we saw (her).'	IP
	e)	*Vous pouvez partir. Revenez demain.*	/vupuvepaʁtiʁ ‖ ʁəvənedəmɛ̃/	'You may leave. Come back tomorrow.'	PU

In the next two sections, we examine two emblematic phenomena of the sounds of French: liaison and the behavior of schwas. Both are associated, at least in part, with the phonological phrase.

---

1) Divide the following utterance into prosodic constituents: *Pierre, son père, il (ne) lui a rien redemandé en échange* 'Peter's father asked nothing in exchange.' What are the places of uncertainty and why?
2) What type of foot structure do the English words *understand* and *desperate* exemplify? Can you find similar examples in French?

2.4.3   The schwa

2.4.3.1   Why call the schwa a schwa?

The schwa or 'neutral' mid vowel, occurs in many languages. In languages such as English and German, the schwa is a non-rounded central vowel, corresponding to the last two vowels in the English word *permanent*, and the final vowel in the German word *Gabe* 'fork'. In French, except for French-based Creole varieties where it is either elided or pronounced /e/, the schwa is pronounced /ø/ before high vowels and glides (*netteté* /nɛtəte/ 'clarity', *atelier* /atəlje/ 'workshop') and at the end of major prosodic phrases (*Dis-le!* /dilə/ 'Say it!'), but it sounds like /œ/ in other contexts, particularly before and after /ʁ/ (*retenir* /ʁətəniʁ/ 'retain', *soufflerie* /sufləʁi/ 'bellows'). While recognizing its merger with mid vowels, we will retain a separate symbol, /ə/, for this vowel rather than using /ø/ or /œ/ to transcribe it. This is because in many cases, e.g. in contexts of hiatus, morphological alternations, diphthongization in Canadian French, and other specific prosodic conditions, the schwa 'behaves' differently from either /ø/ or /œ/, and this makes it necessary to analyze it as a phonologically distinct segment.

Most word-final schwas, spelled *e* in words like *table* 'table' and *lune* 'luna', go back to the Latin word-final /a/, although some emerged due to the loss of other vowels or even of entire syllables. In the northern, i.e. *oïl*, dialects of French, /a/ weakened to a central neutral vowel towards the late seventh century, labialized during the fifteenth century, and finally became silent by the end of the eighteenth century (hora (Latin) > *heure* /œʁ/ 'hour', filia(s) (Latin) > *fille* /fij/ 'girl', stella (Latin) > *étoile* /etwal/ 'star'). This development set northern varieties apart from other Romance languages, including the southern, i.e. *Oc*, dialects, since the latter preserved the Latin /a/ as a full word-final vowel.

2.4.3.2   *Schwa and dialect*

Consider for instance the transcription of an utterance in (10), pronounced by a mountain guide living in the southern Alps. While all word-final schwas bolded and underlined were pronounced by the guide (10a), a hypothetical realization of the same utterance by a northern French speaker (10b) would only contain one word-final schwa in the function word *de* 'of'.

(10)   *Cette corniche nous indique un danger, s'il y a une   chute de neige*
         'This ledge signals danger, if there is a snow fall . . .'
         a) / sɛtəkɔʀniʃə   nuzɛ̃dikə   ɛ̃dɑ̃ʒe   siljaynə   ʃytədənɛʒə/
         b) / sɛtkɔʀniʃ   nuzɛ̃dik   ɛ̃dɑ̃ʒe   siljayn   ʃydːənɛʒ/
                                                (France 2, evening news, 1997)

Thus in terms of prosodic hierarchy (see section 2.4.2), we seem to be dealing with different domains of application of word-final schwa rules. In the southern speaker's speech, word-final schwas emerge within and across word boundaries throughout the phonological utterance, while in the hypothetical northern realization, only one out of the seven potential word-final schwas emerges within a phonological phrase. Thus the prosodic domain of schwa insertion in the southern varieties seems to be the foot (Coquillon et al. 2000), while the appropriate domain in the northern varieties is more likely be the phonological phrase (Walker 2001). However, it has been argued that a 'vestigial' trocheic type of foot still regulates a large portion of word-internal schwa placement in northern varieties of French as well (Montreuil 2002). Nonetheless the 'erratic' behavior of schwa in the northern Metropolitan varieties is probably most easily described with respect to its place in the phonological phrase.

2.4.3.3   *Phrase-final schwas*

Phonological phrase-finally, as we can see in (10b), schwas are elided with virtually no exception in the northern Metropolitan varieties. And yet, there are phrase-final schwas at the end of major discourse units in the French spoken in Paris!

In a chunk of discourse of equal or larger size than a paragraph or a speaker's turn, the strong release of the final consonant (due to the realization of primary stress, see section 2.5.1) can provoke a vowel-like sound after the released final consonant and before a pause. This can also happen at the end of words which, historically, did not contain a reduced final vowel: *Bonjourə!* 'Hello!' (see e.g. Fagyal 1998, Carton 1999). Given that the release of final consonants in French, as opposed to English, is always strong, the 'audible' release of a consonant is not surprising. But in this case the release had vocalized into a 'real' vowel, and is now interpreted as signaling the end of a conversational or discourse unit in colloquial spoken French (Hansen and Mosegaard 2003).

2.4.3.4 Phrase-medial schwas

The general rule accounting for word-internal and word-final schwas that are other than at the end of a phonological phrase is the well-known 'three consonant rule' or *loi des trois consonnes* (Grammont 1939).

This rule states that any schwa surrounded by three pronounced consonants is retained, while schwas not fulfilling this condition are deleted. Word boundaries do not block the process, which is why phrase-internal schwa insertion seems to belong to the domain of the phonological phrase. As suggested by Walker (2001:82), however, referring to 'three' consonants is somewhat a misnomer: the key factor in retaining phrase-internal schwas is not three consonants surrounding the schwa, but at least two pronounced consonants preceding the schwa. The examples in (11) show that schwa deletion routinely produces triconsonantal sequences within the phonological phrase that are nevertheless tolerated because the consonant cluster follows (and not precedes) the schwa. The examples in (12) also show that schwa deletion is blocked in CCəC contexts, i.e. when a consonant cluster precedes and a single consonant follows the schwa.

(11) *cett(e) proposition* /sɛtpʁopozisjɔ̃/ (12) *appartement* /apaʁtəmɑ̃/
      'this proposal'   'apartment'
      sans l(e) sculpteur /sɑ̃lskyltœʁ/   *cercle fermée* /sɛʁkləfɛʁme/
      'without the sculptor'   'closed circle'
      il nous r(e)trouve /ilnuʁtʁuv/   *un apte guerrier* /ɛ̃naptəgeʁje/
      'he finds us'   'a worthy warrior'

There is only one case when consonants following the schwa prevent its deletion: when the schwa is followed by an LG (liquid + glide) cluster as illustrated in (13). In all other contexts, the schwa is deleted as in (14). Individual consonants in clusters resulting from schwa deletion undergo assimilation of voicing and sometimes of place, as we have seen in section 2.3.4.

(13)   *chandelier* /ʃɑ̃dəlje/ 'candlestick'   (14)   *médecin* /metsɛ̃/ 'doctor'
    Vous bouderiez /vubudəʀje/   *salade verte* /saladvɛʁt/
    'You would pout'   'green salad'
    Il faut le lier /ilfoləlje/   *chute de neige* /ʃydːənɛʒ/
    'It needs to be linked'   'snow fall'

So-called rhythmic constraints within the phonological phrase are another powerful conditioning factor for schwa placement in French. This phenomenon is related to prosodic and accentual factors, and as such will be discussed in a later part of this chapter (see section 2.5.1).

2.4.3.5   Phrase-initial schwas

Schwas tend to be preserved in phonological phrase-initial position (see the examples in (18)), and even seem to have been increasing their stability in this prosodic position over the past few decades (Hansen 1994). This might be attributed to the accentual-metric properties of larger phonological phrases (see section 2.5.1), whose first syllable tends to attract 'initial stress' (*accent initial*) and therefore preserve the nucleus of the prominent syllable (Walter 1977).

SCHWAS IN CONTIGUOUS SYLLABLES   When several schwas occur one after the other, often one schwa starting the phrase, they can be deleted when preceded and followed by a single consonant, as shown in examples (15) through (18). Obviously, however, not all schwas can be deleted in such cases, even though the 'three consonant rule' itself would not prevent their deletion. Indeed schwa deletion in contiguous syllables has often been modeled by the cyclic application of the 'three consonant rule': when the first schwa in the sequence is deleted, the second should stay because it is preceded by two consonants, then the third can be deleted again, since the fourth is kept, and so on (see example in (15)).

(15)   . . . *de ce que je te*   /dəskəʒtəpaʁl/   'of what I am talking to you'
    parle . . .

(16)   a)   *Tu ne le fais pas.*   /tynləfɛpa/   'You are not doing it.'
    b)   *Tu (ne) le fais pas.*   /tylfɛpa/

(17)   . . .*que je te revois* . . .   /kəʃtəχəvwa/   'that I see you again'

(18)   *Ne me regarde pas.*   /nəmχəgaʁdəpa/   'Don't look at me.'
    Demain, il pleuvra.   /dəmɛ̃‖ ilplœvʁa/   'Tomorrow, it will rain.'

Some clitics and morphemes enjoy special status with respect to schwa deletion, which shows that the process is also sensitive to morphological information. The schwa in the negative particle *ne* for instance elides in priority when it is not in phrase-initial position, which often triggers the deletion of the entire syllable (16a). The elision of *ne* in turn can set the stage for the deletion of the schwa in the following word (16b). The prefixes *de-* and *re-* are always preserved in priority (see example in (17)).

2.4.3.6 Schwas and morphological alternations

Alternations involving schwas in French are numerous and play an important role in inflectional as well as derivational morphology (see section 3.2.1). The /ɛ/–/ə/ pair is responsible for alternations between verb forms in the infinitive (*appeler* /apəle/ 'to call', *semer* /səme/ 'to seed'), third-person singular (*il appelle* /apɛl/ 'he calls', *il sème* /sɛm/ 'he seeds'), and first-person plural (*nous appelons* /ap(ə)lɔ̃/ 'we call', *nous semons* /səmɔ̃/ 'we seed') of the most productive conjugation class in French: *-er* verbs. This pair is also put to use productively in different types of derivation, for instance: *peler* /pəle/ 'to peel' – *elle pèle* /pɛl/ 'she peels' – *pelage* /pəlaʒ/ 'peeling', and *crocheter* /kʁɔʃte/ 'to pick' – *elle crochète* /kʁoʃɛt/ 'she picks' – *crochetage* /kʁɔʃtaʒ/ 'picking'.

When the half-closed mid vowel is added to the paradigm, we obtain the /ə/–ɛ/–/e/ alternating environment: e.g. *appeler* /apəle/ 'to call', *j'appelle* /apɛl/ 'I call', and *appellation* /apelasjɔ̃/ 'brand'. In each case, each vowel is attributed to a particular verb stem or base word: /ə/ most frequently to infinitives and nouns, /ɛ/ to the stem in first-, second- and third-person singular, and /e/ in first- and second-person plural. Usage-based theories of grammar suggest that forms or associations between forms like these are stored 'as is' in speakers' mental lexicons (Bybee 2001).

---

1) Why is the schwa pronounced in *appartement* 'apartment' and *chambre d'hôte* 'bed and breakfast'?
2) Circle all schwas that can be simultaneously deleted in the following sentence if pronounced by a speaker from a) northern, and b) southern areas of France: *Ce que je te ferai remarquer ne devrait pas être redit à mon père.* 'What I am going to tell you should not be repeated to my father.'

2.4.4 Liaison and enchaînement

2.4.4.1 From forward syllabification to liaison

Consonants between two vowels tend to be linked to the next vowel in French, a tendency we called forward syllabification in section 2.4.1.1. Special conditions apply, however, to word-final consonants.

Many consonants that are pronounced at the end of words are word-final, because in many varieties of French schwas (silent *e*) at the end of these words are no longer pronounced (see section 2.4.3.1). Sometimes called 'protective schwas', these vowels are thought to have historically 'protected' from elision the consonant that preceded them (Posner 1997:263). These cases are predictable from spelling (e.g. *un verre* 'a glass', *une bouteille* 'a bottle') and pose no particular problem for forward syllabification. But there are two other types of 'word-final' consonant in French.

STABLE WORD-FINAL CONSONANTS (*le bec* 'beak', *la dot* 'dowry') are always pronounced even though they are not followed (underlyingly) by a word-final schwa. This is because the motivations behind the historical sound changes that affected these consonants, and shaped them to what they are today, are no longer accessible for speakers. Stable final consonants in words like *chef* 'chief' and *finir* 'to end' result from a "historically documented restoration" process by which word-final consonants in many monosyllabic words were "preserved from extinction" before the sixteenth century. In other words, "graphical" or "fixed" word-final consonants are not the rule but rather fossilized remains of past changes preserved in the lexicon (see Posner 1997 for more detail).

LATENT WORD-FINAL CONSONANTS are pronounced before a word-initial vowel, but not before a word-initial consonant. One such example is /t/ in *petit* 'small', which is pronounced in *petit animal* 'small animal' /pətitanimal/ but not in *petit chien* 'small dog' /pətiʃjɛ̃/. Latent consonants are part of speakers' mental representation of the word, but they only appear when they need to serve as syllable onsets for the initial syllable of the following word. The process by which latent word-final consonants emerge to prevent hiatus between the preceding and the following vowels at a word-boundary is called **liaison**. Thus liaison in general is a specific case of *enchaînement*: it is the 'linking' of latent word-final consonants. In some cases, latent word-final consonants, even if they emerge, are not linked to the following syllable: liaison can happen without *enchaînement* (see below).

There is currently no consensus about the prosodic domain of liaison and *enchaînement*. Many have suggested that the domain of common cases of liaison should be the phonological phrase (Selkirk 1986, Nespor and Vogel 1986), or a prosodic constituent of similar span and complexity (Brown and Jun 2002). Many have also shown, however, that there are problems with both proposals (Post 2000, Fougeron and Delais-Roussarie 2004). All speech styles considered, the situation is even more complex since liaison can cut across large phrase boundaries set off by a pause in conversation (Nespor and Vogel 1986:240), and it can also be blocked by what seems to be a major phrase boundary in formal speech styles (Miller and Fagyal 2005).

2.4.4.2   Liaison and h-aspiré

If liaison is the realization, vowel-initially, of an otherwise silent or 'latent' final consonant, then it can be, broadly speaking, considered an alternation between two forms of a word. Such alternations, specifically involving word-final consonants, are in fact commonly used for gender and number distinctions: e.g. *français* /fʁɑ̃sɛ/ vs. *françaises* /fʁɑ̃sɛz/ 'French', *l'enfant* /lɑ̃fɑ̃/ vs. *les enfants* /lezɑ̃fɑ̃/. But the tendency to avoid hiatus, i.e. to provide each syllable with an onset, is so strong that it can take priority for instance over gender marking.

Consider the words *armoire* 'wardrobe' and *aiguille* 'needle' in the examples in (19) below. They are vowel-initial feminine words that prefer the masculine possessive forms *mon* 'my' and *son* 'your' over the only morphologically appropriate feminine form *ma* and *sa*. Furthermore, vowel-initial masculine words such as *arbre* 'tree' and *ami* 'friend' shown in (20) also necessitate the use of forms that are ambiguous for gender marking (they sound feminine), but which are preferred because they accomplish liaison, and thus prevent hiatus. (NB: The forms *cet* and *bel* in (20) are only gender-neutral in writing; they sound like the feminine forms *cette* and *belle*.) Some have analyzed this behavior of French adjectives and determiners as cases of **suppletion**, i.e. the use of an 'unrelated' morphological form (Tranel 1996), while other proposals stress the fact that using the form of the 'inappropriate' gender (for instance in (19) and (20)) is the only option that resolves hiatus without creating an entirely novel form (Steriade 1999).

(19) *mon armoire* /mɔ̃naʁmwaʁ/ 'my wardrobe' **ma armoire*
      son aiguille /sɔ̃neɡɥij/ 'his needle' **sa aiguille*

(20) *cet arbre* /sɛtaʁbʁ/ 'this tree' **ce arbre*
      bel ami /bɛlami/ 'handsome friend' **beau ami*

(21) a) *nos héros* /noeʁo/ 'our heros' **nos héros/nozeʁo/*
      b) *le hibou* /ləibu/ 'the owl' **l'hibou /libu/*
                                          *morphologically 'correct' but
                                          phonologically incorrect form

One category of words, called **h-aspiré** 'aspirated h' words, behave differently with respect to liaison. These words are a small class of lexical exceptions that require hiatus. To achieve this, they block liaison, as shown in (21a), and

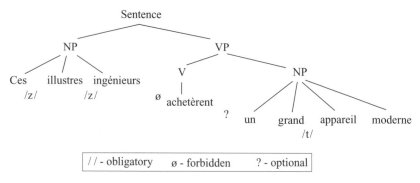

Figure 2.7 Schematic sentence structure and obligatory, optional, and forbidden liaisons in *Ces illustres ingénieurs achetèrent un grand appareil moderne*. 'These renowned engineers bought a big modern device.'

prevent schwa deletion with preceding pronouns and clitics, as illustrated in (21b). Spelled with an *h*, silent since at least the sixteenth century (see section 6.4.1.2), so-called *h-aspiré* words are best represented as vowel-initial words with empty consonantal onsets: phonetically speaking they start with a vowel, but phonologically they behave as if they began with a consonant. Therefore these words do not necessitate having a word-final latent consonant linked to their onset (Tranel 1996).

2.4.4.3 *Liaison and syntax, morphology, and the lexicon*
The most difficult aspect of liaison to model, however, is not lexical exceptions like *h-aspiré* words. It is the fact that liaison is not obligatory between each and every word in a prosodic phrase. Historically, the situation was much easier, since word-final consonants were systematically pronounced before vowels. However, word-final consonants progressively eroded, and have only been preserved in some cases. Thus 'predicting' when liaison occurs is now a complex issue that very likely involves several domains of the grammar as well as language-external factors.

Liaison can be obligatory, optional, or outright forbidden (see section 2.4.4.4). Syntactic structure is thought to play an important role in predicting where liaison is likely to occur, as there is good correlation between liaison and words with strong syntactic ties. Although syntactic trees have not yet been introduced (see Chapter 3), a rough sketch of the structure of an utterance in Figure 2.7 gives a general idea of what syntactic ties mean.

Based on Figure 2.7, we can say that words that are in the same syntactic phrase (NP or VP) are more likely to be bound together by liaison than words in different phrases and at different levels in the syntactic phrase structure.

Thus liaison is obligatory between *grand* 'grand' and *appareil* 'device' as well as *ces* 'this' and *illustres* 'famous' and *ingénieurs* 'engineers' in Figure 2.7, as these words are adjectives and nouns that belong to the same noun phrase (NP). Liaison is uncertain or optional between the verb *achetèrent* 'bought' and the indefinite article *un*, belonging to different syntactic phrases, and it is forbidden between *achetèrent* and the preceding subject noun *ingénieurs* 'engineers', which are separated by a major syntactic phrase boundary. But syntax is 'blind' to many properties of liaison, not being able to predict for instance the fact that nouns are much less prone to liaison with an adjective that follows, *des enfants intelligents* /dezãfãẽteliʒã/ 'intelligent children' than an adjective that precedes the noun: *beaux enfants* /bozãfã/ (also mentioned in section 2.4.2.4).

Lexical frequency is also thought to explain apparently random aspects of liaison. The verb *être* is 91% prone to liaison with a preceding modal verb (e.g. *devoir* 'must', *pouvoir* 'can', *falloir* 'need to') when it is followed by a past participle (*elles doivent être retenues* 'they must be held back'), but the other auxiliary, *avoir*, is only 50% likely to behave in the same way (Bybee 2001:183). Also, the final /t/ of the third-person singular of *être* in present, *il/elle est*, is virtually certain (97%) to have liaison with any following vowel-initial word, while *s* in the first-person plural form of the same verb, *nous sommes* is only 58%, and *j'étais*, the first-person singular imperfect, is virtually unlikely (21%) to do so (Bybee 2001:180). This means that the entire verb phrase has an influence on the occurrence of liaison.

Usage-based models of grammar propose that larger chunks of such frequently occurring and syntactically more or less tightly related expressions such as the ones containing liaison in French are 'constructions', stored in our mental lexicon in ways similar to long words. Although it might be hard to tell what chunks of words form such invariable 'constructions', because these might or might not overlap with syntactic phrases (see Figure 2.7), frequency of use undoubtedly plays a role in liaison.

Another aspect of liaison seems to be morphological, since the type of latent consonant seems to depend on the morphological characteristics of the preceding word. Liaison is achieved by using one of the following six consonants: /z/, /t/, /n/, /ʀ/, /p/, and /g/. As examples (22) through (27) show, each liaison consonant is 'associated' with at least one morphosyntactic context.

(22)   /z/   *heureux_*   'happy birthdays'   plural adjective + noun
             anniversaires
             enfants_adultes   'grown-up children'   plural noun + adjective
             Donnes-en!   'Give some'   second-person sing.
                                                        verb + pronoun

(23)   *je suis̲américaine*   'I am American'   pronoun + verb +
                                                      adjective
      /t/   *Vient-il?*   'Is he coming?'   third-person sing. verb
            Viendra-t-il?   'Will he come?'   + pronoun
            petit ami   'boyfriend'   singular adjective +
            grand amour   'great love'   noun

(24)   /n/ *un/ton exemple*   'an/your example'   article (pronoun) +
                                                   noun
            bon agent   'good agent'   singular adjective +
                                                   noun

(25)   /ʀ/ *léger accueil*   'light reception'   'r' ending singular
            premier empire   'first empire'   adjective + noun
            dernier ennemi   'last enemy'
            parler ainsi   'speak in this way'   infinitive + adverb

(26)   /p/ *beaucoup exagéré*   'exaggerated a lot'   *p*-ending adverbs
            trop aimé   'too (much) loved'   + complements

(27)   /g/ *long été*   'long summer'   *g*-ending adjectives + noun

The most frequent consonants /z/, /t/, and /n/ are observable across all speech styles and varieties, and are associated with several contexts. Liaison was rare with /ʀ/, erratic with /p/, and absent with /g/ in a corpus of several hours of reading and spontaneous conversation between friends at home and at the workplace (Moisset 2000:130). These facts again raise the issue of lexical frequency, as it is likely that some of the liaison morphemes became 'entrenched' in their most frequent morphosyntactic contexts of occurrence.

So-called 'false liaisons' also attest to this possibility. It is widely acknowledged, for instance, that /z/ is "the plural linking consonant par excellence" (Tranel 1987:170), frequently over-generating liaison with numerals that have a plural meaning but no latent consonant word-finally: *huit épreuves* */ɥizepʀœv/, 'eight tests', *quatre erreurs* */katzeʀœʀ/ 'four errors', *mille évèques* */milzevɛk/ 'a thousand bishops' (Tranel 1987:171). Probably due to the high frequency of liaison with the third-person singular form of *être* (*c'est*), false liaisons involving /t/ are particularly frequent in the vicinity of this auxiliary. This phenomenon is played out in *ce n'est pas à toi* 'it's not yours', pronounced jokingly */snɛpatatwa/. (NB: /patat/ is the familiar term for *pomme de terre* 'potato'.) The liaison consonant /n/ is so frequent in determiner + noun contexts that it can, mistakenly, be interpreted as part of the lexical representation of vowel-initial masculine nouns by children acquiring

French as a native language: *navion for *avion* 'airplane', *nordinateur* for *ordinateur* 'computer'.

2.4.4.4 *Liaison without* enchaînement

With all the above aspects taken together, liaison already seems complicated. And yet situational factors also need to be mentioned, as speech styles play a crucial role in determining when and where liaison might occur.

In general, the more formal the speech style is, the more often liaison tends to occur. In formal styles 'optional' liaisons occur in greater numbers, and they tend to involve relatively rare linking consonants as well. A particular case of liaison in formal speech styles, liaison *sans enchaînement* 'liaison without linking' is especially noteworthy in this respect, because its first detailed analysis by Encrevé (1988) revealed stylistic dimensions of liaison largely unknown until that time.

(28)   *il faut* /ə/ # *interdire*   /ilfotə ‖ ɛ̃tɛʁdiʁ /   'one must forbid'

Most of the time, word-final latent consonants are syllabified with the onset of the following syllable within a larger prosodic phrase. Thus, liaison usually means *enchaînement* as well. But the emerging latent final consonant is not necessarily always linked to the onset of the following word. In example (28), /t/ in *il faut* 'one must' remains in the coda of the syllable /fot/ instead of being syllabified in the onset of the initial syllable of *interdire* 'forbid'. The liaison consonant is followed by a schwa-like vowel and a pause. To fill the onset of the syllable at the beginning of the next word, there is often a glottal stop following the pause.

These cases are also interesting because they 'cut across' major prosodic boundaries signaled by a pause and other major pitch events (Encrevé 1988:190). Therefore they do not conform to the model which attributes liaison to the domain of the PhP (see section 2.4.2.4), and as some rightly pointed out, when all types, contexts of occurrence, and speech styles are taken into account, liaison remains one of the most challenging topics of French phonology (Rialland 1988).

---

1) What would be the phonetic transcription and the English translation of the following sentence if liaison would NOT be blocked by *h-aspiré* words? *Nos héros sont en haut, ils halètent très fort.* 'Our heroes are up (there), panting heavily.'
2) What is the difference, if any, between the pronunciations of neuf in *neuf livres* 'nine books', *neuf portes* 'nine doors', and *neuf ans* 'nine years'?

2.5   On stress, accent, and intonation

2.5.1   Stress and accent

The accentual system of French is unlike that of any other Romance language. The primary **stress**ed, i.e. most prominent, syllable in most varieties of French is the final full (non-schwa) syllable of a prosodic phrase, and it is not involved in distinguishing the meaning of words. In a language such as Spanish, on the other hand, the stressed syllable can be in different positions in the word, and it is lexically contrastive (*'número* 'number' vs. *nu'mero* 'I number' vs. *nume'ró* 'she/he numbered'). English is similar to Spanish in that changing the position of the primary stressed syllable in the word changes the meaning of the word (e.g. *'permit* (noun) vs. *per'mit* (verb)).

The physical manifestation of stress, when it makes primary use of the laryngeal frequency (called **pitch**) rather than length and loudness, is called **accent**. Speakers, depending on the height and size of their larynx, the length of their vocal folds, and other physiological characteristics, have a certain range of laryngeal frequencies with which their vocal folds can vibrate at any given time. Within this overall range, variations in pitch are used for communicative purposes (see section 2.5.2).

As in many languages, accent placement in French helps to disambiguate the meaning of sentences (see examples in (29) and (30)). Following the prosodic hierarchy (section 2.4.2), one would readily call the phonological phrase (PhP) the domain of accent placement in French. But, as it turns out, the actual prosodic phrasing of an utterance often differs from predictions one can make based on the syntactic information that is chiefly involved in the definition of the PhP. One possible solution is to redefine the prosodic hierarchy so that it can take into account factors such as the length of the phrase and speech tempo.

(29) $\{[Ceux\ qui\ \underline{savent}]_{\text{PhP}}\ [leur\ souffleront]_{\text{PhP}}\}_{\text{IP}}$
          'Those who know (it) will whisper (it) to them.'

(30) $\{[Ceux\ qui\ savent\ l'heure]_{\text{PhP}}\ [souffleront]_{\text{PhP}}\}_{\text{IP}}$
          'Those who know what time it is will whisper (it).'

Many such models have been proposed for intonation and prosodic phrasing in French. So many, in fact, that even outlining them here would be a daunting task (see Di Cristo 1999, 2000, Di Cristo and Hirst 1998, and Lacheret-Dujour and Beaugendre 1999 for detailed reviews of many models).

2.5.2   A phonological model of French intonation

The model presented here is an autosegmental-metrical (AM) model of French intonation (Jun and Fougeron 1995, 2000, 2002) that subscribes to two

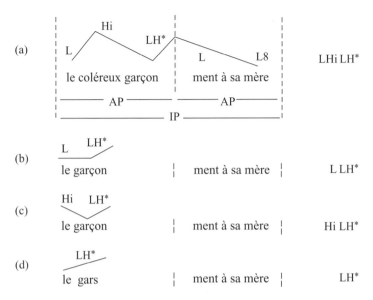

Figure 2.8 Realizations of AP in IP- and utterance-initial positions (utterance in (a) adapted from Jun and Fougeron 2002:154)

important notions, widely accepted in current phonological approaches to intonation. The first is that each utterance has an underlying metrical structure ('meter' from poetry), i.e. some kind of a regular pattern of alternation between stressed and unstressed syllables. The second is that this metrical structure provides 'docking sites' for the physical realization of two types of tonal event: (1) **pitch accents**, which are tonal events (i.e. local pitch maxima (H) and/or minima (L)) associated with prominent (stressed) syllables at the word or phrase level; and (2) **boundary tones**, which are tonal events associated with the edges of prosodic phrases. The intonation contour of an utterance arises from 'continuously moving' from one tonal event to the other, while 'accenting', i.e. pronouncing louder, with higher or lower pitch, and often with longer duration, prominent (stressed) syllables as opposed to less prominent (unstressed) syllables.

Accent is assigned to the most prominent syllables in an accentual phrase (AP). According to the model presented here, the AP has a 'default' LHiLH* accentual pattern, illustrated on the six-syllable AP *le coléreux garçon* 'the angry boy' in the top contour (a) in Figure 2.8. Since an AP in French is made up of tonal elements that can be omitted or realized 'imperfectly' (undershot), this default tonal pattern can have many realizations (see contours (b), (c), and (d) in Figure 2.8).

The default pattern is composed of the following tonal events. First there is an optional L (low) tone on either the first or the second syllable of the AP.

This L tone is frequently realized when the phrase starts with a function word (*le* 'the') or a plurisyllabic lexical word. Next is the optional Hi (high initial) tone that usually falls on the first or the second syllable of the first lexical word (*coléreux* 'angry'). It is a phrasal tone, which means that its primary function is to demarcate the left edge of the AP, although it can also be used to mark emphasis or contrast. In some circumstances, there can be two rises in the AP: the first is then called Hi, the other is marked H (Jun and Fougeron 2002). When the AP is short, i.e. less than three or four syllables, there is no room to realize the Hi tone, and one can immediately proceed with the LH* pitch accent on the primary stressed (final full) syllable of the AP (*çon* of *garçon* 'boy'). This tone is a combination of a low tone (L) and a high tone (H) because it always implies the simultaneous presence of two tonal events: a low point aligned near the onset of the final syllable followed by a high point aligned with the vowel of the primary stressed syllable. The H* tone is starred to indicate that this is the metrically strongest syllable of the accentual domain (here, of the phrase). The full realization of the LHiLH* pattern is also called *arc accentuel* 'accentual arch' (Di Cristo 2000), a metaphor illustrating how the initial and final 'rises' ((L)Hi and LH*) mark the left and right edges of an AP.

That 'rising intonation' at the end of phrases is some kind of a default intonation in French seems intuitively right for learners of French as a foreign language, but it is also supported by evidence from language acquisition: French children's first utterances overwhelmingly display a rise, showing the early acquisition of the LH* pitch accent, while children acquiring English or Japanese do not show such tendencies (Halle et al. 1991, Boysson-Bardies 1999).

This of course does not mean that French speakers always raise the pitch of their voices at the end of an AP. Positing that APs in French have a default LHiLH* pattern helps us derive other possible tonal configurations. Contours (b) and (c) in Figure 2.8 show a LLH* and a HiLH* pattern with, respectively, the Hi and the first L not realized on the three-syllable AP *le garçon* 'the boy', while contour (d) illustrates the typical LH* pattern realized on the two-syllable AP *le gars* 'the guy'.

Words clustered in tightly knit syntactic phrases, i.e. a noun and a determiner in a noun phrase (see section 3.5.3) or a verb and its preceding clitics (see section 3.6.3) in a verb phrase tend to form a single AP. But this does not mean that they always do, and that such constituents cannot be broken up by large phrase boundaries because of disfluency, emphasis, and many other 'accidents' in the actual production of an utterance. The morphosyntactic 'make-up' of an AP and its length are two other important factors determining its accentual pattern. The realization and placement of the initial L and Hi tones, as mentioned earlier, partially depend on word class (lexical vs. function word), and words tend to be grouped into larger APs at a fast speech rate.

2.5.3   Notes on stress clash

Another important restriction to accent placement in general is the tendency to avoid 'clash', i.e. the contiguous realization of two accents within the same prosodic domain; in French, realizing a sequence of adjacent Hi or LH* tones in the same phrase.

Languages find different ways around stress clash. Some of these are salient in the phonological structure (e.g. moving pitch accents, inserting segments), while others involve fine-grade distinctions (e.g. aligning contiguous high tones further apart from each other). English, for instance, moves the pitch accent to the syllable preceding the stressed syllable when the next word also bears lexical stress, as it is the case in the well-known example of '*thirteen* '*men* vs. *thir*'*teen com*'*puters*. In French, the same can be achieved by the insertion of a schwa, whether underlyingly present or not. The famous 'rhythmic rule' of Léon (1992) stating that the schwa has to appear in two-syllable but not three- or four-syllable compounds, can be recast in terms of 'stress assignment' (Charette 1991) and clash resolution (Kassai 2001): a schwa is called up to prevent the clash between two contiguous (LH*) pitch accents in words like *porte-clef* 'key ring', *garde-robe* 'wardrobe', *contre-bas* 'below', and *ours /ə/ blanc* 'white bear', but not in *porte-manteau* 'coat hanger', *garde-frontière* 'border patrol', *contre-mesure* 'counter measure', or *ours polaire* 'polar bear', where the two primary stressed syllables are not contiguous.

What could be the possible realizations of the LHiLH* tonal pattern in an AP such as *C'est anticonstitutionnel.* 'It's against the Constitution'?

2.5.4   Intonation

Accentual Phrases (APs) are further structured into Intonation Phrases (IPs), with their right edges strictly aligned, which means that wherever the higher-level prosodic unit (IP) ends, the lower units (AP) ends, as well. This has implications for the tonal structure of IPs, whose right edges become 'crowded' with two types of tone: they are marked by the LH* pitch accent that comes from the last AP in the phrase, and they themselves contribute to the marking of the IP with a 'high' (H%) or a 'low' (L%) IP-phrasal tone. Further research will determine whether, similarly to languages like English, Japanese, Spanish, Korean, and others, French also has an intermediate phrase (ip) between the AP and the IP. Previous research seems to support the existence of such a phrasal domain, which is why the right edge of major phrases in pitch contours presented here are sometimes marked by an L- (low intermediate phrasal tone) (Jun and Fougeron 2000).

The schematized pitch contour (a) in Figure 2.8 shows a single IP with two APs, in which the final word of the last AP, *mère* 'mother', is also associated with a L% IP-boundary tone. This IP boundary also coincides with the end of the utterance. The way in which this configuration arises is that the LH* AP-boundary tone of the last AP in the utterance is 'preempted', i.e. replaced entirely by the L% IP-boundary tone. But IP boundaries can also occur within utterances, and can be marked by a rise. One such case is illustrated in the pitch contours of Figure 2.9 where the utterances *Le monde privé des ouvriers* 'The world without workers'/'The private world of workers' are uttered in two IPs. The first one ends on the highest and longest rise in the utterance (on *monde* 'world') and therefore is marked by a H% boundary tone. The second, utterance-final IP boundary displays a final rise, and therefore it is marked by a L% tone. The final syllable of an IP also tends to have longer duration than final syllables of APs that are not at the end of an IP. For example in Figure 2.8, the AP-final but IP-medial syllable -*çon* is lengthened to a lesser degree than *mère* which is not only AP but also IP-final. This phenomenon is called **final lengthening**, and it gradually increases at the edge of constituents as we climb up the prosodic hierarchy. Being able to measure such acoustic cues represents strong evidence for a hierarchy of prosodic constituents.

Intonation and phrasing are commonly used to distinguish between ambiguous syntactic structures. Besides the examples shown in (29) and (30), the two pitch contours in Figure 2.9 illustrate how intonation and phrasing can cue different interpretations of a single syntactic phrase. The upper utterance corresponds to a single major prosodic phrase (IP) with two minor prosodic phrases (APs), mirroring the syntactic structure shown in Figure 3.2: a noun phrase (NP) composed of the head NP *le monde privé* 'the private sphere' and its PP complement *des ouvriers* 'of workers'. The lower utterance, on the other hand, shows a greater prosodic (and syntactic) boundary before the adjectival phrase *privé des* 'deprived of': as opposed to contour (a) there is an IP-boundary between *monde* and *privé* in contour (b).

Intonation is also chiefly implicated in the expression of speakers' communicative intent (see Chapter 5). When asking for or requesting confirmation about something, the most common and neutral way of uttering the question or the request is to use 'rising intonation', i.e. a H% IP-boundary tone at the end of an utterance. Such is the case of so-called **total** or **yes-no question**s (*Tu viendras ce soir?* 'Are you coming tonight?') and, contrary to common belief, of many **partial** or **wh-question**s (*Comment vas-tu?* 'How are you doing?') in French. Asserting and ordering, on the other hand, commonly involve 'falling intonation', while other types of utterance are halfway between asking and asserting, so to speak, and display a 'midish' tone, as shown in the so-called stylized calling contour (e) in Figure 2.10. This, however, does not mean that there are no questions with falling intonation, and speakers cannot utter a

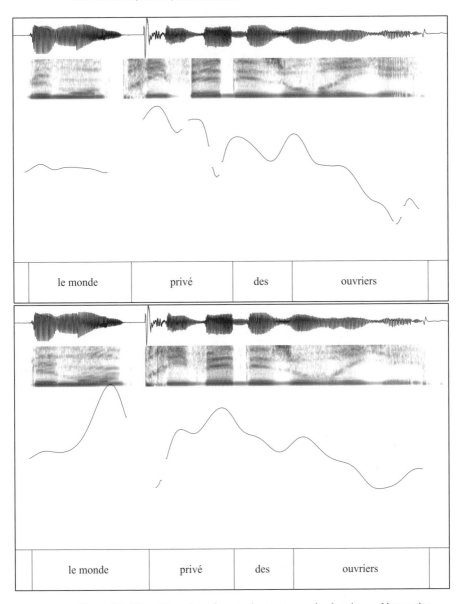

Figure 2.9 Disambiguation of syntactic structures via phrasing and intonation
(The relevant syntactic trees are shown in Figure 3.2.)

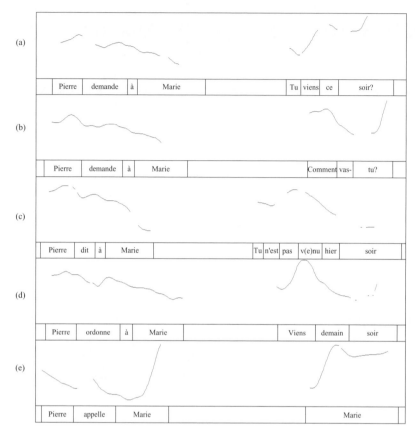

Figure 2.10 Examples of the intonation contours of a canonical 'yes-no' question (a), wh-question (b), declarative (c), imperative (d), and stylized calling (e)

statement with rising intonation. Further details on intonation in conversation will be provided in Chapter 5.

Relatively little emphasis in studies of accent and intonation in French is given to social and geographical variations. There is very little known about social factors influencing the use of prosodic patterns in French, and there is only slightly more known about differences between dialects in this respect. As mentioned previously, Canadian varieties of French differ the from French spoken in France in their treatment of vowel length. One could speculate that since Canadian French tends to put greater emphasis on the strong-weak contrast between syllables through diphthongization and laxing of vowels, such a contrast is the starting point of important prosodic differences as well (Walker

2001). It has been observed, for instance, that there is considerable **pretonic lengthening** (lengthening of the penultimate syllable) in Canadian French, partially due to diphthongization, which might have induced accentual shift from the final to the penultimate syllable in some cases (Thibault and Ouellet 1996). Other varieties of French also cast doubt on the unquestionably final position of the primary stressed syllable, as the authors point out tendencies similar to the Canadian French 'accentual shift' in Cajun French, and working-class varieties of Parisian French (Mettas 1979).

2.6   Exercises

1) Transcribe the following sentences using the symbols of the IPA.

   Jean-Marie de Mounin mourut à la ville de Dun-les-Lapin un vendredi matin le 15 juin 1581. Il disparut près de Quimper, et non pas à Saint-Etienne comme le prétendent quelques-uns de ses concitoyens. Le parfum des vertus dont le défunt était plein, se respirait de loin chez cet homme saint, un individu hors du commun même aux yeux des voisins les plus mesquins.

2) All but two of the missing letters correspond to one vowel. Identify this vowel, as well as the two exceptions. What variety of French is exemplified by these examples?

   Ad . . . le, si tu all . . . à Paris en T.G.V., tu verr . . . le Châtel . . . , la Tour . . . ffel, le Pal . . . Royal, le Musée d'Ors . . . , les Ar . . . nes de Lut . . . ce, la Madel . . . ne, la salle Pl . . . yel, le Mar . . . , la Sainte-Chap . . . lle, l'Eglise S . . . nt-Germ . . . n-des-Pr . . . s.

3) Cite examples where word-final *p*, *t*, *k*, *b*, *d*, and *g* are and are not pronounced.

4) Circle sequences that 'correspond' to the nasal vowel /ɑ̃/, and find at least one word in the text in which a vowel + *n/m* letter sequence does not correspond to a nasal vowel. Explain why this is the case.

   Les enfants ont vu un paon dans le jardin de leur voisin Adam qui est parti pour Cannes le week-end, mais qui reviendra à temps dans une semaine.

5) Use the sonority hierarchy to explain why an invented sound sequence like /rbasm/ cannot belong to a single syllable.

6) Analyze the following words in terms of onset, nucleus, and coda. Find the words that contain either a syllable with 'a complex onset' or 'a branching coda':

   masque, pneu, émeraude, strident, crique, sprint, Xavier, turque, extraordinaire, j'reviens, je r'viens, j'travaille

7) Errors might have slipped into the phonetic transcription of the following short sentences. Identify the spelling of each word, and correct the errors, if any: /tʁijele/, /ʒɛmleljɔ̃/, /kɛskilja/, /kijadisa/.

8) Certain speakers might pronounce *mettre* 'to put' and *maître* 'master' differently. What is the difference?

9) Are there geminate consonants in French? Justify your answer.

10) Find the phrases with geminate consonants: *la veuve verte, le champion olympique, c'est agrammatical, il courra, tu l(e) liras.*

11) Transcribe the following words, and justify the absence or presence of liaison: *les hors-d'œuvre, des hommes, ces hollandais, un hibou, mon honneur.*

12) Show the phonological status of *h-aspiré* in *les halles, en haut, des héros.*

13) Mark all possible (i.e. obligatory and optional) liaisons in the following sentences:

> *Vous avez explicitement mentionné que beaucoup de rares oiseaux entament leurs grands voyages migratoires à travers le continent américain beaucoup plus tard que le siècle dernier. Ce comportement des hirondelles et des oies canadiennes indique que le réchauffement de la planète est une réalité incontestable.*

14) There are several cues to gender distinction in written French, one of which is silent *e* at the end of adjectives such as *grand, -e* 'big'. What is the situation in spoken French? Can listeners 'hear' grammatical information encoding gender in French?

15) Transcribe the following sentences in standard French. To what style do these pronunciations belong? What alternative pronunciations are possible?
[imadikivjẽdʁɛ]
[ɛmdi ‖ ifodʁɛʁvwʁseʒɑ̃]

16) What is one of the phonetic consequences of schwa elision for surrounding consonants?

17) Is the following rendition of the phrase *On va à la pêche ce soir* 'We go fishing tonight' possible in French: [ɔ̃va:alapɛs:əswaʁ]? And how about this case: [ɔ̃va:alapɛs:waʁ]?

18) Segment the following sentence into potential Accentual Phrases (APs) and Intonation Phrases (IPs). Give at least two different tonal configurations for the first two APs that you identify: *Marianna et son amie nous retrouveront à l'entrée de la piscine.*

19) What changes in the prosodic structure of the following utterances lead us to arrive at the two readings: *Gal, amant de la reine alla, tour magnanime* and *Galamment de la reine à la tour Magne à Nîmes*?

20) How do the meanings of *je n'vaux rien* 'I am worth nothing' and *jeune vaurien* 'little devil' ('good-for-nothing young person') reflect in the intonational structure of the two expressions?

3 Topics in morphology and syntax

3.1 Preliminaries: words and morphemes

Just as Chapter 2 was concerned with the minimal units of sound, this chapter is concerned with the identification, classification, and possible combinations of minimum units of meaning. These minimal units of meaning, called **morphemes**, can be either **bound** or **free**. Morphemes such as **affixes** (e.g. **prefixes** and **suffixes**) are said to be bound because they cannot occur in isolation. By contrast, free morphemes can manifest themselves independently of other morphemes; in such cases, the overlap between a morpheme and an individual word is one hundred percent: *très* 'very', *pour* 'for', *garçon* 'boy', *rouge* 'red', *tant* 'so much', *hélas* 'unfortunately' are all simultaneously single morphemes and single (written) words. Free morphemes also frequently occur with one or more bound morphemes, as in for instance the verb stem *chant* of the verb form *chantait* '(he) was singing' or the base word *nation* in the adjective *international* that also contains the prefix *inter-* and the suffix *-al*. Thus the verb form *chantait* has at least two morphemes: the verb stem *chant-* 'to sing', and the inflection *-ait*. The adverb *heureusement* is a single written word that can be broken down into three morphemes: *heureux* /œʁ/ 'happy' + feminine gender /øz/ + adverbial suffix /mã/ (on the concept of 'word', see section 4.1).

> In the above paragraph, identify five cases where written French words correspond to single morphemes. Which French word contains the most morphemes? Explain your choices.

The study of morphology concerns the study of the permissible shapes, combinations, and distributions of bound and free morphemes within words. The study of syntax concerns the study of the linear distribution of and the relationship between morphemes which constitute phrases and sentences.

To begin our inventory of the principal morpheme classes, let us first consider what are commonly referred to as 'word classes'. There are traditionally eight word classes inherited from the Latin grammatical tradition: nouns, adjectives, articles, pronouns, verbs, adverbs, prepositions, and conjunctions.

Nouns, adjectives, verbs, and adverbs are often called **lexical morphemes**, since they appear to carry the principal ideas within a sentence or utterance and are open-ended categories, i.e. they can be added to or subtracted from our mental **lexicon**, and be included in dictionaries over time. Articles, pronouns, prepositions, and conjunctions are referred to as **grammatical morphemes**: they constitute a fixed inventory of forms in the language, and appear to function primarily as links between lexical morphemes.

Let us begin by examining nouns and adjectives. A rather old-fashioned definition of both 'parts of speech' – another term for word classes – can be found, for instance, in Grevisse's *Bon Usage*, a traditional prescriptive French grammar:

Le nom ou *substantif* est le mot qui sert à désigner, à 'nommer' les êtres animés et les choses; parmi ces dernières, on range en grammaire, non seulement les objets, mais encore les actions, les sentiments, les qualités, les idées, les abstractions, les phénomènes, etc.: *Louis, chien, table, livraison, colère, bonté, néant, absence, gelée.* [. . .] L'adjectif est un mot que l'on joint au nom pour exprimer une qualité de l'être ou de l'objet nommé ou pour introduire ce nom dans le discours. (Grevisse 1980:223, 366)

'The noun or substantive is a word serving to identify, to 'name', animate beings and things; among the latter we usually find, grammatically speaking, not only objects but also actions, feelings, qualities, ideas, abstractions, phenomena, etc., as in *Louis*, *chien* 'dog', *table* 'table', *livraison* 'delivery', *colère* 'anger', *bonté* 'kindness', *néant* 'nothingness', *absence* 'absence', *gelée* 'jelly'. [. . .] The adjective is a word that is joined to a noun in order to express the quality of a being or of an identified object, or to insert a noun into speech.'

To the extent that they rely on rather general semantic characteristics to indicate word-class differences, definitions such as these are often contradictory. In this instance, saying that both adjectives and nouns express 'a quality' does not allow us to distinguish between the two word classes. A more promising approach might be to look for cases that tell us where nouns and adjectives can appear in sentences/utterances in relation to each other and to members of other word classes. Note that the attempt to separate nouns and adjectives into distinct categories is a relatively recent phenomenon in the history of grammars: during the height of importance of Latin, because of their shared declensional endings both nouns and adjectives were collapsed into a single category, that of 'substantive'. However, with regard to present-day French, the pertinent questions we need to ask ourselves are:

1) Are nouns and adjectives different as far as their sound structure is concerned?
2) Can they be distinguished from each other on the basis of their morphologies?
3) Are their syntactic uses sufficiently different to justify two different labels?

On the phonological level one cannot point to any particular combinations of sounds as being typical of either word class in French. This is also true of English: whereas stress patterns can be used to differentiate between nouns and verbs (e.g. 'permit vs. per'mit, see section 2.4.2.1) there are no such patterns which differentiate between adjectives and nouns. On the morphological level we note that both nouns and adjectives can be marked for gender through different kinds of **inflection**: e.g. *-eur/euse* in *chanteur/chanteuse* 'singer', *-ier/ière* in *fermier/fermière* 'farmer', *-e* in *petit/petite* 'little', *-se* in *gros/grosse* 'fat', and *-ne* in *bon/bonne* 'good' (inflections can also mark tense and number alterations). Yet many nouns and adjectives do not vary in gender. The vast majority of nouns in speech have a single gender (e.g. *un dossier* 'a file', *une chaise*, 'a chair'), and so do many adjectives, even in their written forms (e.g. *mince* 'thin', *jeune* 'young').

As for plurality, we find it widely expressed in both nouns and adjectives, although much less frequently in their oral than written forms. For example, in speech, without the presence of preceding **determiners**, the singular and plural forms *intérêt/intérêts* 'interest(s)' and *page/pages* 'page(s)' are indistinguishable, as are *grise/grises* 'grey' and *mince/minces* 'slim'. Our quick conclusion, therefore, is that on the whole nouns and adjectives cannot be put into rigidly separate categories based on inflectional morphology alone.

Turning to derivational morphology, the same situation pertains. For instance, nouns can be created by the **suffixation** of a noun (e.g. *argent* 'silver' > *argenterie* 'silverware', *moule* 'mold' > *moulin* 'mill') and also by the suffixation of an existing adjective (e.g. *grand* 'big' > *grandeur* 'greatness', *content* 'happy' > *contentement* 'satisfaction'). Similarly, both nouns and adjectives serve as bases for derived adjectives: respectively, *volcan* 'volcano' > *volcanique* 'volcanic', *argent* 'silver' > *argentin* 'silvery' are examples of noun **bases**, i.e. adjectives derived from nouns, whereas *proche* 'near' > *prochain* 'next', *malade* 'sick' > *maladif* 'sickly' illustrate adjective bases, i.e. adjectives derived from other adjectives. Among derived verbs, we again find no clear-cut predominance of noun bases over adjective bases. Verbs such as *pasteuriser* 'to pasteurize' or *baser* 'to found' have obvious noun bases, whereas *blanchir* 'to whiten' and *bavarder* 'to chat' can only come from adjectives. Finally, the derivation of adverbs from both noun and adjective bases is attested, although adjective bases clearly predominate: *vif* > *vivement* 'lively' and *douce* > *doucement* 'softly' represent the more frequent cases of adverb formation, whereas *diable* 'devil' > *diablement* 'fiendishly' and *vache* 'cow' > *vachement* 'bloody' seem more the exception than the rule. (Note that not all of the latter group would occur at every level of usage.) Thus our conclusion is that the derivational behavior of both nouns and adjectives is also similar, even though in some cases, e.g. adverbs derived from nouns, there is a clear-cut preponderance of one type. (For more on derivation, see section 4.6.1.)

To complete the overall picture of criteria that might distinguish nouns from adjectives, we also need to look at possible contrasts of syntactic usage, i.e. where the two word classes occur within sentences or parts of sentences. Once again we find a great number of similarities. For instance, noun phrases (henceforth NPs) can have as their 'centerpieces' either a noun (e.g. *le/ce/mon garçon* 'the/this/my boy') or an adjectival phrase (*le/ce/mon surdoué* 'the/this/my little genius'). In the so-called 'predicate' position, i.e. after *être*, we can find both nouns and adjectives: *Georges est un homme* 'George is a man', *Georges est grand* 'George is tall'. A noticeable formal difference in the use of the two word classes, however, is that nouns in predicate position usually require a determiner (i.e. a preceding 'article'), while adjectives do not. We can also find nouns and adjectives in so-called 'appositives': e.g. *M. Untel, député maire, vient d'arriver* 'Mr. Doe, vice mayor, has just arrived', *M. Untel, terriblement malade, vient de partir* 'Mr. Doe, terribly sick, has just left.'

In NPs consisting of two consecutive words, both nouns and adjectives can occur as the second member next to the **head** of such constructions: *le camion-remorque* 'trailer truck', *le camion russe* 'Russian truck'. Similarly, and at least superficially, *une voiture Peugeot* 'a Peugeot car' does not look much different from *une voiture rouge* 'a red car'. When it comes to nouns that occur with adverbs, the similarities continue: *nous sommes très amis* 'we are very good friends', *il est très beau* 'he is very handsome'; while in adverb + noun combinations we have e.g. *la non-violence* 'non-violence' and *la presque totalité* 'almost totality'. We find further similarities in the combinations of verbs and nouns or adjectives: e.g. *tenir parole* 'keep a promise' and *demander pardon* 'ask (for) forgiveness' illustrate noun-related combinations, while *parler bas* 'speak low' and *voir clair* 'see clearly' represent combinations with adjectives. Finally, pronominalization, i.e., the substitution of pronouns for nouns and adjectives, works in similar ways: e.g. *Voilà le garçon* 'Here is the boy' can be pronominalized as *Le voilà* 'Here he is', just as *Etes-vous marié?* 'Are you married?' can be answered with *Oui, je le suis* 'Yes, I am.'

What are we to conclude from all of the above? One would first say that there seems to be tremendous overlap between nouns and adjectives in both form and syntactic behavior. But what might not be readily apparent are also frequencies of occurrence. Double-gendered nouns (*fermier/fermière* 'farmer') are considerably less common in written texts than double-gendered adjectives (*vert/verte* 'green'). According to Brunet (2003), in a list of the 1,499 most frequent words in written sources, 61 (52%) of the 117 adjectives show double gender in either their spoken or written forms, whereas only eleven (2%) of the 608 most frequent nouns do. Adverb formation is also more frequent with adjective bases (*énorme/énormément* 'enormous(ly)') than with nouns (*bête/bêtement* 'stupid(ly)'). Compound nouns in which the second member is a noun (*camion-remorque* 'trailer truck') occur less frequently than the combination of noun + adjective (*une fille intelligente* 'an intelligent girl'). This situation has led some linguists to propose the additional morpheme categories of 'noun-adjective' for such cases of overlap (see Marty 1975). The remaining nouns would stay in the 'noun' category and be defined by a specific context such as *Le _____ est ridicule/beau/superbe*, while the remaining adjectives would be identified by a structure such as *Ce _____ garçon vient de partir* or *Cette _____ fille vient d'arriver*, with additional contexts to take care of adjectives that are placed after the noun. Our system is not perfect in that it allows for some seemingly anomalous utterances (e.g. **Le beau est superbe*), but is probably as close as we can get to a definition of these word classes. Another way to account for the morphosyntactic properties of these word classes is to study the ways in which they can be combined into larger syntactic units, called phrases (see section 3.1).

---

1) Give examples of nouns and adjectives in which we can 'hear' the plural.
2) Give examples of nouns and adjectives 'behaving' similarly in syntactic phrases.
3) What can we say about head and modifier in double-noun compounds such as *autoroute* and *voiture-balai*?

3.2   Topics in inflectional morphology

3.2.1   *The morphology of the verb*

Of all the types of lexical morphemes previously identified, by far the most complicated in French is the verb. Thus, it should come as no surprise that students of French can find entire books filled with elaborate and extensive tables illustrating the multiple written forms of verbs. However, such manuals usually cover only the written verb forms. But the number and distribution of oral forms correspond only partially to those of their written counterparts, as illustrated below with a verb from the first traditional conjugation: *chanter* 'to sing'. Since not all of the traditionally-named **tenses** (cohesive groups of six verb forms) are consistently used in speech, we shall illustrate only the following forms: present indicative, imperfect, future, conditional, present subjunctive, infinitive, and the present and past participles.

Table 3.1 shows that, orthographically, there are a total of twenty-four different forms for the verb *chanter* 'to sing', whereas orally, these forms can be reduced to twelve or thirteen, depending on the dialect of French and the register (formal or informal) used by the speaker. (All verb forms are cited without overtly indicated noun or pronoun **subject**s since the only classificatory consideration here is the morphological 'shape' of the verb form.) As

Table 3.1 *Written and oral forms of the verb* chanter *'to sing'*

Written form	Oral form	Person, number, and tense
chante, chantes, chantent	/ʃɑ̃t/	first-, second-, and third-persons singular, and third-person plural present indicative and present subjunctive
chantons	/ʃɑ̃tɔ̃/	first-person plural, present indicative
chantez, chanter, chanté	/ʃɑ̃te/	second-person plural present indicative; infinitive; past participle
chantais, chantait, chantaient	/ʃɑ̃te/ or /ʃɑ̃tɛ/*	first-, second-, and third-persons singular and third-person plural imperfect
chantions	/ʃɑ̃tjɔ̃/	first-person plural imperfect and present subjunctive
chantiez	/ʃɑ̃tje/	second-person plural imperfect and present subjunctive
chanterai, chanterez	/ʃɑ̃t(ə)ʁe/	first-person singular, second-person plural future
chanterais, chanterait, chanteraient	/ʃɑ̃t(ə)ʁe/ or /ʃɑ̃t(ə)ʁɛ/*	first-, second- and third-persons singular and plural conditional
chantera, chanteras	/ʃɑ̃t(ə)ʁa/	second- and third-persons singular future
chanterons, chanteront	/ʃɑ̃t(ə)ʁɔ̃/	first- and third-persons plural future
chanterions	/ʃɑ̃təʁj(i)ɔ̃/	first-person plural conditional
chanteriez	/ʃɑ̃təʁj(i)e/	second-person plural conditional
chantant	/ʃɑ̃tɑ̃/	present participle

*form non-existent in some dialects

Table 3.1 reveals, the distribution of the oral forms is skewed or uneven: rather than five or six separate orthographic forms for a single tense, a single oral form /ʃɑ̃te/ for instance can represent up to six orthographic forms in dialects where the front unrounded vowels /e/ and /ɛ/ are merged (see section 2.2.1.3). These oral verb forms are distributed among two tenses and two individual forms (present indicative, imperfect, infinitive, past participle).

Since there are fewer forms to contend with in the oral versions and since there is no consistent one-to-one correspondence between oral and written forms, it seems useful to attempt a reorganization of verb types based solely on the spoken forms. There is not enough space in this text to treat the entire gamut of French verbs; consequently, we will limit our description to fifty verbs which are among the most frequent in the general word count list of Brunet (2003), which was compiled using a large number of written sources. The rank of each among the 1,499 entries in the list is indicated in parentheses:

être (5), *avoir* (8), *faire* (30), *dire* (32), *aller* and *vouloir* (58), *voir* (59), *venir* (61), *pouvoir* and *devoir* (67), *prendre* (70), *trouver* (82), *donner* (83), *falloir* (88), *parler* (90), *mettre* (95), *savoir* (97), *passer* (99), *regarder* (102), *aimer* (107), *croire*

(110), *demander* (121), *rester* (126), *entendre* (129), *penser* (149), *arriver* (151), *connaître* (156), *tenir* (166), *comprendre* (168), *rendre* (170), *attendre* (174), *sortir* (175), *chercher* (198), *revenir* (203), *appeler* (210), *partir* (215), *perdre* (250), *commencer* (251), *paraître* (252), *marcher* (254), *écouter* (283), *monter* (289), *jouer* (331), *manger* (350), *lire* (417), *travailler* (452), *rentrer* (455), *payer* (463), *acheter* (648), *laisser* (unranked).

The first theoretical hurdle is deciding how many separate morphemes are present in the various forms of these (or any other) verbs. The traditional textbook approach is to divide them into a **stem** or 'base' + **suffix** or 'ending': *parl* + *ons, fin* + *issez, donn* + *é*, etc. Most divisions seem rather obvious and much the same can be done with oral forms, but there is far from one hundred percent agreement on exactly where the cuts should be made in every case, and whether some forms are more logically described as, say, two or three separate morphemes.

A possible 'two-way cut' could be applied to *entendre* 'listen' (i.e. possible infinitive base) + *ons* (first-person plural ending for many tenses) or the 'cut' *entend* (base useful for *entendent*) + *rons* (universal first-person plural, future tense ending). An example of a 'three-way cut' would be *fin* + *iss* + *ons* 'to finish' with *-iss-* treated as **infix** between stem and ending. The position adopted here will be to reject the infix description as not absolutely necessary, and to choose the 'two-way' approach, after having identified all reasonable possibilities. But even with these problems taken care of, there remains the issue of final consonants and liaison. Certain consonants, such as the *-t-* of the interrogative form *parle-t-il*, for instance, are not accounted for in the forms proposed for either the stem or the ending. Does the schwa between the stem and the ending in *chanterions* /ʃɑ̃t(ə)ʀjɔ̃/, if it is realized at all, belong to the stem or to the ending? In general, what should be the morphemic analysis of forms with endings that contain a latent final consonant that can undergo liaison? One of the answers could be a lexical account, as explained in 2.4.4.3. Briefly stated, in the lexical account, frequent constructions, including pronouns and verbs such as *je suis* 'I am' + *vowel initial word*, would be stored in our memories 'as is', i.e. as single lexical items, as opposed to being reassembled on an as-needed basis from stems and endings and following certain rules.

Another approach would be a purely morphemic account, identifying the maximum number of alternate forms, called **allomorphs**, of stems and endings. Below, the fifty verbs we selected from Brunet (2003) are classified according to this account:

SINGLE-BASED verbs are in the majority: there are 21 in the above list. These include all verbs with an *-er* ending, except for *aller, acheter*, and *appeler* which have two or more bases.

TWO-BASED verbs constitute a group of seven: *acheter, appeler, attendre, croire, entendre, perdre, rendre*. This group must be further broken down into subgroups since the distribution of the two stems is not always the same. In SUBGROUP I *acheter* and *appeler* are similar in that each has one stem, /aʃɛt/ and /apɛl/, for fourteen of the twenty-four written manifestations of the previously named tenses and forms, whereas the ten remaining forms utilize the second base, /aʃ(ə)t/ and /ap(ə)l/, with optionally pronounced schwa (see section 2.4.3). SUBGROUP 2 consists of four verbs with similar stem distributions: *attendre, entendre, perdre*, and *rendre*. As an example, *attendre* has a short stem /atã/ occurring in only two forms of the present indicative; all other forms use the longer stem /atãd/. SUBGROUP 3 has only one member, *croire* 'to believe': the stem /kʁwa(j)/ is used for all written forms except the past participle *cru*, which is represented by /kʁ/, with the past participle ending analyzed as /y/, as it is also in subgroup 2.

THREE-BASED verbs include six from the list: *dire, lire, mettre, partir, sortir*, and *voir*. But of these six, only two, *partir* and *sortir*, have the same stem distribution. For *partir* 'to leave' these stems are /paʁ/, /paʁt/, and /paʁti/. One might wonder, again, why we need to identify two closely related stems, /paʁt/ and /paʁti/ when one might seem to do. The answer lies in our intention to describe the future and conditional endings as consistently as possible across all verb types, i.e. as /ʁe/~/ʁɛ/, /ʁa/, /ʁɔ̃/, /ʁjɔ̃/, and /ʁje/.

The three stems of *dire* 'to say' are: /di/, /diz/, and /dit/. The first accounts for a number of oral forms, such as *dis, dit, dire, dirai(s)*; the second is needed, e.g. for *disons, disiez*, and *disant*, while the final one accounts only for *dites*. *Mettre* 'to put' also has three stems: /mɛt/ is the most widely utilized; /me/~/mɛ/ occurs only with *mets* and *met*, and /m/ forms only the past participle *mis*. The three stems of *voir* 'to see' are /vwa/, /vɛ/, and /v/; the second forms the future and conditional forms, and the third is restricted to the past participle *vu*. Forms like *voyons* and *voyez* get their endings /jɔ̃/ and /je/ added to the base /vwa/. Finally, *lire* 'to read' also has three stems, /l/, /li/, and /liz/, but their distribution among the tenses is not exactly the same as any of the other verbs in this group: the first helps form the past participle *lu*, similarly to *vu* in *voir*, but the two other stems are much more evenly divided between the remaining tenses and forms than are /vɛ/ and /vwa/.

FOUR-BASED verbs include *connaître, devoir, falloir, paraître, revenir, tenir*, and *venir*. The latter three have similar bases with identical distributions, as in /ʁəvjɛ̃/ for *reviens* and *revient*; /ʁəvjɛn/ for *revienne, reviennes, reviennent*; /ʁəv(ə)n/ for *revenons, revenez, revenions, reveniez, revenais, revenait, revenaient, revenant, revenu, revenir*; and /ʁəvjɛ̃d/ for all of the future and conditional forms. *Connaître* 'to know' and *paraître* 'to seem' have identical stem distributions; for *connaître* the stems are /kɔnɛ/ or /kɔne/, /kɔnɛs/, /kɔn/ and /kɔnɛt/, the two least used being /kɔnɛ/ for *connais* and *connaît* and /kɔn/ for *connu.* The stems for *devoir* 'should' are /d/ (for *dû*), /dəv/, /dwa/, and /dwav/. *Falloir* 'should/must' is, of course, as restricted orally as it is in written form: /fo/ corresponds to *faut*; /fod/ to *faudra* and *faudrait*; /fal/ to *falloir*; and /faj/ to *faille*.

FIVE-BASED verbs are four in number: *prendre* 'to take' and *comprendre* 'to understand' with identical stem distributions; *savoir* 'to know' and *vouloir* 'to want' with differing distributions. For the former pair we find /kɔ̃pʁɑ̃/, /kɔ̃pʁɛn/, /kɔ̃pʁən/, /kɔ̃pʁ/, and /kɔ̃pʁɑ̃d/. As for *savoir* and *vouloir*, their five oral bases are listed here in the order of increasing frequency: /so/, /sav/, /saʃ/, /se/~/sɛ/, and, /s/ (for the past participle); /vul/, /vud/, /vœj/, /vø/, and /vœl/, the latter being restricted to the single form *veulent*.

ARRIVING NOW AT SIX-BASED verbs, we are squarely in the area of what are traditionally called 'irregular' verbs, based on both orthography and pronunciation. The verb *aller* 'to go' has the following stems: /al/, /i/, /aj/, /va/, /vɛ/, and /vɔ̃/. The verb *avoir* 'to have' has the distinction of using a zero base for the /y/ ending of the past participle *eu*. The five other verb stems are unevenly distributed: *avoir* 'to have' has /av/, /a/, /ɔ/, /e/, and /ɔ̃/ for *ont*; *faire* 'to do' has /fə/, /fəz/, /fas/, /fe/~/fɛ/, /fɔ̃/ for *font*, and /fɛt/ only for *faites*.

THERE ARE TWO VERBS WITH AT LEAST SEVEN BASES: *être* 'to be' and *pouvoir* 'can'. The former uses three bases singly, /sɥi/, /sɔm/, and /sɔ̃/, accounting for the entire verb form (including the endings). Following this method all the way through, the four remaining bases are /s(ə)/ and /ɛt/ for *être*. *Pouvoir* needs seven bases in order to accommodate the *peux/puis* register alternation in the first person of the present tense. The more formal *puis* yields a unique base: /pɥi/. The other bases are /pø/, /pœv/, /p/ for *pu*, /puv/, /pɥis/, and /pu/.

There remains the question of verb endings, which is a difficult aspect of morphemic analysis. The problem is interesting especially in light of liaison consonants that create alternations of the type identified above, e.g. when *je suis* is pronounced as /ʒəsɥiz̲/ or /ʒəsɥi/, depending on the numerous factors influencing liaison (see 2.4.4). A purely morphemic analysis would state: if /z/ in *je suis* /ʒəsɥiz̲/ is not included in the inventory of various endings, then the phonemic rules are unable to insert the correct consonant between verb ending and the following word in case of liaison. But if /z/ is tagged as 'verb ending', we run into contradiction when we see /z/ function as a plural marker in noun phrases, such as *heureuses amies* 'happy friends'. A mixed, lexical and rule-based, account would propose that frequently occurring irregular verb forms are stored and accessed 'as is' from our mental lexicon, while other, regular

Table 3.2 *'Standard' and 'non-standard' verbs (following Marty 2001, Martinet 1969)*

Standard form		Substituted form	Possible analogy with
/apɔljɔ̃/	*appelions*	/apɛljɔ̃/	*emmêlions* /ɑ̃mɛljɔ̃/, *appelle(s)* /apɛl/
/swa/	*soit*	/swaj/	*soyons* /swajɔ̃/, *soyez* /swaje/
/vwa/	*voie*	/vwaj/	*voyons* /vwajɔ̃/, *voyez* /vwaje/
/nɛtwa/	*nettoie(s)*	/nɛtwaj/	*nettoyons* /nɛtwajɔ̃/, *brille(s)* /bʁij/
/aʃɛtʁa/	*achètera(s)*	/aʃtʁa/	*achetons* /aʃtɔ̃/, *acheter* /aʃte/
/kʁɛv/	*crève*	/kʁœv/	*crevons* /kʁœvɔ̃/, *crevez* /kʁœve/
/dɔʁ/	*dors, dort*	/dɔʁmi/	*finis, finit* /fini/
/kuʁːa/	*courra(s)*	/kuʁiʁa/	*finira(s)* /finiʁa/
/dit/	*dites*	/dize/	*parlez* /paʁle/
/fɛt/	*faites*	/f(ə)ze/	*faisiez* /f(ə)zje/
/f(ə)ʁa/	*fera(s)*	/f(ə)zʁa/	*faisons* /f(ə)zɔ̃/
/mœʁ/	*meurs, meurt*	/muʁ/	*mourons* /muʁɔ̃/
/pløvwaʁ/	*pleuvoir*	/pløv(ʁ)/	*pleuvra* /pløvʁa/
/ply/	*plu*	/pløvy/	*pleuvoir*/pløvwaʁ
/ve/–/vɛ/	*vais*	/va/	*va(s)* /va/

forms, have their stems and endings stored and accessed in a more rule-based fashion (Bybee 2001). Thus purely phonemic analysis seems less appropriate for the former rather than latter, which can be well illustrated, for instance, with the imperfect indicative, a relatively regular conjugation pattern. Without possible liaisons, we have /e/~/ɛ/ for the singular and third-person plural forms, depending on the dialect, /jɔ̃/ and /je/ for the remaining first- and second-person plural. Using such an account, one can determine what the endings will be for any of the other tenses of the fifty verbs listed above by simply 'subtracting' a given stem from the most fully pronounced form of a given verb: *(il) doive* would be subjunctive stem /dwav/ + zero ending, and *(il) revenait* would be imperfect stem /ʁəvən/ + ending /e/ or /ɛ/, depending on the dialect.

Given the complexity of the pattern of verb stems and endings, it should not come as a surprise that native speakers often make 'errors' in constructing their oral verb forms in the context of, say, a normal informal conversation. A list of some expressions of this type are shown in Table 3.2. Note that not all forms are of equal frequency: the 'incorrect' forms of *courir*, *dire*, and *faire* are much more common than e.g. *nettoyer* (probably restricted to the subjunctive and unlike similar verbs such as *aboyer* or *envoyer*, quite regular) or of *acheter* (not like similar verbs with a mute-e in the stem, such as *cacheter* or *amener*, also regular).

Other common substitutions consist of replacing an 'irregular' verb, i.e. one with numerous stems or with a stem and endings relatively difficult to recall, with a 'regular' verb or verbal expression, usually one with an infinitive ending in *-er* and a single oral base. Some of the numerous examples include *casser* or *briser* for *rompre* 'to break', *fermer* or *clôturer* for *clore* 'to close', *avoir peur* for *craindre* 'to fear', *retrouver* or *rattraper* for *rejoindre* 'to join', *augmenter* for *croître* 'to increase'. A decreased frequency of usage might co-occur with a register differentiation, with irregular verbs being predominantly used in formal registers, e.g. the appropriate verb for 'closing' a session at a meeting is, in all cases, *clôturer (une session)* as opposed to *fermer*. Thus each pair of verbs should be examined for differences in meaning, since synonyms are often not as 'synonymous' as they seem (see section 4.3.1).

And yet it is not just irregular stems, or stems and endings, that prevent speakers from successfully forming a number of highly 'irregular' verbs such as *être, avoir, faire, savoir*, and *aller*. High frequency of use starting with children at a very early age usually overcomes the obstacle of complication caused by irregularity. Irregular forms, according to some accounts, become part of children's vocabulary rather soon, as they acquire their native language (see e.g. Clark 1986).

---

1) The verb *sembler* is not always a perfect substitute for the verb *paraître*. Find an example in support of this statement.
2) Are the English verbs *be* and *have* as morphologically complex as French *être* and *avoir*?

3.2.2   The morphology of other morpheme classes

Compared with verbs, other morpheme classes in French have considerably less in the way of morphemic variation. If variations involving singular–plural number (e.g. *va/vont; chantais/chantions*), masculine–feminine gender (*couvert/couverte; dit/dite*), and first, second and third persons (*mangerai/mangeras; allez/vont*) in the verb result in multiple forms, alternating forms associated with determiners (*l'/le/la/les; ce/cet/cette/ces*), pronouns (*je/me/moi*), adjectives (*vert/verte*), nouns (*cheval/chevaux*), conjunctions (*parce que/parce qu'*), adverbs (*bien/facile/; bien_aimable*), and prepositions (*sans résultat/sans_ami*) are still considerably fewer in number and certainly more randomly distributed.

A category of morphemic variation called **case** applies to personal and clitic pronouns in French (see also section 6.3):
– **accusative** or 'direct object' (*me, te, le, la, nous, vous, les*);
– **dative** or 'indirect object' (*me, te, lui, nous, vous, leur*) and;
– **ablative** or 'object of a preposition' (*moi, toi, lui, nous, vous, eux*).

Overt gender marking is present in the oral forms of the singular of determiners, also called definite and indefinite articles: *le/la, un/une*; in the forms of demonstrative and possessive adjectives: *ce/cet/cette; son/sa*; 'demonstrative' and 'possessive' pronouns: *celui/celle, mien/mienne*; and 'personal' pronouns: *il/elle*. Nouns alternating in gender are typically names of profession and kinship, e.g. *chanteur/chanteuse* 'singer', *boucher/bouchère* 'butcher', *veuf/veuve* 'widow(er)', but also *traître/traîtresse* 'traitor', all based on natural sex distinctions. Gender marking in most adjectives is a bit more complicated, due to their large number and the variety of interpretations that have been proposed. The following analysis is based on data mostly from Rigault (1971).

The formation of feminine adjectives by the realization of a latent final consonant or semi-consonant is frequent: /t/ – *petit/petite, vert/verte*; /s/ – *gros/grosse, doux/douce*; /d/ – *bavard/bavarde, grand/grande*; /ʃ/ – *frais/fraîche, blanc/blanche*; /g/ – *long/longue*; /l/ – *soûl/soûle*; /j/ – *gentil/gentille*. In some cases, addition of the final consonant is accompanied by a vocalic change: /ʁ/, with /e>ɛ/ – *premier/première, léger/légère*; /t/, with /o>ɔ/ – *idiot/idiote, sot/sotte*; /n/ with a nasal vs. a corresponding oral vowel /ɛ̃>ɛ/ – *ancien/ancienne*, /ɔ̃>ɔ/ – *bon/bonne*, /ã>a/ – *roman/romane*, /ɛ̃>i/ – *fin/fine*. There are also a few cases in which the final consonant of the masculine form is 'exchanged' for another consonant: /v>f/ – *vif/vive, neuf/neuve, bref/brève*; /k>ʃ/ – *sec/sèche*; and a few more where the changes show no direct vowel–consonant relationship: *beau/belle, nouveau/nouvelle, mou/molle, vieux/vieille*. And by treating the past participle as an adjective in some contexts, one more consonant, /z/, can be added to the list: *acquis/acquise, mis/mise, inclus/incluse*. Of course, a number of the above examples can see the masculine/feminine contrast neutralized in favor of the feminine form in the case of *enchaînement*, such as in *petit_oiseau* /pətitwazo/ when the linking of /t/ renders the pronunciation of the masculine form the same as of the feminine form *petite*. This phenomenon, called **suppletion**, is discussed in section 2.4.4.2.

Despite all of the examples in the preceding paragraph, there remains a large number of paired masculine and feminine forms that are only marked for gender in writing; the distinction can be lost in oral forms: e.g. *joli/jolie* 'pretty', *public/publique* 'public', *réel/réelle* 'real', *cher/chère* 'dear/expensive', *pareil/pareille* 'same'.

Overt number marking is rare in the oral forms of nouns. About thirty nouns ending in /al/ show the *cheval/chevaux* pattern (e.g. *journal, bocal, caporal*), while others do not (e.g. *bal, chacal, festival*), and yet another dozen transform /aj/ into /o/ (e.g. *bail, corail, travail*). A much smaller group has more radical changes involving vowel and consonant alterations: *oeuf/oeufs* /œf/~/ø/, *boeuf/boeufs* /bœf/~/bø/, *oeil/yeux* /œj/~/jø/, *ciel/cieux* /sjɛl/~/sjø/, *os/os* /ɔs/~/o/. The plurality of nouns in French is marked more consistently by the determiner that, with only a few exceptions, always precedes the noun: *le/les chaise(s), ce/ces garçon(s), mon/mes_amis, tout_animal/tous_azimuts.* Distinct oral forms of adjectives are equally hard to come by without the aid of preceding determiners and/or a following noun that is vowel-initial (thus allowing obligatory liaison to come into play): *les différents_agendas, de grands_amis, certains beaux_enfants.* Liaison consonants in these cases might function as plural morphemes to be inserted before the vowel-initial noun (see section 2.4.4 for more detail).

A few adjectives ending in *-al*, such as *national*, retain a distinctive plural ending without having to rely upon an immediately following vowel or a preceding determiner (*les monuments nationaux*). For a more precise view of the actual frequency of gender and number markers both in the contents of an entire dictionary (*Le Petit Robert* 1989) and in two sample running texts, the well-known plays *Huis clos* and *Rhinocéros,* see Marty (2001).

---

1) How many types of gender marking are there in the written and oral forms of French adjectives?
2) Some nouns cannot be openly marked for plural, while others exist only in the plural. Give one example for each case in French and in English.

3.3   Topics in syntax

3.3.1   Definitions

Syntax has been loosely defined as the linear arrangement of words, single morphemes, or a combination of two or more morphemes, to form phrases and sentences. Sentences form even larger units such as paragraphs and entire texts. There are a number of syntactic theories claiming to supply definitive answers for what constitutes the underlying basis for the surface, i.e. immediately apparent, sentence structure of languages, but there is still no total convergence on many basic details. In lieu of a survey of current theories or an in-depth discussion of several topics in the technical literature, this chapter will touch upon a few issues in French syntax. The motivated reader is encouraged to keep an open mind and delve further into syntactic topics in both traditional-prescriptive grammars, for instance Grevisse's (1980) *Bon usage*, and more contemporary treatises such as Jones' (1996) *Foundations of French Syntax*.

3.3.2   Surface and deep structures

A syntactically simple sentence is commonly divided in two immediate **constituent**s, and expressed by the rule: S → NP + VP. This division corresponds to the traditional grammarian view, partitioning sentences into a **subject** and a

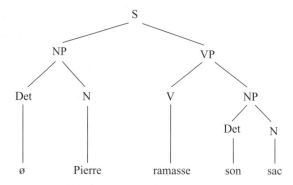

Figure 3.1 Schematic syntactic tree of *Pierre ramasse son sac*. 'Peter picks up his bag.'

predicate. In example (1), *Pierre* 'Peter', a **noun phrase** (NP), is composed of a single noun, and it is the subject, while *ramasse son sac* 'picks up his bag', a **verb phrase** (VP), which is 'centered' around a verb, is the predicate. It is assumed that this fundamental division can be applied to such diverse sentences, written or oral, as examples (1) and (2) (see below). A schematic, graphic representation of the phrase structure of sentence of (1) in the form of an upside-down tree is shown in Figure 3.1.

Let us say, as a first approach to the structure of French sentences, that the sentence (S) in example (1) is split into a subject NP, *Pierre*, and a predicate VP, *ramasse son sac*. As shown in Figure 3.1 and as discussed later in this chapter, these categories can be further divided. The question is, however, how to represent (2), which seems to be missing its subject. The comma between *attention* and *mes bagages* intuitively suggests a fundamental division but, even with this, the two parts do not correspond to the NP + VP pattern in (1). In order to recognize the underlying structural similarity between the two sentences, one needs to reconstitute the ostensibly missing but intuitively understood parts, which in (2) could be: *(Vous) faites attention à mes bagages!* Once the subject and predicate are overtly expressed, the pattern observed in (1) once again emerges: NP *(Vous)* + VP *(faites attention à mes bagages)*.

(1)   *Pierre ramasse son sac.*
        'Peter picks up his bag.'

(2)   *Attention, mes bagages!*
        'Watch out, my luggage!'

The above analysis of example (2) shows the need to describe some kind of structure that gives us information about the 'missing parts' of an utterance. Thus, we need to look for what syntacticians call an 'underlying' or 'deep structure' of syntactic phrases, intuitively clear to native speakers as they hear or read the words arranged and expressed in a linear order (the linear ordering is referred to as the 'surface structure' of an utterance). Besides 'filling in' the missing parts in an **elliptic** sentence like (2), the phrase structure similar to the one in Figure 3.1 will also help us analyze the order of words in French sentences in which adverbs and negatives are in the vicinity of verbs. In section 3.7.2 the intuitively true, but yet sketchy, underlying structure shown in Figure 3.1 will be completed with a so-called Inflection (I) 'node', an abstract notion that we will use to model the behavior of inflected verbs in French, and to represent seemingly unrelated structures in a more unified way.

To gain a better understanding of how sentences are 'built' in French, however, we first need to introduce the various morpheme categories mentioned at the beginning of this chapter. Then we can show how these categories relate to each other when put together in larger structures. Plainly put, if one states that in its simplest form, an NP (e.g. *le garçon* 'the boy') consists of a determiner (*le* 'the') and a noun (*garçon* 'boy'), with the noun acting as the **head** of the NP, i.e. the centerpiece of the phrase, and with the determiner as its subordinate element, one first has to introduce the categories of nouns and determiners. The same is true for VPs, so let us start with the introduction to the verb.

---

1) Draw a schematic syntactic tree similar to the Figure 3.1 for the reconstructed context of *Attention, mes bagages* in example (2).
2) In French, can the head of an NP composed of a single noun ever stand alone, i.e. with no determiner? If yes, in what context(s)?

3.4   The verb

3.4.1   The arguments of the verb

When, in the search for the underlying structure of French sentences, we begin the partition of the sentence into a subject and a predicate, as discussed above, we quickly realize that the two concepts tell us more about function than about form. Using an example, it is easy to see what is meant by this: *Pierre* 'Peter' and *son sac* 'his bag' are both noun phrases or NPs 'built' around a proper noun and a common noun, respectively, and yet in example (1), *Pierre* is the subject, while *son sac* is what grammarians refer to as the direct object of the verb *ramasser* 'to pick up'. Relational categories like subject, the person or thing that does something to something or someone in the sentence, and direct object, the thing that undergoes the action of the subject, are considered manifestations of the **arguments** of verbs.

Table 3.3 *Sentence functions, syntactic expressions, and lexical manifestations of three arguments of* mettre *'to put' in the sentence* Marie met son sac par terre *'Mary puts her bag on the floor.'*

Argument	Relational category	Syntactic category	Lexical manifestation
Agent	subject	NP (proper noun)	*Marie* 'Marie'
Theme	direct object	NP (article + noun)	*son sac* 'her bag'
Optional:			
Goal	modifier	PP (preposition + noun)	*par terre* 'on the floor'

The arguments of verbs come from the meaning of verbs: they are pieces of information represented by one or more lexical items (words and phrases) that must be syntactically expressed for the sentence to be semantically complete; in short they must appear in the sentence so that the sentence will make sense.

For instance, the verb *ramasser* 'to pick up' in example (1) involves, by definition, two arguments or components of meaning: 'the one that picks up', referred to as the Agent, and 'the one that is being picked up', called the Theme. The first, realized by an NP, is the subject of the sentence, while the second, also realized by an NP, is a direct object. The verb *travailler* 'to work' in *Pierre travaille* 'Peter is working', on the other hand, has only one argument (it involves only one 'participant'): it is the Agent that 'is working'. The Agent is also the subject in (1), and it is morphosyntactically speaking an NP.

Verbs such as *mettre* 'to put' can have three arguments: an Agent that 'puts', a Theme that is 'being put', and a Goal or the place where the Theme is being put by the Agent. Agent, Theme, and Goal are called thematic or **theta-roles** and refer to semantic, i.e. meaning-related, relations between the verb and its arguments. Although such semantic nuances related to the verb can be multiplied at will depending on those aspects of the meaning of the verb one wishes to emphasize, lexical meaning plays an important role in syntactic expressions: the subject of a sentence, for instance, can be an Agent 'that acts' in the verb *donner* 'to give', it can be an Experiencer 'that feels' in *sentir* 'to smell', or a Possessor in *détenir* 'to hold/keep'. Syntactic structures that express such thematic roles are referred to as the **complements** of verbs (see Table 3.3).

One might also wonder whether such complex categories are needed at all. As it turns out, the distinction between arguments and their syntactic realizations is an important tool when it comes to explaining, for instance, certain points about the syntactic behavior of French verbs. For instance, consider the examples in (3) and (4). The 'rejection' of the *Maman la lettre* 'Mother the letter' word order in (4) in French would be difficult to explain if one could not distinguish between arguments and complements of verbs: in English, it is acceptable to have so-called double-object constructions (sentences that have two direct objects) similar to the English translation of (4), where the first object NP expresses the Goal (*à Maman* 'Mother'), while the second object NP expresses the Theme (*la lettre* 'the letter') of the verb *donner* 'to give'. French, on the other hand, does not allow verbs to have more than one direct object; therefore, the Goal necessarily has to be expressed as an 'indirect' object, such as a Prepositional Phrase (PP), as in (3).

(3)   *Le facteur a donné la lettre à Maman.*
        'The mailman gave the letter to Mother.'

(4)   **Le facteur a donné Maman la lettre.*
        'The mailman gave Mother the letter.'

Many similar insights can be gained in other areas of the grammar, as well, by referring to the arguments of verbs and their various manifestations. As we will see in section 5.4.3.1, the choice between certain perception verbs such as *sembler* and *paraître* in French has implications for the role attributed to the Experiencer in perceiving the event reported by the Agent and/or grammatical subject of an utterance.

But let us examine beforehand a traditional syntactic classification of verbs following the grammarian Grevisse (1968).

Analyze the reconstructed (non-elliptical) version of example (2) in terms of arguments and complements of the verb *faire* 'to do'.

3.4.2   Verb types and complements

French verbs can be classified, in traditional grammars as well as contemporary syntactic theories, as follows:

'COPULA' VERBS: linking subjects and predicate nouns/adjectives together as e.g. *être* (*je suis malade* 'I am sick'), *rester* (*elle reste assise* 'she remains sitting'), *devenir* (*elle devient folle* 'she becomes mad'), and *tomber* (*il tombe amoureux* 'he falls in love').

TRANSITIVE VERBS: associated with either direct objects (*il conduit l'aveugle* 'he is guiding the blind person'), indirect objects (*j'obéis à mes parents* 'I obey my parents'), or both (*je donne des vêtements aux pauvres* 'I donate clothes to the poor').

INTRANSITIVE VERBS: never associated with direct or indirect objects (*le chien dort* 'the dog is sleeping', *la Terre tourne* 'the Earth spins').

PRONOMINAL VERBS: the subject and the direct or indirect object refer to the same person. The four subcategories are: (a) *reflexive* (*il se blesse* 'he injures himself'), (b) *reciprocal* (*ils se battent* 'they are beating each other', *ils se parlent* 'they talk to each other'), (c) so-called *illogical*, in which the object *se* has no precise semantic referent (*il se moque* 'he makes fun of'), and (d) *passive* (*le blé se vend bien* 'wheat is selling well').

IMPERSONAL VERBS, existing only in the third person singular, introduced by the 'impersonal *il*' as the subject (*il pleut* 'it is raining', *il arrive un malheur* 'a misfortune occurs').

However, by taking into account only the possible complements French verbs can have, a somewhat different picture of verb types emerges:

I. VERBS NOT TAKING ANY COMPLEMENTS: drawn from intransitives, illogical pronominals, and impersonals that cannot have what is often called an 'attribute' (i.e. link a subject to a nominal or adjectival predicate like copula verbs do; see above) or any other complement, e.g. *déjeuner* (*il déjeune à la maison* 'he dines at home'), *s'écrouler* (*le bâtiment s'écroule* 'the building collapses'), *pleuvoir* (*il pleuvait* 'it was raining').

II. VERBS TAKING AN ATTRIBUTE OR INDIRECT OBJECT: a mixture of copula verbs and impersonals, e.g. *être* (*il est fou* 'he is crazy'), *rester* (*il lui reste un euro* 'he still has one euro'), *paraître* (*il paraît neuf* 'it seems new').

III. VERBS TAKING ONLY A DIRECT OBJECT: same as the traditional category of transitive verbs, e.g. *connaître* (*elle connaît le chemin* 'she knows the way'), *rentrer* (*j'ai rentré la voiture* 'I put the car inside').

IV. VERBS TAKING ONLY AN INDIRECT OBJECT: a mixture of intransitives, impersonals, and 'illogical' pronominals, e.g. *obéir* (*il obéit à son chef* 'he obeys his boss'), *songer* (*elle songe à son ami* 'she is thinking about her friend'), *venir* (*il m'est venu à l'esprit de* 'it came to me to'), *se souvenir* (*elle se souvient de vous* 'she remembers you').

V. VERBS TAKING A DIRECT OR AN INDIRECT OBJECT BUT NEVER BOTH AT THE SAME TIME: e.g. *penser* (*je le pense* 'I think so', *je pense à lui* 'I think of him'), *manquer* (*Pierre manque à Jeanne* 'Jeanne misses Peter', *j'ai manqué la cible* 'I missed the target'), *courir* (*il court les rues* 'he roams the streets', *il court après elle* 'he runs after her'). (NB: All meanings of *manquer* and *courir* are subsumed here under single dictionary entries.)

VI. VERBS SIMULTANEOUSLY TAKING BOTH DIRECT AND INDIRECT OBJECTS: drawing mostly from transitives, e.g. *laver* (*je me lave les mains*, 'I am washing my hands'), *aider* (*il m'aide à la tâche* 'he is helping me with the task').

Further refinements can be made to this classification based on whether any of the verbs in groups II through VI could occur either without any of the complements mentioned, or obligatorily with at least one or two such complements. Thus *rentrer*, compatible only with direct objects (*je rentre la tente* 'I put the tent inside'), can also occur alone (*Rentrons!* 'Let's go home!'), whereas *songer* always requires an indirect object, at least in contemporary usage (*nous songeons à l'avenir* 'we think about the future'). Similarly, *intéresser* is necessarily associated with either a direct object (*cela m'intéresse* 'it interests me') or simultaneously with a direct and an indirect object (*je m'intéresse à cela* 'I am interested in that'), but never without one of these (**j'intéresse, *cela intéresse*). Other examples may appear to contradict the classification of some of the verbs in categories II through VI: two verbs in *je pense, donc je suis* (categories V and II, respectively); *j'ai dit* declared at the end of an *explication de texte* (category VI).

3.4.3   Adverbials as modifiers

Adverbials (*compléments adverbiaux, complements circonstanciels*) differ from the above in that they do not express the arguments of the verb, but rather convey optional information about the circumstances in which the action depicted by the verb is performed. Such constituents are referred to as **modifiers**. As opposed to complements, modifiers can be freely added or taken away from the minimal sentence, can be quite numerous (see (5)), and can be placed at different locations within the sentence in varying sequences (6). Adverbs that modify the entire sentence rather than just the verb will be discussed later in this chapter. For cases in which adverbials can be difficult to distinguish from direct and indirect objects, consult Molinier and Levrier (2000).

(5)   *Pierre ramasse son sac <u>tous les jours/à l'entrée/dès qu'il sort de l'école.</u>*
       'Peter picks up his bag every day/at the entrance/as soon as he exits the school.'

(6)   *<u>Tous les jours/dès qu'il sort de l'école</u> Pierre ramasse son sac <u>à l'entrée</u> .*
       'Every day/as soon as he exits the school/Peter picks up his bag/at the entrance.'

Modifiers come in a variety of syntactic structures, some of which are illustrated in (5) and (6): NPs (*tous les jours*), PPs (*à l'entrée*), and even entire clauses (*dès qu'il sort de l'école*). They can also convey a vast array of semantic nuances (translated from Grevisse 1968):

TIME: *partir <u>dans trois jours</u>* 'leave in three days'
CAUSE: *agir <u>par jalousie</u>* 'act out of jealousy'
PLACE: *rester <u>chez nous</u>* 'stay at our house'
MANNER: *marcher <u>à pas pressés</u>* 'walk briskly'
INSTRUMENT: *percer quelqu'un <u>de sa lance</u>* 'pierce someone with his lance'

CONCESSION: *reconnaître malgré l'obscurité* 'recognize despite darkness'
CONSEQUENCE: *s'ennuyer à mort* 'to get bored to death'
WEIGHT: *peser dix livres* 'to weigh ten pounds'

The danger of such classifications is that they often seem too general, and especially infinitely expandable. Depending entirely on how much detail one wishes to convey, one could invent a new category for virtually any unique concatenation; thus, WEIGHT could be expanded into POUND (*peser deux livres*) or KILO (*peser trois kilos*).

3.4.4   Clauses as modifiers and complements

In example (5), we noticed that an entire 'clause', i.e. a simple sentence containing a lexical verb, *dès qu'il sort de l'école* 'as soon as he exits school', can be used as a modifier. Thus (5) can be analyzed as an embedded or 'complex sentence' that contains two clauses: a matrix or 'main clause', *Pierre ramasse son sac* 'Peter picks up his bag', and a so-called 'subordinate clause' that is joined or 'subordinated' to the main clause of which it modifies certain aspects. In contrast with so-called coordinated clauses, e.g. *Pierre ramasse son sac et il sort de l'école* 'Peter picks up his bag and exits the school' where both clauses are of equal importance, in subordinate clauses the embedded clause is a complement or a modifier of the main clause, adding to its meaning in some way. Of the many different possibilities, let us illustrate a few cases.

The complementizer ('conjunction' in traditional grammar) *dès que*, joining the embedded clause to the main clause in (6), adds temporal information to the action that the subject performed. Other complementizers of this type can include *parce que* that indicates a causal relationship, *de façon à* that adds information about 'manner', and *à moins que* that conveys a concession to the meaning expressed in the main clause. In each case, both clauses in the complex sentence could, a priori, stand on their own.

In some cases, however, the embedded clause becomes 'invested' in the expression of the attitude of the speaker towards the situation or action described. In short, if the main clause contains any of the following types of verbs, the embedded clause has to be in a 'special', so-called 'subjunctive mood', as opposed to 'indicative mood', for which we have seen examples so far:

> WISHING OR DESIRE: *desirer* 'to desire', *empêcher* 'to prevent', *ordonner* 'to order', *préférer* 'to prefer', *vouloir* 'to want'
>
> OPINION (often in negative constructions): *penser* 'to think', *songer* 'to reflect', *croire* 'to believe', *douter* 'to doubt', *nier* 'to deny', *savoir* 'to know', *soupçonner* 'to suspect'

PERCEPTION (also in negative constructions): *voir* 'to see', *s'étonner* 'to wonder', *admirer* 'to admire', *sembler* 'to seem', *paraître* 'to appear'

FEELING: *se réjouir* 'to rejoice', *être fâché/heureux/content* 'to be angry/happy/satisfied/

The above categories list some typical verbs that require the subjunctive mood in their embedded clauses, although the categories are not necessarily clear-cut. Notice for instance that *sembler* 'to seem' can be just as well listed as a verb of OPINION as a verb of PERCEPTION. These verbs illustrate the idea that there is some kind of 'emotional speaker involvement' in the message to be conveyed: e.g. in (7) the use of the subjunctive allows the speaker to express doubt (uncertainty, insecurity) about the arrival of a friend. One must be careful, however, because not all verbs denoting speaker attitude allow the subjunctive: the verb *parier* 'to bet' in (8), for instance, requires the indicative in the subordinate clause. In fact, the subjunctive mood, at least at this point in the history of French, is typical with the matrix verbs of volition and expressions of attitude illustrated above, and it is also required after certain complementizers such as *avant que* 'before', *pourvu que* 'in order to', or *sans que* 'without'. But otherwise it is rather erratic in the speech of uneducated speakers, and rarely contrastive with the indicative. Rather, it has become part of the lexico-semantic property of certain verbs and complementizers.

(7)   *Je ne pense pas qu'il puisse venir.*
        'I don't think he can come.'

(8)   *Je parie qu'il ne viendra pas.*
        'I bet he will not come.'

Subordinate clauses can also be complements of verbs. They can fulfill the role of a direct object (9) and can even be in the subject position of the sentence (10). The complementizer *que* 'that' in these cases introduces declarative subordinate clauses which, when in subject position, require a pronominal trace (*le* 'it'), i.e. repeating the expression of the object function of the clause. As a typical construction in French, when the subject of the subordinate and main clauses refer to the same subject (*je* 'I' in (9)), the verb of the subordinate clause becomes an infinitive (as opposed to be a 'finite' or 'inflected' verb), and causes the complementizer *que* to be omitted.

(9)   *Je crois que je le vois. / Je crois le voir.*
        'I think that I can see him/it.'

(10)   *Que son frère ait fait une bêtise, Marie le sait fort bien.*
        'That her brother did a stupid thing, Mary knows (it) quite well.'

3.5   Noun phrases

3.5.1   Expanding the NP

The examples of NP discussed so far (*Pierre, le facteur*) have been short in terms of the number of words involved, and seemed transparent at first glance, at least as far as their structure and meaning were concerned. But what about all the other possible NPs? How long and complicated can NPs get before they become implausible and unclear? What other classes of morphemes are involved besides articles and nouns or proper names?

The shortest NP imaginable is, of course, a proper name, as we have seen in example (1) above. It begins with a capital letter, and is unaccompanied by what linguists refer to as a determiner, and traditional grammars call an 'article'. The longest NP is, in theory, infinite: adjectives could be endlessly added after the principal, so-called head noun of the phrase in a basically coordinative structure (11). The same holds for English, the only difference being the position of the adjectives with respect to the head noun: in French NPs the head is 'left', while in English NPs it is 'right'.

(11)   *les flottes anglaise, américaine, française, russe, chinoise, japonaise*
         'English, American, French, Russian, Chinese, Japanese fleets'

In a subordinative-type structure, theoretically speaking, there are also no limits, but in practical terms the subordination rarely goes beyond a few immediate sublevels (shown in (a) through (c) in (12) below). In a mixture of subordinative and coordinative structures, one cannot exceed more than three or four post-head syntactic elements, as exemplified in (13a–c), in which *organique* and *extraite* stand in a progressively subordinative relationship to *matière*, i.e. *matière + organique*, then *matière organique + extraite*, and finally *matière organique extraite +* the coordinated group *incolore ou de couleur différente*.

(12)   *la flotte (a) anglaise (b) amarrée à Bordeaux (c) qui fut arrivée deux jours plus tôt . . .*
         'The English fleet anchored in Bordeaux which arrived two days earlier . . .'

(13)   *une matière (a) organique (b) extraite (c) incolore ou de couleur différente*
         'an extracted, organic substance uncolored or of different color'

3.5.2   Post-head position in the NP

What modifiers, elements adding meaning to another element, can be in post-head position? Besides nouns (e.g. *film événement*, 'important film'; *moissonneuse-batteuse*, 'harvester-thresher'), we find:

– adjectives, as in example (12);
– prepositional phrases (PPs) (e.g. *les vins de France* 'the wines of France');
– subordinate clauses (e.g. *les vins que j'ai bus* 'the wines I drank');
– NPs (e.g. *l'entretien Chirac-Jospin* 'the meeting between Chirac and Jospin');

and, of course, any number of combinations of these: *une avalanche impressionnante de records dont 57 records du monde,* 'an impressive avalanche of records of which 57 (were) world records', with an adjective/present participle (*impressionnante*), a PP (*de records*), and a subordinate clause (*dont 57 records du monde*). Further, when coordination of modifiers is present, i.e. when the post-head elements are linked together with 'and' or another similar conjunction, these may or may not be similar in structure. For instance, the constructions in example (13) are a common type with post-head modifiers being the same word class (adjective), but other combinations would not be out of the question: e.g. *une attaque nucléaire* (adjective) *ou par représailles* (PP) 'a nuclear attack or (one launched as) a reprisal'.

There is, strictly speaking, no formal order among multiple post-head modifying adjectives, as in the pre-head situation. In coordinative-type structures, i.e. when words are juxtaposed to each other, the order is of little direct importance, as *les flottes anglaise et française* would not mean anything essentially different from *les flottes française et anglaise*. In a subordinative-type structure, such as *des efforts britanniques extraordinaires* 'extraordinary British efforts' we note that the first adjective, *britanniques*, modifies the head noun *efforts*, then this group is further modified by the more 'distant' adjective: *extraordinaires*. The order is governed by the meaning to be conveyed. But where French uses word order, English might use intonation. For instance, the final adjectives are contrastive in *les carrés verts réguliers* 'regular green squares' vs. *les carrés verts irréguliers* 'irregular green squares', and in *les carrés réguliers verts* 'regular green squares' vs. *les carrés réguliers jaunes* 'regular yellow squares' in French but not in English.

Rules governing the relative order of subordinative post-head modifiers must in particular take into account semantic ambiguity when adjectives and PPs ostensibly 'collide', i.e. when both are contiguous in immediate post-head position. For example, does *les camps de prisonniers classiques* mean 'classic camps for prisoners' or 'camps of classic prisoners'?

First of all, if the order of post-head modifiers is adjective + PP, few such problems arise: *une enquête immédiate sur place* can only mean 'an immediate

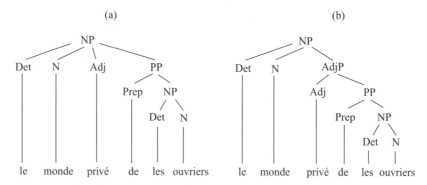

Figure 3.2 Schematic syntactic trees of the two meanings of *le monde privé des ouvriers*: (a) 'the private (non public) sphcrc of workers', (b) 'the world deprived of (left without) workers'

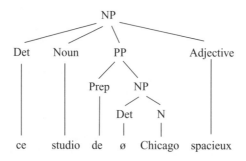

Figure 3.3 Schematic syntactic tree of the only possible meaning of *ce studio de Chicago spacieux* 'this spacious studio (situated) in Chicago'

on-the-spot inquiry'. Similarly, *le cadeau typique de Noël* is unambiguously 'the typical Christmas present'. However, *le monde privé des ouvriers* (see Figure 3.2) leaves some doubt as to precise meaning: (a) 'the private sphere of workers' or (b) 'the world deprived of workers'?

In many of these cases, prosody and the context of the NP or the reader's (or hearer's) knowledge or perception of the world comes into play to resolve the ambiguity. An example of disambiguation by prosodic means of the syntactic structures shown in Figure 3.2 is discussed in section 2.5.4.

The sentence *ce studio de Chicago spacieux* 'this spacious studio (situated) in Chicago' (see Figure 3.3) is unlikely to be interpreted as 'this studio in spacious Chicago' despite the immediate contiguity of *Chicago* and *spacieux*, a potential NP in itself. Similarly, expressions like *la jauge d'essence réparée* are restricted to a single interpretation, in this case 'repaired gas gauge', as nobody would imagine a meaning that has to do with 'repairing' the 'fuel' (*essence réparée*) of a vehicle. In the same way, when a post-head modifier forms a compound with the preceding head noun, they both act as the head of the NP, which is why *son mètre de sable carré* is agrammatical, and *son mètre carré de sable* 'his square meter of sand' is the only possible word order for the intended meaning.

Another example when the order of complements is governed by an especially strong semantic link between the head noun and the PP following the noun is *la main d'oeuvre étrangère* 'foreign workforce', demonstrating the inseparability of *main* and *d'oeuvre,* thus eliminating the possibility of interpreting *oeuvre* as being modified directly by *étrangère.*

The role of likely semantic interpretation also governs successive post-head PPs, as in *les échanges de professeurs entre pays* 'exchange of professors between countries' and in *2000 euros de retraite par mois* '2000 euros of retirement per month'. In the first case, the unlikely interpretation is 'exchanges of teachers (caught traveling) between countries' in contrast to the more reasonable 'exchanges of teachers to take place between countries'. In the second case, 'a retirement payment of 2000 euros made every month' obviously wins out over 'a payment of 2000 euros paid for every month of retirement'. Linear order, then, can occasionally mask the true semantic interpretation of the entire NP, provided the latter is considered totally out of context.

---

1) Explain how prosody (see the pitch tracks in 2.5.4) can disambiguate between the two meanings of the phrase *le monde privé des ouvriers.*
2) An expression of contrasting surface and deep structures in English is 'flying planes can be dangerous'. One possible interpretation of this sentence involves a modifier and a head noun: which one is it, and in what position is the modifier in the NP?

3.5.3   Pre-head position in the NP

Turning now to elements preceding the head noun, the options are much more limited but no less complex. As opposed to easily expandable post-head NPs, there is a practical limit to the number of determiners that can occur in front of the head of an NP.

Consider examples (14) and (15): while the former, a maximal leftward extension of an NP, falls into the realm of acceptable structures, the latter – although 'grammatically correct' and understandable with a little effort – stretches credibility. But even within shorter and more restrictive NPs, syntactic rules need to be established in order to allow the creation of common structures, all the while preventing impossible structures such as *les toutes autres trois filles*, *les petites jolies filles*, or even *trois toutes autres les filles*.

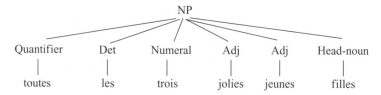

Figure 3.4 Schematic diagram illustrating the order of several pre-head modifiers (NB: The interpretation of *jeunes filles* as a compound noun is also
acceptable.)

(14)   *toutes les trois autres jolies jeunes filles*
         'all the other three pretty (young) girls'

(15)   *toutes les mêmes six premières nouvelles jolies petites jeunes filles*
         anglaises de Londres qui viennent d'arriver et dont je vous ai parlé
         'the same first six pretty new (young) English girls who have just
         arrived and about whom I was talking to you'

There are essentially five groups of pre-head modifiers, the last three of which
are further subdivided into other subcategories. A syntactic tree exemplifying
at least one element from each of these groups is shown in Figure 3.4.

GROUP I consists of *tout/tous*, used as a determiner, i.e. quantifying an NP
as in e.g. *tous les gens (le disent)* and, according to some grammarians, the
adjective *seul*, as in *seules les filles (sont venues)*. These two items, if present,
always occupy the leftmost spot before the head noun. They are unique in
that they are capable of being displaced to other positions in a sentence with no
change in meaning. This process, illustrated in (16) and (17) is called **quantifier
floating**, and it is frequent in informal spoken speech styles in French. Notice,
however, that floating the adjective *seules* to the last position in the sentence in
(17) changes the meaning from 'only the girls came' to 'the girls came alone',
showing the limits of floating *seul* in French.

(16)   *Tous les garçons sont venus.*
         'All the boys have come.'
         Les garçons sont tous venus.
         Les garçons sont venus tous .
         'All the boys have come.'

(17)   *Seules les filles sont venues.*
         'Only the girls have come.'
         Les filles seules sont venues.
         'Only the girls have come.'
         Les filles sont venues seules .
         'The girls came alone.'

Another source of variation with respect to floating quantifiers seems to be dialectal. Examples such as (18), in which the quantifier *toute* appears with plural NPs without agreeing with them in number and gender, are acceptable in Canadian French, but not in Metropolitan French where *tout(e)* cannot modify a VP (De Cat 2000).

(18)   *J'ai toute mangé les chocolats.*
         'I have eaten all the chocolates.'

GROUP 2 consists of all other determiners: the definite 'article' *le* 'the' as in *tout le village* 'the whole village', the possessive *mon/ma/mes* 'mine' as in *mes deux parents* 'my two parents', and the demonstrative *ce/cet/cette* as in *cette belle phrase* 'this nice sentence'.

GROUP 3 consists of a series of four related subgroups, beginning with:
– cardinal numbers, e.g. *les trois filles* 'the three girls';
– ordinals, including *dernier* and *prochain*, e.g. *le premier ami* 'the first friend';
– *seul, moindre* e.g. *la seule/moindre* histoire 'the only/least affair';
– *autre, même*, e.g. *les autres/les mêmes filles* 'the other/same girls'.

Possible combinations of these elements are subject to semantic compatibilities, which is why **les moindres dernières pages* 'the least final pages' is not felicitous.

GROUP 4 also contains some of the so-called preposed or, using a well-known label, 'BAGS' adjectives, expressing meaning related to **B**eauty, **A**ge, **G**oodness, or **S**ize. As opposed to most adjectives in French, these adjectives are or can be prenominal, i.e. placed in pre-head position: *pauvre* 'poor', *cher* 'dear', *nouveau* 'new', *ancien* 'old', *vrai* 'true', and *faux* 'false'. Again, there are possible (*mon pauvre cher ami* 'my poor dear friend') and impossible combinations (*cette vraie fausse affirmation* 'this true false statement').

GROUP 5, based on the possible linear ordering of items, has at least five subclasses of pre-head adjectives: *bon* 'good' and *mauvais* 'bad'; *beau* 'handsome' and *joli* 'pretty'; *gros* 'large/fat'; *vieux* 'old' and *jeune* 'young'; and *petit* 'small' and *grand* 'big'. Thus, typical examples are: *les bons vieux temps* 'the good old times', *une pauvre petite chose* 'a poor little thing', and *une grosse vieille voiture* 'a big old car'.

When otherwise postposed descriptive adjectives are added to this mix, one finds that they are placed after adjectives from Groups 1 and 2 but before Groups 4 and 5: e.g. *la silencieuse vieille demeure* 'the quiet old home'; *un sale vieux chien* 'a dirty old dog'; *cet insaisissable petit detail* 'this inconceivable little detail'. The relative order of a complex NP combining preposed and postposed adjectives can be seen in the following attested example: *une délicieuse petite vieille bonne femme* 'a delicious good little old lady'.

Occasionally these ordered classes are rearranged when a different semantic nuance is to be conveyed. In *une petite jeune fille* 'a small (young) girl', we note a 'violation' of the linear order of elements in Group 5, since the 'size' adjective *petit* is supposed to follow the adjective expressing age. Also, in *un gros vrai diamant* 'a huge real diamond', the 'size' adjective from Group 5 precedes the intensifier from Group 4. In *les dernières vingt-quatre heures* 'the last twenty-four hours', the cardinal number follows the ordinal, as opposed to preceding it, as usual.

In these cases, we are usually dealing with a tightly-knit **compound**, which consists of an adjective and a noun and which does not allow for any intervening modifiers. Thus, with *main d'oeuvre* 'work force', expressions like *jeune fille* 'girl', *bonne femme* 'woman', and *vingt-quatre heures* 'twenty-four hours' are essentially inseparable, so-called 'semantic wholes' that can force the remaining adjectives in the NP to be placed in an otherwise atypical position.

---

1) Give an example of quantifier-floating in English.
2) Compare the meaning of the adjectives *ancien* 'old', *grand* 'big', and *sale* 'dirty/nasty' in pre-head and post-head positions. What do you notice?
3) Pre-head modifiers can acquire semantic nuances when they occur with a given head noun. Why are *bon homme* and *bonne femme* in French good examples of this?

3.5.4   'Determiners'

In the above discussion of NPs, we have used traditional terms such as 'definite', 'indefinite', and 'partitive' articles (*le, la, les*; *un, une*; *du, de la, des*); 'demonstrative', 'possessive', 'indefinite adjective' (*ce, cet, cette, ces*; *mon, ma, mes* [plus the other persons]; *quelque(s), plusieurs*), and 'adjective' (e.g. *nouveau* 'new', *bon* 'good', *séculaire* 'ancient', *intelligent* 'intelligent', *mou* 'soft'). But occasionally, we tried to capture the general properties of all these words by a single label, such as 'modifier', 'quantifier', or 'determiner', as it would seem from the examples of NPs discussed so far that some of these categories have a lot in common. Thus they could also be grouped under a single label. There is also the consideration of open and closed categories: while the number of articles and indefinite adjectives is limited, descriptive or qualitative adjectives form an open-ended group that can be expanded by the creation of new words, just as much as the list of nouns or verbs can be.

With these points in mind, linguists may create an all-purpose syntactic category that unites all the grammatical elements listed above. This all-encompassing category is then broken down into different subcategories depending on the type of syntactic approach and on the basis of criteria such as: (a) the number of elements allowable in a given NP, (b) their order vis-à-vis each other when there is more than one present, and (c) what they seem to have in common from a semantic point of view. Approaches vary with respect to the labels that they adopt. In what follows, and despite more nuanced analyses that one can make, we will refer to the all-purpose syntactic category of words expressing the type of referent(s) of a noun as **determiners**. In other words, we extend our current category of 'determiners', also called 'articles' (definite, demonstrative, possessive etc.), to refer to all types of words, diverse as they might be, whose grammatical 'function' is to express the reference of a noun, including its definiteness, location, quantity, etc. Thus our sub-categories will be composed of:

– articles (*le, la, un, une . . .*) expressing whether the referent(s) of a noun is/are identified or not (*le, un . . .*);
– demonstratives (*ce, cet, cette, ces . . .*) indicating the spatial, temporal, or discourse location of the referent(s) of the noun;
– possessives (*mon, ta, ses, notre . . .*) expressing relationships of possession between the noun and its referent(s);
– quantifers (*tout, seul, de* [as 'partitive article'] . . .) conveying the definite or indefinite quantity (number or amount) of referent(s) of nouns,

together with single-item categories and other groupings that we retain here for their possible combinations with other 'determiners':

– *quel* 'which', *je ne sais quel, n'importe quel* 'which ever'/ 'whatever' and variants
– *maint* and its variants (mostly of formal written style with no article possible between it and the head noun, e.g. *maintes fois* 'multiple times')
– *chaque, un, nul, aucun,* and feminine variants (used only in the singular and incompatible with determiners: *chaque occasion* 'every occasion', *nul ennemi* 'no enemy', *aucun ami* 'no friend')
– ordinal numbers (can be preceded by another determiner, e.g an article, *ma première année* 'my first year')
– *quelques, plusieurs,* and cardinal numbers (used only with plural NP heads, with or without preceding determiners: *(les) quelques livres* '(the) few books', *plusieurs assiettes* 'several plates', *(ces) trente années* '(these) thirty years')
– *tel, certain, autre, même,* and variants (in singular or plural, with or without a preceding determiner, e.g. *telle chose* 'such (a) thing', *un certain nombre* 'a certain number', *les autres pages* 'the other pages', *la même situation* 'the same situation').

All these elements still await definitive classification based on mutual affinities and compatibilities, as we have tried to demonstrate with respect to the position and scope of quantifiers such as *tout* and *seul* (see section 3.5.3).

1) What semantic properties might *tel*, *certain*, *autre*, and *même* have in common?
2) Possessives and demonstratives usually agree in gender with the noun that they modify (*mon livre* 'my book', *cette amie* 'this (female) friend'). What is the situation in English where nouns are not marked for grammatical gender? Do determiners in English agree in some way with the following noun? Explain.

3.6   Pronouns

3.6.1   *Subject pronouns of* être

A major challenge for contemporary French morphosyntax has been the 'competition' between the demonstrative pronouns *ce* and *cela* (and their abbreviated version *ça*) and the personal pronouns *il* and *elle,* and impersonal *il*, when these occur – most often just preceding a form of the verb *être* – in the subject position as in (19) and (20):

(19)   *Cela/Ça fait vingt euros.*
        'That will be 20 euros.'

(20)   *Il/Elle est avocat(e).*
        'He/She is a lawyer.'

These pronouns appear at first glance to fulfill the communicative need to 'refer back' to a so-called antecedent, overtly expressed either in the same sentence/utterance or, more frequently, in a preceding sentence/utterance. This referential property of pronouns is called **anaphora**. Thus, *cela/ça* in (19) refers back to a just-previously mentioned concept or physical event, e.g. a sales clerk holding an object in his hands when saying (19) for instance can be thought of as referring back to the object for which he had already checked the price. Similarly, *il* and *elle* in (20) refer to gender-specific antecedents, typically proper names.

There are also cases of 'forward reference', called **cataphora**, with *ce* and *ça*, as shown in (21), with the underlined clause introduced by *que* as the co-referent, and in (22) and (23) with the underlined infinitives as co-referents.

Pronouns assuming such 'forward' referential function in the sentence/utterance often correspond to 'traces' left behind when a word is moved or a simple sentence is expressed by other means. The *c'est . . . que* construction in (21) and the pronoun *elle* referring to *la dame* in (24), for instance, are means of focusing on a word or a constituent in the sentence/utterance. In both cases the pronouns are 'placeholders' for the element put in the spotlight. The sentence in (21) is called a **cleft sentence**, i.e. a complex sentence in which a simple sentence (*il ne peut pas venir*) is embedded using a subordinate clause (*c'est . . . que*). The structure in (24) is referred to as **dislocated**: the subject noun (*la dame*) is moved to the end of the utterance, set off from it by a comma (representing level intonation), but leaving a pronominal copy (*elle*) in subject position.

(21)   *C'est dommage qu'il ne puisse pas venir ce soir.*
         'It is too bad that he could not come this evening.'

(22)   *Cela/Ça fait du bien de se baigner ici* .
         'It is good to take a bath here.'

(23)   *Il fait bon de se promener* .
         'It is good to take a walk.'

(24)   *Elle parle bien, la dame!*
         'She speaks well, the lady.'

The use of *ça/cela* with *être* is restricted to just a few environments, principally 'modal' (or auxiliary) verbs such as *devoir* and *aller* (25, 26). The pronoun *ça/cela* is used for emphasis in place of *ce* in idiomatic expressions as in (27), or as an initial and/or final element in dislocated sentences/utterances (28).

(25)   *Qu'est-ce que c'est? – Ça doit être le train.*
         'What is it? It must be the train.'

(26)   *Qui fera la conférence? – Ça va être le professeur Dubois.*
         'Who will give the lecture? That will be Professor Dubois.'

(27)   *A-t-il terminé son travail? – Oui, ça y est.*
         'Is he done with his work? Yes, that's it.'

(28)   *Je pourrai emprunter la voiture de mon père. – Ça, c'est à voir, ça!*
         'I could borrow my father's car. That remains to be seen.'

In general, however, the main competition occurs between *il(s)/elle(s)* and *ce* in morphosyntactic environments where the pronoun is in subject position preceding *être* or, less often, another **copular verb** such as *devenir* 'to become', *rester* 'to stay'. Copular verbs deserve particular attention when it comes to the use of subject pronouns in French, since the different types of construction in which they participate often determine which pronoun should be used. They represent a 'special' group of verbs that associate ('couple') certain properties with a distinct subject entity (an individual or an object), rather than describing relationships between them, as other verbs do. In (29) for instance the complement of *être* associates a given property ('being king of Spain') to 'someone unique', called Juan-Carlos. Such structures are called 'identificational' constructions, and are abundant with *être*. So-called 'predicational' constructions, on the other hand, state or 'predicate' something specific about the subject, as *un bon roi* 'a good king' in (30):

(29)   *Juan-Carlos est le <u>roi</u> de l'Espagne.*
        'Juan-Carlos is the king of Spain.'

(30)   *Juan-Carlos est un bon <u>roi</u> .*
        'Juan-Carlos is a good king.'

When a given entity (individual or object) is referred to for the first time in a given discourse context, its identification is done with the pronoun *ce* (31). The gender-neutral *ce* is preferred when the pronoun 'refers back' to a preceding masculine (32) or feminine (33) inanimate NP. In these examples, *il* or *elle* would yield ungrammatical results (see *). The pronoun *ce* is also favored when its antecedent in the preceding sentence is an animate attribute (predicate of *être*) (34).

(31)   *<u>C</u>'est une baleine blanche.*
        'This is a white whale.'

(32)   *J'ai vu le nouveau film de ce réalisateur. <u>C</u>'est un film d'action. *Il est un film d'action.*
        'I have just seen the new movie of this director. It is an action movie.'

(33)   *Nous venons d'acheter une voiture. <u>C</u>'est une Renault. *Elle est une Renault.*
        'We just bought a new car. It is a Renault.'

(34)   *Je connais le voisin. <u>C</u>'est un homme honnête.*
        'I know the neighbor. He is an honest man.'

But when the complement of *être* is a bare noun (35), as is the case with e.g. professional titles in French, or with a PP following *être* (36), then the use of personal pronouns (*il* or *elle*, depending on the gender of the antecedent) is mandatory. The gender-neutral *ce* is also likely when the pronoun 'refers back' to a preceding masculine (32, 34) or feminine NP (33), whereas 'technically' one would expect *il* or *elle*.

(35)   *Je connais Pierre/Marie. Il/elle est <u>professeur</u>.*
        'I know Peter/Maria. He/She is a teacher.'

(36)   *J'ai rencontré ta sœur. Elle est charmante./Elle est <u>dans le jardin</u>.*
        'I met your sister. She is charming./She is in the garden.'

The difficulty sometimes lies in making the right choice of a subject pronoun in contexts such as the one in (37) and (38). Little, if anything, seems to separate the meaning of the two sentences, but in reality, there is a subtle difference: the use of *ce* denotes a reference to the general idea or content conveyed by the clause, while the personal pronoun is a reference to a certain property of the antecedent. Thus the meaning in (37) is that 'it is a nice idea to have a hat', while the meaning in (38) is 'this particular hat looks nice'.

(37)   *Que pensez-vous de ce chapeau ? C'est bien!*
       'What do you think of this hat? It is nice!'

(38)   *Que pensez-vous de ce chapeau ? Il est bien!*
       'What do you think of this hat? It looks nice!'

As we will see with respect to politeness strategies in conversation (see section 5.4), speakers sometimes chose generic reference similar to *ce* in (37) to avoid a direct answer to questions or to receive or pay a compliment.

3.6.2   Impersonal il *and* ce

'Impersonal' *il* is a so-called subject **clitic**, i.e. a word that 'clings' to a verb (see more in section 3.6.3) but, unlike a subject or object pronoun, it does not refer to anything specific.

It is, so to speak, an 'empty placeholder' put in subject position when no reference to an Agent, an Experiencer, or any such argument of the verb is required. It is typically the case with meteorological verbs (*Il pleut* 'it is raining') or passive-like constructions in which the Agent is not expressed (see section 3.9.1). The number of contexts in which it never interchanges with *ce*, *cela*, and *ça* is limited to certain idiomatic expressions, such as *Il est quatre heures* 'It is four o'clock' and *Il fait beau* 'The weather is nice.'

The pronoun *ce*, on the other hand, appears in:

1. Cleft sentences in which the complement under focus can be any complement, including PPs (39), infinitives (40), or even subordinate clauses (see (21)), often with a genderless antecedent.

   (39) *Ce cadeau, c'est pour les amis de nos amis que nous l'avons acheté.*
        'This gift, it is for the friends of our friends that we bought (it).'

   (40) *Voir, c'est croire.*
        'Seeing is believing.'

In addition, we find alternation between *ce* and *il/elle* when considerations of register come into play: *Il est bon de pouvoir lire* is a more formal, while *C'est bon de pouvoir lire* is a more informal way of stating 'It is good to be able to read.'

2. One group has a gendered referent in the context and is constructed with *être* + adjective, adverb, or infinitive:

(41) *Voulez-vous boire votre <u>café</u> ? – Je veux bien mais <u>c'</u>/<u>il</u> est trop chaud.*
'Would you like to drink your coffee? I would like to but it is too hot.'

(42) *A-t-il fini de composer son <u>opéra</u> ? – Non, <u>c'</u>/<u>il</u> est toujours à <u>faire</u>.*
'Has he finished composing his opera? No, it is still to be done.'

3. The other group contains an 'impersonal' *il* or *ce* + *être* + adjective:

(43) *<u>Il</u>/<u>C'</u>est <u>évident</u> que ce problème est difficile .*
'It is obvious that this problem is difficult.'

(44) *Jean est arrivé, <u>il</u>/<u>c'</u>est <u>vrai</u> , bien en retard.*
'Jean has arrived, it is true, quite late.'

4. The alternation of 'impersonals' can also occur between *il* and *cela*/*ça*, with *il* once again representing the more formal register:

(45) *<u>Il</u>/<u>Ça</u> m'amuse <u>de voir tant de gens</u> .*
'It amuses me to see so many people.'

(46) *<u>Il</u>/<u>Ça</u> se peut <u>qu'elle ait menti</u> .*
'It might be that she lied.'

Regarding the last two categories, Hollerbach (1994) remarks that with certain impersonal structures and with certain 'formal' verbs the only possibility is *il*: *Il advient que . . .* 'It happens that', *Il s'ensuit que . . .* 'It follows that . . . ', *Il arrivera un grand malheur . . .* 'A big misfortune will occur . . . ' (but note: *Il/Ça m'arrivera de . . .+ infinitive*) 'It will happen to me . . . ', *Il me manquera cent euros* 'I'll be short 100 euros', *Il a été déduit des sommes importantes* 'Large sums have been deducted'.

---

1) Give an example of the anaphoric (refers back) and cataphoric (refers forward) use of personal pronouns.
2) With respect to dislocated sentences structures (see (24)), people often talk about comma intonation. What does that mean, and what is it used for?

3.6.3   Clitic pronouns

One of the 'specialties', and no doubt sources of major difficulties, of French syntax is clitic pronouns. A few of their many characteristics will be pointed out in this subsection. Clitics can be thought of as short pronominal 'traces' to dislocated or unexpressed complements of verbs 'clinging' to the inflected verb of a VP in rigorously predefined orders. Consider for instance (47), (48), and (49), illustrating some aspects of clitic placement in French.

(47)   *Pierre offre une poupée à sa sœur* > *Pierre la lui donne.*
         'Peter offers a doll to his sister.'

(48)   *Pierre offre ce livre ancien à notre famille* > *Pierre nous le donne.*
         'Peter offers this book to our family.'

(49)   *Pierre parle de ce problème à la réunion* > *Pierre y en parle.*
         'Peter speaks about this problem at the meeting.'

The object clitics *la* 'it (fem.)' in (47) and *le* 'it (masc.)' in (48), the dative clitics *lui* 'to him' in (47) and *nous* 'to us' in (48), as well as the adverbial clitics *y* 'to there' and *en* 'of it' in (49), despite their differences, have at least two common properties: (a) in indicative mood (see 4.4), all clitics are attached to the inflected verb, and (b) their grammatical functions (object, adverbial, etc.) are directly 'imprinted' in their forms, as all clitics in French are marked for **case** (see also section 3.2.2).

In compound tenses in indicative mood the clitics should also be placed to the left of the inflected verb, as would the case in e.g. the *passé composé* form of (47): *Pierre la lui a donné.* 'Peter gave it to her.' In imperatives, however, clitics are moved to the right of the verb, as in e.g. *Donne-la-lui.* 'Give it to her.' In yet another strange twist, though, the same does not hold for negative imperatives, at least as far as the standard written language is concerned: in that particular mood, clitics 'stack up' on the left of the inflected verb, following the negative particle *ne*: *Ne la lui donne pas* 'Do not give it to him/her.' Spoken French, however, conspicuously dropping the negative particle *ne* in informal register (see section 3.8), tends to regularize clitic placement in the latter contexts by moving all remaining clitics after the verb, as in positive imperatives: * ~~Ne~~ *Mets le pas là!* 'Don't put it there.'

Although clitics are marked for case, and thus their order could be variable, they nonetheless observe a very strict order (see Table 3.4). Two generalizations are particularly important:

– clitics have to 'stick' to their own categories, which means that clitics of the same column cannot be combined;
– when a dative clitic from column II is used, it cannot be combined with a clitic from column IV. In practical terms this means that the sentence in (50) is ungrammatical if *nous* is also marked for 'dative', pronominalizing an indirect object such as e.g. *à notre association* 'to us in our association'.

(50)   *Tu nous lui présentes.*
         *You DAT DAT introduce.
         '*You to us to him introduce?'

Table 3.4 *Order of clitics before the finite verb in declaratives (following Jones 1996:253)*

I NOMinative	II ACCusative / DATive	III ACC	IV DAT	V and VI PRO-PP
je	*me*			
tu	*te*			
il		*le*	*lui*	
elle		*la*		
nous	*nous*		*y*	*en*
vous	*vous*			
ils				
elles		*les*	*leur*	

Clitics combine with, and are sometimes replaced by, so-called disjunctive pronouns *moi* 'me', *toi* 'you', *lui* 'her/him', *nous* 'us', *vous* 'you (pl.)', *eux* 'them (masc.)', *elles* 'them (fem.)'. An example of their combination/replacement is when cliticization is prevented, because a complement of the verb cannot be both pronominalized and extracted from a constituent in the sentence. For instance in (51), the complement *mon frère* 'my brother' can be replaced by a disjunctive pronoun, *lui* 'him', but it cannot be moved out of the *ne . . . que* restrictive construction. This phenomenon is called **PP-island constraint**, which states that in French no single item can be extracted from a prepositional phrase (PP). This constraint applies to other constructions as well, e.g. coordinating and subordinate clauses, which of course does not mean that the entire PP cannot be moved, as in (52). When it is moved, however, a special 'extraction' device, usually *c'est . . . que* construction has to be used (see section 3.6.1).

(51)   *Je n'ai parlé qu'à mon frère. > Je n'ai parlé qu'à lui. > *Je ne lui ai parlé que.*
        'I only spoke to my father. > I only spoke to him.'

(52)   *Ce n'est qu'à mon père que j'ai parlé.*
        'My father was the only one I spoke to.'

Another important restriction for French clitics is that they are generally not allowed to 'leave' the verb to which they are attached, even if the verb becomes an infinitive and clitics would, in many other languages, readily 'migrate' to the inflected verb in the sentence. While in Spanish and other languages, for instance, one can say the equivalent of 'Him I go to see' (53), in French **clitic climbing**, i.e. the clitic *le* 'lo/him' 'climbing up' to the inflected modal auxiliary *aller* results in an agrammatical sentence. The clitic is attached to the main verb as follows: *Je vais le voir.* 'I will go to see him.'

(53)   **Le je vais voir/ * Je le vais voir.*
         'Lo voy a ver.'
         'Him I go to see.'

   One possible explanation for this special behavior of clitics in French could be that pronominal clitics in French are lexical rather than syntactic phenomena. According to Miller and Sag (1997), for instance, clitics in French behave more like inflectional morphemes that, although 'cliticized', i.e. formally separated from the verb, still act like affixes to the verb. This interpretation is consistent with the fact that clitics are marked for case (like inflectional morphemes are) in French (see section 3.2.2), and would explain why it is impossible to move clitics out of a 'clitic + auxiliary' construction. According to this view, lexical rules rather than syntactic movement would account for the specific ordering of clitics within a template: e.g. *Je te le donne* as opposed to **Je le te donne*, etc. A template-based approach to subject + clitic-complement + clitic-verb sequences have also been proposed by others (see Watson 1997), suggesting that clitic sequences are special grammatical units or 'kernel sentences' in which constituent elements follow a given order. Thus, rather than syntactically derived, French clitics are better understood as "template-formed morphological agreement markers" (Watson 1997:69), i.e. cliticized bound morphemes. A similar view has been advocated with respect to clitics in Italian (Crysmann 2003).

The clitic pronouns *y* and *en*, in declaratives and imperatives, are always the last elements of a sequence of clitics. What might motivate the 'ungrammatical' order of clitics in spoken French imperatives, such as: *Donnes-en-moi*?

3.7   Adverbs

3.7.1   *The intensifiers* si, tant, *and* tellement

The word class called adverb, with its various subcategories, is commonly defined based on meaning and distribution. Consider for instance the three adverbs *si*, *tant*, and *tellement*, generally translated as 'so', 'such', and 'so much' or 'so many', according to context. They are also called degree adverbs or degree modifiers, expressing 'strong intensity' of the element that they modify. Despite their semantic resemblance, these adverbs do not appear in exactly the same contexts. Consider the following examples (mainly from Lehmann 1959):

SI

(54)   *Elle en avait si envie.*
        'She wanted it so much.'

(55)   *Ces conditions sont si contre nature.*
        'These conditions are so contrary to nature.'

(56)   *Son esprit est si supérieur!*
        'His mind is so superior!'

(57)   *On ne l'achète pas si facilement.*
        'You can't buy it so easily.'

(58)   *Vas-tu me pardonner d'être si 'petite fille'?*
        'Are you going to pardon me for acting so much like a little girl?'

TANT

(59)   *J'aimais cette maison où j'aurais dû tant m'ennuyer.*
        'I liked this house where I ought to have been so bored.'

(60)   *Il n'ose pas parler, tant il est timide.*
        'He doesn't dare speak, he's so timid.'

(61)   *Elles ont tant besoin d'admiration.*
        'They need so much to be admired.'

(62)   *Enfin . . . elle est partie . . . et tant mieux!*
        'Finally . . . she's gone . . . and so much the better!'

TELLEMENT

(63)   *Il a un esprit tellement supérieur aux autres.*
        'His mind is so superior to that of others.'

(64)   *Je l'aime tellement!*
        'I love him so much!'

(65)   *Il se sent tellement mieux maintenant.*
        'He's feeling so much better now.'

(66)   *Elle ne voulait pas y penser, tellement cette idée lui paraissait inadmissible.*
        'She didn't want to think about it, this idea seeming so inadmissable to her.'

(67)   *C'est moi qui suis tellement au-dessus d'eux!*
        'I'm the one who is so much above them!'

(68)   *Nous étions tellement amis!*
        'We were such (good) friends!'

(69)   *Ça n'avait pas tellement d'importance.*
        'That wasn't so important/. . . didn't have so much importance.'

If we look strictly at the immediate context of surface structure, we are tempted to say that only *tant* and *tellement* can modify a verb: e.g, . . . *tant m'ennuyer* in (59), and . . . *aime tellement* in (64). This, despite the label 'adverb' which, strictly speaking, means 'adjoined' to a verb, i.e. 'ad + verb'. What kind of adverb is *si*, therefore? Apparently, *si* can co-occur with many complements: nouns (54), prepositional phrases (55), adjectives (56), other adverbs (57), and NPs (58). But note, too, that *tant* and *tellement* can also co-occur on the surface with a variety of words in a variety of structures. In addition to the verbs cited above, either *tant* or *tellement* co-occur with adjectives (63), with prepositional phrases (67), with nouns (61), or with other adverbs (65), entire clauses (60), or they can become a lexicalized expression such as *tant mieux* (62).

And yet a number of these surface analyses might leave us dissatisfied. For instance, it could be argued that in (60) and (66), we are dealing with an entirely separate set of words, i.e. *tant* and *tellement* as conjunctions, not adverbs. We would do this, of course, at the risk of ignoring the semantic similarity of, for instance, *tant*, adverb, and *tant*, conjunction. Another observation: instead of 'superficially linking' *tellement* only with a following prepositional phrase, such as *au-dessus d'eux* (67) and *d'importance* (69), one could argue that the adverb modifies a larger group of words, such as *être au-dessus d'eux* and *avoir de l'importance*. And if we do so, we may account for *si + petite fille* in (58) by saying that *si* modifies the verbal expression *être petite fille* 'be childish' rather than just *petite fille* 'little girl'. The only way to settle such problems is to observe the behavior of such expressions in many other contexts, quite apart from their association with the adverbs *tant* and *tellement*. In the end, one must conclude that the three adverbs are not completely interchangeable, despite considerable syntactic overlap and semantic resemblance. One has to account for the fact that *si* can never have a 'zero complement', i.e. it can never occur independently as in the hypothetical follow-up to **Oui, si* to (54), while *tellement* occurs with comparative (*tellement plus simple*) and superlative (*il est tellement le plus fort*) adjectives, but *si* and *tant* do not (**tant/si plus simple*, **tant/si le plus fort*).

How are such restrictions handled in a grammar? It often depends on the syntactic theory. Some propose that such restrictions have to be encoded as particular features of the lexical item(s) in question since, as we have just seen

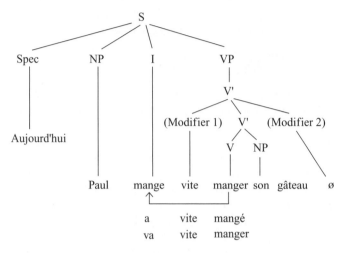

Figure 3.5 Schematic syntactic tree of *Aujourd'hui Paul a/va vite mangé/ manger son gâteau*. 'Today Paul quickly ate / will quickly eat his cake.'

with respect to degree adverbs, the type of word class which such items can modify depends on the adverb itself. Others suggest that such properties should be built into rules of a more general nature and should be useful for describing other syntactic phenomena.

3.7.2   Sentence and VP adverbs

The term adverb suggests that this word class is closely related to the verb. But we have also seen that the **scope** of degree adverbs can be much wider and more diverse than the verb. In fact, many adverbs can modify not just one element, but the entire sentence.

In a simple sentence like *Paul mange son gâteau* 'Paul is eating his cake' in Figure 3.5, adverbs can be inserted in different locations. One such spot in French, and in many languages, is at the beginning of the sentence. Elements that select this location come in different shapes. They can be sentence adverbs (*aujourd'hui* 'today'), NPs (*cette année* 'this year') or PPs (*à neuf heures* 'at nine o'clock'), but they are all elements defining the place, the time, or the mode of the events described in the sentence. Generative theories of syntax call this spot 'specifier' or 'spec position', and refer to it when they analyze other complements in other contexts, as well (e.g. wh-words in interrogatives, see section 3.10.2). Through the insertion of the sentence adverb *aujourd'hui* 'today' in our previous example, we obtain *Aujourd'hui, Paul mange son gâteau*.

The case of adverbs modifying the verb seems more complicated. The adverb *vite*, for instance, can be placed after the verb, yielding *Aujourd'hui Paul mange vite son gâteau*, which is not a preferred structure in English: *'Today Paul eats quickly his cake'. English can place the adverb before the verb it modifies, as in 'Today Paul quickly eats his cake', or it can place it at the very end of the sentence, as in 'Today Paul eats his cake quickly.' The adverb *vite* can also be placed at the end of the sentence in French *Aujourd'hui Paul mange son gâteau vite,* with no change in meaning in comparison with *Aujourd'hui Paul mange vite son gateau.* But when *manger* is put in a complex tense (e.g. *a mangé*), *vite* in French is placed between the auxiliary and the past participle: *Aujourd'hui Paul a vite mangé son gâteau* 'Today Paul quickly ate his cake'. The same is also possible in English: 'Paul had quickly eaten his cake thinking his sister would finish it all.' Can these phenomena be captured in both languages simultaneously in a unified way?

To find an answer, we would have to adopt a more formal way of thinking about the structure of these utterances. The deep structure of the sentence in Figure 3.5 shows two possible 'docking sites' for adverbs modifying the inflected verb (*mange*) and its complements (*son gâteau*) in the above sentences. The first spot is referred to as Modifier 1, the second as Modifier 2. English VP adverbs can select the first slot, i.e. the one before the inflected verb ('quickly eats his cake'), but French VP adverbs cannot: **Aujourd'hui Paul vite mange son gâteau*. French VP adverbs, on the other hand, can go in the second, Modifier 2, position (*mange son gâteau vite*), as can English VP adverbs ('eats his cake quickly'). But how do we account for the structure, in French, in which the VP adverb appears between the inflected verb and its complement in both simple (*mange vite son gâteau*) and complex (*a vite mangé son gâteau*) tenses? And how do we interpret the fact that English does not select the first possibility when the inflected verb is in a simple tense (**'eats quickly his cake'), but allows VP adverbs in that same position when the verb is in a complex tense ('will quickly eat his cake')?

It turns out that if we adopt what, in some syntactic theories, is called the 'split-inflection hypothesis', we can capture all these structures in a unified way. As shown in Figure 3.5, the split inflection hypothesis postulates that in the deep structure of the above utterances there is a syntactic 'slot' called the 'Inflection' or I node which, in French, would either harbor a verb in a simple tense (*mange vite son gâteau*) or serve as a site for an auxiliary or modal verb modifying the main verb (*a vite mangé/va vite manger son gâteau*).

Thus, instead of saying that VP adverbs are placed after the inflected verb in French, which does not explain why they can sometimes also be inserted before it, it is better to formulate a rule in terms of the movement of the verb. A rule like this in French would say: when there is a VP adverb in Modifier 1 position in the sentence (between the subject and the verb), then the verb is moved out of its unmarked syntactic position into the I position 'across' the adverb (see Figure 3.5) to acquire its inflections: *il vite _manger_ son gâteau → il _mange_ vite son gâteau. The raising of the verb to the I position, therefore, excludes structures such as *il _vite_ mange son gâteau, in which the inflected verb does not precede the adverb. Thus the difference between French and English can be captured as follows. In English, the auxiliary or modal verb in complex tense forms moves to the I position, but there is no such verb raising with simple tense verbs. In French, on the other hand, verb raising always takes place, whether the inflected verb is in simple or complex tense form. Moreover, by supposing such a scenario, we can also grasp the seemingly 'illogical' behavior of adverbs before verbs in the infinitive. The fact that a VP adverb is always between the subject and the infinitive in sentences such as _Je lui ai dit de vite manger son gâteau_ 'I told him to quickly eat his cake' is due to the fact that the infinitive is not an inflected verb form, therefore it does not have to raise to the I node to acquire its inflection: the VP adverb can stay in Modifier 1 position.

---

1) For what syntactic phenomenon is the sentence _Joe will quickly finish his homework_ a good example?
2) Find adverbs, synonyms of _tellement_, _tant_, and _si_, that are used as intensifiers in informal registers of spoken French.

3.8   Negation

3.8.1   Negatives and their positions

The word 'negation' evokes a number of concepts. For instance, one can find polar opposite semantic pairs of various types of morphemes, referred to technically as **antonyms**, such as prepositions (_avec/sans_), adjectives (_possible/impossible_), and adverbs (_beaucoup/peu_). Beyond contrasts of this sort that are 'built into' the lexicon of the language (see section 4.3.1), syntax looks for negation expressed by structural, not just lexical means.

Structures similar to _ne ... pas_ are numerous, as the following list of negative adverbs and **particles**, one-time adverbs with no transparent meaning in Modern French, demonstrates. They consist for the most part of pairs of morphemes, each complementing the other: _ne . . . pas_ 'not', _ne . . . plus_ 'not anymore', _ne ... personne_ 'nobody', _ne ... rien_ 'nothing', _ne ... jamais_ 'never', _ne ... guère_ 'hardly', _ne . . . aucun(e)/nul(le)_ 'none', _ne . . . nullement_ 'not at all', _non plus_ 'neither'. In addition, there is an occasional single item such as _non_ 'no' and a few old constructions like _ne ... point_ 'not', supposedly stronger than *ne . . . pas*, but now characteristic only of the written language and of some dialects, *ne . . . mie* ('breadcrumb'), *ne . . . goutte* ('drop'), and *ne . . . grain*.

'Total negation', i.e. the negation of the whole sentence, is usually expressed by *ne . . . pas* or *ne . . . point* (in more formal styles) (70). 'Partial negation' focuses on a particular element in the sentence (71), the time reference of the action described by the verb (72) in the sentence, or some combination of the two (73).

(70)   *Il n'y pense pas* [informal]. *Il n'y songe point* [formal].
        'He does not think about it.'

(71)   *Il ne pense pas au train (car il prend toujours la voiture).*
        'He does not think about the train (because he always takes the car).'

(72)   *Il ne pense jamais.*
        'He never thinks.'

(73)   *Il ne pense jamais à aucune conséquence de ses actions.*
        'He never thinks of any consequence of his actions.'

In formal styles and in the 'standard' written language negative adverbs are incompatible with *pas*: **Je ne ferai pas rien* 'I will not do anything', **Elle ne se sent pas nullement offensée* 'She does not feel offended at all' are unacceptable.

Within the framework demonstrated for VP adverbs (see section 3.7.2), the position of negatives to the verb becomes easy to explain. Similar to *not* in English, both *ne* and *pas*, would be, by default, inserted before the verb. The negative adverb *pas,* as well as 'not', occupies the Modifier 1 position before the verb, while the negative particle *ne*, which is not an adverb but more like a clitic, would be attached to the left of the I ('Inflectional') position (see section 3.7.2). Verbs in simple tense forms 'rise' to the I position to acquire their inflectional features, thus ending up between *ne* and *pas*: **(Pierre) ne pas venir demain* > *(Pierre) ne viendra pas demain* 'Pierre will not come tomorrow.' The process is essentially the same for complex tenses, as the auxiliary is the inflected verb form, and therefore the one rising to the I position: **(Pierre) ne pas être venu hier* > *(Pierre) n'est pas venu hier*. Other negative adverbs such as *rien, jamais, plus*, and *guère* behave similarly to *pas* in both simple (74) and complex (75) tense forms.

(74)   *Nous ne (le) trouverons jamais/plus/guère .*
        'We will never/neither/hardly find it'

(75)   *Nous ne (l')avons jamais/plus/guère trouvé.*
        'We have never/neither/hardly found it'

The negatives *aucun, personne*, and *rien* enjoy a somewhat special status. *Aucun* functions as a determiner, i.e. it occurs, with a negative meaning, in pre-head position (76). *Personne* and *rien* can be analyzed as pronouns that can be the objects of verbs (77) or subjects (78) in the sentence. As opposed to *personne*, however, when *rien* is the object of the verb, as it is in (79), it is 'floated' to the position before the inflected verb, just like *pas* (see above), or VP adverbs (see section 3.5.2).

(76)   *Ce n'est faisable en <u>aucune</u> manière.*
        'It is not feasible in any way.'

(77)   *Je n'ai vu <u>personne</u>./Je n'ai <u>rien</u> vu.*
        'I have not met anybody.'

(78)   *<u>Personne/Rien</u> ne bouge.*
        'Nobody/nothing moves.'

Some support for the default pre-verbal position of negatives in French comes from the fact that both *ne* and *pas*, and variants, remain before the verb when the latter is an infinitive, an uninflected verb form that does not 'need' to rise to the I node to be inflected (79). Interestingly enough, the two negatives get separated if the second one is further modified by a reinforcing expression (*du tout* 'at all') placed immediately after it (80), or if *aucun(e)*, i.e. a determiner, is the second member (81).

(79)   *Je compte <u>ne</u> <u>rien</u> faire la semaine prochaine.*
        'I intend not to do anything next week.'

(80)   *Je vous conseille de <u>ne</u> leur envoyer <u>rien</u> <u>du</u> <u>tout</u> .*
        'I recommend that you do not send them anything at all.'

(81)   *Le Président prétend <u>n</u>'avoir parlé à <u>aucun</u> conseiller.*
        'The president alleges not to have been talking to any counselor.'

3.8.2   *Meaning and scope*

An interesting meaning effect of two complete negations within a single sentence is that they act as an intense affirmation: the two *ne . . . pas* 'not', each modifying a verb in (82), act as a reinforcement of the opposite interpretation, synonymous with (83).

(82)   *Il s'agissait d'une dispute qui <u>ne</u> pouvait <u>pas</u> <u>ne</u> <u>pas</u> éclater.*
        'That was a fight that could <u>not not</u> occur.'

(83)   *Il s'agissait d'une querelle qui allait certainement éclater.*
        'That was a fight that had to occur.'

There is perhaps a stylistic effect, possibily negative politeness (see section 5.4.3) when one chooses to say, e.g. *Ne croyez-vous pas qu'il ne vaut pas la peine d'y aller?* 'Don't you think that it is not worth the trouble going there?' instead of the equivalent *Croyez-vous qu'il vaille* (or *vaut*) *la peine d'y aller?* 'Do you think it is worth going there?' In the first instance the speaker might simply be asking for confirmation, as if the sentence had read *Il ne vaut pas la peine d'y aller, n'est-ce pas?* 'It is not worth the trouble going there, right?', whereas in the second case we have a 'true' question to which either a positive or a negative answer could be given.

There is also a positive meaning of negatives in a complete two-word negative structure preceding the second, false negative, as in *Il ne veut pas que rien (i.e. quoi que ce soit) ne se fasse sans lui* 'He does not want that anything (whatever) be done without him', meaning 'He wants everything to be done in consultation with him.'

Some constructions are more subtle. For instance, the fact that in *Il ne faut pas faire cela* 'One must not do this' it is not the verb *falloir* 'must' that is negated, despite what is written, but rather the verb *faire* 'do', making the 'real' meaning equivalent to *Il faut ne pas faire cela* 'One must not do this.' This discrepancy between surface structure and deep meaning also occurs with other modal verbs (*Je ne pense pas le revoir* 'I don't envision seeing him' (= *Je pense ne pas le revoir* 'I envision not seeing him'). The statistically dominant pattern seems to be to negate the modal verb rather than the infinitive.

But it should not be assumed that a negated modal + infinitive structure is always interchangeable with a modal + negated infinitive structure. The sentence/utterance in (84), for instance, is not equivalent to (85):

(84)   *Je n'espère pas le revoir.*
        'I have no hope of seeing him again.'

(85)   *J'espère ne pas le revoir.*
        'I hope not to see him again.'

The above sentences have unequivocally different meanings because the two morphemes (*ne . . . pas*) modify two different verbs, i.e. their scope (in French *la portée*) is different: in (84) the scope of *ne . . . pas* encompasses *espère*, in (85) it targets *revoir*.

Another example of the value of the concept of scope can be seen in the following three contrastive sentences in which the 'partitive article' *de* varies in form between the expected reduced form *de* and the unexpected full forms *du/de la* depending upon its distance from the initial negative (examples from Marty 1975):

(86)   *Il ne veut pas de vin.*
        'He does not want wine.'

(87)   *Il ne veut pas boire de vin.*
        'He does not want to drink wine.'

(88)   *Il ne veut pas essayer de boire du vin.*
        'He does not want to try to drink wine.'

In the last example one might say that the scope of the negatives applies to the partitive immediately following the negated verb and also to the one accompanying the verb right after it, but not to any verb + partitive article at a greater distance away (*boire du vin*). A similar situation can be seen in (89) through (91), where the negative *aucun* becomes progressively more separated from *ne*. As the distance between the two negatives increases, the acceptability of the sentence decreases: (91) might seem a 'stretch' to many native speakers of French (Muller 1984):

(89)   *Max n'a parlé à aucun ministre.*
        'Max did not speak to any secretary.'

(90)   *Max n'a parlé au chef de cabinet d'aucun ministre.*
        'Max did not speak to the chief of staff of any secretary.'

(91)   *Max n'a parlé au conseiller du chef de cabinet d'aucun ministre.*
        'Max did not speak to the counselor of the chief of staff of any secretary.'

The importance of scope can also be seen in sentences in which the negative elements and the 'partitive article' are virtually contiguous, yet the fuller form(s), *du*, *de la*, or *des* are maintained. Thus, sentences such as *Je n'ai pas de pain* 'I don't have bread' are commonplace, but others with the fuller forms of the partitive article, are often labeled as 'exceptional' (from Marty 1975):

(92)   *Ça ne ressemble pas à de l'encre.*
        'This does not look like ink.'

In all of these cases the scope of the negation is not on the verb but on complements of the verb, such as the 'indirect' object as in (92): 'This object does look like something, but it is not ink.' These kinds of negative sentences are also sometimes referred to as partial negatives, in that they restrict some part of the sentence other than the expected part, i.e. the principal verb. This can be seen again very clearly in this live interchange on TV between Alain Juppé and Jacques Chirac, concerning the latter's difficulties with supposed under-the-table cash payments and his immunity from prosecution as President:

AJ – *Vous avez de la chance!* 'You are lucky.'
JC – *Je n'ai pas de la chance, je suis protégé.* 'I am not lucky, I am protected.'

By using the negation and the full form of the partitive, Chirac is simply denying Juppé's assertion and stressing the fact that he enjoys the special protection of presidential immunity, as if he had said: 'luck has no role to play in this matter'. All this shows that the description of the relative positions of the two-part negatives is a critical part of a complete description of negation.

3.8.3   Negatives and style

An important stylistic characteristic of negatives is the frequent omission of *ne* in informal styles of spoken French. Its elimination is most prevalent with a preceding subject pronoun, such as *il (n')a pas voulu que je le fasse* 'he did not want me to do it' or *elle (n')a rien vu* 'she hasn't seen anything'.

Negative adverbs such as *pas, jamais,* and *rien* in informative negatives (i.e. when conveying a content-related message) often bear emphatic accent in French, while they seem less prominent in remedial contexts, e.g. apologies, justifications, etc. The degree of prosodic prominence that a negative receives, however, also depends on cultural factors and **stance**, i.e. the supportive or adversial attitude of the speaker (Yaeger-Dror 2002). The particle *ne/n'*, which is often contracted and behaves like a clitic (see section 3.6.3), is more likely to be unaccented in continuous speech. Thus the negative adverb in French today becomes the primary carrier of negation, completely reversing the historical situation in which *ne* began as the only truly negative element, while *pas, point, mie*, etc. were full nouns meaning 'step', 'dot', and '(bread)crumb', respectively. The reversal of the historical situation between the two negatives has gotten so far as to make some linguists declare that *ne* has become a 'hyper-style variable' typical of formal, and mostly written, styles of French (Coveney 1996), but no longer characterizing the spoken language transmitted from generation to generation by the normal process of acquisition. Support for this fact comes from the observation that children who barely used the particle before, start acquiring it when they start learning written French in school (Armstrong 2001:160).

The retention of *ne*, although in more formal styles, is most characteristic in the following environments (examples from Hollerbach 1994 and Armstrong 2001):

– after a full NP (*les profs n'ont pas la loi* 'teachers aren't in control');
– after an accented demonstrative or disjunctive pronoun (*et eux n'acceptent pas les Continentaux* 'and they don't accept the Continentals');
– after *ce + être (c(e) (n)'est pas à nous de le faire* 'it's not up to us to do it');
– pre-formed, lexicalized sequences such as *n'importe* 'doesn't matter', *ne serait-ce* 'if only').

1) Support the statement that a 'double negative' is sometimes a 'positive'.
2) In English, there are words and expressions that are not negative themselves, and yet they can occur in negative sentences. Two such examples are *ever* and *any*. Find examples of such so-called 'negative polarity' items in French.

3.9   Passive 'voice'

3.9.1   Types of passive construction

The formal link between the sentences in (93) and (94) might not be immediately apparent, but few would dispute that these sentences represent different ways of expressing the same event or action. In traditional grammar, the term VOICE refers to grammatical means allowing the arguments of the verb (participants of an action or event) to be expressed in different ways. The active and passive constructions illustrated in (93) and (94) represent such means of expression.

(93)   *Une balle lui a fracassé la mâchoire.*
         'A bullet broke his jaw.'

(94)   *Sa mâchoire a été fracassée (par une balle).*
         'His jaw was broken by a bullet.'

The passive in (94) arises by two operations, of which the first is the crucial one: (a) the subject (*une balle*), which is also the agent of the action, of an active verb (*fracasser*) is suppressed and optionally expressed as a complement of the verb using the prepositions *par* or *de*; (b) the direct object of the active verb then moves to the empty subject position, and is expressed as the subject of the 'passive verb'. The latter is formed as a combination of *être* + past participle of the active verb.

Short passives, i.e. when the 'logical' subject (the subject of the active sentence) is not expressed (e.g. (94) without *par une balle*), might be preferred from a stylistic point of view, for instance when a speaker or writer wishes to emphasize what (s)he considers to be the 'main topic' of the sentence. Thus the passive can serve as means of **topicalization**, i.e. foregrounding one constituent or aspect rather than another. In (94) the writer might wish to emphasize the body part ('the jaw') that was hit, as opposed to the object that caused the injury ('the bullet'). This stylistic device is prominent in journalistic styles and official communications, predominantly concentrating on the 'results' and 'effects' of actions rather than the 'means' by which the action was performed.

There are many other types of passive construction that, in general, vary with respect to their means of expressing the agent of the action. In impersonal passives (95) the reference to the action is so general that there is no overt expression of an Agent: the impersonal pronoun *il* 'it' is moved to the subject position of the sentence. Such highly formal expressions are frequent in written French, e.g. in legal documents, minutes of meetings, and scientific treatises. Some passives formed by means of a reflexive pronoun, such as the one in (96), could be analyzed as a way of making the logical subject the object of the action performed: 'the ice broke itself (the ice)'. This, however, would lead to contradiction with respect to (97) where the reflexive construction can clearly not be interpreted as 'the pie eats the pie'.

(95)   *Il a été procédé à l'autopsie.*
       'An autopsy has been performed.'

(96)   *La glace s'est brisée sur le lac.*
       'The ice broke on the lake.'

(97)   *La tarte aux pommes se mange chaud.*
       'Apple pie is eaten warm.'

3.9.2   Tense and aspect in passives

Passive constructions are not simple 'transformations' of an active sentence into a passive one. As examples (98) and (99) illustrate, there can be mismatches of tense and aspectual meaning between the two: for instance the imperfect *était* in the passive structure (98) corresponds to a *passé composé* or a *plus-que-parfait* in the active sentence (99), rather than the expected imperfect form in (100). One can see why this is the case: if the imperfect verb form occurred in the active structure, it would denote 'continuing or repetitive action' that would be incompatible with the permanent result implied by *était meublé avec goût*.

(98)   *L'intérieur était meublé avec goût.*
       'The inside was furnished with (great) taste.'

(99)   *On a (avait) meublé l'intérieur avec goût.*
       'They (had) furnished the inside with (great) taste.'

(100) *On meublait l'intérieur avec goût.*
       'They were furnishing the inside with (great) taste.'

Although exact tense correspondences do occur, see (93) and (94), when mismatches arise, they are treated more often as **aspectual** rather than a matter of **tense**. The active sentence in (101) shows a single action in present time, but the expected passive in (102) loses those characteristics: through the use of

the sentence adverb *aujourd'hui* it implies a specific instance of an otherwise
repetitive action: e.g. 'Mike is the one who usually paints the room, but today
it is Max.' In place of (102), we would more likely expect something like
(103):

(101)   *Aujourd'hui Max repeint la chambre.*
         'Today Max is repainting the room.'

(102)   *Aujourd'hui la chambre est repeinte par Max.*
         'Today the room is being repainted by Max.'

(103)   *Aujourd'hui la chambre est en train d'être repeinte par Max.*
         'Today the room is being repainted by Max.'

3.9.3   *Passive verbs and their complements*

Verbs in idiomatic expressions or with a metaphorical meaning do not have a
passive form. For instance the abstract meaning in (104) is entirely lost in the
concrete, physically oriented sense of the active sentence in (105).

(104)   *L'enfant était (a été) attaché à sa mère.*
         'The child was fond of its mother.'

(105)   *On a (avait) attaché l'enfant à sa mère.*
         'They tied the child to its mother.'

Copular verbs (*être* 'to be', *devenir* 'to become', *rester* 'to stay'), since they
are not transitive, never allow passive constructions:

(106)   *Il est devenu pilote.* > **Un pilote est devenu de lui.*
         'He became a pilot.' > *'A pilot became of him.'

Measure verbs (*peser* 'to weigh', *coûter* 'to cost', *mesurer* 'to measure')
(107), as well as verbs taking an inalienable object (e.g. body parts) as their
complement (108), also repel the use of passive, probably because the complement of the verb (*pilote*, *80 kilos*), often called the Theme, has to be a direct
object external to the physical body of the Agent. The meaning of the incorrect
passive shown in (108), for instance, suggests that Marie is lowering someone
else's eyes. In the same vein, direct objects preceded by generic or partitive
articles also cannot become subjects of passives (109).

(107)   *Il pèse quatre-vingts kilos.* > **Quatre-vingts kilos sont pesés par lui.*
         'He weighs eighty kilograms.' > *'Eighty kilograms are weighed by
         him.'

(108)   *Marie baissait les yeux.* > **Les yeux étaient baissés par Marie.*
        'Marie lowered her eyes.' > *'The eyes were lowered by Marie.'

(109)   *Les chats boivent du lait.* > **Du lait est bu par les chats.*
        'Cats drink milk.' > 'Milk is drunk by cats.'

Other formal restrictions apply to complements or 'themes' of passive verbs. Although technically in object position in the active sentence, complements cannot be a relative clause (110), an infinitive (111), or even include a possessive adjective as part of the NP (112), probably because the reference of *son* cannot be established until later in the sentence.

(110)   *Il juge que le tapis est trop cher.* > **Que le tapis est trop cher est jugé par lui.*
        'He thinks that the rug is too expensive' > *'That the rug is too expensive is judged by him.'

(111)   *Il désire la rencontrer.* > **La rencontrer est désiré par lui.*
        'He wishes to meet her.' > *'To meet her is wished by him.'

(112)   *Paul m'a prêté son livre.* > **Son livre m'a été prêté par Paul.*
        'Paul lent me his book.' > *'His book was lent by Paul to me.'

As mentioned, the expression of the logical subject is optional in passives, but when it is expressed, it is done so in most cases by the preposition *par* (see e.g. (94) above). Certain verbs denoting long-term 'static' states, however, have their logical subjects expressed by the preposition *de* rather than *par*. The sentence in (113) exemplifies an emotional state of the subject, but the meaning of the verb can also convey the 'physical' arrangement of an animate subject (114).

(113)   *Pierre semble être aimé de ses amis.*
        'Peter seems to be liked by his friends.'

(114)   *L'enfant était bordé de coussins.*
        'The child was surrounded by pillows.'

---

1) Some pronominal verbs might give the impression of passive constructions. Discuss this statement with respect to the sentence *Ce pain se mange chaud* 'This bread is supposed to be eaten warm.'
2) Why is it ungrammatical to translate the English sentence 'I cut my finger' as **J'ai coupé mon doigt* in French? Where does the 'passive meaning' lie in the correct form *Je me suis coupé le doigt*?

Table 3.5 *Possible syntactic structures of different question types with a subject NP (*Paul*) in written and formal 'standard' spoken French*

	Yes-no question	Partial question		
		adverbial	subject	direct object
S + V order	*Paul vient?*	*Paul va où?*	*Qui vient?*	*Paul voit qui /quoi?*
Simple inversion	–	*Où va Paul?*	–	–
Subject-clitic inversion	*Paul vient-il?*	*Où Paul va-t-il?*	–	*Qui/Que Paul voit-il?*
Est-ce que . . .	*Est-ce que Paul vient?*	*Où est-ce que Paul va?*	*Qui/Qu'est-ce qui vient?*	*Qui/Qu'est-ce que Paul voit?*
Tag	*Paul vient, n'est-ce pas/ hein?*	–	–	–
	'Is Paul coming?'	'Where is Paul going?'	'Who/What is coming?	'Who(m)/What does Paul see?'

3.10   On interrogatives

3.10.1   Yes-no questions

Questions can be asked in many ways in French. According to Di Vito (1997) "native-speaker choice of interrogative syntax depends not only on the speech mode (spoken or written), but [. . .] on the discourse type, question type, and nature of the subject and verb in question". Of this array of variation, Table 3.5 illustrates a few the syntactic forms of the most common question types, and the following discussion reveals a few interesting points.

The first distinction to be established in between **yes-no questions**, i.e. questions that elicit a yes/no answer, accompanied or not by additional information supplied by the person answering, and questions called **partial questions** (also called wh-questions) that elicit a specific piece of information.

Yes-no questions aim at soliciting information/confirmation about the entire statement that they inherently contain (see Chapter 5). In other words, *Est-ce que Paul vient?* 'Is Paul coming?' questions the entire assertion 'Paul is coming', as opposed to some elements of it. Yes-no questions can take a variety of forms. In informal contexts they can be formulated, with no loss of meaning, with default subject + verb word order, and uttered with rising intonation on the final syllable, e.g. *Paul vient?* 'Is Paul coming?' In more formal registers, a syntactic process called (simple) **inversion**, takes place and the original statement becomes a question. The term inversion, on the surface, suggests that the order of the subject and the following inflected verb is inverted: the linear order of 'subject + verb' becomes 'verb + subject'. As we will see below, there are other ways to account for the underlying structure of such sentences.

Although possible in English with auxiliary and modal verbs ('Is Paul coming?', 'Can Paul come?'), the inversion of a full NP results in an ungrammatical sentence in French: *Vient Paul?* Simple inversion in French is only possible when the subject is expressed as a pronoun: *Vient-il?* 'Is he coming?', *Vient mon garçon?* 'Is my boy coming?' Inversion is 'reserved' to formal registers, and sometimes resorts to suppletion, i.e. borrowing a morphologically 'unrelated' stem (see section 2.4.4.2). This is the case with the verb *pouvoir* 'can', for which there is an alternative first-person form *Puis-je?* instead of *Peux-je?* 'May I?' Inversion of the first person of the present tenses of *devoir* 'must', *être* 'to be', *pouvoir* 'can', and *savoir* 'to know' is found today only in literary texts in the form of *Dois-je . . .? Suis-je . . .? Puis-je . . .? Sais-je . . .?* Inversion with demonstrative pronoun subjects is only possible when the verb is *être,* and the pronoun is in the third-person singular form in the present tense: *Est-ce possible?* 'Is it possible? *Est-ce elle?* 'Is it her?' Thus it is ungrammatical to say: *Doit-ce être vrai?* 'Should this be true?' and *Sent ça mauvais?* 'Does this smell bad?'

The way to get around the difficulties of inverting a full subject NP with the verb is called subject-clitic inversion. The process consists of inserting a clitic pronoun as the placeholder of the full NP after the inflected verb, and leave the NP in sentence-initial subject position: *Paul vient-il?* The fact that the subject clitic is placed after the inflected verb is important, since in compound tenses, the clitic appears after the inflected auxiliary or modal verb: *Paul est-il venu?* 'Has Paul come yet?' *Paul peut-il venir?* 'Can Paul come?' Although such sentences might give the impression of dislocated structures, with the subject topicalized on the left and the predicate repeated on the right, they are nonetheless neutral, although quite formal, ways of asking a question.

'Inverting' the subject pronoun and the inflected verb clearly implies 'movement'. Of the two possibilities, namely moving the subject clitic rightward across the inflected verb, or moving the inflected verb to the left, the second is usually preferred, since it enables syntacticians to account for some 'non-standard' question types (see below).

To elicit a yes or no answer, one can also use the periphrastic interrogative construction: *est-ce que.* The advantage of using this is that the rest of the sentence remains in the default subject + verb word order, thus not necessitating inversion. It is customary to derive *est-ce que* 'is it' from the declarative construction *c'est que* 'it is because' by applying subject-clitic inversion to the latter: *c'est que > *ce est que > est-ce que* for reasons that will be explained below (see section 3.10.3).

A fifth, common way of asking for confirmation is to use a so-called tag question. Tags are very frequent in informal registers of spoken French and English. They are numerous, and are used in a wide variety of contexts (see Chapter 5 for more details). Syntactically speaking, the advantage of using them is that tags are not, technically, part of the sentence (i.e. they are not attached to the highest sentence node (S) in the underlying syntactic structure). Sentences are, literally 'tagged' by them, i.e. attached to the right, but also set off from the rest of the utterance by a typical intonation pattern (see 2.5.2).

The sentence *Sent ça mauvais? is also incorrect when translated as *'Smells this bad?' What syntactic process, already encountered in this chapter, can we recognize in the correct translation 'Does this smell bad?'

3.10.2   Partial questions

When an adverbial is the principal focus of the question, we find the possibilities illustrated by *où* 'where' in Table 3.5. This class of interrogatives is made up by other words, some of which are referred to as wh-words, i.e. words starting with the letter sequence 'wh' in English: *who, when, why,* etc., but also *how.*

3.10.2.1 The atypical pourquoi 'why'
While *Où va Paul?* 'Where is Paul going?' and *Quand arrivent tes amis?* 'When are your friends coming?' are acceptable as inversion patterns, **Pourquoi travaille Paul?* 'Why is Paul working?' is never found. Questions with *pourquoi*, found not only in formal but also in informal registers, also show a peculiar behavior. For instance, while *Paul va où?* and *Les amis arrivent quand?* are common in everyday informal speech styles, **Paul travaille pourquoi?* is judged awkward. Some linguists have looked for an explanation in the two-syllable length of *pourquoi*, as opposed to the monosyllabic *où* and *quand*, but the indisputable existence of simple inversion with *comment* 'how', e.g. *Comment va votre ami?* 'How is your friend doing?' contradicts this interpretation. Note also that the closely related *Pour qui travaille Paul?* is acceptable.

3.10.2.2 Simple inversion and the complements of verbs
Whenever a direct object is introduced into the simple inversion pattern, e.g. **Où ces paquets trouve Paul?* *'Where these packages finds Paul?', the results are unacceptable because one fails to unambiguously identify the sentence functions of *Paul* and *ces paquets*. One possible explanation for this might be that, according to some syntactic theories, wh-movement, i.e. the placement of the 'question word' at the beginning of the sentence, is derived by moving

a complement of the verb to the SPEC position (for this position, see section 3.7.2).

In such cases the position of the wh-word would be the leftmost edge of the sentence or VP, just as *aujourd'hui* 'today' and *vite* 'quickly' are in Figure 3.5. The adverbial *dans son bureau* 'in his office' in the sentence *Paul trouve ces paquets dans son bureau* 'Paul finds these packages in his office' is moved 'out' to the beginning of the sentence in the form of a wh-word (*où*). In order to understand who is the subject and who is the object after the wh-movement takes place, word order in the VP has to remain unchanged. This means that *ces paquets*, the direct object of the verb, has to remain in object position within the VP, and cannot be topicalized to the left, as in the above example. Thus the correct order, using subject-clitic inversion, yields: *Où Paul trouve-t-il ces paquets?* 'Where is Paul finding these packages?'

3.10.2.3 Questioning the subject

The interrogative pronoun *qui* is used to question the identity of a human, regardless of its sentence function: a subject *Qui vient?* 'Who is coming?', an object *Qui as-tu invité?* 'Who(m) did you invite?', or a complement of a preposition *De qui parles-tu?* 'Whom are you talking about?' Unity of form, however, can be a problem for reference, as questions such as *Qui voit Marie?* are potentially ambiguous in French: they can mean 'Who(m) does Mary see?', with Mary as the subject, and 'Who is seeing Mary?', with Mary as the object.

When the **subject**, or some aspect of it, is being questioned, there is a considerable number of interrogative patterns missing, at least when compared with other groups outlined in Table 3.5. The most important gap is the absence of inversion, i.e. structures such as **Vient qui?* If one assumes, however, as some theories do, that *qui*, as a wh-word, is moved to the SPEC position (see section 3.7.2) at the very beginning of the syntactic phrase (see Figure 3.5), one can understand why there is no need for inversion: the interrogative pronoun, a 'placeholder' for the subject, is in the leftmost position in the phrase, i.e. the default subject + verb linear order of elements is reproduced. At the same time, the interrogative meaning is also present: it is conveyed by the pronoun *qui*.

Another 'question word', *quel(le)(s)* 'which', can also be used to question the subject or object of an utterance. It can either fulfill the role of a determiner (see section 3.5.4), i.e. questioning some aspects of the head of an NP, e.g. *Quelle chemise as-tu choisie?* 'Which shirt did you pick?', or it can question the complement or 'attribute' of the copula verb, as in *Quelle est ta réponse?* 'What is your answer?' But unlike English, when *quel(le)(s)* is used in French, the 'modified' complement (the head noun) has to be present in the sentence, or else the form is *le(la)quel(le)(s)*: *Laquelle?* 'Which (one of the shirts)?' This is so even if the speaker can tell, based on the immediate context, whether the conversation is about shirts or not.

3.10.2.4 Questioning the object

With questions requesting information about the direct object of a verb, one can find three types of pattern: default word order, subject-clitic inversion, and *est-ce que* (see Table 3.5). When, in questions with default word order, the interrogative pronoun remains in object position within the VP, i.e. there is no wh-movement, the pronoun is realized as *quoi*: *Paul fait quoi?* 'What does Paul do?' When it is moved into SPEC position in the phrase, it changes to *que*: *Que fait Paul?* In informal styles of speech, however, it is customary to see the use of a single form in both positions: *quoi* is 'extracted' from its object position and moved, as is, to the beginning of the sentence, using the expression *c'est... qui*. In such cases, dislocated constructions also often arise: *C'est quoi qu'il voit, Paul?* The *quoi* form of the interrogative object pronoun is also the only possibility when questioning the complement of a preposition, e.g. *De quoi parles-tu?* 'What are you talking about?' The formal register, on the other hand, prefers the use of the full interrogative structure *qu'est-ce que*, with default word order following. For animate objects, the only possible form of interrogative pronoun is *qui* or *qui est-ce que*, depending on styles and register: *Paul voit qui?*, *Qui voit Paul?*, with the latter being potentially ambiguous, or *Qui est-ce que Paul voit?* 'Who(m) does Paul see?'

3.10.3   Questions, styles, and register

The preceding sections made use of the distinction between the formality and informality of registers and styles, which figures predominantly among the determining factors in the use of question forms in French. Since all possible constructions cannot be illustrated here, the interested reader is invited to consult e.g. work by Coveney (1996), McCool (1994), and Di Vito (1997) for a more complete picture of possible variations.

The many question types observed so far can be divided, on the whole, into two major categories: those that make use of inversion, and those that avoid it. Although inversion exists in informal styles, it is less frequent than in formal styles, and characterizes sentences in which there is a need to invert the default subject + verb word order to place a long informative complement at the end of the sentence: e.g. *Où sont les toilettes dans cet immeuble immense?* 'Where are the restrooms in this immense building?' Most of the time, however, subject-verb inversion is avoided at all costs. The means to achieve that, as we have seen, are diverse.

Using intonation is a common way to formulate questions with no 'cost' of moving syntactic constituents. In very informal styles, for instance, not only yes-no questions, but also some partial questions can be uttered with the default subject-verb word order and rising intonation on the final syllable of the phrase: e.g. *Tu (ne) dis rien?* 'Aren't you saying anything?', *Tu vas où?* 'Where are you going?' Another way to avoid inversion is through the use of the periphrastic expression *est-ce que* or its variant *c'est que*. As mentioned earlier (see section 3.10.1), it is customary to suppose that *est-ce que* 'is it' derives from the declarative construction *c'est que* 'it is because' through subject-clitic inversion. Although the meanings of the two constructions are the exact opposite of each other – *est-ce qu'il vient?* can mean 'is he coming?' while *c'est qu'il vient* can mean 'because he is coming' – the surface structure of several 'non-standard' question forms show that there is, indeed, a possible link between the two. Among these forms are (115) and (116), both making use of the construction *c'est que*, with the interrogative pronoun within the construction (115), or in SPEC position (see section 3.7.2) on its left (116).

(115)   *C'est quand qu'il vient?*
         'When is it that he is coming?'

(116)   *Qui c'est qu(e) t(u) as vu à la fête?*
         'Who(m) have you seen at the party?'

The interrogative construction *qui est-ce qui* is also often uttered with no inversion of *être* and the demonstrative *ce*, as in sentences such as (117) and (118), which are very frequent in everyday informal speech styles. In fact, example (118) is an attested utterance of a French mother scolding a child who fell off an object at the playground.

(117)   *C'est qui qui t'a dit ça?*
         'Who told you that?

(118)   *Qui c'est qui t'a dit de monter là-haut?*
         'Who told you to get up there?'

Some analyses of 'non-standard' question types (see e.g. Hollerbach 1994) mention the insertion of a so-called 'intrusive' *que* after the wh-word, possibly a reduced form of *est-ce que* or of *c'est que*, as in (119), while others quote the well-known 'particle *-ti*' of working-class French, possibly an analogy of the linking /t/ 'heard' in some subject-verb inversion patterns (*part-il?* 'is he leaving?', or *pousse-t-il?* 'is he pushing?').

(119)   *Pourquoi que le gars est venu?*
         'Why did the guy come?'

(120)   *Quand c'est-ti qu'il part?*
         'When is he leaving?'

Finally, we should note the existence of structures that are characterized by the complete absence, at least on the surface, of the major portion of a question (121). The interrogative meaning must then be inferred from context: *Si j'y allais? (=Que diriez-vous si j'y allais?)* or *Et s'il n'est pas là? (=Que faut-il faire s'il n'est pas là?).*

(121)   *Et si tu lui disais non . . .?*
          'And what if you were to say no to him/her . . .?'

Given this proliferation of interrogative constructions, it is not surprising that speakers attempting to formulate standard, perceived as 'correct', question forms often actually make a mistake by combining syntactic means that do not normally combine. Such utterances represent a sort of 'overkill', known to linguists as **hypercorrection**. In (122), for instance, *est-ce que*, a construction that does not necessitate subject-verb inversion, is combined with subject-clitic inversion. Example (123), a similar combination of an *est-ce que* phrase and simple inversion, has been attributed to General de Gaulle, who had the reputation of always using very formal style in his public speeches.

(122)   **Est-ce que les Français ne sont-ils pas un peu . . .?*
          'Are not the French a little . . .?'

(123)   **Qu'est-ce qu'a pensé votre père . . .?*
          'What did your father think . . .?'

---

1) Translate the following question into French in as many different ways as you can. Consider all styles and registers: 'Who told you to go there?'
2) What is the difference, in terms of the complements of *être*, between: *Quelle est la situation en ce moment?* 'What is the situation right now?' and *Comment est la situation en ce moment?* 'How is the situation right now?'

3.11   Exercises

1) Isolate and classify all the morphemes that you find in the following utterances. Which words turn out to be the most difficult to analyze from this point of view?
   a *Les Haïtiens réclament le départ du président Aristide.*
      'The Haitians are calling for the departure of President Aristide.'
   b *Le bicentenaire de l'indépendance est l'occasion d'un sombre bilan.*
      'The bicentennial of Independence is an opportunity to make a sad assessment.'
   c *L'architecte aéronautique américain a choisi une date symbolique.*
      'The American aeronautical architect chose a symbolic date.'
   d *Ce journaliste a prétendu que le maire a accepté des pots-de-vin.*
      'This journalist claimed that the mayor took bribes.'

2) Apply the morphological and syntactic criteria delimiting nouns and adjectives to those delimiting prepositions and conjunctions. What difficulties come up? What overlap is there with other word types?

3) What criticisms might one make of the following definitions of a 'part of speech' by the traditional grammarian Grevisse (1968)?

   Le pronom est un mot qui, en général, représente un nom, un adjectif, une idée, une proposition. 'The pronoun is a word that, in general, represents a noun, an adjective, an idea, a proposition.'

4) Determine the oral endings for the following verb forms: a) present tense of *perdre* 'to lose', b) present subjunctive of *croire* 'to believe', c) future of *rendre* 'to give back', d) imperfect of *sortir* 'to go out', e) conditional of *comprendre* 'to understand', f) the four forms of *falloir* 'must'.

5) What would be the advantage(s) and disadvantage(s) of dividing verb forms like *finissons, finisse, finissait, finissiez* into stem + infix + ending?

6) Work out the stems and endings of the following verbs: *rire* 'to laugh', *mourir* 'to die', *s'asseoir* 'to sit', *joindre* 'to join', *dormir* 'to sleep', *suivre* 'to follow'.

7) Try to find a more 'regular' verb to substitute for the following largely 'irregular' verbs: *émouvoir, dissoudre, distraire, faillir, contraindre, mouvoir, acquérir, haïr, peindre.*

8) Here are five erroneous (*) oral or written verb forms: */suʁja/ for *(il) souria*; */kɔ̃klya/ *(il) conclua*; */ʁezɔlvəʁɔ̃/ *(ils) résolveront*; */vule/ *(ne m'en) voulez (pas)*; */pʁɑ̃dy/ *prendu* (past participle of *prendre*). What are the errors, and what models are probably responsible for them?

9) Why could the following NPs have a problem of semantic interpretation (see section 3.5.2)? Reflect on these examples in both oral and written French.

   des peintures sur verre espagnoles, la distribution des carburants en France, la fabrique d'accessoires de Londres

10) Define the following two concepts, and give an example of each in French and in English: a) clitic placement, b) quantifier floating.

11) Draw a schematized syntactic tree of the following sentence. Circle the complements of the verb: *Les petits enfants gentils donnent un cadeau à leur grand-parents* 'The nice little children give a present to their grandparents.'

12) Analyze the syntactic structure and possible register of the following question: *C'est qui que tu dis qu'elle a remarqué?* Find a real-life situation in which such a question could be uttered.

13) Transform the following sentence into an a) *impersonal* and b) *passive* construction: *Le marchand a compté les pièces* 'The salesman counted the change.'

14) Name three essential properties of passive constructions.

15) There are numerous adverbial constructions in French. Give a few examples of as many types as you can. Make frequent comparisons with English.

16) French routinely uses structures called 'double negation' in English. Compare some French and English negatives, with special emphasis on standard and non-standard forms.

17) Where does the negative meaning come from in the following two sentences? What is the technical term linguists use to refer to such constructions? a) *Hier, je n'ai pas fait grand-chose.* 'Yesterday I did not do much of anything.' b) *Il n'a pas la moindre idée des conséquences de ses actions.* 'He does not have any idea of the consequences of his actions.'

18) Translate the sentence 'Jack is a plumber' into French. How can the obvious surface difference between the English and the French renditions of identificational constructions be analyzed in terms of constructions with the verb *être*?

19) Give a short definition and an example of the following English terms: morpheme, noun phrase, and complementizer.

20) Morphosyntactic structure tightly interacts with the phonological structure of French. Illustrate this statement by one example.

21) *Je ne peux pas partir* means 'I cannot leave.' Change the scope of the negative, and report the meaning you obtain.

4   Lexicology and derivational morphology

4.1   Preliminaries

Lexicology is the study of words and their relationship to each other. A first step, then, is the determination of the boundaries of a word. While we all have an intuitive sense of what a word is, defining the term in a scientific manner is much more difficult. The typesetter might describe the word as any unit surrounded by spaces, in which case *don't* is one word but *do not* is two. This leads to such questions as: Do compound forms of a verb (*I shall have eaten*) constitute one word or three? Is the term *arc-en-ciel* 'rainbow' one word or three? We see that lexical units, sometimes referred to as **lexemes**, might include more than one 'word'.

At the same time, a single form might represent different words. The verb *lead* /lijd/ is a different word from the noun *lead* /lijd/ 'dog's leash'. Even within the same grammatical category, *ball* (sporting equipment) is a different word from *ball* (a formal dance). Given these problems, Touratier (1998) proposed a set of defining characteristics to distinguish the 'word' from a 'morpheme', insisting on the autonomy of the word. Through the characteristic of 'moveability', a word can be moved about in its sentence context, while bound morphemes cannot be (see section 3.3.1). The second criterion is 'separability', by which we recognize that a word is independent because it can be separated from the surrounding constituents of a phrase, i.e. it is not part of a fixed phrase. Following his proposal, we shall adopt the working definition of the word as a lexical unit as follows: the word refers to a single notion (*arc-en-ciel* 'rainbow' denotes [**denotation**] a single idea, as does *avoir peur* 'to fear') and its related forms refer to the same notion as the word itself, e.g., *j'ai vu* 'I saw' and *je vois* 'I see' both refer to the act of seeing.

We have seen in Chapter 3 that the same word can take many different forms by inflection. In this chapter we will study different aspects of the word: how they mean, how new meanings are formed, and how new words themselves are formed.

Some words have meaning by imitation (**onomatopoeia**), but most do so by a completely arbitrary connection between sound and meaning. New meanings are created by metaphorical and figurative usage. New words are created by such processes as **affixation**, **compounding**, **truncation**, and **acronyms**, while others are introduced into the language by **borrowing**. In all these processes there are perceived or imposed norms, which will lead us to examine the regulation of word usage, both informal and formal.

The vocabulary of French, and of any language, is the most volatile component of the language. Meanings can change quickly, sometimes radically. Words come rapidly in and out of use, as evidenced by the ceremonies each year that attend the announcement of new words to be included in the latest editions of the Larousse dictionaries. Patterns of word formation and of borrowing are similarly affected by changes in society. The feminizing suffix *-eresse* was quite common in the Middle Ages but has now taken on negative **connotations**, which is why the terminological commissions trying to find a term for 'female doctor' chose *docteure* over *doctoresse*. Borrowings from Italian, such as *balcon* 'balcony' and *pantalon* 'trousers', were extremely common in the sixteenth century. Today borrowings from English, for example *cool* 'cool' and *pullover* 'sweater', are omnipresent, particularly in advertising and some technical fields, and borrowings from Arabic (*toubib* 'doctor', *bled* 'village') are a prominent feature in the speech of French youth. The rapid expansion of science and technology in the twentieth century led to similar expansions in scientific and technical vocabulary.

Last but certainly not least, word choices vary both geographically and socially within the French-speaking world. *Char* 'tank' is a military vehicle in France, but an ordinary automobile in Quebec. Terms for common aspects of our lives, such as the automobile, vary radically in terms of **register**: *automobile, voiture, bagnole*; all refer to the same object, but in different speech styles.

4.2   Analyzing the meaning of words

The meaning of words can be one of simple referentiality: *book* = object with pages bound together. The meaning of simple words is usually unmotivated, or arbitrary, in that there is no reason why the combination of sounds in *cat* /kæt/ should mean a feline. However, in some instances, simple words can be seen as partially motivated, in that certain sounds convey somewhat vague meaning, a phenomena known as 'phonesthetics' '*phonostylistique*' (Léon 1993). For instance, many words in French that begin with /gʁ/ have a negative or unpleasant connotation (*grief* 'grievance', *grognon* 'grumbler', *grommeler* 'to mutter', *grimace* 'grimace'), much as a similar series starting in /sl/ in English (*sleazy, slime, slob*, etc.). However these are not absolutes, as evidenced by *grenier* 'attic', *gré* 'liking' in French and *sleek* and *slender* in English (see Van den Berghe 1976).

The most extreme case of sound symbolism is onomatopoeia, in which the word imitates a sound: *cocorico* in French and *cock-a-doodle-doo* in English represent the crowing of the rooster. These processes are relatively rare, though, and most words are considered arbitrary. As we shall see, however, arbitrariness is also relative.

While some words have only **referential meaning**, for instance *magnétoscope* 'VCR', others also have connotation, i.e. connotative meaning. *Ivrogne* 'drunkard' has a different connotative meaning from *alcoolique* 'alcoholic'. The motivation to avoid undesirable connotative meanings is a driving force behind the social-linguistic practice known as 'political correctness', but it also plays an important role in the development of scientific vocabulary and legal definitions. Connotative meanings are harder to pin down than are referential or denotative meanings, as they leave more an impression of a feeling about the referent, rather than denoting the referent itself. From the contexts in which a word is used, we can usually distinguish a core meaning of the word, to which certain features are added in a specific context (see sections 5.1 and 5.2). Defining that core meaning is not a simple task. One approach would be to list all the items that might be designated by that term. For instance one could say that *chair* includes 'armchair', 'stool', 'rocking chair', 'recliner', etc. This approach is called definition by inclusion. In such a system *chair* is said to be the **superordinate** or **hyperonym**, and the list of objects that are subsumed under the term *chair* are said to be **hyponyms**.

Look up the following words in a French-French dictionary, and compare the connotative meanings of the following pairs of words: *ivrogne – alcoolique; simple – niais; mécano – garagiste.*

4.2.1   Semic analysis

A second approach would be to identify features that these items have in common, such as +seat, +one person, +legs, and point to other features that distinguish one type of chair from another: +arms, +four-legged, +back, etc. This approach is called **componential analysis** or **semic analysis**. These minimal units of meaning should in principle be finite in number and comparable across languages. However, the search for universal components of meaning (see Wierzbicka 1996) has not gained widespread following. Instead, most linguists have focused on language-specific studies of categories of meaning.

One problem with feature analysis is determining what the distinctive traits will be for a given language. In French some terms for 'commercial establishments where one can have something to drink' are: *café, bar, guinguette, buvette*

Table 4.1 *Possible semes for a componential analysis of French words denoting 'commercial establishments where one can have something to drink'*

	(1) Drink	(2) Commercial	(3) Seated	(4) Standing	(5) Private	(6) Public	(7) Outdoor	(8) Rural	(9) (Social) class	(10) Dancing
café	+	+	+	−	+	−	−	−	−	−
bar	+	+	+	+	+	−	−	−	−	−
guinguette	+	+	−	+	+	−	+	+	+	+
buvette	+	+	+	+	−	+	−	−	−	−

(see Table 4.1). A *bar* is distinguished from a *café* by its physical form, the former requiring a counter where one drinks standing or seated on a high stool. A *guinguette* is distinguished from the others by its lower-class clientele and by the activity of dancing along with drinking. A *buvette* is located in a public space, such as a train station. Not all of these characteristics are absolute for each term, however. In particular the seated/standing opposition has exceptions. One might add for instance a category concerning the principal type of drink served in these establishments, with *bar* and *guinguette* more oriented towards alcoholic beverages, *café* and *buvette* more towards non-alcoholic beverages, although all four serve both. Another category could be the social group that would use each term. Of the four words above, only *guinguette* could be marked for class differentiation, but this is more a reflection of the likely clientele; the word is known and used by all classes of society. As these examples show, it is hard to fit these distinctions into a universal scheme or to develop a language-specific scheme that is not perceived as arbitrary.

This type of lexical semantic analysis permits us to establish the relationships between words of the same lexical category, or class. In Table 4.1, **semes** 1 and 2 establish the basic characteristics of the class. Semes 3 through 10 are used to establish the relationships between the various members of the class.

A problematic aspect of componential analysis is that there is circularity in the establishment of the semes between lexicographic accounts and lexicological analysis. Dictionary writers, called lexicographers, generally establish definitions through a less formal, more intuitive sense of the oppositions expressed by these semes. Lexicologists, who approach these problems through theories of meaning, generally establish their oppositions based on dictionary definitions. Only recently, with the establishment of large corpora of written and spoken language, have we been able to test the intuitions of the lexicographers, and therefore the oppositions established by the lexicologists. One example of such a collection is FRANTEXT, a collection of, mostly literary, texts focusing on the nineteenth and twentieth centuries, on which the *Trésor de la langue française* dictionary is based. This permits us to find examples that can test classifications such as the ones supplied above.

Applying the new techniques to one of the examples above, the case of *guinguette* is instructive. The definition in *Le Petit Robert* (1989) is: *café populaire où l'on consomme et où l'on danse, le plus souvent en plein air dans la verdure; Guinguette au bord de l'eau* 'working-class coffee house where one can drink and dance, usually in the open air surrounded by nature; riverside (waterside) *Guinguette*'. There are eighty-six examples of *guinguette* in the database, the earliest dating to the second half of the eighteenth century, the most recent to the 1950s (the database is limited to texts before 1960). Some representative examples are:

Mirabeau (1755): *Le bas artisan court à la guinguette, sorte de débauche protégée, dit-on, en faveur des aides.*
  'The unskilled craftsman runs to the *guinguette*, a safe place to unwind, one might say, for assistants (helpers).'
Maupassant (1886): *C'était le père Malivoire qui cria: Eh! Mon pé, j'vous invite à bé une fine. Et ils s'assirent devant la table d'une guinguette installée en plein air.*
  'Father Malivoire shouted: "Hey! Pops! I invite you to drink a shot." And they sat down at a table of an open-air *guinguette*.'
Alain (1936): *Mais aucun des détails de la parure aristocratique ne serait supporté par le peuple. Les grands décolletés n'entreraient point dans un bal de campagne, ni de guinguette.*
  'But none of the details of aristocratic appearance would be tolerated by the common people. Deep cleavage would not be admitted in country people's balls or in a guinguette.'

From these we can clearly see the features listed in the dictionary definition: place to drink, working class, dancing, open air, in the country. An element missing from the dictionary definition is the often temporary nature of the *guinguette*. Frequently the *guinguette* is open only on Sundays and holidays, as evidenced by the following examples from the FRANTEXT database:

Restif de la Bretonne (1776): *L'ouvrier supporte jour et nuit les plus rudes travaux, dont il sait que rien ne peut l'affranchir que la mort, dans l'espoir d'aller le dimanche à la guinguette, boire du vin détestable, avec le grossier et peu ragoûtant objet de son amour.*
  'Day and night a worker puts up with the harshest labor, from which he knows his only escape is death, in the hope of going, Sunday, to the *guinguette*, to drink horrible wine accompanied by the vulgar and disgusting object of his affections.'

Romains (1939): *Antonia reconnut le village de Saint-André. Elle me désigna une guinguette, qui était un de ces bals du dimanche auxquels elle avait pensé.*

'Antonia recognized the village of Saint-André. She pointed out a *guinguette*, which was one of these Sunday balls that she had had in mind.'

But this is not always the case, as we see in the following example:

Bosco (1945): *Avec quelques camarades nous allâmes à une guinguette, dans les champs. C'était un vendredi soir.*

'With some friends we went to a *guinguette*, out in the fields. It was Friday night.'

The country location is frequently further specified by proximity to water; this aspect is hinted at by the example given in *Le Petit Robert* (1989), but not included in the definition.

Zola (1891): *Emmener à une guinguette du bord de l'eau la fille qui passe, jouir de tout ce qui se vend, de la paresse et de la liberté?*

'Take the girl passing by to the *guinguette* near the water, enjoy everything that is sold, laziness and freedom?'

As we can see, one of the difficulties of the componential analysis of individual words is that many of the supposedly distinguishing semes are not obligatory: the *guinguette* might or might not be open only on Sundays or holidays; it might or might not be next to a river; it might or might not serve meals as well as drinks.

Use semic analysis to distinguish the following words denoting types of vehicles: *voiture – moto – mobylette – vélo – cabriolet – poussette – traineau*.

4.2.2   Prototypes and stereotypes

To get around the problems with componential analysis, modern lexical semanticists have tried two related approaches: that of the 'prototype' and that of the 'stereotype'. Each of these is primarily concerned with the notion of how classes of objects are related to a specific name. According to a theory of meaning that dates back at least to the Greek philosopher Aristotle (384–322 BCE), objects belong to a given lexical class because they share the same properties. Sharing these properties is a necessary and sufficient condition for membership. While this sounds straightforward, some words seem to belong to a given class even if they lack the primary characteristics of the class. For instance, one might define a 'table' as 'a piece of furniture with a flat surface and legs on which objects can be placed', but there are tables with one leg (*guéridon* 'pedestal table'). Others that seem to have all these characteristics might be commonly excluded from the category 'table', for example, a desk. Furthermore, some objects are perceived to be more 'table-like' than others: a dining-room table seems more 'table-like' than a bedside table. All members of a category are not equal. Finally, some characteristics that seem necessary may not be. 'Ability to fly' may seem the most characteristic element of the definition of a bird, but there are birds that do not fly.

Given these problems with the Aristotelian definition of classes, scholars have explored other ways to conceive of categories. One such way is to adopt a psychological perspective, and pursue the notion of 'prototypes' (see e.g. Kleiber 1990). Prototypes are seen as a way to conceptualize categories without having recourse to rigid lists of properties. Instead of having in mind a list of necessary properties, the human brain would instead retain a model of the best example of a certain category, and see other objects as more or less closely related to it. Thus all objects on which one sits might be compared to a model 'chair', with some such objects ('armchairs', 'dining-room chairs') being perceived as closer to the core conception, while others ('stools', 'bean-bag chairs') are perceived as more peripheral. Instead of emphasizing the elements that distinguish one category from another, this approach insists on relative similarity. It is linked to a branch of science called cognitive science, which studies the structures and functioning of the human brain.

The second approach is more oriented towards pragmatics (see Chapter 5). The notion of stereotypes emphasizes the negotiation of meaning between speakers of a language, conceiving of language as a set of conventions agreed upon by those speakers. Once again the similarity is stressed over difference, but the source of the similarity is different. Here it is the agreement between speakers on a mental model of a certain concept. Speakers agree that the stereotype of a cherry might include the characteristic 'red', but this stereotype does not exclude yellow cherries (Rainier variety).

The difference between a prototype and a stereotype in this context is that the stereotype is derived from usage, from the use of the term in a specific discourse context, rather than from the psycholinguistic image of the prototype.

All these approaches to meaning assume uniform usage within a linguistic community. They distinguish the elements of meaning in the relationship between the word and the object referred to by that word. Another kind of meaning is established by usage, one that establishes a connection between the word and the speaker as a social actor. To return to some examples given above, *guinguette* tells us that the 'thing' referred to is frequented primarily by people of the working class. *Zinc* would tell us that the speaker using the term is of the working class. It might also tell us the geographic origin of the speaker. As noted above, 'car' in France is usually *voiture*, but in Canada it was commonly (until the intervention of terminological commissions) *char*. A dilapidated car in France is a *bagnole, tacot,* or *guimbarde*, while in Quebec it is a *bazou, cancer,* or *citron* (= 'lemon'). Words thus convey not only referential meaning, but also social meaning. We will revisit this question when we look at the creation of new words in section 4.6.

Draw a car. What are the characteristics of the vehicle you draw that contrast it with others one might call a car (e.g. 'minivan', 'convertible')?

4.3   Semantic relations

Having established the meaning of words from the techniques described above, we will now turn our attention to the relationships between words in French. We can identify several types of such relationships: synonyms/antonyms; superordinates/hyponyms; and holonyms/meronyms. The first pair describe words of equivalent stature, while the next two pairs express a hierarchical relationship.

4.3.1   Synonyms and antonyms

Synonyms are words that mean the same thing, or almost the same thing. Synonyms can be absolute when they are perfectly interchangeable, without any change in meaning. This is most often the case when learned scientific terms have popular equivalents, for example *mouche des vendanges* for *drosophile* 'fruit fly'. Another source of full equivalents is word-borrowing, as in the English expression *last will and testament*, where English and French terms for the same thing were paired during the period when French was used in the English justice system.

Synonyms are also newly coined, either officially or unofficially. Official **neologisms** have been created by terminological commissions, in the hope of fending off foreign terms that have entered the French language in France and other French-speaking countries. The French terminological commission created *baladeur* for 'walkman', both referring to the same object: a portable music player. The creation of new synonyms is also part of the movements for the rights of traditionally disfavored groups, in the hope that a new name will avoid the negative connotations of the original, for example, *demandeur d'emploi* for *chômeur* 'unemployed' or *technicienne de surface* for *femme de ménage* 'cleaning lady'. The success of such governmental intervention in word creation is varied. While there have been some successes (e.g., *logiciel* for 'software'), there have been many more failures (e.g., *transbordeur* for 'ferry').

Alongside these official means of creating new vocabulary, there is the unofficial creation of new synonyms as well. Historically, attitudes toward unofficial neologisms have varied from the enthusiasm of the Renaissance to the condemnation of purists in later centuries. Today a new wave of neologisms is entering the general usage, with the spread of some terms invented in the word play of *verlan* (see section 4.9.2). The gradual acceptance into mainstream usage of terms such as *beur* 'Arab' reflects both changing attitudes towards language, and changing attitudes towards linguistic authority. The battle over who has the right to create new words, and the concurrent battle over who will use the new words, dates back many centuries (see Chapter 6). In either official or unofficial lexical creation, newly minted words are more likely to disappear within a few years than spread to general use.

Do synonyms really have the same meaning? More frequently, words have the same general sense, but differ in some respect, whether it be the tone, register, or some precision of meaning. These are known as partial synonyms. *Robber* and *thief* are both people who steal, but the former implies, more often, violence or the threat of violence, while the latter contains more a notion of deception. Similarly in French, *bandit* and *voleur* are synonyms, both signifying 'someone who steals', but at the same time *bandit* implies violence, while *voleur* does not.

Antonyms have opposite meanings. *Joyeux* 'happy' is the opposite of *triste* 'sad'. A very few words are their own opposite, such as *hôte*, which can mean 'guest' or 'host'. This phenomenon is known in French as *énantiosémie*, from the Greek word *enantios* 'contrary'. Sometimes antonyms are created through predictable derivational processes, such as the adjectives *honnête/malhonnête* 'honest/dishonest'. Noun antonyms are most frequently partial, differing in one key respect but being similar in many others: *garçon* 'boy' and *fille* 'girl' are both young human beings, differing only in gender.

Some antonyms are complementary, in the sense that the negation of one term is the equivalent of the other. *Mary is a foreigner* is the equivalent of *Mary is not a native*. Other antonyms do not offer the same type of opposition. *Mary is not rich* is not the same as *Mary is poor*, because there are varying degrees of wealth and poverty. Distinctions between various points along a continuum of meaning are known as 'scalar', as opposed to black and white 'binary' distinctions. Some antonyms, particularly those relating to family, social, or spatial relations, are said to be reciprocal. *Mary is in front of John* is equal to *John is behind Mary*. Switching the arguments (*John, Mary*) requires switching to the opposite term (*in front of, behind*).

4.3.2 *Hierarchical relations*

The reciprocity of synonyms and some types of antonyms is possible because they are at the same level in the **lexical hierarchy**. This means that another type of relation between words is hierarchical, between superordinates or hyper-onyms and hyponyms (see also section 4.2). Superordinates are more general terms that include a number of hyponyms, i.e. more specific words. *Chien* 'dog', *chat* 'cat', and *éléphant* 'elephant' are all hyponyms of the superordinate *animal*. The positive reciprocity of synonyms (all fruit flies are drosophilae, all drosophilae are fruit flies) and the negative reciprocity of some antonyms (a foreigner is not a native, a native is not a foreigner) does not apply in this case: while one can state that *all cats are animals*, the converse is not true (**all animals are cats*).

This fact has important pragmatic implications for the structuring of discourse: a superordinate can serve an anaphoric function for its hyponym, where the opposite is impossible. In (1a) the word *athlète* 'athlete' refers back to *sprinter* 'sprinter':

(1a)   *Le sprinter est accusé de dopage. L'athlète proclame son innocence.*
        'The sprinter is accused of   The athlete claims he/she is
        doping.   innocent.'

The reverse process, however, is not acceptable:

(1b)   **L'athlète est accusé de   Le sprinter proclame son innocence.*
        dopage.*
        'The athlete is accused of   The sprinter claims he/she is
        doping.   innocent.'

Restrictions also apply to the order of hyponyms and superordinates in coordinated constructions. The hyponym must always come first, as it does in (2a), but not as in (2b):

(2a)   *Les agents ont accusé de dopage le sprinter et d'autres athlètes.*
        'The officials accused the sprinter and other athletes of doping.'

(2b)   **Les agents ont accusé de dopage l'athlète et d'autres sprinters.*
        'The officials accused the athlete and other sprinters of doping.'

Psycholinguists (see e.g. Wisniewski 1995) have been studying aspects of the adult language acquisition of superordinates and hyponyms, and computer scientists (see e.g. Keane and Costello 1997) have analyzed the structure of compound nouns with respect to hierarchical relations: why do we say *soccer mom* instead of *sports mother*? We will return to this question when we study French compounding below.

In the superordinate/hyponym relationship, the hyponym is an example of the general class represented by the superordinate. Therefore all hyponyms must possess the characteristics of the class of the superordinate. *Chiens* 'dogs', *chats* 'cats', and *éléphants* 'elephants' all possess the characteristics of 'animalness'. In the relationship of meronymy, the **meronym** is a part of the whole; for instance, the *beak* is part of a *bird*, or a *headlight* is part of a *car*. The larger object (*bird*, *car*) is called the **holonym**. The meronym does not possess the characteristics of the holonym, but rather constitutes a part of the holonym. *Pattes* 'paws', *queues* 'tails', *yeux* 'eyes', *oreilles* 'ears' are not animal-like; instead they are parts of some animals. Psychologists and psycholinguists recognize such part-whole relationships as a fundamental part of human cognition and human linguistic development. Wierzbicka (1980) considered 'part' one of the thirteen original semantic primes on which her system of universal componential analysis was based (see section 4.2.1).

Cruse (1986) proposes four types of meronomic relations, based on the principle of necessity. (All examples are from ATILF [see References]):

> FACULTATIVE-FACULTATIVE: a cow is part of a herd, but not all cows are in herds nor are all herds composed of cows (*troupeau: ensemble d'animaux domestiques*);
>
> CANONICAL-FACULTATIVE: a corridor is a part of a building: all corridors are in buildings but all buildings do not have corridors (*corridor: passage plus ou moins étroit, mais plus long que large, qui, dans une habitation, donne accès, de plain-pied, à une partie de l'édifice*). Here we are dealing only with the literal and not with the figurative meaning of 'corridor', excluding thus such usage as 'the Danzig corridor' *le corridor polonais/le couloir de Dantzig*;
>
> FACULTATIVE-CANONICAL: a page is part of a book: all books have pages, but not all pages are in books (*livre: assemblage de feuilles en nombre plus ou moins élevé*);
>
> CANONICAL-CANONICAL: all corneas are in the lenses of eyes, and all lenses of eyes have a cornea (*cornée: partie de la cuticule transparente et dure qui forme la lentille*).

Another classification (simplified from Priss 1996) is based on the types of quantification that are possible with a given set:

> SUBSTANCE/OBJECT (meat is what goes into a sausage: meat is a mass noun, sausage is a count noun);
>
> SUBSTANCE/MASS (salt is part of seawater; both are mass nouns);
>
> ELEMENT/MASS (cells make up the skin; cells are count nouns while skin is a mass noun);
>
> MEMBER/SET (a tree is part of a forest; a chapter is a subdivision of a book; both terms in each set are count nouns).

Once again, these distinctions play out differently in different languages. Some words considered **mass nouns** in one language will be **count nouns** in another. A number of words are mass nouns in English and count nouns in French. For instance, *news* in English is a mass noun, for which we use another noun to express the parts: *a piece of news*, *news item*; in French, *information* is a count noun, so the singular *information* is the part of the whole: *les informations*. Sometimes this relationship is expressed simply by changing the determiner used, say from an indefinite to a definite article: while in English *an advertisement* is part of *advertising*, in French *une publicité* is part of *la publicité*.

The semantic relations within the **lexicon** are thus structured by several different types of opposition that vary, in their application, from language to language. The study of these structures and how they are expressed draws on anthropological, psycholinguistic, and sociolinguistic perspectives and permits us to understand fundamental differences between French and other languages.

4.4   Homonymy and polysemy

We recognize intuitively that French *sang* 'blood', *cent* 'hundred', *sans* 'without', and the verb forms *sent* 'she/he feels' and *sens* 'you (sing.) feel' are different words, though pronounced identically. These are **homonyms**, with very different **etymons**, from Latin *sanguis, centum, sine, sentit,* and *sentis*, respectively. They can have the same phonetic form, such as *tente* 'tent' and *tante* 'aunt' (**homophones**), or be spelled identically, such as *(la) tour* for 'tower' and *(le) tour* 'turn' (homographs), but in both cases are unrelated in meaning.

In other cases words that are spelled the same and have the same etymon seem to have become different words. Such cases are examples of **polysemy**, literally 'multiple meanings'. Technical words are designed to have only one specific meaning (e.g. *modem*), and as such are labeled monosemic, but many non-technical words are polysemous. This fact becomes a problem in such domains as the law, in which jurists attempt to give technical meanings to non-technical terms. *Robbery, theft,* and *larceny* have specific legal definitions, and are much more restricted than in ordinary usage.

Distinguishing between words that are different but sound the same, and words that look the same but have taken on different meanings, is not as simple as looking at the historical origins of the word. The etymological approach to distinguishing homonyms from polysemous words would lead us to the conclusion that *bank* (of a river) and *bank* (Bank of England) are the same word, as both are derived ultimately from the same Old Teutonic root, whether or not speakers recognize them as the same word.

The boundaries between homonyms and polysemous words are hardly clear, as is evidenced by widely varying practice in dictionaries. Consider the French noun *feu* 'fire'. Through a variety of processes (**metaphor, metonymy, synecdoche**) which we shall discuss further below, the characteristics of combustion, light, and heat contained in this word have led to its use to designate 'light' ('traffic light' *feu de circulation*, 'lamp light' *feu de la lampe*), 'inhabited house' (for taxing purposes) *feu* (e.g. *ce village a 400 feux* 'this village has four hundred taxable households'), 'brilliance' (*le feu d'un rubis* 'the brilliance of a ruby'), 'shooting' (*cessez-le-feu* 'ceasefire'), and 'aflame' (*avoir les joues en feu* 'have red cheeks'). All of these are derived from the same etymon, so the historical approach to distinguishing between them does not work.

In *Le Petit Robert* (1989) (henceforth PR) all of these meanings of *feu* ('light', 'fire', etc.) are listed under one entry, with four major subdivisions:

> PR^1: *Dégagement d'énergie calorifique et de lumière accompagnant la combustion* 'the release of caloric energy and light when combustion occurs'
>
> PR^2: *Coup de feu* 'shot' (of a gun)
>
> PR^3: *Toute source de lumière* 'any source of light'
>
> PR^4: *Se dit de ce qui est ardent* 'used to describe something that is burning'

In this approach, if the meanings of the word can be linked by rhetorical processes, such as metaphor and metonymy, they should remain linked in a single entry. In the preceding example, *feu* 'combustion' becomes *feu* 'the noise accompanying combustion', by metonymy. Similarly *feu* 'combustion' becomes *feu* 'the light given off during combustion', and *feu* 'warmth' 'the product of combustion' – *les joues en feu*.

In the *Dictionnaire du français contemporain* (henceforth DFC) by Larousse, a very different approach is taken, in which polysemous words are separated into as many entries as there are distinct meanings. *Feu* has six entries in the *DFC*:

> DFC^1: *Dégagement simultané de chaleur et de lumière produit par la combustion d'un corps* 'the simultaneous release of heat and light produced by combustion'
>
> DFC^2: *Ardeur des sentiments* 'the warmth of feelings'
>
> DFC^3: *Sensation de chaleur* 'the sensation of heat'
>
> DFC^4: *Décharge d'une ou de plusieurs armes, entraînée par la combustion, instantanée d'une manière explosive* 'the discharge of one or more weapons, produced by instantaneous and explosive combustion'
>
> DFC^5: *Signal lumineux conventionnel* 'a conventional signal light'
>
> DFC^6: *Maison familiale* 'a family house'

The basis for making such different decisions by these dictionaries was outlined by Jean Dubois, an editor of the *DFC*. A first technique is to compare the syntactic distribution and possible **collocations** of different meanings. Syntactically, only the meanings PR^1, DCF^1, and DCF^2 are used as the object of a verb without an article (*prendre feu* 'catch fire', *faire feu* 'light a fire'). Morphologically, PR^4, DFC^2, and DFC^3 cannot be plural. Finally certain collocations are only possible with specific meanings or entries, for example:

> *Les feux de la Saint-Jean* (PR^1, DFC^1) 'summer solstice bonfires'
>
> *Être tout feu* (PR^4, DFC^2) 'to be passionate about'
>
> Part of the body + *en feu* (PR^4, DFC^3) 'flushed (face)', 'burning (cheeks)'

Another type of morphological distinction concerns possible derivations. For instance, the DFC distinguishes two words *fruit*: *organe végétale* 'part of the reproductive system of a plant' and *profit, avantage* 'profit'. The first has derived adjectives *fruité* 'fruity', *fruitier* 'fruit-bearing', the derived nouns *fruiterie* 'storeroom for fruit', *fruitier* 'greengrocer', *fruitière* 'cooperative dairy', *fructification* 'fructification', and the verb *fructifier* 'to bear fruit'. The second has the derived adjectives *fructueux* 'profitable' and *infructueux* 'unprofitable', the adverbs *fructueusement* 'profitably' and *infructueusement* 'unprofitably', and shares the verb *fructifier* with *fruit[1]*. The combination of these features – syntactic, morphological, and collocational – allows lexicologists and lexicographers to distinguish words, as in the DFC, or meanings of a single word, as in the PR. These organizational choices are not to be dismissed as mere notational variants; they represent an important scientific decision concerning the relative importance of the history of the language for the description of its present state.

4.5   Change of meaning

Reading texts from the medieval period makes it obvious that many words have changed meaning over the years. *Soie* 'silk' comes from Latin *seta*, meaning the long, coarse hair of an animal. In the earliest French texts it was specifically the hair of a pig, then the hair of the mane of a horse. The first instance of *soie* being used to designate 'silk', the threadlike substance produced by moth larvae (silkworms) dates to the thirteenth century. Now only brush makers remember the first usage, and *soie*, in everyday usage, only designates the luxury fabric. Metaphorically, then, the term has become equivalent to the notion of luxury itself, as in the expression *jours tissés de soie* 'happy days', which literally means 'days woven in silk'.

While the change in meaning of *soie* has taken centuries, other changes occur much more rapidly. Until the 1950s, *holocauste* was a fairly obscure word signifying a sacrifice. Since the 1950s, through a process of specialization, it has become a common word with specialized meaning, signifying the genocide of Jews during World War II. Social change, historical events, the influence of other languages, and the whims of lexical fashion are among the many factors that can effect meaning changes.

Meaning change takes place through processes that have traditionally been described as figures of rhetoric and confined to literary analysis. Many figures of rhetoric involve larger constructions and therefore are beyond the scope of this chapter, so we shall focus on metaphor, metonymy, and synecdoche. These processes are, in fact, much more than literary figures, and have a crucial function in the nature of language and the process of language development (see Lakoff and Johnson 2003).

4.5.1   Metaphor

In metaphor, we find a similarity between certain features of two concepts, and then substitute one for the other. This might start as a **simile**, in which the comparison is overt:

(3)   *Il est fort comme un bœuf.*
        'He's strong as an ox.'

(4)   *C'est un bœuf.*
        'He's an ox.'

In so doing, we select certain features of the animal, and ascribe them to the human being. In a simile the feature of similarity is explicitly stated; in a metaphor it is understood. Very frequently, once a metaphor has been established, we 'forget' that it is even a metaphor. The verb *chanceler* is based on the noun *chancel*, the space around the altar in a church, frequently enclosed by a lattice or railing. The Latin etymon means 'trellis'. It was the intersecting lines of the trellis or lattice that led to the notion of zigzag movement and thus, in modern usage, 'walking unsteadily'. The original imagery of *chanceler* has been lost, and we do not now recognize it as a metaphor.

Metaphors can take us from one concrete concept to another, or from a concrete concept to an abstract concept. In the first instance, the concrete concept of the *ruche* 'beehive' is taken metaphorically for any place where there is a lot of activity: *cette usine est une vraie ruche* (DFC) 'this factory is a beehive of activity'. In the second, the concrete concept of a *clef* 'metal object one inserts in a lock' becomes the abstract concept 'crucial element': *clef de l'énigme* 'solution to the puzzle', *clef de voûte* 'keystone'.

In each case we could consider this process as the identification of similarity between one or two semes (smallest units of meaning) from one **sememe** (the cluster of semes forming a meaning of a word) and those of another. *Ruche*, cited above, has the characteristics of 'bees' *abeilles*, 'shelter' *abri*, 'site of great activity' *lieu d'activité frénétique*. In its metaphoric application to a workplace, only the last two semes are exploited, while the seme of 'bees' has been left aside.

4.5.2   Metonymy

In metaphor it is the similarity between two items that leads one to be used for the other. In metonymy it is the proximity between two items. Many types of relations are subsumed under this category, such as:
– material for object (*cuivres* = brass instruments);
– surface for what is on the surface (*toile* = woven fabric > painting on canvas);

- place for thing located there (Washington = the US government);
- instrument for what it produces (*langue* 'tongue' = *langue* 'language');
- container for what is contained (*prendre un verre* = drink what is contained in the glass);
- characteristic for event (*aube* 'white' > 'dawn' the time of day when the first light appears);
- function for object performing the function: *porte-avions* 'aircraft carrier' (ship).

The list could go on and on. Unlike metaphoric usage, metonymy frequently passes from the abstract to the concrete, particularly with respect to **deverbal nouns** (see section 4.6.1.2). *Fortification*, the act of building up defenses, becomes the physical defense structure itself. It can also work in the other direction: *bureau* 'desk' > *bureau* 'room', 'office' > *bureau* 'place where one works', e.g. *je vais au bureau* 'I'm going to work'.

In this example we see that sometimes one metonymy builds on another, creating chains of metonymy. In the case of *bureau* we can see the connections between the various links in the chain, but frequently these links are not obvious. *Campagne*, 'stretch of land', 'countryside' was first extended to a military expedition that conquered territory, such as in *la campagne de Napoléon en Russie* 'Napoleon's military invasion of Russia'. It now encompasses any activity organized to obtain something: *une campagne publicitaire* 'an advertising campaign'. The relationship between the land and the military operation can be understood, but the relationship between the third term, the activity of a publicity campaign, and the first, land, is not transparent.

4.5.3   Synecdoche

Synecdoche is a particular type of metonymy, one in which the specific relationship is not just of contiguity, but of being a component part of the larger term. In some cases the part is given for the whole. Synchronically this is reflected in the concept of 'heads of cattle', in which 'head' substitutes for the entire body. In this respect, it is instructive to revisit the example of *feu* discussed in section 4.4. As each house used to have a hearth, one could refer to houses as *feux*, a practice very common in taxation practices in the *Ancien Régime* 'France under the monarchy (prior to 1789)'. In other cases, the member of the set is substituted for the set. A diachronic example of this process is the transformation of the meaning of *fabrique* 'forge' > *fabrique* 'small factory'.

The procedures can be reversed as well: the whole for the part, the set for the member of the set. For instance, the French noun *cheptel* used to designate all moveable property, but now is restricted to 'livestock'. English has gone a step further: *cattle* used to designate any moveable property, then all livestock, and now is generally restricted to bovines. English also has the word *chattel*, legally any type of moveable property, but more specifically in modern usage, it refers to slaves. All of these terms are ultimately derived from the Latin word *capitalis*, which has been reintroduced in modern financial vocabulary, e.g. *capital campaign* in fundraising. This term, in turn, is derived from the Latin word *caput*, 'head' (French *chef*), with the result that 'head of cattle', our original example, ultimately is a 'head of things with heads'!

All of the processes listed above are ways in which the meanings of the existing word stock are expanded. The development of polysemy through the use of metaphor, metonymy, and synecdoche increases the range of our expressivity, and establishes new relational structures between meanings and words. In the next section, we turn to processes for creating new lexical items through derivation and word compounding.

4.6 Word formation

The creation of new vocabulary takes place through **derivation** and **composition**. In the first case, one word is derived from another, frequently, but not exclusively, by the addition of prefixes or suffixes. For instance, the root *dire* 'to say' can become *médire* 'to speak ill' and then *médisance* 'slander'. In these instances, a free morpheme combines with one or more bound morphemes. In the second case, composition, two free morphemes are joined: *après-rasage* 'after-shave', *clairvoyant* 'clairvoyant' ('able to see the future').

Both processes require, at least at the outset, some degree of transparency, so that the person who hears the word for the first time can guess at its meaning. For instance, if we know what *possible* means, and we know that *im-* is a common negating prefix, we can guess what *impossible* means. For this reason, while the meaning of root words is generally unmotivated – there is no reason the sequence of sounds/diʁ / should signify 'to say' – the meaning of derived words and word compounds is, at least initially, partially motivated: the sum of the parts allows us to guess the meaning. Sometimes the original root is lost, or has changed meaning, and this transparency is lost. At that point the derived word has lost its 'motivation', and has become a root word.

Psychologists and psycholinguists studying the mental lexicon assume that we store our vocabulary in bound and unbound morphemes, and combine them according to rules we have learned about our language. This approach associates derivational processes and inflectional processes (see Chapter 3). In this book we discuss the two phenomena separately, an approach that permits us to recognize social differences in how these processes are used, but psychologically they may ultimately turn out to be identical. This is still an area of much scholarly debate (see e.g. Temple 1996 and Beard 1995).

4.6.1   Derivation

A study of the words listed under the letter A of the *Petit Larousse* dictionary found that sixty-eight percent of those lexical items were formed by the addition of derivational suffixes (Dubois 1971:138). This gives some indication of the importance of derivation as a process of lexical creation.

The first step in determining whether words are simple or complex is to see if the root can be separated from the affixes (see section 3.2). This can be accomplished through a set of substitution exercises. Consider the noun *contradiction*. By comparing *contradiction* with *interdiction* 'prohibition' we can see that *contra* and *inter* are both affixes, in this case prefixes because they come before the word. By comparing *contradiction* with *contradictoire* 'contradictory' we can identify -*(t)ion* and -*oire* as suffixes.

These roots and affixes can have variable forms according to the context in which they are found. The root *dict* /dikt/ alternates with *dic* /dis/, as in words like *indicible* 'unspeakable' and *dit* /di/ in the noun *contredit* 'objection'. The affix *contra-* /kɔ̃tra/ in *contradiction* alternates with *contre-* /kɔ̃trə/, e.g. in *contredit*. Such variations are called allomorphs (see section 3.2.1). Usage-based models of grammar propose that we actually do not store these forms separately from the most frequently occurring lexical items that contain them.

As we can see from the above examples, both roots and affixes can be free or bound morphemes. The allomorphs /dikt/ and /dis/ of the root never occur independently, but /di/ does in *je dis* 'I say'. The allomorph /kɔ̃tra/ never appears independently, but the allomorph /kɔ̃trə/ does, e.g. in *contre toute attente* 'against all expectations'. Most affixes are bound, as in the case of the prefixes *in-* and *inter-*, and the suffixes -*(t)ion*, -*(i)ble,* and -*oire*, above.

The formation of words by derivation can include many layers of derivation. In the case of *contradictoirement* one could start with the base verb *dire* 'to say', from which we derive *contredire*, whence *contradictoire*, and finally *contradictoirement* 'contradictorily'. Some of these layers may have disappeared over time, or may never have existed. While *indicible* 'unspeakable' would presumably be derived from **indire*, or *dicible*, the verb *indire* is not attested in French, and the logical Latin root, *indicere* 'to proclaim' does not carry the negative meaning expressed by *indicible*. *Dicible* is newer, and much less used than *indicible*, indicating that it was in fact derived from *indicible* by **back formation**. The formation of a word by the simultaneous addition of both a prefix and a suffix is known as **parasynthesis**, which we will discuss further below.

While the analysis of these elements seems straightforward, appearances can be deceiving. Some words that look like complex forms are not easily analyzable. In some cases we can sense a root, but the affix apparently attached to that root is one of a kind. For instance, the noun *mensonge* 'lie, falsehood' seems to be constructed of the root *men(t)-* from the verb *mentir*, but the suffix *-onge* is not attested in any other word. In *rallonge* 'extension' (< Latin *longus*) and *éponge* 'sponge' (< Latin *sponga*), *-onge* is not a suffix. In other cases, we sense a compound word, the presence of an affix, without a clear sense of what the root might be. *Délabré* means 'in ruins', and a division into the common prefix *dé-* and the root *labré* seems reasonable, but there is no positive equivalent *labr-*. The best guess by etymologists is that the *-labr-* root is the same as the one that gives us *label*, originally a 'ribbon'. This might then come undone, giving the sense of *délabré*. However, such historical reasoning does not play a role in the understanding of the ordinary speaker, who is unaware of such connections. The segmentation of words is thus not always as obvious as it might first appear.

4.6.1.1   Derivation by affixation

As we have seen, words can be formed by adding affixes to a root. Such processes can change the grammatical category of the word, such as the creation of a verb from an adjective (*rougir* 'to blush' from *rouge* 'red'), a noun from a verb (*rougissement* 'reddening, blushing' from *rougir* 'to blush'), or a noun from an adjective (*rougeur* 'redness, blotch' from *rouge* 'red'). Others maintain the same grammatical category (*rougeâtre* 'reddish' from *rouge* 'red'). All new words created by the addition of prefixes are limited to the same grammatical category: *voir* 'to see', a verb, can only give another verb by prefixation – *revoir* 'to see again', *entrevoir* 'to glimpse'.

Affixes that are still being used to create new words are called **productive**. In recent years the problem of defining productivity has come under close scrutiny (see Bauer 2001, Corbin 1987, Dal 2003). The productivity of affixes varies over time. To demonstrate the productivity of French suffixes, Dubois (1962) studied the words included under the letter A in dictionaries from 1906 and 1961. The nominal suffix *-ose* is primarily related to medical vocabulary, and thus words with *-ose* have become more common as medical science has grown (*tuberculose* 'tuberculosis', *artériosclérose* 'arteriosclerosis'). At the same time, there is only one new noun in his database ending in *-oir(e)* (*arrachoir* 'puller [of teeth]'), and by the end of the twentieth century it had gone out of use along with others that had already disappeared by 1961, such as *affenoir* 'trapdoor of a hayloft', *amusoire* 'toy, amusement'.

A synchronic study of the language does not consider productivity over the course of the centuries, but rather focuses on current capability. Following Bauer (2001), we can say that while productivity and creativity are both types of innovation, productivity is rule-governed and distinguishes itself in this way from creativity, which for her, is limited to conscious borrowings from foreign languages. Thus the comic who coined the term *ministresse* to designate a 'female minister (of government)' was playing with a productive suffix recognized in such words as *duchesse, princesse*. Breaking the rules, thus opening the way to new rules, is a matter of creativity: the use of the term *marathon* to designate the long-distance race was a simple matter of metonymy (place for the event that happened at the place), but the first use of the suffix *-thon* to designate any long event, e.g. *tricothon*, 'a knitting contest', was creating a new suffix, which has since become quite productive (see Aleong 1984).

Why does this distinction between productivity and creativity matter? In linguistic description we attempt to find generalizations, sometimes referred to as 'rules' or 'laws' about linguistic behavior. Creativity emphasizes unpredictable exceptions to rules and new combinations of existing elements, while morphological productivity is a matter of rules, of judging which affixes still have the potential to create new words.

In the following section we shall present a representative sample of productive affixes, classified by the category of the newly formed word and subcategorized by the category of the source word. Thus 'denominal adjectives' are adjectives formed from nouns, 'deverbal nouns' are nouns formed from verbs, 'deadjectival verbs' are verbs formed from adjectives, and so forth. We shall explore in some depth the formation of nouns, providing an introduction to the methods used to understand those processes. For the formation of verbs, adjectives, and adverbs, consult Thiele (1987) and Dubois and Dubois-Charlier (1999).

Affixes can be used to form new nouns by suffixation, prefixation, and parasynthetic combinations of the two. The most common of the three processes is suffixation, which can form nouns from other nouns (*colonne* 'column' > *colonnade* 'colonnade'), nouns from verbs (*servir* 'to serve' > *serveur* 'server, waiter'), and nouns from adjectives (*pur* 'pure' > *pureté* 'purity'). The creation of new words in this fashion often involves a change to the base word, i.e., an allomorph of the base. For instance, *americain* /amɛrikɛ̃/ 'American' alternates with the base /amɛrikan/ in the formation of *américanisme* 'Americanism'.

4.6.1.2 Deverbal nouns
Nouns created from verbs are called **deverbal nouns**, and they express:
- the action or the result of an action (suffixes *-age, -ment, -ion, -ison, -ure, -ade, -at, -erie, -is, -ing*);
- the agent of the action (*-eur/euse/teur/trice, -ard/arde, -oir/oire, -ier/ière, -on/onne, -ant/ante*);
- the instruments used in an action (*-eur/euse/teur/trice, -ard/arde, -oir/oire, -ier/ière, -on/onne, -ant/ante, -ail/aille, -et/ette*);
- the place where an action occurs (*-oir/oire*).

These semantic categories can be subdivided on several morphological, syntactic, and pragmatic criteria. First, morphologically, the nominalizing suffixes can be distinguished by the forms of verbs that can be used as bases, and by the gender of the resulting noun. With rare exceptions, verbs with the infix *-ifi-* or *-is-* are limited to the nominal forms in *-ion* (*rectifier* 'to correct' > *rectification* 'correction', *réaliser* 'to achieve' > *realisation* 'accomplishment'). The nominalizing suffix *-erie* is limited to verbs of the *-er* conjugation (e.g. *moquer* 'to make fun of' > *moquerie* 'mockery'). The suffix *-ing* is productive in the sense that new words are created in French using this suffix, but only if the base has been borrowed from English. Most French nouns in *-ing* have an English verb base, even if they do not correspond to English usage (*lifting* 'a cosmetic surgery operation', *pressing* 'a dry-cleaning business' or more recently 'putting on pressure' in sports); sometimes, the English root word is not even a verb (French *footing*, as in *faire du footing* 'to go jogging').

In the category 'action/result of an action', *-age, -ment, -at, -is,* and *-ing* produce masculine nouns while *-ion, -ison, -ure, -ade* and *-erie* produce feminine nouns. It is important to note that as a result of social practice, now rapidly changing, the agentive nouns with masculine and feminine forms do not necessarily refer to the same function. A *repasseur* is a person who sharpens blades, while a *repasseuse* is a woman who does ironing.

Sometimes the same verb can combine with different suffixes to produce the same semantic result. *Accrochage* 'hooking, catching' has competed with *accrochement, finissage* 'finishing' with *finition*. As an indication of the trends, *accrochage* is attested fifty-two times in the FRANTEXT database, *accrochement* only six, and most recently in 1896. Similarly, *finition* appears four times and *finissage* only once. These competitions can end in a semantic distinction. *Doublage* is the dubbing of a film (adding a second soundtrack) while *doublement* is doubling the quantity of something by two (*doublement des recettes* 'doubling the money received').

Syntactically, the deverbal nouns can be distinguished by the type of verb from which they are formed, typically **transitive** (5), **intransitive** (6 and 7), and pronominal (8). Consider the following transformations:

(5)   *M. Dubois gère cette entreprise.*   > *M. Dubois est le gérant de cette enterprise.*

      'Mr. Dubois runs this enterprise.'   'Mr. Dubois is the director of this enterprise.'

(6)   *une machine qui imprime*   > *une imprimante*
      'a machine that prints'   'a printer'

(7)   *une machine qui agrafe*   > *une agrafeuse*
        'a machine that staples'   'a stapler'

(8)   *il se comporte mal*   > *il a un mauvais comportement*
        'he misbehaves'   'he has bad behavior'

Instrumental nouns are derived from prepositional constructions (9), and some deverbal nouns are also derived from *être* + adjectival constructions (10) (Dubois and Dubois-Charlier 1999:25).

(9)   *on agrafe des feuilles avec cet* > *on agrafe des feuilles avec*
        outil   *une agrafeuse*
        'one staples pieces of paper with   'one staples pieces of paper
        this tool'   with a stapler'

(10)   *Pierre est irrésolu, cela me*   > *l'irrésolution de Pierre me*
        retarde   *retarde*
        'Peter is undecided; this is   'Peter's indecisiveness is
        holding me back'   holding me back'

The syntactic structure underlying the root and affix combination thus permits us to distinguish the appropriate frames in which different suffixes can be used. Deverbal nouns in *-age* (11) have as their complement the inanimate direct object of the verb in question, while the paired nouns in *-ment* (12) have the animate subject of the verb as their complement. The expansion of a noun exposes the underlying syntax, allowing us to understand the choice of suffix, and the types of complements nouns with those suffixes can take.

(11)   *Le bûcheron abat les arbres, cela* > *L'abattage des arbres par le*
        a lieu à l'automne.   *bûcheron a lieu à l'automne.*
        'The lumberjack cuts down trees;   'The harvesting of trees by
        this takes place in autumn.'   the lumberjack takes place in
                                             autumn.'

(12)   *Paul est abattu après ce résultat,* > *L'abattement de Paul après*
        ça m'inquiète.   *ce résultat m'inquiète.*
        'Paul is depressed after this   'Paul's depression after this
        result; I'm worried about it.'   result worries me.'

Some endings are more common in certain domains (science, law, industry), while others are more general. New creations in the scientific domains tend to use the *-tion* suffix (*l'aération des poumons* 'aeration of the lungs'), while the deverbal nouns concerning industrial processes most frequently call on the suffix *-age* (*l'aérage d'une mine* 'ventilation of a mine'). Also, in general usage one uses the term *vendeuse* 'seller, saleswoman', but in the legal world the older *venderesse* is standard.

4.6.1.3 Deadjectival nouns

Nouns formed from adjectives, called **deadjectival nouns**, express the quality of the adjective. The most common suffixes for expressing a quality are as follows (all of these suffixes produce feminine nouns):

-esse	*délicat* 'delicate'	>	*délicatesse* 'delicacy, tact'
-eur	*grand* 'large, tall'	>	*grandeur* 'size, grandeur'
-ice	*injuste* 'unjust'	>	*injustice* 'injustice'
-(er)ie	*drôle* 'funny'	>	*drôlerie* 'joke'
-ise	*mignard* 'dainty'	>	*mignardise* 'daintiness'
-ure	*droit* 'straight'	>	*droiture* 'rectitude'
-ance/-ence	*abondant* 'abundant'	>	*abondance* 'abundance'
-ion	*abject* 'abject'	>	*abjection* 'abjection'

Of the suffixes expressing system or ideology, *-isme* produces masculine nouns (*national* > *nationalisme*) while *-iste* produces nouns that can represent both genders (*national* > *nationaliste*). Nouns expressing qualities are generally not countable, but in French, more easily than in English, these nouns can frequently be used in the plural to express specific instances of a quality. For example, *bêtise*, from *bête*, can express the quality of being stupid, or a specific instance of being stupid or acting stupidly (13)–(14). Some nouns ending in *-esse* or *-ité* are collective nouns, expressing all the people who belong to a group: *nationalité, noblesse*.

(13) *La bêtise de cette politique nous étonne.*
'The stupidity of that policy astonishes us.'

(14) *Ce garçon fait beaucoup de bêtises.*
'That boy does many naughty things.'

The underlying structure of deadjectival nouns can be 'N is Adj' or 'N which is Adj'. The former is a global evaluation with durative aspect, while the latter is more punctual. In the case of *bêtise* above, (13) is a global and timeless characterization of the policy, while (14) is a punctual evaluation of specific acts of behavior.

4.6.1.4 Denominal nouns

Nouns formed from other nouns, called **denominal nouns**, can represent agents or instruments, sometimes expressing pejorative or diminutive attitudes towards them. Such nouns can also refer to a state, status, or professional category, as well as collectives, which include nouns derived from numbers. Representative examples for each type of suffix are:

AGENTS:

-ier/-ière	cuisine 'kitchen'	cuisinier 'cook'
-iste	piano 'piano'	pianiste 'pianist'
-ien/-ienne	histoire 'history'	historien 'historian'
-aire	livre 'book'	libraire 'bookseller'

usually depreciative:

-eux/-euse	théâtre 'theater'	théâtreux 'untalented actor'

usually pejorative:

-ard/-arde	chauffeur 'driver'	chauffard 'bad driver'

STATE/STATUS/PROFESSION:

-at	partenaire 'partner'	partenariat 'partnership'

can also express territory:

	emir 'emir'	émirat 'emirate'
-age	esclave 'slave'	esclavage 'slavery'
-ure	candidat 'candidate'	candidature 'candidacy'

can also express territory:

	préfet 'prefect'	prefecture 'prefecture'

COLLECTIVES:

-at	professeur 'professor'	professorat 'teaching corps'
-ée	cuillère 'spoon'	cuillerée 'spoonful'
-age	feuille 'leaf'	feuillage 'foliage'

plants:

-aie	cerisier 'cherry tree'	ceriseraie 'cherry orchard'

numerals:

-aine	quinze 'fifteen'	quinzaine 'about fifteen'
-erie	gendarme 'police agent'	gendarmerie 'police station'
-ure	magistrat 'judge'	magistrature 'judiciary'

A special class of denominal nouns is composed of derivations from abbreviations. Abbreviations can become the basis for new nouns, using suffixes. A member of the *CGT* (*Confédération Général du Travail*) is a *cégétiste*. A person receiving the minimum wage, the *Salaire Minimum Interprofessionnel de Croissanc*, is a *smicard*. A student at the *École Nationale d'Administration* is an *énarque*.

4.6.1.5 Derivation by prefixation

Prefixation is less common in French than suffixation, but still an important means of creating new nouns. Prefixes are frequently prepositions or allomorphs of prepositions, and many are learned, taken directly from Greek or Latin, and only used in technical vocabulary that is drawn directly from those two languages, e.g., *hypoderme* 'hypodermic'. Sometimes the combinations of bases and prefixes that are from specialized intellectual domains are considered cases of compounding rather than prefixation. The prefixed form *télévision* (Greek prefix and French base) is distinguished from the compound *téléphone* (Greek prefix and Greek base) and the compound *téléfilm* 'movie made for TV' (*télé* is a shortened form of *télévision*, combined with *film*; Lehmann and Martin-Berthet 2000:116–117).

Thus we see that in some cases it is hard to distinguish clearly between prefixation and **word-compounding**. Another problem is when the two elements, the prefix and the base, are both free morphemes, as in the case of *avant-bras* 'forearm' or *après-midi* 'afternoon'. Orthographic and printing conventions are not much help. Some prefixes are always joined to their base words by hyphens (*avant-*, *sous-*, *hors-*) while others never have hyphens (*sur-*, *pro-*, *anti-*) or are variable (*contresens* 'misconception' but *contre-courant* 'counter-current, against the current'; *soucoupe* 'saucer' but *sous-marin* 'submarine'). Why then should *malvoyant* 'with poor eyesight' be a derivation by prefix while *clairvoyant* 'clairvoyant' is a compound word? The most important reason is that *mal-* is a negative prefix to many words (*malveillant* 'malevolent', *malaise* 'malaise', *malnutrition* 'malnutrition', etc.) while *clair-* is not. The division between prefixation and compounding combines questions of origin (diachrony) and of productivity (synchrony), and ultimately should be considered more a continuum than a binary classification. Prefixes can be divided into eight semantic classes (Thiele 1987):

– spatial (*sur-*, *sous-*, *sub-*, *hors-*, *entre-*, *inter-*, *anti-*, *avant-*, *pré-*, *arrière-*);
– temporal (*avant-*, *pré-*, *ex-*, *arrière-*, *post-*, *après-*, *entre-*, *co-*);
– opposition (*anti-*, *contre-*, *para-*);
– sympathy for an idea or person (*pro-*);
– privation (*an-*, *sans-*);
– negation (*in-*, *non-*, *dé-*, *dis-*, *mal-/mé-*);
– intensity (*archi-*, *hyper-*, *méta-*, *super-*, *sur-*, *ultra-*, *sous-*, *vice-*, *re-*);
– intensifiers (*demi-*, *hemi-*, *mi-*), (*semi-*, *pén-*, *presque-*, *quasi-*), and (*tout-*).

4.6.1.6   Parasynthetic nouns

Parasynthetic formation of nouns is rare in French. True **parasynthetics** are those in which a prefix and a suffix are added at the same time to a nominal base, to form another noun. Consider for example the word *intonation*. There is no noun *inton nor *tonation. Both the prefix *in-* and the suffix *-ation* have been added to the nominal base *ton* at the same time to produce the word *intonation*.

> Explain how *emprisonnement* and *atterrissage* are parasynthetic constructions.

4.6.2   Truncation

Truncation is a process in which the new word is formed by leaving out part of the base word. If the end of the word has been dropped, then it is termed **apocope** (*laboratoire* 'laboratory' > *labo*); if the first part of the word is lost, it is called **apheresis** (*autocar* 'intercity bus' > *car*). Some words have both apheresis and apocope: *automobile* + *omnibus* > *autobus* 'city bus', with a subsequent reduction (by apheresis) to *bus*. Sometimes the division of the word is at a morpheme boundary (*automobile* > *auto*), but this is not always the case, as we see in *laboratoire* > *labo*, where the morphemic boundary would be between *labor-* and *-atoire*.

Once a truncation has been made, the new word can be the foundation of new series of words. Words using *euro* (< *Europe, européen*) have proliferated following the creation of the European Union, and even more since the creation of the euro as a monetary unit: *eurocrat* 'bureaucrat working for the European Union', *eurodollar* 'US currency held in European banks to pay international transactions' (EuroDicAutom: the European Union's multilingual term bank), *euromarché* 'Euromoney market' (EuroDicAutom).

Another type of truncation is known in English as **back formation**. Nouns are created from verbs by the loss of the verbal inflection: *offrir* 'to offer' > *offre* 'offer', *oublier* 'to forget' > *oubli* 'neglect'. Older forms may exhibit changes in the morphology of the base, reflecting morphological alternations in the verb at an earlier period of the language: *espérer* 'to hope' > *espoir* 'hope'.

4.6.3   Conversion and reduplication

Conversion is the change of grammatical category without any change in the form of the word. The most common type of conversion is the use of an adjective as a noun: *français* 'French' > *un Français* (French person), *le français*

'French language'. Also common is the conversion of a participle to a noun, for example *étudiant* 'student', *penchant* 'penchant' (present participle) or *fiancée* 'fiancée', *crainte* 'fear' (past participle). Infinitives are also frequently used as nouns: *les parlers régionaux* 'regional languages'. Sometimes whole phrases serve as nouns: *le rendez-vous* 'meeting', *un certain je-ne-sais-quoi* 'a certain something'. Similarly nouns can be used as adverbs: *point* 'not at all', *personne* 'no one', *rien* 'nothing' serving as the second element of negation.

The formation of new nouns by **reduplication** is typical of children's speech, and of adults' speech to children. It can also express, among adults, an attitude, frequently pejorative or certainly depreciative, towards the object designated. Simple reduplication repeats the same syllable: *jouet* 'toy' > *joujou* 'toy' (child's language), *chou* 'cabbage' > *chouchou* (only in the figurative sense 'darling'), *dormir* 'to sleep' > *dodo* 'sleep'. In partial reduplication, so-called **echo-words**, only the consonant + vowel part of the original syllable is repeated, with the consonant remaining in the second syllable: *biche* 'darling' > *bibiche* (also 'darling'). While the formation of nouns by reduplication is usually denominal, there are some examples of deverbal reduplication: *cache-cache* ('hide and go seek'). A variation on reduplication alters the vowel: *zigzag* 'zigzag', *bric-à-brac* 'odds and ends'.

4.7   Compounding

One of the most prolific sources of new nouns today is the combination of two free morphemes, with or without an intervening preposition. Compounds can have many forms, as illustrated in the following, non-exhaustive, list:

Noun + Noun:	*bateau mouche* 'passenger boat on a river'
N + Prep + N:	*pomme de terre* 'potato'
Verb + Noun:	*gratte-ciel* 'skyscraper'
Adjective + Noun:	*pur-sang* 'thoroughbred horse'
	rouge-gorge 'robin'
Infinitive + Infinitive:	*savoir-faire* 'know-how'
Sentences:	*rendez-vous* 'meeting'
	sot-l'y-laisse 'tastiest morsel of chicken'
Two numbers:	*quatre-quatre* 'four-wheel drive car'
Number + Noun:	*deux roues* 'two-wheeled vehicle'
Preposition + Noun:	*à-côté* 'aside' (remark), 'side issue'

Some have ascribed the popularity of the noun + noun construction to the influence of English, complaining that the absence of prepositions that might explain the relationship between the two nouns in such a construction is unclear. The widespread influence of English is relatively recent, though, and these constructions are far from new in French: *chêne-liège* 'cork oak tree' was first attested in 1600; *porte-fenêtre* 'door with window' in 1676; *papier-monnaie* 'paper money' in 1727; and *bateau mouche* 'passenger boat on a river' itself, 1870 (Noailly 1990: 208). The rapid increase in such constructions might be a natural development, indicating that French has reached the end of the line of its movement towards an **analytic** language, and the pendulum is starting to swing back towards **synthetic** constructions.

In the following examples two consecutive nouns appear without any intervening words:

un bateau mouche	'passenger boat on a river'
un oiseau chanteur	'songbird'
une épée baïonnette	'sword which doubles as a bayonet'

In all of these examples the first noun is analyzable as the principal one (or head) of the whole construction. This makes the second noun subordinate to the first, i.e. it serves as a modifier of the first noun, as for instance in these expanded versions of compounds (see section 3.5):

bateau qui ressemble à une mouche (par sa taille)	'boat that resembles a fly (based on its size)'
oiseau qui sait chanter	'a bird that sings'
épée qui sert aussi de baïonnette	'a sword also used as a bayonnette'

Adjectives are even more commonly found in NPs in which the noun acts as the head:

un bateau anglais	'an English boat'
un oiseau délicat	'a delicate bird'
une épée impressionnante	'an impressive sword'

Differences apparent in the paraphrases reveal underlying structures that remain hidden in the surface structure. Thus, understanding compounding requires us to look at all such NPs to see what the structural limits and semantic interpretations are.

Two of the most prolific categories today are in fact those represented by *bateau mouche* and *épée baïonnette*. In the first case the second noun stands in a metaphorical relationship to the first (= *bateau qui ressemble à une mouche par sa taille*). The second represents more a kind of coordination, in which there is essentially identity of the two objects mentioned (= *objet qui est à la fois épée et baïonnette*).

For the first category, consider the following wide range of metaphors:

meeting monstre	'huge meeting'
bac(calauréat) poubelle	'throwaway, i.e. worthless, high school diploma'
justice escargot	'slow-moving justice', i.e. as slow as a snail
chou-fleur	'cauliflower', i.e. a cabbage that looks like a flower
mot-clef	'keyword'
budget accordéon	'constantly changing budget'

The possibilities are almost endless and new formations are appearing all the time (Picone 1996). As for the second category, coordination, it is open-ended as well:

comédie-ballet	'play + ballet in a single performance'
paysan fermier	'peasant + farmer'
climatisation-chauffage	'heating + cooling'
service-volée	'service + volley play (in tennis)'
point-virgule	'semicolon', i.e. period + comma

The pattern exists even with proper names: *Poquelin-Molière*, the real name and pseudonym of the well-known dramatist (1622–1673). It should also be pointed out that not all such constructions are immediately transparent from their meaning: out of context, does *jean carotte* mean 'jeans with legs tapered like a carrot' or 'orange-colored jeans'? Is a *cravate ficelle* a tie that is thin like a string or one whose color resembles that of string, i.e. white or grey? Or, finally, consider *bec papillon*, '(gas) burner with a flame resembling butterfly wings'. Without specific context or explanatory note, the relationship between the two nouns can be rather obscure, sometimes even for native speakers.

Further complicating the semantic interpretation of such structures, corresponding nouns and adjectives are not always equivalent, e.g. *mystérieux* in *homme mystérieux* 'mysterious man' may not carry the same semantic force as *mystère* in *homme mystère* 'man of mystery', somewhat similar to the English equivalents. Similarly, *catastrophe* 'catastrophe' in *arrivée catastrophe* 'a catastrophe of an arrival' seems to be a stronger, more forceful modifier than *catastrophique* 'catastrophic' in *arrivée catastrophique* 'catastrophic arrival'.

Word formation by derivation and compounding is one way to expand the vocabulary available to describe new things or concepts, or attitudes towards these two. In the above we have only treated such processes with respect to the creation of new nouns, but the same processes can be applied in the creation of new words in other grammatical categories. Some of these we will explore in the exercises at the end of the chapter. Now we will turn our attention to another way to expand the vocabulary of French: borrowing from other languages.

4.8   Borrowing

A large portion of French vocabulary has simply continued from Latin and Germanic forms, but other words are more recent borrowings from those languages. Distinguishing between these two sources accounts for the classification of some words as 'learned', i.e. later borrowing unaffected by phonetic changes that occurred in the intervening period. Often this gives rise to **doublets**, words that have the same source but different forms because they entered the language at different periods. For instance, *hôtel* 'hotel' and *hôpital* 'hospital' are both derived from Latin *hospitalem*, but the longer form was borrowed later (twelfth century), and therefore does not show the loss of the unstressed medial syllable. However, both have lost the *s* of the first syllable, which reappears in the later construction *hospitalité* 'hospitality' (thirteenth century).

Forms that have been borrowed are, at first, recognized as foreign. As time passes they are assimilated into French, and can become the source for further production of new words. The English word *look* first appeared in French in the 1970s, meaning 'style' or 'appearance'. Now the verb *se relooker* 'to get a makeover' has been created, and the pronunciation of the base form has been changed to make it sound more French (/luk/ English /lʊk/). Another, common way of nativizing borrowings is direct translation from the donor language, a process known as **loan translation**. Some well-known words that belong to this category of **calques** in French are *gratte-ciel*, the word-by-word translation of the English 'skyscraper', as well as *lune de miel* from 'honeymoon', and *jardin d'enfant* (Canadian French) from 'kindergarten'.

French has taken in words from over a hundred languages, in part a legacy of the colonial empire, e.g. *bled* 'small town' from Arabic, *hamac* 'hammock' from an indigenous language of the Caribbean, and in part a reflection of trade routes and economic and political power. In the early Renaissance, the city-states of Italy were the wonder of Western Europe. French kings invaded northern Italy on several occasions, and brought back thousands of Italian courtiers and artists, including Leonardo da Vinci. As a result, thousands of words were borrowed from Italian in the sixteenth century. Many of them have since disappeared, but a number remain, such as *balcon* 'balcony' and *salon* 'living room'. Even a few suffixes have come to French from Italian: *-esque* (*romanesque* 'romanesque') and *-ade* (*colonnade* 'colonnade').

In the nineteenth and twentieth centuries, the political and economic power first of the British empire and then of the United States has led to a large number of borrowings from English. The recognition of such borrowings is complicated by the fact that large numbers of English words were borrowed from French following the Norman Conquest of 1066. Some of these words have now come back into French, with meanings far different from those that evolved on French territory. Modern French *tunnel* is a borrowing from English, but the English term itself is derived from Old French *tonel*, which gave *tonneau* 'cask' in Modern French.

Borrowing of foreign terms to designate objects or concepts that were previously unknown or had no term in French has generally been accepted, but the use of borrowings when French equivalents exist has led to some concern in the French-speaking world. While the first concerns were voiced in the nineteenth century, the increased numbers of English borrowings became a political issue after World War II, as first Alfred Sauvy and then René Étiemble sounded the alarm against Anglo-American influence. The first period after the war was dominated by private movements, such as the Défense de la Langue Française, founded in 1953 as the Cercle de Presse Richelieu, and the Office du vocabulaire français (1957), which grew out of the journal *Vie et langage* (1952).

In Canada, the private movements and the political issues were quite different, but the results were similar. The driving private organization was not the political left, but the political right, and in particular the religious organization Société Saint-Jean-Baptiste (SSJB). This society was founded in 1834, and after World War II focused its attention on language issues. In the late 1950s the SSJB pushed to have French accepted in public places, such as hotels and restaurants. In the 1960s, as the 'Révolution tranquille' turned less tranquil, the SSJB was passed by, as the Parti Québécois took form and pushed a stronger linguistic agenda.

Government intervention came earlier outside of France. The Fichier français was created in Switzerland in 1959, the Office du bon français in Belgium in 1961, and the Office de la langue française in Quebec, also in 1961. In France, Étiemble's book *Parlez-vous franglais?* appeared in 1964. Its publication helped to transform the private movements of the 1950s into the governmental interventions of the 1970s (terminological commissions formed from 1972, Loi Bas-Lauriol in 1975). This political concern has led to considerable discussion in the francophone world as to how one might distinguish 'necessary' from 'superfluous' borrowings. The terminological commissions created in a variety of francophone countries serve to create new French words for English terms, in essence an attempt to make the English terms superfluous. One difficulty is that French, Belgian, Swiss, and Quebecois terminological commissions have sometimes arrived at different solutions. This topic will be pursued further below, in our discussions of variation in the lexicon and of state intervention.

4.9   Lexical variation

4.9.1   Regional variation

Regional variation in French vocabulary has sometimes been valued as a source of enrichment, as when the sixteenth-century poet Ronsard encouraged his compatriots to take words freely from the various dialects of French. More often, however, regional variation was criticized as providing unnecessary synonyms for words that already existed in the standard variety. This gave rise to many commentaries on 'flandricisms', 'gasconisms', etc. that teachers sought to eliminate from their students' vocabulary. In the nineteenth century the scientific study of lexical variation began with a number of dialectal studies, which led to the compilation of a linguistic atlas of French by Jules Gilliéron and Eduard Edmont (1902–1920). The *Atlas linguistique de la France* studied the use of specific words and pronunciations, mostly relating to rural life, across hundreds of points throughout francophone Europe, including Belgium and Switzerland.

Describing a word as 'regional' requires, first of all, a definition of the region. Many studies have limited themselves to the particularities of regions as small as a single village, while others have taken a broader sweep, such as Poirier's *Trésor de la langue française au Québec* (see http://www.tlfq.ulaval.ca/). In general, the definition of a regional variety of French has been with reference to a mythical 'Parisian French', 'international French', *'français commun'* or *'français de référence'*. Poirier (1995) prefers to use as his point of comparison the *'français des dictionnaires'*, by which he means the words found in the most widespread French dictionaries, *Petit Robert, Grand Robert, Trésor de la langue française, Lexis, Grand Larousse de la langue française, Grand dictionnaire encyclopédique Larousse*, etc. This has the advantage of providing a verifiable point of comparison, but the disadvantage of ignoring the peculiarities in the way these dictionaries were compiled, and the sociolinguistic status of the words.

Each region has its specific historical and political connection to this reference point. Because France is a political unity, speakers using regional lexical variants in northern France are usually conscious of the norm represented in the standard dictionaries, because they have attended schools in which that norm is taught, and interacted with a government for which it is the official language.

French speakers in Quebec live in a province in which French is the official language, and the language of education, but the reference point is not necessarily that of the *français des dictionnaires*, at least those dictionaries that are produced in Paris. Indeed, new dictionaries in Quebec, such as the *Dictionnaire du français plus*, incorporate words specific to the North American context, but only those that meet with official approval, while still omitting many words, particularly Anglicisms, whose use is discouraged by the government and its educational system. For instance, in the *Dictionnaire du français plus* one will find a long explanation of the difference between the use of *bleuet*, 'blueberry' in Quebec, 'blue-bottle plant' in France, but common Anglicisms such as *braker* 'to brake (a car)' are omitted.

French speakers in Haiti and the Caribbean departments and territories of France use French as their official language and the language of education, but speak as their native language a French-based Creole. The group of Creole speakers also includes African-Louisianans, some 20,000–30,000 descendants of slaves in southern Louisiana. The boundaries between Creole and French may be difficult to determine. There is no scientific way to determine when a word crosses the boundary between a different pronunciation, and becomes a different word, just as it is hard to distinguish between a dialect and a regional language. In Louisiana Creole, *kwit* (*français de France* (FF): *cuit*) is a word that exists in French, and is pronounced close to its French equivalent, but in this region it refers to the culturally specific sugar cane syrup. Other words have a close equivalent in French but are sufficiently different that they might not be recognized: *parkwa* is the Louisiana Creole equivalent of *(il n'y a) pas de quoi* 'you're welcome'. At the far end of the spectrum, no historically related French equivalent exists for *rakatcha* 'spur' (FF: *éperon*).

French speakers in the Côte d'Ivoire (Ivory Coast) and other West African and Central African countries have had all their education in French, and French is the official language of the government, but French is not the native language of the speakers, nor the language most frequently spoken in the street. Here the distinction between French and the mother tongue is easier than in the Creole situation, but the distinction among the types of French is equally thorny. In these countries, the French used can be further subclassified into, for example, 'French in the Congo (Zaïre)', 'French of the Congo', and 'Congolese French' (see Nyembwe 1995). These represent not just historical steps, but can also be concurrent linguistic situations. The first is the French language used in a country or region, without taking into account the local context. This can be identical with or closely resemble the *français de référence* 'RP French'.

The second still resembles *français de référence*, but includes a number of terms – borrowings from local or international language(s), neologisms created within the framework of French derivation, or changes in the meaning of French words – to accommodate local cultural and natural specificities (political, culinary, zoological, or botanical, for example). Throughout West and Central Africa *foufou* (sometimes spelled *fufu*) has been added to French vocabulary to designate a paste commonly eaten in the region. From this term a French derivative has been created: *foufoutière*, to designate a restaurant in which this food is served. Borrowings are not necessarily from local languages, but can also be from other European languages that have had an influence in the region. Togolese French, for example, has borrowings also from Portuguese (*cabécère* 'port administrator') and from the English of neighboring Ghana (*highlife* 'a type of popular dance music'; see Anzorge 1995). As for changes in meaning, in the Congo *bière*, a French word meaning 'beer', has come to mean a 'tip' (*pourboire*).

The third is a form of French that has become sufficiently autonomous that the link with the *français de référence* is no longer important to the speakers. This variety of regional French is different enough from the *français de référence* that the northern French speaker would have difficulty understanding such speakers. This might well include syntactic and phonological variation, in addition to the use of different words, or the change in meaning of existing words.

This tripartite division is not exclusive to overseas situations of language contact. One might distinguish equally well 'French in Marseille', the 'French of Marseille', and 'Marseillais French', with *provençal* being the contact language instead of Lingala or other Congolese languages. These varieties may all exist simultaneously among different social groups in the society.

Regional variation might be caused by the influence of the local language on words or expressions originally in the dominant language (in this case French), or might be words from the local indigenous language borrowed into the variety of French spoken. The historical and political relations between French and the local languages play a decisive role in determining how such influences are perceived. After the Revolution, the goal of the French educational system was to eliminate such variation within French territory, and external linguistic policy (*Alliance française*, *Alliance israélite*) sought to establish or to maintain the status of the *français de référence* for regions not under French control. Since World War II, and particularly with the revived interest in regional identity and regional folklore in the 1960s and 1970s, local variation has been perceived in a more positive light, with the result that dictionaries of regional French (e.g. Rézeau 2001) have become quite popular.

4.9.2   Social variation and word games

Social variation has long been recognized in French dictionaries through the use of a number of usage markers such as *bas, familier,* and *populaire* or by reference to specific groups, particularly the usage of lawyers (*le palais*). The *Trésor de la langue française informatisé*, the on-line version of the dictionary that fills sixteen large volumes, lists some 6,914 words or meanings as *familier*; 2,993 as *populaire* (some of these are both *familier* and *populaire*); and 120 as *vulgaire*; at the other end of the scale we have 4,336 listed as *littéraire* (for example: *écharpe aux sept couleurs* = *arc-en-ciel* 'rainbow'); 280 as *poétique* (*moisson* 'harvest' used to replace *an* 'year'), 4 as *savant* ('learned'), and only 1 as *soutenu* 'formal' (*fer* for 'any weapon that cuts'). It is not an accident that dictionaries do not specify words that are 'bourgeois' or 'aristocratic'; the assumption is that all the words included in the dictionary are known by or suitable for the wealthier part of society, and usage indicators are necessary only when the privileged enter other realms, social or artistic. These indicators of usage are not explained or justified. The long introduction to the print version of the *Trésor de la langue française* does not explain how these terms are used, nor does the much shorter introduction to the *Grand Robert*. Some recent research on usage indicators in older dictionaries has appeared (Wionet (2004) on the first edition of the *Dictionnaire de l'Académie Française* (1694), Seguin *et al.* (1990) on Féraud's *Dictionnaire critique* (1787)), and other studies have focused on 'slang' (*argot*) or lexical creation, such as *verlan* (see below), but much remains to be done in the scientific investigation of social variation in the lexicon.

In all times, word formation processes also included language games. The most popular assignment in introductory computer programming classes is one of the oldest language games: producing 'pig Latin', *igpay atinlay*. The rules are simple: words that begin with a consonant have all their initial consonants up to the first vowel moved to the end of the word, then *ay* is appended to the word (*pig* > *igpay*), while vowel-initial words simply have the 'suffix' *way* added to the end (*animal* > *animalway*).

Such 'cut and paste' types of derivational processes are widely used in all languages to produce cryptic languages, i.e. existing words purposely altered so that people outside a group have difficulties deciphering them. In French, some of these 'languages' are now almost forgotten, while others are enjoying a growing reputation, and even becoming a symbol of identity in some social groups. Linguists have studied the almost forgotten *largonji*, from the word *jargon*, which appears to be one of the oldest cryptic word formation processes in French, and so-called 'cant' languages in England. As a "real code of *voyous*", according to Merle (2000), largonji arose in the Parisian *milieu* 'mob' during the nineteenth century, but fell out of use in the 1930s. Picked up by several professional groups during its existence, the largonji became associated with the *louchebem*, the *bouchers* 'butchers' of the French capital who supposedly made extensive 'corporate' use of it. This language game operates by replacing the first consonant in a word with an /l/, *boucher* > *loucher*, *sac* > *lac*, then moving the replaced consonant to the end of the word, *loucher* > *loucheb*, *lac* > *lac(c)*, and following it with the word-initial suffix, *-em* or *-se*, *loucheb* > *louchebem* or *-é*, *lac* > *lacse*. The following list from Plénat (1985) illustrates some regular and irregular forms. Among the latter are *aimable*, a vowel-intial word in which the target of the consonant replacements is the second syllable, and *bout* and *beau*, in which the sibilant *s* of the suffix elides before the bilabial stop consonant *b*:

coq	> *loquecem*	'rooster'
passer	> *lassepem*	'to leave'
aimable	> *ailabem*	'friendly'
sac	> *lacsé*	'bag'
bout	> *loubé*	'end, a bit'
beau	> *laubé*	'handsome'

It seems, however, that in running speech, only some content words were subject to such transformations.

Rather than taking the word as its unit, the *javanais* word-game targets syllables within words: it consists of inserting *-va* between each syllable in each word of a sentence. Thus *Parlez-vous français?* 'Do you speak French?' gives *Pavarlévez vouvous fravançaivais?* Similar to largonji, javanais was very popular in Paris during the nineteenth century, so much so that at the height of its popularity entire newspapers were published in javanais (Rigault 1888).

By far the best known language game in French, however, is *verlan* which, over the second half of the twentieth century, also became a symbol of identity of the working-class youth living in the ghettoized areas of big cities.

To put it simply, 'verlanizing' words consists of inverting the order of the syllables in the word. Similar to largonji, only content words undergo such a transformation. Contrary to popular belief, and apart from a few exceptional cases of verbal bravado reported by ethnographers (Lepoutre 1997), speakers do not verlanize each word in their utterances. Many words from verlan are now part of mainstream spoken French vocabulary, but verlan nonetheless remains a spoken derivational process.

Because of its essentially spoken use, whenever a verlanized word is written, it is the rule to spell it as close to its phonemic representation as possible. Once verlanized, for instance, the vowel /e/ in *tomber* was represented by the letter -é- rather than the original, and more complex, letter sequence *-er* (see 2.1.2), and gave *béton*. The rule, which consists of inverting the order of syllables within the word, is rather straightforward in bisyllabic words:

copine	> *pinco*	'female friend' (slang)
bizarre	> *zarbi*	'strange'
bagnole	> *gnolba*	'voiture' (slang)
pourri	> *ripou*	'rotten', 'corrupt individual'
tomber	> *béton*	'to fall'
français	> *céfran*	'French'

But even in these cases, there is often more to verlan than a simple inversion of syllables. To begin with the name of the game, *envers* 'backwards' first yields 'vers' + 'en' > *veran* to which a so-called linking consonant is added to arrive at the final form *verlan*. On the other hand *bouteille* 'bottle', which yields a perfect *teibou* /tɛjbu/ when inverted, is often simplified by dropping the glide in the first syllable of the word: *tébou* /tebu/. Therefore, word-initial syllables in verlanized words are not always 'light', as they tend to be in the other word formation processes discussed earlier (see section 4.6.3). There seems to be, however, a common tendency for most verlanized forms to map words into a 'bisyllabic word template' (Scullen 1997). This becomes evident in the verlanization of monosyllabic words. Since there is, one would say, only one syllable in the word *bête* 'animal', the word would not be verlanized unless obeying a much stronger constraint, which forces underlying schwas (/ə/) to surface in word-final position, yielding *bê-te* /bɛtə/. Since the schwa, underlyingly present or not, is pronounced as a front rounded vowel in French (see section 2.2.1.3), monosyllabic words, when verlanized, often contain a front rounded vowel in word-initial position:

bête	> *teubé*	'animal', 'a very pretty woman'
louche	> *chelou*	'weird'
lourd	> *relou*	'heavy'

Variation is attested, however. The front vowel /e/ can be substituted for /œ/ in some words and different variants of a particular word:

bande	> *déban*	'gang'
clope	> *péclot*	'cigarette' (slang)
rap	> *péra*	'rap music'
Black	> *quebla/keubla/kébla*	'non-white individual'

But even the 'bisyllabic template' has exceptions, because not all monosyllabic verlan words are monosyllabic. Some frequently used terms are formed through the inversion of the onset and coda consonants, and the substitution of the original vowel of the word with /œ/:

mec	> *keum*	'guy'
femme	> *meuf*	'woman'
frère	> *reuf*	'brother'
soeur	> *reus*	'sister'
père	> *reup*	'father'
mère	> *reum*	'mother'
fou	> *ouf*	'crazy'
bus	> *sub*	'bus'

Other words, also frequently attested, undergo only consonant inversion, not vowel substitution. It is likely, however, that the kinship terms shown above (*reuf, reus*, etc.) have been formed as analogical extensions of a pattern rather than a productive process, because more recent forms of verlan called *veul* – often based on already verlanized forms – revert to the bisyllabic template. The now mainstream word *beur* 'man of North-African immigrant origin' was originally derived from *arabe* 'Arabic' through the **clipping** of the first vowel, then a consonant inversion and vowel substitution, *rabe* > *beur*, but the most recent form *rebeu* is bisyllabic (although some sources cite yet another recent clipped form: *reub*). The same seems to have happened to the word *femme* which becomes *femeu* at the end of the same lengthy process: *femme* > *meuf* > *feumeu* (Goudailler 1997).

Plurisyllabic words can also be verlanized, *cigarette* > *garetsi*, although they are not frequently attested. Rules to determine the exact order of the syllables in these words have not been established; it seems to depend solely on speaker preference (Azra and Cheneau 1994). Bisyllabic words also sometimes 'develop' plurisyllabic verlanized forms by taking up an additional linking sound. A common word of this sort is *racaille* verlanized to *caillera*. The word *racaille* denotes the worst elements (drug dealers, etc.) of the marginalized youth population. It has three known pronunciations: a bisyllabic one, /kajʀa/, and two trisyllabic ones /kajøʀa/ and /kajeʀa/.

The media hype targeting verlan since the early 1980s will probably result in further reports of lexical innovation of these types. But contrary to some of the interpretations that also emerge, verlan is not something entirely new, and historically not even limited to the working classes. It is a little-known fact, for instance, that the famous eighteenth-century French writer Voltaire (1694–1778) reportedly formed his pseudonym by the inversion of the two syllables of the toponym *Airvault* /ɛʀvolt/ > *Voltaire* /vɔltɛʀ/, the closest city to the village Saint-Loup-sur-le-Thouet in the Poitou region where his grandfather was born (from Merle 2000). Thus verlan, like other derivations, is a testimony to the remarkable continuity and richness of word-formation processes in French.

---

1) Try to 'crack' the following sentence written in largonji: C'est *lanqué lémem lûrdé* de *larlerpé largonji*.
2) In veul, *feumeu* means 'woman'. Explain the steps of word formation that led to this contemporary form of verlan.

4.10   State intervention in French vocabulary

State intervention in vocabulary has a long history, dating back to the revision of *coutumiers* ('compilations of laws') in the sixteenth century. At that time, the requirement that these previously oral documents be written down, a process overseen by the *Parlement* ('court') in Paris, brought much, though not total, uniformity to legal language throughout France (see Smedley-Weill and Geoffroy-Poisson 2001). In general, however, state intervention in language issues was generally concerned with status issues (relations between French and other clearly distinct languages such as Alsatian or Breton) rather than corpus issues (language questions internal to French).

The Académie Française, founded in 1635, is often cited as an arm of the state in the regulation of the French language. However, the Académie Française has never had that kind of authority. It is currently producing the ninth edition of its dictionary, of which the first edition appeared in 1694. This dictionary does not pretend to be complete, and is particularly lacking in the technical and scientific terms that have become increasingly a part of everyday life. The main source of the Académie's authority now is the veto power it holds over the terminological recommendations produced by the ministerial commissions.

The increasing dominance of English as an international language, first felt in the scientific and technical areas, and later spreading throughout the society, has led to a number of efforts in the twentieth and twenty-first centuries. The first scientific conference devoted to the 'threat' of English took place in Liège (Belgium) in 1905. The presence of British Commonwealth and American troops in France in World War I accelerated the process, as did the dominance of American and British industry over the war-ravaged production facilities of continental Europe. A group of French scientists and engineers formed, in 1937, the Commission de la terminologie du français moderne. The same year a group of French linguists and cultural figures, led by the linguist Ferdinand Brunot and the poet Paul Valéry, founded the Office de la langue française.

After World War II, these private efforts started up again. In the scientific and technical domains, Georges Duhamel, a medical doctor and novelist, and Louis de Broglie, a Nobel prize-winning physicist, launched the Conseil du langage scientifique, a group that would gain the official sponsorship of the Académie des sciences in 1955 (renamed the Comité consultative du langage scientifique). In the early 1950s the Association française de normalisation (AFNOR) was founded, as well as the Cercle de Presse Richelieu, which would become Défense de la langue française; both of these organizations are still active early in the twenty-first century. In 1952 Alain Guillermou started publication of the new journal *Vie et langage*, and in 1955 the republication of Rémy de Gourmont's *L'esthétique de la langue française* (first published in 1899) spurred even more interest in the effect of English borrowings on the French language. These private campaigns culminated in the publication of René Étiemble's *Parlez-vous franglais?* (1964), which, along with the establishment of state offices relating to the French language elsewhere (e.g. in Quebec the Office de la langue française, 1961) inspired modern state intervention in France in matters of vocabulary.

On 31 March 1966, President Charles de Gaulle and his Prime Minister Georges Pompidou created by decree the Haut Comité pour la défense et l'expansion de la langue française. Citing the 'bastardization of French vocabulary' (*l'abâtardissement du vocabulaire*), Pompidou asked this committee to use its influence to correct bad usage and to suggest legislation and other regulations to remedy the situation.

The following year, the Conseil International de la Langue Française (CILF) was formed, with the mission to make sure French was fundamentally the same everywhere it was spoken. It has the goal of enriching French vocabulary and harmonizing technical terms throughout all of *la Francophonie*. In 1970, after Pompidou succeeded de Gaulle in the presidency, his Prime Minister, Jacques Chaban-Delmas, ordered the creation of terminological commissions in each ministry. By the end of the year, four had been created, and their mission was outlined in a decree of 7 January 1972. The words they would create were to be used in all governmental work. In case the commissions came up with different solutions for the same problem, the CILF would decide which term should be used, and the Académie Française would provide its opinion. Although these decisions had no legal force with respect to private usage, the press generally went along with the recommendations.

In the early 1970s, the justification for the creation of new words moved away from the intense nationalism of the preceding period, towards consumer protection and social unity. In a speech delivered on 7 February 1975, Jacques Chirac, then Prime Minister under the presidency of Valéry Giscard d'Estaing, argued:

En luttant contre la complication et la prétention des vocabulaires spécialisés, en luttant contre le snobisme du mot étranger – souvent incompréhensible – on contribue, en réalité, à des rapports sociaux plus faciles et naturels, plus humains, et, par conséquent, plus détendus.

'By fighting the obscure and pretentious nature of specialized vocabularies and the snobbish use of foreign – often incomprehensible – words, one contributes, in reality, to the creation of an easier, more natural and human, and therefore more relaxed, social atmosphere.' (from Chansou 2003:96)

These sentiments led to the elaboration of a law 'relating to the use of the French language', finally passed on the last day of 1975, and commonly referred to as the Loi Bas-Lauriol, after the co-authors, Pierre Bas and Marc Lauriol. This law aims at protecting the French citizen rather than the French language. The targets are documents relating to the sale of products or the provision of services, contracts, and public signs. Because this law was widely seen as ineffective, in part because the fines imposed on those breaking the law were so minimal, a new law, the Loi Toubon, after Minister of Culture Jacques

Toubon, was developed in the early 1990s, and passed in August 1994. Both laws prescribe the use, by government officials, of terms chosen by the terminological commissions and approved by the Assemblée nationale 'Congress'. These terms are printed in the official record of the Assemblée and distributed in dictionaries such as the *Dictionnaire des termes officiels* (Délégation générale à la langue française 1994) and the *Répertoire terminologique* (Commission générale de terminologie et de néologie 2000).

With some notable exceptions (*ordinateur* 'computer', *logiciel* 'software'), the imposition of neologisms has had limited success. One explanation is the time required to produce a new term. The minimum time required for a word to be deliberated on first by the ministerial terminological commission, then the general terminological commission, then the Académie française, and finally by the Assemblée is about fourteen months (Candel, private communication 2003). During that time, the term already being used, most often an English word, has had plenty of time to become part of the working vocabulary of those concerned. Furthermore, cooperative work with Canadian, Belgian, and Swiss terminological commissions does not always lead to uniformity across *la Francophonie*. For instance, the official equivalent for the internet function of 'chat' in France is *causette*, while in Canada it is *clavardage*.

4.10.1   A case study: the feminization of professional titles

The work of terminological commissions is not directed solely at the protection of French from English borrowings. Changes in society affect language as well, and one of the most dramatic changes in society in the last part of the twentieth century was the opening of new professional opportunities for women. In a language that has distinct masculine and feminine forms, such as French, these changes present new challenges to the language. The addition of the feminizing *e* does not always work, as the addition of *e* to the masculine term *médecin* 'doctor' would lead to confusion between the existing *médecine* 'medicine' and the new term *médecine*, presumably 'female doctor'.

One argument, put forward by the Académie française, among others, is that no feminine forms are needed, since the masculine form is the 'generic' form that applies to people of both sexes. However, the use of masculine forms has served as justification for the exclusion of women in the past. The law of 1810 defining the functions of different participants in the legal process used the masculine term *avocat* 'lawyer'. When, at the end of the nineteenth century, the first women trained as lawyers asked for the right to take the lawyer's oath, the Assemblée argued that "when the 1810 law used the term *avocat* in the masculine, it excluded women from the profession" (cited in Baudino 2001:22). Similarly, when, in 1935, the Conseil d'État refused women the right to vote, the explanation was as follows (NB: French women got the right to vote in April 1944, and used it for the first time in 1945):

Le législateur, en donnant le droit de vote "à tous les Français" n'avait pas pensé aux femmes.

'The legislators, when giving the right to vote to "all the French (masc.)" did not have women in mind.' (cited in Baudino 2001:21)

The Office de la langue française in Quebec issued an opinion in 1979 recommending that feminine forms be established for all professions and titles. Their guide, *Titres et functions au féminin: essai d'orientation de l'usage* appeared in 1986. In France a Commission relative à la féminisation des noms de métiers was formed in 1984, and a ministerial circular distributed in 1986. However, these efforts were rejected by popular opinion, and a renewed effort was made in 1998. This resulted in the report *Femme j'écris ton nom* which provides equivalents for hundreds of words, and explains particular points of difficulty. Similar documents have been produced in Belgium (*Mettre au féminin*, 1994).

Particularly challenging for these commissions was the formation of feminine forms for masculine words ending in *-eur*. French provides a number of alternatives: adding *-e* (*professeur/professeure*), changing *-eur* to *-euse* (*confiseur/confiseuse*), changing *-teur/deur* to *-trice/drice* (*ambassadeur/ambassadrice*), changing *-eur* to *-oresse* (*pasteur/pastoresse* [Switzerland; elsewhere, *pasteure*]), or most simply, changing the article but not the noun itself (*la professeur* – the solution preferred in Belgium and Switzerland). As we see from these examples, the solutions were not always uniform. In some cases many optional forms were attested in the history of the language. *Doctrice, docteuse*, and *doctoresse* are all attested as feminine equivalents to *docteur*, in addition to the official recommendation for *docteure*. Sometimes multiple forms are retained, with distinct meanings. *Une enquêteuse* is a female police investigator, while an *enquêtrice* is a woman who conducts surveys.

Unlike some other areas of linguistic intervention, the most common feminine forms have been adopted by the public almost without thought. Newspapers and magazines have quickly taken up this new usage. It is proof, along with the Canadian example, that the success of state intervention in lexical matters depends primarily on the will of the speakers to make these words part of their active vocabulary.

4.11   Exercises

1) Using what you learned in morphology and in this chapter, define what the expression 'open class lexical items' means. Give examples.
2) Read the following statements about sound symbolism. Find examples that prove and contradict the claims made.

Schuchardt: the group f(v) + l(r) occurs again and again in words which convey the idea of motion round a fixed point; compare French *flotter, flatter* (un cheval), English *flutter*, Rumanian *fluture* 'butterfly', etc.

Ullmann: Si l'on ajoute la labiale f, 'élément souffle, à la latérale, expression de la liquidité', on obtient un effet de fluidité.

3) Perform a semic analysis on the following words, and then create a table that brings out the differences between the terms:
   voiture – automobile – bagnole – taxi – char – véhicule – moto – limousine – vélo.

4) Are the following terms synonymous? Explain your answer: *voiture/automobile, vélo/bicyclette, policier/gendarme.*

5) Find all terms relating to the terms *chaud* and *froid* and place them in the order of 'degree of heat'. What traits distinguish them?

6) What are the meanings of the word(s) *bande*? What are the advantages or disadvantages of treating the different meanings as one word?

7) Find all the possible meanings of the following words: *paille* 'straw', *cavalier* 'horse rider', *gorge* 'throat'. What processes (metaphor, metonymy, etc.) link the meanings?

8) What prefixes can make an adjective negative? (Example: *content~ mécontent.*) Find three examples for each prefix. Why is one prefix chosen instead of another in each case?

9) What are the pejorative suffixes in French? Are they equally productive?

10) Based on the following examples, trace the use and meanings of the new suffix *-rama*. What is the order of their appearance in French? *cinerama, diorama, discorama, panorama, télérama*

11) What is the origin of each of the following truncations? Are the same processes used in each case? Define each word: *dico, métro, apéro, prolo.*

12) Provide two examples of each of the following types of compounding: Noun + Noun, Noun + Preposition + Noun, Verb + Noun, Adjective + Noun, Sentence.

13) List five words that end in *-ing* in French. What is the relationship with the original English word?

14) What is the difference between the Quebecois and Metropolitan French meaning of the following words: *génie, soie, mitaine, carrosse, appointement*?

15) Find the language of origin of the following words, and the date of their first attestation in French: *camelot, mammouth, ginseng, coche, châle, nadir, goéland, chamane*. Has the meaning changed between the language of origin and the word's current use in French?

16) When, where, and with whom would you use the following terms: *godasses/chaussures, rafistoler/réparer, claudicant/boiteux*

17) What do the following echo-words mean, and by what means of word formation were these words formed? *Glou-glou, bing-bing, zin-zin, coucou, Loulou*

18) Form nicknames for the following first names: *Yann, Yannick, Anne, Annick, Marie, Charles.* Are some processes better than others for these names? Why?

19) Can the word *flic*, argot for 'policeman' be verlanized? If yes, how?

5   Pragmatics

5.1   Preliminaries

Up until this point, we have been primarily concerned with the description of various levels of linguistic structure ranging from individual sounds to syntactic phrases. But 'structure' obviously does not end here; if it did, we would be incapable of communicating in any consistent manner. For instance, any linguistic analysis that would not analyze the relationship between successive sentence/utterances would neglect meaningful links that hold utterances together in discourse and conversation. Let us take samples of exchanges to highlight this point at the supra-sentential level (adapted from Falkin 1988):

(1)   S1: *Il a quel âge?*
            'How old is he?'

        S2: *15 ans.*
            'Fifteen.'

(2)   S1: *J'aime bien Valérie.*
            'I like Valérie.'

        S2: *Moi aussi.*
            'Me too.'

(3)   S1: *Mettons-nous à table.*
            'Let's sit down at the table.'

        S2: *D'accord.*
            'All right.'

(4)   S1: *Salut ça va?*
            'Hi how are you?'

        S2: *Oui ça va, merci . . .*
            'I'm fine, thanks.'

The exchanges in (1) through (4) are **adjacency pairs**, which typically contain one intervention from a speaker and one from an **addressee** who typically assume each other's role in the following **turns** of the conversation. Adjacency pairs can bring together a question and a direct answer (1), a remark followed by an evaluation (2), an offer and its acceptance (3), or a greeting followed by another greeting (4) analyzed in terms of **speech act** or **conversational move**. But while these categories account for a great deal of semantically linked interchanges, they do not exhaust all possible combinations. Conversational **openings** such as (4), for instance, are sometimes not followed by a direct answer, a related evaluation or any answer at all to what had been initiated by the other speaker. In (5), S2 does not pick up on the topic initiated by S1, because he/she might be interested in pursuing his/her own agenda by starting out with a new topic. This move could earn him/her the reputation of being rude and disrespectful for not preserving the **face** of the interlocutor (see politeness principles in section 5.5.3). An alternative interpretation of this example is **implicature**: S2 might be diverting the conversation because she/he is trying to suggest or 'imply' to the other that it is a sensitive topic that he/she is unwilling to discuss (see section 5.2.3).

(5)   S1: *Mais pourquoi faire une chose pareille?!*
             'But why do such a thing?!'

         S2: *Tiens, il pleut.*
             'Look, it is raining.'

Conversational exchanges, however, rarely correspond to isolated adjacency pairs. Most of the time they involve more than two participants and more than one turn, as several participants of a conversation might take turns in assuming the role of the speaker and the **hearer**, sometimes with considerable overlap or 'parallel talk'. Speakers do this following a ritualized code of behavior called **turn-taking**. Knowing when to take, hold, and yield the floor presupposes, to a large extent, the anticipation of the speaker's communicative intent (what he/she wants to say). Particular roles that speakers assume in face-to-face interactions can also be quite complex. The distinction between the concepts of hearer and addressee, for instance, enables us to account for the fact that an utterance is sometimes directed to an individual who 'overhears' a conversation rather than being its actual addressee (Clark and Carlson 1982). Hearer-directed exchanges like (6) are typical in situations of 'indirect communication' when the speaker asserts something (e.g. having paid for a piece of merchandise in a different check-out line), but his/her intent is to convey a message different from the literal meaning of the utterance (e.g. the cashier at this check-out line is too slow). A hearer can also 'jump in' and take a turn that a speaker initially yielded to another participant of the exchange, as in (7).

(6)   S1   (loudly to S2 while standing in the check-out line n°3):
             L'autre jour j'ai passé la caisse en moins d'une minute, moi!
             'The other day I checked out in less than a minute!'

(7)   S1   (to the male child): *Tu es en troisième?*
               'Are you in third grade?'

        S2   (mother answers for him): *Non en quatrième! C'est un grand
               garçon, hein?*
               'No, in fourth grade. He is a big boy, right?'

Although these illustrations and the overview of linguistic pragmatics (LP) in this chapter cannot do justice to new advances and remaining problems in the field, they attempt to present some basic concepts to the reader. Conversation analysis (CA), a closely related field studying linguistic communication in context, will also be mentioned but not be dealt with here. While LP grew out of the work of twentieth-century philosophers studying the linguistic processes that underlie human cognition (Austin 1962, Searle 1969, Grice 1975), CA comes from ethnomethodology, a branch of sociology that deals with the codes and conventions played out in everyday social interactions (see Sacks 1992, Silverman and Sacks 1998). One important difference between the two is that in LP, communicative interactions are viewed through the structure of the language, as LP aims at understanding how linguistic properties of sentence/utterances carry meaning in real-life interactions. This 'meaning-making' process is regarded as 'cognitive' in essence, i.e. it relies on people's perception and processing of each other's perceived beliefs, intentions, goals, and plans for action. CA also looks at the use of language in context, but while doing so it focuses on 'social action' rather than linguistic structure. Although CA shares several principles with LP, it conceptualizes them differently (see Sacks 1992). For instance, approaches to CA and LP both agree that speaking is performing particular 'acts' with language (see section 5.2) and that these 'acts of speaking' presuppose reasonable social actors cooperating in conveying 'meaning' through interaction. As opposed to LP, however, studies in CA do not resort to the method of introspection by using invented examples that are validated only by the researcher's knowledge of the language, and therefore lack the complexities of real-life interactions. Rather than highlighting facts about grammar, CA considers speech just another form of social (inter)action, similar to any action performed by humans in society, and is therefore interested in studying speech communication as a whole, not just as a particular manifestation of speakers' and hearers' mental grammar in action. On an imaginary continuum of pragmatic approaches to conversation, studies in LP would, therefore, be closer to philosophy and social cognition, while research methods applied in CA are to be linked with sociology and anthropology.

5.2   Referring and indexing

Linguistics goes a long way towards formalizing how words mean in context. This might sound peculiar, at first, because what else would words do if not refer to things in the context of a speech event? But as previous sections in Chapter 4 have shown, there are many types of words, and also many ways in which these words can convey meaning. In this section, we come back to the notion of **referential** meaning, i.e. the way in which words denote existing things in the world (see section 4.2.4).

As explained earlier, the link between words and the objects that they denote is largely arbitrary (onomatopoeias are exceptions). We call a fire *fire* because this is the word we learned on our mother's lap and/or because everybody else around us calls it a *fire* (Green 1996:7). This idea of the arbitrariness of linguistic signs had been a major insight in structuralist approaches to language (see Saussure 1916) but early work in LP also identified another important component of meaning in context: the referent.

Words like *magnétoscope* 'VCR' refer to a particular thing serving a particular purpose in the world, and as such it has an easily identifiable referent: the machine that we use to view movies. To interpret the meaning of the word *lemon* or *croûte* 'crust', 'painting of bad quality', however, we need more than just the words, since these words also have connotative meaning, i.e. meaning that goes beyond their literal referent (a fruit called *lemon* in English or 'bread crust' called *croûte* in French). What we need for identifying the intended referent of such expressions, first of all, is a wider discourse context: a series of preceding utterances that supply sufficient background information for us to interpret what the speaker meant when he/she chose to say *lemon* instead of *car*. What is important here is the need for 'interpretation' of the meaning of words in context. For a long time, and as far back as antiquity, philosophers and linguists thought that words refer to things in the world in a transparent and direct way. As the following examples will show, however, meaning is not handed to us on a plate: more often than not it has to be found out, derived (later we will say 'inferred') from what had been said earlier and/or what the speaker might have intended. In fact, the referent of a linguistic expression is underdetermined, by definition. It becomes unambiguous as a function of the larger discourse context.

5.2.1   Indexical expressions

LP, in its narrowest sense, is the study of linguistic expressions whose reference is a function of the context. The most typical expressions of this kind are so-called indexical expressions, e.g. personal pronouns (*je* 'I' and *ce* 'this') and adverbs (*ici* 'here' and *demain* 'tomorrow'), whose referents can only be identified from context because, plainly put, there is no other way to find out who 'I', 'you', 'this', and 'that' are, and when 'here' and 'tomorrow' take place than outside the literal meaning of the utterance (see Bar-Hillel 1954, Benveniste 1966). Thus the hearer most go beyond what information is available from the utterance to find out what is being referred to. It is crucial to realize, however, that indexical expressions do not merely refer to speakers as actors or participants of the communicative process, but also to many of their social and relational attributes, i.e. they also have 'social indexical meaning'. The choice between the personal address pronouns *tu* 'informal you' and *vous* 'formal you' in French, for instance, implies not only pointing to a person other than the speaker but also to the nature of the relationship between the speaker and the addressee, as well as their relative social status within the community (see section 5.4.2.1).

5.2.2   Deictic reference

Indexical expressions can be **deictic**, derived from the verb meaning 'to show' in Greek, when they involve pointing to an object in the world and naming it by a certain linguistic form. The deictic pronoun *ça* 'that' in (8), and the deictic adverb *ici* 'here' in (9) fulfill such a function.

(8)   *Oui, je vois ça!*
        'Yes, I can see that!'

(9)   *C'est ici et maintenant, et pas demain!*
        'It is here and now, and not tomorrow!'

But even spatial reference denoted by deictic adverbs like *ici* 'here', *là* and *là-bas* 'there' can be ambiguous since contrary to what one might think these adverbs do not unambiguously refer to a certain well-determined location in time and space. The place adverb *ici* 'here' only symbolically refers to the space and time of enunciation, as a letter sent to an addressee that contains the sentence *Je n'aime pas la nourriture ici* 'I don't like the food here' is an obvious reference to the writer's relative time and space of enunciation or writing. The adverb *là-bas*, on the other hand, is not a simple reference point in the addressee's space but rather a location distant from the speaker's space that he/she however expects the addressee to be able to identify. In (10), the park to which Sandy reportedly cannot find the way is referred to by the adverbial clitic *y* 'there', carrying the meaning 'somewhere but not here', as it refers to a location that is not indexed with reference to the speaker but to anyone other than the speaker. Interestingly enough, recent studies came to similar conclusions with respect to the place adverb *là-bas*, claiming that *là-bas* does not refer to the addressee's space in any straightforward way, but it should rather be regarded as an opaque (non-transparent) indexical symbol (Brault 2004) that changes its indexical reference depending on the context.

(10)   *Sandy veut aller au parc, mais il ne sait pas comment y aller.*
         'Sandy wants to go to the park, but doesn't know how to get there.'
         (translated from Green 1996:23).

5.2.3   Other types of references

Instead of pointing to something in the world, as deictic expressions do, speakers can use **anaphoric** reference to link two related linguistic forms in discourse, one of which occurred earlier and one which refers to it in the present context. As argued in 3.6.1 and 3.6.3, pronouns typically represent one such word class by acting as 'traces' of complements of nouns and verbs. But determiners like *le* 'the' in *le menteur le plus odieux* 'the most hideous liar' in (11) refer to 'the sister-in-law', 'the neighbour down the block' or anybody else to whom the speaker intended to refer once the referent, 'hinted on' by the determiner, had been correctly identified by the hearer. In (11), the overhearer (S3), who is not the addressee but who is joining the conversation, realizes that he/she missed out on the intended anaphoric referent of *le* 'the' from the preceding context:

(11)   S1: *Je te jure que c'est le menteur le plus odieux que tu n'aies jamais vu!*
          'And I swear he's the most hideous liar you've ever seen!'

        S2: *Je veux bien croire!*
          'Oh but I can perfectly believe that.'

        S3: (walks in while S2 is speaking) *Vous parlez de qui?*
          'Who are you talking about'?

As we have discussed earlier (see section 3.6.1), cataphora is reference to an upcoming full complement in the syntactic structure, and as such it is different from anaphora in the directionality of the reference: it points to a complement that follows, as opposed to referring back to a complement that precedes. Metaphor (see section 4.5.1) or metaphora is reference by 'evocation': a particular object or event in the world is described, and sometimes deictically pointed to, but what is meant is what this object or event evokes or symbolizes. For instance, a ship *cutting through* the waves is metaphorical reference to a particular way in which a ship's movements are perceived and depicted, as the choice of the verb *to cut through* refers 'by evocation' to a smooth and steady movement. Metaphoric reference, often in the form of lexicalized idioms, is more common in everyday communication than one might think: expressions of doing something easily, i.e. *comme une lettre à la poste* 'a walk in the park', represent such reference by evocation. Metonymy, another 'figurative' way of referring to objects in the real world (see also section 4.5.2), is also common in everyday language use. When pointing to a CD case and asking *Have you listened to this?* the speaker is obviously inquiring about the music recorded on the CD and not the CD case itself. How such an 'implicit' understanding about the intended referent between the speaker and the hearer arises will be discussed in 5.2.3.

Sometimes finding the referent in context is not straightforward. Indexical expressions can have several possible referents in context. In such cases the meaning intended by the speaker is identified either according to certain rules or it has to be inferred from the participants' **shared knowledge** or 'beliefs', i.e. what had been established and become known to them from previous turns of a conversation or discourse. In French, as in other languages, there are means by which such cases of **co-reference** (co-referentiality) can be indicated with clarity: using *celui-ci* 'the latter' instead of *il* 'he' makes *Yann* and not *Pierre* the intended referent in (13) vs. (12)

(12)   *Quand Pierre a appelé Yann pour lui montrer une photo, il n'a rien révélé.*
         'When Peter called Ian to show him a picture, he said nothing.'

(13)   *Quand Pierre a appelé Yann pour lui montrer une photo, celui-ci n'a rien révélé.*
         'When Peter called Ian to show him a picture, the latter said nothing.'

In these cases indexicals are put in service of the 'semantic thread' or 'general topic' that runs through the dialogue or written paragraph, holding together the intended discourse, and helping the hearer/addressee to comprehend successive units and their contents. Morphemes such as indexical expressions are designed to help the interpretation of the general semantic thread, assuring coherence in the text or discourse. As we will see, they do not denote by themselves but are put in use by the speaker as 'tools' to formulate hypotheses about what the other means in the interaction.

This brings us back to our initial point: understanding what words mean requires active involvement from the hearer in comprehending what the speaker had in mind when uttering those words. Thus there is an active, cognitive dimension to linguistic communication: using words to talk about the world presupposes one's ability to interpret and anticipate the intentions and plans of action of those involved in the communicative process. This mental activity received the name of **enunciation** (*énonciation*) in the French pragmatic tradition, and sprung specifically from the study of indexical expressions initiated by linguists like Benveniste (1966) who writes:

*. . . ces formes pronominales ne renvoient pas à la « réalité » ni à des propositions « objectives » dans l'espace ou dans le temps, mais à **l'énonciation**, chaque fois unique, qui les contient . . .*

'. . . these pronominal forms do not refer to "reality" or propositions existing "objectively" in space and time, but to the always unique [act of] enunciation that contains them . . .'
(1966, 254)

Work by Benveniste and his successors in France represented a first step towards the integration of *l'énonciateur*, the subject or cognitive agent, in models of *énonciation*:

> *L'énoncé contenant « je » appartient à ce niveau ou type de langage [. . .] qui inclut, avec les signes, ceux qui en font l'usage.*
>
> 'Utterances that contain *je* ['I'] belong to this level or type of language [. . .] that includes, together with [linguistic] signs those who make use of them.'
>
> (Benveniste 1966, 252)

Further elaborated by Culioli (1995), the theory of *énonciation* gained wide acceptance in the francophone pragmatic tradition (see Cervoni 1992). Although there are differences in details of definition, as some do not view *énonciation* as just a cognitive process referring to speakers' mental representations, but also as building speakers' actual utterances (see Roulet et al. 1985, Jeanneret 1999 and the Geneva school of pragmatics, e.g. Roulet 1995).

Who could be the intended referent(s) of *il* 'he' if the following sentence is uttered, and why? *Le patron a licencié son employé parce qu'<u>il</u> a découvert son secret.* 'The boss fired his employer because he discovered his secret.'

5.3   Speech acts and models of communication

5.3.1   *The Code Model of communication*

Linguistic communication was traditionally viewed as a seamless process of translation of thoughts into words that convey direct meanings to participants viewed in similarly idealistic ways (see Blanchet 1995, Ludwig 1997). In what came to be known as the 'Message' or 'Code Model' of communication, several centuries of philosophical thought on language merged into a model of communication in an 'ideal' world (see the critique by Sperber and Wilson 1986).

According to the Code Model, speakers are 'transmitters' who encode what they have to say, while hearers are active 'receivers', decoding what they hear or read. Communication by way of words is, therefore, pictured as an exchange of messages via speech or writing that serve as 'channels' for ideas to be transmitted. While such a model is useful in understanding many instances of purposeful communication, e.g. giving and following directions, instructing and learning facts, and so on, it is incomplete when communicative situations are less straightforward.

WHEN THE MESSAGE IS AMBIGUOUS: The Code Model does not offer means of disambiguating between possible meanings of a syntactic phrase, such as *le monde privé des ouvriers* 'the private (non public) sphere of workers' vs. 'the world deprived of (without) workers', analyzed in 2.5.2 and 3.5.3. While it is true that intonation and prosodic phrasing help distinguish between the two meanings, knowing what intonation and phrasing goes with what syntactic structure does not mean knowing which one of the two meanings of these syntactic phrases applies felicitously to what situation. This is because being able to tell what meaning the speaker intended in a given context requires more from the hearer than just 'decoding' the literal meaning of the utterance (see section 5.2.2).

WHEN SPEAKING IS PERFORMING CERTAIN 'ACTS': The second series of problems with the Code Model is that communicating a particular message is not always the objective of linguistic communication. As pointed out by Austin (1962) in his seminal book *How to Do Things with Words*, one of the foundational studies of LP, our remarks sometimes stand as pure 'acts' rather than descriptions of our thoughts. Particular words pronounced in social rituals, such as firing, baptizing, and marrying someone or taking an oath from somebody are good examples of 'institutional speech acts', which involve effectively 'doing' something with words. The act of uttering *I now pronounce you husband and wife* is clearly not some kind of a translation of the thoughts of an individual but rather the public declaration of a mutually binding, legal obligation between two people.

Also, by each utterance that they pronounce, speakers do not only perform a **locutionary act**, i.e. use their speech organs to say something, but also an **illocutionary act**, i.e. indicate how the hearer should interpret what is said, e.g. whether the utterance is to be taken as a question, a request, or an order. Doing so can achieve one or several **perlocutionary acts**, i.e. 'act upon' the hearer/addressee or overhearer. This connects us to a third series of problems with the Code Model, which is when what is said is intended to mean something more, or even something different from what stands as the literal meaning of the utterance.

WHEN SPEAKING INDIRECTLY AND NON-LITERALLY: Certain utterances mean more than what they literally convey. Nobody in a dinner conversation would, for instance, utter a response similar to S2 in (14), and not act upon the polite request of handing the cheese tray over to S1. Thus S1's question, which might even have been uttered with sharply rising intonation, as typical yes-no questions are in French (see section 4.5.2), is not a query about the hearer's physical ability to reach the tray, but a polite request to do so (see also 5.5.3).

(14)   S1: *Tu peux me passer le plateau de fromage?*
             'Can you pass the cheese tray?'

        S2: *Oui, je peux.*
             'Yes I can.' (not followed by action)

Similarly nobody would suppose that a car driver entering a car repair shop would utter the words *J'ai un pneu crevé* 'I have a flat tire' with the intention of chatting about the day's most memorable events. Reasons for this will be discussed in 5.2.3, but let us retain for now the idea that in many cases of indirect and non-literal communication, the illocutionary force of an utterance seems to be a matter of (social) convention, a code of behavior that the hearer expects the speaker to follow. Consider the construction *si* 'if' + conditional in (15).

(15)   *Si on allait au cinéma . . .*
        'Why don't we go to the movies . . .'

Despite what its syntactic structure suggests, the illocutionary act in (15) is not a statement in the conditional: the speaker does not intend to explore what would happen if he/she and the hearer would go out that night, e.g. explore possible consequences of going out in terms of potential costs, chosen means of transportation, etc. Instead, *si* + conditional is a syntactic structure typically chosen for polite requests and suggestions in French, with the *why* + indicative construction as its typical English equivalent. Searle (1975) called such expressions 'speech act idioms', i.e. constructions carrying a conventionalized, indirect illocutionary force in different languages. The idiomatic – language-dependent – nature of such expressions becomes obvious when translating the English expression literally to French: *Pourquoi on ne va pas au cinéma?* is no longer a polite suggestion but sounds more like an accusation or a resentment. The Code Model cannot account for requests being uttered as interrogatives as in (14) and suggestions worded as hypothetical statements as in (15).

> Another, so-called indirect, speech act arises when actual orders are uttered as yes-no questions. Can you think of an example of such a, not particularly polite, speech act?

5.3.2   *Inferential models of communication*

Linguistic communication, as we have seen, necessitates the active cognitive involvement of speakers and hearers, as the meaning conveyed by the words in an utterance might not provide sufficient indication about the speakers' intended referent(s). In such cases, the referent has to be 'inferred'. Thus the connection between what speakers want to convey, that is, their 'communicative intents' and sounds and words that vehicle those intents is necessarily inferential: the speakers' wants and goals in communication are filtered through the perception and understanding of them by their hearers and addressees. Despite their differences, current approaches to linguistic communication now depart from the assumption that meaning in context is not a given but a matter of interpretation. Speakers and hearers rely on many simultaneous sources of information (word meaning, gesture, intonation) and actively use these to generate hypotheses about what the other might have intended (see Grice 1957, Bach and Harnish 1979, Sperber and Wilson 1986, Toolan 1996).

Linguistic communication is successful – as metaphors in our everyday language use also point out – when the participants are 'on the same wavelength', i.e. when they are successful in inferring each other's communicative intents from what they communicate to each other. Thus we can compare linguistic communication to some kind of joint problem solving that relies on, and tries to further develop, an established common ground or system of shared knowledge and beliefs. Philosophers, linguists, and cognitive psychologists had long been divided, however, on how we 'know' what **inferences** and **presumptions** we can make about certain speakers and situations. One hypothesis is that in the course of learning to speak our mother tongues, humans not only learn words, intonations, and sentence structures, but also learn how to communicate with them in real life. This means that humans have/acquire/share a variety of presumptions about each other, which then enable them to successfully communicate.

LINGUISTIC PRESUMPTIONS: Unless otherwise indicated (e.g. we meet someone who does not speak our language, has a specific impairment, or is mentally ill), we presume that those with whom we enter into communication are capable of determining the meaning and intended referents of our expressions in the context of our utterances. The shortest way to formulate this presumption is: 'we speak the same language'.

COMMUNICATIVE PRESUMPTIONS: When engaged in a communicative process, we also suppose that others who communicate with us do so with an identifiable intent in mind. This brings us back to the question of the illocutionary force of utterances: speakers and hearers suppose that by uttering certain words in a certain way they are instructing each other on how to interpret the utterance (question, request, suggestion), which also implies that hearers/addressees are confident that those intents are recognizable to others. Briefly: 'reasons why we communicate should make sense'.

CONVERSATIONAL PRESUMPTIONS: Instrumental in the elaboration of a third set of presumptions that humans make when they communicate was Grice's (1957, 1975) seminal work on meaning and conversation. One of Grice's important contributions was to 'free' the discipline of LP from its long-time fixation on the rules of classical logic in analyzing linguistic communication. As Grice pointed out, the main reason why natural languages do not essentially work like rules of classical logic is because instances of natural language use are simultaneously situated speech acts and linguistic forms. Thus the principles of human communication cannot be pinned down by abstract 'operations' ('and', 'if', 'but') derived from classical logic, because they are grounded in a series of social acts and conventions that might work differently from the principles of classical logic. Concentrating only on the linguistic form of expressions disregards the fact that in conversing, humans follow scenarios common to social actors in general.

5.3.3   The Maxims of conversation

Grice's alternative proposal to this view is that in every kind of communicative process humans follow a 'behavioral dictum' (Green 1996:90) that states: "Make your contribution such as is required, at the stage at which it occurs, by the accepted purpose or direction of the talk exchange in which you are engaged" (Grice 1975:45). This principle, called the **Cooperative Principle**, is not specific to linguistic communication, but is common to cooperative social behavior among humans in general. Thus communication via language would be based on the same assumptions as any rational human behavior. As far as principles underlying conversation are concerned, they can be decomposed into four or five main and several minor 'Maxims', which represent particular 'behavioral consequences' that the burden of successful communication puts upon communicating social actors. (The following presentation of the Maxims is adapted from Green 1996 and Akmajian et al. 1997):

QUANTITY – Be informative!
            Agents will do as much as they must to achieve their goal.
            Agents will not do more than is required.
QUALITY –   Be truthful!
            Agents will make assertions that are true.
            Agents will not say what they believe to be false.
            Agents will not say that for which they lack adequate evidence.
RELATION – Be relevant!
            Agents' actions will be relevant and relative to their intentions.
MANNER –   Be perspicuous!
            Agents will make their actions relevant to others' goals with
               whom they share a joint intention.
            Agents will not speak obscurely when attempting to
               communicate.

> Agents will act so that intentions they wish to communicate
> can be unambiguously reconstructed.
> Agents will spend no more energy on actions than is necessary.
> Agents will execute sub-parts of a plan in an order that will
> maximize the perceived likelihood of achieving their goal.

These principles might at first seem so trivial that they appear to have no explanatory force at all, and seem more like guidelines on how to speak and write in an ideal world rather than principles that would underly and explain 'problematic cases' in linguistic communication. At first glance, it is hard to see how their predictions would differ for instance from the Code Model of communication (see section 5.2.1): as long as interlocutors respect these Maxims, literal and direct communication, modeled as adequately by the Code Model as they are by Grice's Maxims, should take place.

But the way in which the Cooperative Principle works is best seen when it is violated. The Cooperative Principle is such a fundamental assumption of successful communication, Grice suggests, that it becomes obvious only when speakers' observed behavior does not conform to it. What happens then is the following. Since the speaker is assumed, following the Cooperative Principle, to act as a reasonable social actor when communicating, when he/she does not, the hearer will look for 'hidden' intentions or meaning behind his/her statements. This is when **conversational implicature**, i.e. meaning conveyed without being made explicit, arises and naturally 'falls' out of the Maxim(s) that have been violated.

Consider, for instance, the exchange in (16), which is an adaptation of a classical example that Grice considered typical of conversational implicature.

(16)   S1: *A mon avis il ne se mariera jamais.*
         'I think he will never get married.'

         S2: *Il rend fréquemment visite à quelqu'un en ville.*
         'He often visits somebody in town.'

As far as their semantic contents are concerned, the two utterances could be entirely unrelated. Each speaker could have spoken independently from the other without any connection between their statements, if it had not been within the same adjacency pair. But the fact that S2 utters his/her statement right after S1's and yet his/her utterance bears no obvious relationship to what S1 said sets the implications of the Cooperative Principle in motion: S2's statement constitutes a violation of the Maxim of Relation. And the inferential process, a consequence of the violation of the Cooperative Principle, starts immediately: S1 assumes that S2, who is presumed to be a reasonable social actor abiding by the Cooperative Principle, must have meant something that S1 has to be able to understand or infer correctly from what had been said. The most straightforward hypothesis of what S2 might have meant is that he/she gave an implicit comment on S1's statement. Thus S1 assumes that there is a connection – despite any obvious signs of one – between the two statements. S1 thinks that the man to whom he/she is referring by *il* 'he' in his own statement is the same man who S2 says is frequently visiting somebody in town. And since S2's comment is being taken as an answer to S1's comment, the man who visits someone has to be visiting with the intention of trying to find a wife. Thus the implicit meaning of S2's seemingly unrelated utterance falls out of the violation of the Maxim of Relation: it is inferred automatically by S1 who is in search of a reasonable interpretation of S2's communicative behavior.

Exchanges like (5) and (16) in which one speaker 'changes the topic' exploit the hearer/addressee's automatic assumption that the utterance should conform to the relevance maxim despite any such signs. The hearer can see such a conversational strategy as a way of avoiding talking about social taboos, answering unwanted questions, or engaging in unwelcome interactions. In other words "a person's behavior will be interpreted as conforming to maxims, even if it appears not to, because of the assumption of rationality or goal-directedness" (Green 1996:97) attributed to each and every communicating actor.

5.3.4   *Applying the Maxims*

The Cooperative Principle aims to be a general principle of interactive social behavior that also governs conversational interactions. Beyond its philosophical implications, namely that humans are inherently cooperative social beings, its application has been widespread in LP and beyond. Some of them are reviewed here.

MAXIMS ARE NOT LAWS OR NORMS: The Maxims of conversation defined by Grice have to be considered illustrations of the Cooperative Principle. They do not constitute the principle, they only 'exemplify' it by showing the consequences of the assumption that individuals interact in accordance with their communicative goals. Being only illustrations, the Maxims often seem not sufficiently discrete. For instance, how should 'lying' be considered? Is it a violation of the Maxim of Quantity (e.g. being truthful but not telling everything) or of the Maxim of Quality (e.g. being untruthful in everything that is said) or both? Such overlaps are inevitable, and have been a topic of much debate (see e.g. Sperber and Wilson 1986, Leech 1983).

MAXIMS SOMETIMES 'HAVE TO BE' VIOLATED: There might be situations in which the speaker is simply unable to respect all or most of the Maxims listed above. Two examples are:

- A representative who speaks at a town hall meeting to people who might not have heard of a legislative bill under discussion. The representative has to fill that hole in some people's background information by being especially prolix and therefore violating the Maxim of Quantity by giving more detail than necessary for some people in the audience.
- The police chief is interviewed by a local radio station about the criminal case that he is handling. He might chose to violate the Maxim of Quantity and voluntarily 'omit details' about what he knows, because telling the whole truth could inform, say, a serial killer, on actions taken by the police.

'OPTING OUT' OF A MAXIM: In cases similar to those mentioned above, language can provide lexicalized forms by which speakers explicitly tell hearers/addressees that they are unable or unwilling to conform to a conversational Maxim.

- The representative mentioned above might repeat many times that he/she needs to speak longer or in more detail than his/her time would allow: *Je n'ai vraiment pas le temps d'expliquer ça, mais en gros . . .* 'I really don't have time to get into this, but in short . . .'.
- The chief of police might literally opt out of the Maxim of Quantity by presenting an excuse for not observing it: *Je n'ai pas le droit de dire plus, mais l'enquête suit son cours.* 'I am not allowed to say more but the investigation is following its due course.'

There are also implicit ways of signaling that one or more Maxims will not be respected. Meaning 'less' than what one is saying, i.e. implying that one is less knowledgeable than one really is, means violating the Maxims of Quality (being 'false') and of Quantity ('hiding important pieces of information'). And yet doing so is a common conversational and 'face-saving' politeness strategy (see section 5.4.3.2), called **hedging**:

- Someone trying to 'repair' a worsening relationship might chose to hedge (words underlined) a critique of his/her partner: *Peut-être que tu pourrais être un peu plus comprehensive parfois et au moins dire "Excuse-moi"* . . . 'Maybe you could be a little more understanding sometimes and at least say "I am sorry" . . .'

On the other hand, speakers can use linguistic means by which they implicitly 'warn' hearers/addressees that they are about to violate the Maxims of Manner, of Quantity, and therefore of Quality by saying more than what they should be saying:

- A journalist having no evidence of stating what she will state, chooses to introduce her reporting by saying: *Ce n'est peut-être que des rumeurs, mais . . .* 'These might just be rumors, but . . .'.

MAXIMS AND 'FIGURES OF SPEECH': Some violations of the Maxims became conventionalized ways of expressing speakers' attitudes towards the content of the message conveyed. Such expressions are part of an inventory of stylistic means that are routinely used in all genres of language production from everyday casual speech to literary writings. For instance, overstatements consist of saying much more than is required to convey a given piece of information to hearers/addressees. Thus they constitute a violation of the Maxims of Quantity. And yet the way in which S1 expresses his/her feelings of frustration towards parental authority in (17) is very common in everyday language use, allowing him/her to communicate not only a message but also an 'attitude' with that message. Metaphors, proverbs, and understatements (litotes) represent other 'figures' of speech that, although they violate conversational Maxims, are a good way of communicating a message and the speakers' emotional state.

(17)   S1: *Tu ne fais jamais rien pour moi, mais tu veux que je fasse*
toujours tout ce que tu dis! Tu es comme un pacha qui donne des
ordres à ses serviteurs!
'You never do anything for me, but you always want me to do what you tell me to do! You are like a king giving orders to his subjects!'

S2: *Ah tu exagères!*
'Oh you are exaggerating!

MORE MAXIMS: As mentioned above, the Maxims of conversation given by Grice have to be considered illustrations of the Cooperative Principle, 'exemplifing' it by what happens when we assume that humans interact in accordance with their goals. Therefore, there can be many more Maxims depending on the ways in which speakers' goal-oriented behavior can have an impact on an interaction. The exchange in (18) is a violation of the Maxim of Quantity, but it is also a violation of what other authors called the 'Maxim of Politeness' or politeness rules in conversation (see section 5.4), because S2's refusal to participate in the conversation sampled in (18) might in fact go beyond that single interaction, and signal S2's refusal to collaborate with S1 all together.

(18)   S1: *Tu veux du pain?*
'Do you want bread?'

S2 (no answer)

S1: *Je te demande si tu veux du pain.*
'I am asking you if you want bread.'

S2 (no answer)

S1: *Mais réponds, enfin!*
'Come on! Answer me.'

5.3.5   Beyond the Model Speaker

Grice's contribution to a better understanding of the principles of human communication is unquestionable, but current research has gone beyond some of his proposals and questioned some of its assumptions.

CULTURAL FACTORS: One area which has been largely recast in contemporary research on social interaction is the view of the Model Speaker as an isolated, atomic component of society who makes conscious choices about what he/she says. According to many, this Western view of the world is biased towards seeing individuals as autonomous and independent social actors. In many cultures, the individual is given a role or a status only through her/his interaction with, or belonging to, a larger group. Communicative, and therefore linguistic, choices of a female member of a family in Japan for instance are bound to the hierarchy of her family and wider social relations. Therefore she, as a speaker, cannot be considered an individual member of that culture, acting independently from the expectations that her culture puts on her (see Scollon and Scollon 1995). Thus general models of behavior in communication need to account for the fact that speakers' intentions, beliefs, goals, and plans in interaction with others are sometimes filtered through those speakers' roles and status in social groups and 'communities of practice' (see e.g. Eckert and McConnell-Ginet 1998).

THE PRODUCT OF COMMUNICATION: Another assumption often questioned with respect to Grice's Maxims is the product of the communicative process. As mentioned in 5.2, the origins of LP reach back to classical logic and philosophy, which viewed communication as a transmission of propositions, i.e. kernels of succinct, literal information encoded in words. But a great deal of everyday communication through language or other means does not aim at communicating the maximum amount of information in the most effective way. By placing a hateful comment in an exchange, offering flowers, or uttering thanks, speakers fulfill social expectations and signal attitudes rather than conveying a meaningful proposition through a well-chosen set of words.

POSITIVE SPEAKER ORIENTATION: Related to the previous critique is the challenge to Grice's fundamental proposal that perfect communication would be some kind of norm. The implicit agreement between speakers and hearers to cooperate, many say, cannot be taken for granted, because Grice's Cooperative Principle is in fact a strong philosophical stance in favor of social actors with a positive attitude towards each other. Maybe, as some suggest, positive orientation towards others is not more fundamental than, say, the expectation that communicating with someone will be full of difficulties and misunderstandings (see Sifianou 1992, Scollon and Scollon 1995). The existence and therefore the theoretical 'problem' of non-cooperative behavior for a Gricean model of communication (see Eelen 2001) brings us to the discussion about theories of politeness.

> Give an example when an individual speaker might speak from within a social, cultural hierarchy of relationships, rather than as an individual speaker and social actor.

5.4   Politeness

The idea that speakers construct hypotheses about what others' actions mean in conversation led to the development of a subfield of pragmatics that analyzes conversational interaction in terms of politeness. Building on Grice's Cooperative Principle, namely on the fact that deviance from others' expected cooperative behavior leads to the (re)construction of some meaning to the utterance, Brown and Levinson (1986) theorized that there might be good reasons why speakers violate Maxims in conversation. Borrowing on earlier work in linguistic anthropology, these reasons can be summed up as the speaker's desire to 'save face'.

Brown and Levinson (1986) view politeness as a certain amount of 'verbal repair work' performed by individuals to minimize the threat that their utterances represent for others' **face** in conversation. Face is a symbolic notion that refers to an image or a view of one's self that is emotionally invested and that can be lost, maintained, or enhanced through interactions with others (see Goffman 1967). In simplistic terms, one can say that 'indirect speech acts' (see section 5.4.3.1) are minimizations of 'face threatening acts' (FTAs) in conversation, because they are carried out to preserve others' face or image of themselves: "one powerful and pervasive motive for not talking Maxim-wise is the desire to give some attention to face" (Brown and Levinson 1986:95). Critiques of the concept of face in politeness accounts, however, prefer the term 'rapport-management' rather than face-saving act, because it would capture the delicate balance between the wants of the 'self' (i.e. of the speaker) and the wants of the other (i.e. of the hearer/addressee), while 'face' focuses only on the concerns of the self (see Spencer-Oatey 2000, Mills 2003).

Going back to three of our previous examples, (5), (14), and (15), politeness accounts of these interactions would argue that speakers who violated one or several of the conversational Maxims in those contexts did so to minimize the

FTAs that their utterances would have performed on the other speaker, had they been presented 'up front'. For instance S2 in (5) adheres to an avoidance strategy by switching to another topic rather than risking antagonizing the hearer/addressee by directly asking him/her to drop the topic (see section 5.1). Asking about somebody's physical abilities rather than directly requesting something, as in (14), or suggesting something rather than giving directives as in (15) amounts to more 'work' for the speaker in stating what he/she wants to state, but it also shows a more positive overall attitude towards the other than not using such indirect strategies.

Brown and Levinson's politeness account of communication relies on Grice's view of participants of a conversation as cooperating communicative agents, whose behavior follows rational behavioral guidelines that are valid for collaborative social actors in general. Firstly, in politeness accounts it is assumed that individuals who are engaged in a communicative process are "face-bearing rational agents" (1986:91), which means that they are individuals who tend to act reasonably and have some kind of a view of their own 'self'. Second, it is assumed that these rational agents tend to minimize the face threat that their utterances might represent for others in conversation after having rationally assessed or 'inferred' these face risks. So far, nothing more is stated than what inferential models of communication have been advocating as well (see section 5.3.2). What Brown and Levinson's work added to models of inferential processes in communication is an attempt to formalize some of the social aspects of the relationship between the speaker and the hearer/addressee, such as degree of familiarity or distance ('D factor') and power ('P factor'). According to Brown and Levinson, when choosing a politeness strategy in conversation, speakers take into account, at a minimum, these two social factors.

5.4.1   Bald-on-record

The bald-on-record communicative strategy means speaking in conformity with Grice's Maxims. It is linguistic communication in its unmitigated, 'crude' form, and therefore it could represent a potential open FTA for the hearer/addressee.

Speakers and hearers tend to communicate in an unmitigated way, i.e. disregarding face-threat, when maximum efficiency in communication is in their joint interests. For air-traffic controllers, adding 'please' to their utterances while instructing pilots on emergency landing is understandably not a priority. Thus in politeness terms, FTAs conveyed by imperatives such as *Reduce speed* or *Choose track 23* are irrelevant given the urgency of the situation, and therefore they are ignored by the participants.

Another type of bald-on-record communication in which face-threat is ignored is when speakers speak in the sole interest of hearers/addressees. Even though it is considered impolite to talk to strangers in France, friendly warnings such as *Vos phares sont allumés!* 'Your headlights are on' or *Vos collants ont filé!* 'You have a run in your stocking' are hardly taken as intrusive or face-threatening from anybody.

A third type of unmitigated statement is called 'attention-getter' by Brown and Levinson (1986:96). Attention-getters allow speakers to 'simulate' emergency situations by implying that for the sake of maximum efficiency in communication the hearer has to disregard the potential FTA carried by the utterance, and accept that the speaker has to speak directly. *Écoute!/Écoutez!* 'Listen (to me)' uttered at a turning point in a conversation signals, for instance, that there is discordance between the participants of the conversation. It suggests that very little or "nothing so far had been constructed in the process of co-enunciation" between the speaker and the hearer/addressee, and therefore the latter is "constrained to listen again to what he/she has not yet been able to perceive or understand" (Morel and Danon-Boileau 1998:96). And yet *Écoute!/Écoutez!* tends to be perceived as the speaker's commitment to building a consensus with the hearer/addressee rather than an intrusion in his 'face-wants' (image of the 'self'). In fact when the message to be communicated warrants such a bald-on-record communicative strategy (e.g. the speaker reformulates his/her positions after having been evasive), this strategy comes across as constructive. When it serves as means of constraining the other to rethink his/her positions, however, it represents a forceful way of arguing, shown for instance in example (19), adapted from Morel and Danon-Boileau (1998):

(19)   S1: *Et le résultat, mon père, je vais vous le dire, c'est la fin de l'enseignement libre.*
        'And the result, Father, I am telling you, is the end of free education.'

        S2: *Prévu.*
        'Intended.'

        S1: *Non.*
        'No.'

        S2: *Écoutez!*
        'Listen (to me)!'

        S1: *Ce sera la fin de l'enseignement libre au profit de l'enseignement privé.*
        'It will be the end of free education thereby profiting private education.'

        S2: *Alors **écoutez**, Christine Ockrent, moi je ne suis pas le chef d'un lobby . . .*
        'Well listen, Ms Ockrent, I am not the head of a lobby group . . .'

Exchanges such as in (19) are bald-on-record statements that can be taken as a mark of sincerity rather than a face-threat. Thus the assumption that politeness in conversation always functions as 'repair' or 'compensation' for the rudeness of being too direct could be a consequence of an Anglo-centric view of society (see Sifianou 1992). Some cultures, in fact, seem to value it more when speakers speak directly and literally, i.e. when they follow the Maxims of conversation, and it is precisely the avoidance of direct communicative strategies that is looked upon as manipulative and undesirable. Some work in cultural anthropology suggests that lack of direct communication in French culture is perceived with suspicion, as it can be viewed as signifying lack of sincerity and validity of others' statements and intentions (Carroll 1987). Despite its positive semantic content, the expression *Il est très gentil!* 'He is very nice!' in French sometimes amounts to devastating criticism of an individual who comes across as weak and too preoccupied with others' face-wants. The act of *faire une boutade* 'making a joke', on the other hand, which can be roughly circumscribed as issuing a mild attack on the others' arguments in conversation, is culturally accepted in France as long as it serves the need to communicate 'face off', i.e. earnestly but with no restraint. It is generally taken as a benign offense or teasing, because it is perceived as a 'rush' of sincerity, an uncontainable urge to be authentic and showing 'care' about the matter under discussion.

5.4.2   Positive politeness

Positive politeness strategies in face-to-face interactions consist of shaping one's discourse in such as way as to show 'active' care and attention for others' face-wants. In Brown and Levinson's words "anointing the face" of hearers/addressees by claiming common ground, intimacy, and reciprocity with them (1986:101–129). Among the numerous positive politeness strategies there are: "notice, exaggerate, and intensify interest" to the hearer, "use in-group markers, in-group dialect, jargon", "seek agreement", and "presuppose/raise/assert common ground". The most important common feature in all these strategies is the active demonstration of 'care' for the other's face in the interaction. A short-cut to this strategy could be the expression: B E D I R E C T !

Ways in which such attitudes can be conveyed through language are numerous, and cannot be discussed in length here, but they include e.g. switching to the local accent or dialect, using in-group and/or casual expressions or regional lexical forms (see section 4.9.1), increasing the informality and directness of the exchange by frequently dropping the negative particle *ne* (3.8.3), avoiding optional liaison (2.4.4), and passive constructions (3.9). The choice between the impressive array of different interrogatives illustrated in 3.10.3 also entails the selection of a question form and the type of intonation that accompanies it (see section 5.5), depending on social distance and power relations, communicative intent, and stylistic-situational appropriateness. The following subsections present two typical means of positive politeness strategy, i.e. direct speaker involvement in the minimization of FTAs.

5.4.2.1   *Informal* tu *and formal* vous

Address pronouns *tu* (informal 'you') and *vous* (formal 'you') in French demonstrate different degrees of closeness and intimacy between the speaker and the hearer/addressee. As a positive politeness strategy, the use of either *tu* or *vous* gives speakers the opportunity to show, sometimes even to negotiate, their attitudes towards others' status and presumed or perceived face-wants.

As argued by Brown and Gilman (1960) for many European languages that developed an informal (T) vs. formal (V) pronominal address system (abbreviations taken from the Latin *tu* and *vos*), *tu* in French grants speakers less social distance and formality with hearers/addressees than *vous*. As these authors claimed, the determining factors in the emergence of either address form are 'power' and 'solidarity'. In a much simplified way, the strategies are as follows: speakers with superior social status ('power') over other speakers in a conversational exchange tend to use *tu* (informal 'you') and receive *vous* (formal 'you'), while speakers with lesser social status mirror this behavior by using *vous* and receiving *tu*. Between speakers with roughly equal 'power' ('solidarity'), on the other hand, the use of informal or formal address pronouns is usually reciprocal. Although the concepts of power and solidarity are somewhat coarsely defined in this model, it seems intuitively true that non-reciprocal social relations are conducive to non-reciprocal use of address forms (e.g. when there is considerable age difference between speakers), and vice versa (e.g. when two young French speakers accidentally meet in a foreign country). When examined more closely, however, the second-person pronominal address system in French is more complex than this.

First, the age and sex of the participants of an exchange are less important predictors of the emergence of either form than previously thought (Gardner-Chloros 1991). Instead, explicitly negotiated deference and/or intimacy between the speaker and the hearer/addressee, as well as their mutual beliefs about each other's social standing within the community play a crucial role. For instance informal *tu* 'you' is sometimes 'forced' onto the hearers/addressees when the age difference between older and younger colleagues or the social distance between employees of different socio-economic background are explicitly played down for the benefit of intimacy and solidarity (e.g. 'ask' the other to use *tu* or *se tutoyer*). In the same vein, maintaining distance to show greater respect and esteem for the other is also often negotiated with the use of *vous* between speakers of similar age and socio-economic background. Ethnic and cultural differences sometimes stand in the way of effective negotiations of such 'local' social conventions of use. Morford (1997:22) reports, for instance, that speakers of ethnically white French origin have difficulties imposing the use of formal 'you' on workers of North African origin who tend to say *tu* 'too readily' once they are on familiar terms with their supervisors. Speakers might also 'juggle' social-indexical values of address forms from one situation to another: e.g. lawyers who work together and address each other by *tu* switch to *vous* when they plead opposite cases in court. Multiple examples of this kind suggest that address pronouns in French might be negotiated each time in conversation to refer to locally significant social meanings, as well as wider social conventions of use.

5.4.2.2   *Generic* tu, vous, *and* on

The analysis of politeness strategies that presumably underlie the use of address pronouns in French is further complicated by the so-called indefinite or 'generic' meaning of *tu* and *vous*. Although indefinite *tu* and *vous* are of relatively recent historical origin (Posner 1997:76), they are widespread in many varieties of French spoken in France (Ashby 1992, Coveney 2003) and imperceptibly but massively replacing the generic pronoun *on* 'one' in Quebec French (see Blondeau 2001).

One crucial pragmatic factor in the indefinite use of these pronouns is the degree of novelty of their intended referent. The referent in (20) is no doubt an indefinite or generic one, as the hearer (addressed by *tu*) has probably never won money by betting on horses (example from Gadet 1992:78). But when rephrasing the referent with *on*, as in (21), the speaker's intended referents (those 'pointed at' by the pronoun) become only inclusive of a group of hearers/addressees with the exclusion of others (see Deshaies 1985).

(20)   *Au Quinté Plus, quand tu gagnes, ça déforme les poches.*
        'At Quinté Plus, when you win, it makes your pockets bulge.'

(21)   *Au Quinté Plus, quand on gagne, ça déforme les poches.*
        'At Quinté Plus, when one wins, it makes one's pockets bulge.'

Indefinite *vous* is more difficult to disentangle from its definite uses, although one factor that favors the use of indefinite *vous* is the introduction of discourse-new information. The emergence of a new referent in (22), namely the reference to the Frantel restaurant chain, is achieved by indefinite *vous*. Once the referent is discourse-old, however, evaluation and further description are carried out using indefinite *on* (from Ashby 1992:147):

(22)   *Alors là, ça dépend du chef, et puis du gérant, du directeur. Parce que vous avez un, un exemple, **vous** avez un Frantel, c'est une chaîne aussi euh à Bordeaux où on mange très très bien . . .*

'Well that depends on the chef and the manager. Because <u>you</u> have
an, an example, <u>you</u> have a Frantel, which is also a chain in uhm
Bordeaux where **one** can eat very very well . . .'

One motivation behind the indefinite use of personal pronouns such as *tu*,
vous, and *on* is positive politeness strategy, since second-person address pronouns give the 'literal means' to the speaker to draw the hearer/addressee into
the actual process of co-enunciation more actively and extensively than other
discourse strategies would allow. Saying *vous avez un Frantel* 'you have a Frantel' rather than *il y a un Frantel* 'there is a Frantel' in (22), for instance, not
only allows the speaker to introduce a new discourse topic but also to 'call
on' the hearer/addressee (i.e. use a personal pronoun) to picture the restaurant chain Frantel mentally, and therefore participate actively in the referential
process.

The utterance in (23), on the other hand, illustrates another type of definite use of *on* (example from Coveney 2004). When uttered in context, (23)
conveys a well-recognizable imperative meaning with the speaker's attitude
having 'special connotations' or a particular attitudinal meaning interpreted as
condescending. Thus the utterance accomplishes an indirect speech act, it is
an actual order syntactically 'put' as a declarative, but with some 'added connotations' to it. This connotation arises from the use of *on* that is commonly
used as inclusive of both the speaker and the hearer(s)/addressee(s). When this
pronoun appears in an indirect request or imperative such as (23), however, it
allows the speaker to direct the perlocutionary force of the utterance (the action
to be undertaken) solely to the hearers/addressees ('you' need to calm down),
while continuing to claim inclusive or 'in-group' status with the latter (see also
Deshaies' 1985 study of adolescents' pronominal address forms in the city of
Quebec).

(23)   *On se calme, les amis!*
        '(One needs to) calm down!'

Inclusion vs. exclusion of the hearer and others from the referential process
together with the type of reference (definite/indefinite) have been identified
as the main factors determining the use of *on* as equivalent of either *nous*
'we' or *tu/vous* 'you' (see Laberge and Sankoff 1979). In fact, despite earlier
claims to the contrary (see e.g. Oukada 1982), together with its 'long form',
l'on, traditionally attributed to formal contexts, the pronoun "*on* can apparently
replace almost any of the other personal pronouns in particular situations"
(Coveney 2004:101), even though many of these are marked stylistically, and
often convey particular speaker attitudes.

5.4.3   Negative politeness

Negative politeness encompasses linguistic manifestations of distance and formality in conversation. It is "redressive action addressed to the addressee's
negative face: his want to have his freedom of action unhindered and his
attention unimpeded. It is the heart of respect behavior . . ." (Brown and
Levinson 1986:129). In other words, negative politeness strategies comprise
communicative means of 'avoidance' and assurance that the speaker will minimize imposition on the hearer/addressee. This type of strategy or speaker attitude could be expressed as: BE INDIRECT!

5.4.3.1   Indirect speech acts

As mentioned in section 5.4, indirect speech acts allow speakers to perform
a particular speech act while showing no 'direct' signs of acting in the way
they intended. Instead of going on record issuing an imperative, for instance,
speakers – 'verbatim' – are merely asking a question: *Tu peux fermer la fenêtre?*
'Can you close the window?' Thus indirect speech acts soften face-threatening
acts or imposition that the utterance constitutes for the hearer, and preserve the
'negative' face of hearers/addressees.

In example (23) in section 5.4.2.2, the speaker resorted to syntactic/semantic
means to convey one type of meaning: addressing the hearer by *on* that is a
priori inclusive of both participants (synonymous to 'we') while simultaneously
pronouncing the utterance with prosodic means reminiscent of imperatives (see
Figure 2.10(d)). With respect to the utterance in example (14) in section 5.3.1,
we determined that an answer *Oui, je peux* 'Yes I can' to the indirect request
Tu peux me passer le plateau de fromage? 'Can you pass the cheese tray?'
is inappropriate, because speakers and hearers/addressees equally share the
conventional knowledge that the trigger utterance represents an indirect request
('Please pass the cheese tray!') rather than an inquiry about the capacity of the
hearer to lift the cheese tray. The indirect meaning comes from the fact that the
utterance bears the intonational marks (final rise) of a yes-no question while its
syntactic structure is that of a declarative.

Such indirect acts are thought to be idiomatic in languages, and therefore
could not be accessible to speakers and hearers of other cultures. The possibly benign statement *Il fait froid ici* 'It is cold here' might or might not elicit
the reaction of turning on the heat in the room from speakers of French or
other cultures and **communities of practice**. Such 'cultural misunderstandings' due to misinterpretations of speech acts are well known and fill the books
on linguistic communication. But just how much certain styles of politeness,
including indirect speech acts, are universal is a hotly debated topic in pragmatics and interactional sociolinguistics today. Brown and Levinson (1986:230)
point out cultural specificities of politeness rules when classifying interactions

characteristic of members of certain societies as 'positive politeness cultures' (e.g. Anglo-American) and 'negative politeness cultures' (e.g. Japanese). Others denounce the 'Eurocentrism' advocating certain models of politeness as universals and stress the need for further studies (Sifianou 1992, Scollon and Scollon 1995, Spencer-Oatey 2000). Some studies have shown that even within a seemingly unified 'culture' such as the United States, styles of interruptions, and therefore perceptions of politeness and impoliteness, vary in terms of geographic location: Tannen (1990), for instance, found that speakers of similar age and socio-economic background (upper-middle-class professionals) from the east coast of the United States tend to interrupt, and therefore come across as more unpolite, than west coast speakers do in otherwise friendly dinner conversations. Thus different 'subcultures' and communities could have different linguistically transparent roles of polite behavior, and be judged negatively by outsiders. But cultures and/or communities are not the only social factors to play a role. Ways in which French and English speakers tend to put, or on the contrary minimize, prosodic prominence on negative adverbs and particles, for instance, depends on **register** (i.e. type of situation), speaker **stance** (adversarial vs. supportive attitude) and the information status of the negative (informative or remedial). Based on a speech corpus recorded from the French and American English media, Yaeger-Dror (2002) found that informative negatives, i.e. when the matter is about disagreement on content, tend to be more emphasized prosodically, thus are potentially more face-threatening in French speakers' public speech, while prosodic prominence on informative negatives tends to be 'downplayed' in American English. In remedial contexts (apologies, explanations), however, the situation is exactly the opposite: in most situations in French remedial negatives have been found to be less prominent prosodically than their English equivalents. Similar large-scale corpus studies are needed to establish how these and other variables (possibily age and gender) play a role in the perceptions of politeness and impoliteness within and across different cultures (Mills 2003).

5.4.3.2   Hedging and indirectness

Politeness theories assume that ordinary speech acts, such as asking someone to do something or even stating something can represent threats to cooperative interaction, because such acts assume something about others' motivations and investment in the matter at hand. To quote Brown and Levinson directly: "For to ask someone to do something is to presuppose that they can and are willing to do it, and have not already done it; to promise to do something is to admit that one hasn't already done it, to assume that the addressee wants it done and would prefer you to do it – and so on . . .". Thus 'minimizing' the way one's background assumptions are expressed linguistically can be an important 'disarming routine' of potential blunders and rebukes in interactions.

Words and expressions, called **hedges**, are introduced as a way of mitigating (weakening) the certainty with which speakers 'mean' something. Hedges typically convey a non-committal or lessened speaker attitude towards the content of the utterance. Although there are many ways in which one's arguments can be 'softened' in conversations and narratives, and they are communicated simultaneously with words through other channels of communication (e.g. kinetic or non-verbal), 'hedging with words' is probably the most widespread and conventionalized way of indirectly 'caring' for the speaker's positive face in discourse.

PERFORMATIVE HEDGES are analyzed as 'illocutionary force modifiers', i.e. weakening the force with which an utterance conveys a certain prepositional meaning. Adverbs such as *vraiment* 'sincerely' and *réellement* 'really', shown in the example in (24), but also adverbials like *en fait* 'by the way', *d'une certaine façon* 'to some extent', modify the verb in the syntactic phrase. 'Hedging' the verb can convey the speaker's intention of mitigating the conviction or 'force' with which the utterance is pronounced.

(24)   *Il n'a vraiment/réellement rien voulu faire de mal.*
         'He sincerely/really did not want to do anything bad.'

But as analyses of actual corpora indicate, it is often difficult to decide which modifier or adverbial expression functions as a 'strengthener' or as a 'weakener'. For instance, most adverbials that Brown and Levinson (see e.g. 1986:147) consider hedges on speakers' sincerity are regarded as intensifiers, i.e. 'strengtheners' in London teenagers' everyday conversations (Stenström et al. 2002). It is difficult to tell whether this mismatch is due to dialectal differences or to language change (there is more than fifteen years of difference between the two books). But it should alert us to the fact that deciding between what is 'weak' or 'strong' remains a matter of interpretation until some form of input from the speakers can help decide between the two competing interpretations.

QUALITY HEDGES convey that the speaker does not take full responsibility for the truth of the proposition conveyed by the utterance. Utterances such as (25) indicate that the speaker's commitment to the truth is less than what Grice's Maxim of Relation and/or Quantity would require. However, the use of verbs such as *penser*, *sembler*, and *paraître* instead of a simple 'be' verb (*être*) translate exactly what negative politeness strategies would require speakers to do: mitigate the force of the assumption conveyed to the other by "humbling one's self and one's capacities" (Brown and Levinson 1986:185) to assert the truth.

(25)   *Il semble que le directeur ait volé de l'argent.*
         'Apparently the manager stole some money.'

It is noteworthy that the speaker's choice of the perception verb *sembler* in (25) is itself a type of 'quality hedge' to the extent to which it contrasts with other possible lexical choices, e.g. *paraître*, that the speaker could have made. Briefly stated, *sembler* implies indirect 'perceiving' of the event (the manager's theft), and thus could be taken from the speaker's part as delegating 'reliability' for the statement that is uttered about the event.

According to the dictionary *Le Petit Robert* (1989), the meaning of *sembler* is marked by 'a nuance of imprecision and subjectivity' (*une nuance d'imprécision ou de subjectivité*) compared to *paraître* 'to appear'. Although both *sembler* and *paraître* are perception verbs, which means that both convey that a Perceiver/Experiencer, presumably the Agent himself (for these terms see section 3.4.1) who is also the grammatical subject (*il* 'he') in (25), is or was connected with a perceived event in some way, but the way in which the act of 'perceiving' has been carried out (e.g. by direct perception or reported from someone else) is decisive when chosing either verb. In the case of *paraître*, the Perceiver's relationship to the perceived event is more direct than in the case of *sembler*. Based on dictionary definitions, *paraître* means *se présenter à la vue* 'appear at sight', i.e. it is in close relationship with *se montrer/devenir visible* 'to show up/to become visible'. The meaning conveyed by *sembler*, on the other hand, already involves reference to the mental representation of 'perceiving' the event, as it is defined as 'occurring under certain appearances to someone' (*se présenter (faire une telle apparence) à quelqu'un*). A comparative analysis of nineteen French translations of Lewis Carroll's *Alice in Wonderland* reveals, for instance, that *paraître* is preferred over *sembler* when translating the verb 'to seem' in contexts that involve physically 'viewing' an event (Kibbee 1995:78), and even if in both cases, i.e. *paraître* or *sembler*, the certainty of the speaker is attenuated with respect to the perceived event.

Thus it is not suprising that *il paraît* rather than *il semble* is used when reporting an event that is based on rumours, i.e. it means that the actual 'hearing' or 'viewing' of the reported piece of information has been carried out by an Agent that is not the grammatical subject of the utterance. According to *Le Petit Robert* (1989), *il paraît qu'on va doubler les impôts* 'it seems that taxes will be doubled' is synonymous with *le bruit court qu'on va doubler les impôts* 'there are rumours that taxes will be doubled' (1989:1354). As discussed with respect to impersonal constructions in the Syntax chapter (see section 3.6.2), the pronoun *il* in *il paraît* is an 'empty placeholder' in subject position for an unspecified Agent or Experiencer. The 'pragmatic meaning' of such constructions is often referred to as **evidentiality**, which in simplified terms means 'conveying various speaker attitudes towards knowledge'. Thus to come back to the initial purpose of this discussion, lexical hedges are devices of evidential marking in languages: they signal the degree with which speakers are sure of what they say, or in other words the 'degree of liability' they are ready to admit with respect to their statements. (Thus the zero degree of evidentiality would be to go on record and state 'I am absolutely certain of what say.')

Although some languages can express evidentiality by morphological means (e.g. Quechua), evidential marking in French seems to resort to syntactic (e.g. impersonal and passive constructions) or lexical means. Interestingly enough, in cases of bilingualism and/or prolonged linguistic contact, lexical evidential markers are heavily borrowed from the dominant language (King and Nadasdy 1999).

REFERENCE HEDGES: Avoiding direct reference to hearers/addressees in formulating utterances that could be taken as potentially face-threatening is probably one of the most common negative politeness strategies expressed via linguistic means. One way of avoiding overt reference to hearers/addressees is using passive constructions.

As we have seenn in section 3.9, arguments of the verb which are participants of an action or event can be expressed in syntactically different ways. Active (26) and passive (27) constructions represent such means of expression of the same propositional content.

(26)   *Un camarade de classe a poussé le petit garçon dans l'escalier.*
        'A classmate pushed the little boy down the stairs.'

(27)   *Le petit garçon a été poussé dans l'escalier.*
        'The little boy was pushed down the stairs'.

The passive in (27) arises from the suppression of the grammatical subject, and the agent of the action, *un camarade de classe* 'a classmate' of the verb *pousser* 'push'. The direct object of the active verb, *le petit garçon* 'the little boy', is moved to the empty subject position and is expressed as the subject of the 'passive verb', which is formed as a combination of the 'be' verb and the past participle of the active verb: *a été poussé* 'was pushed'. Although such passive constructions can serve as means of **topicalization**, i.e. foregrounding one piece of information rather than another, they also function as means of 'mitigating' direct reference to Agents when such reference is either undesirable in or irrelevant to the context. When trying to find out in the hospital what caused the injuries suffered by the little boy in the fictional utterance in (27), for instance, concentrating on the results of being pushed rather than on the agent who perpetuated thte action can be simultaneously face-saving (towards the boy and supposedly his parents) but also more desirable and efficient in getting quick medical help. As mentioned in section 3.9, passivization is prominent in journalistic styles and official communications that routinely concentrate on 'results' and 'effects' rather than the 'means' by which the action was performed.

5.4.4   Discourse particles

If "talk is an ongoing joint creation in which both forms and meanings are subject to continual negotiation and interpretation" (Schiffrin 1987:67), then it is not surprising that there are linguistic forms specifically for directly instructing the hearer/addressee on how to interpret elements of that negotiation process. Although it is often difficult to tell how the use of certain particles presented in this section qualifies as a type of politeness strategy, e.g. whether it is a positive or a negative, a direct or an indirect way of 'managing' the other's 'face-wants', **discourse particles** and **markers** (*mots du discours* [Ducrot 1980], *ponctuants* or *marqueurs discursifs* [Morel and Danon-Boileau 1998]) in general have been shown to serve (directly or indirectly) to enlist the active collaboration of the hearer/addressee in the construction of the spoken discourse (process of 'co-enunciation'). They do so by seeking agreement or confirmation by the hearer/addressee, while trying to avoid major disagreements by checking upon the understanding of a particular intent or proposition.

Thus discourse particles can be regarded as a linguistic means of 'discourse management' and ostensible means of mediating politeness (see e.g. Beeching 2002). They derive from 'regular' lexical words and expressions that have been **grammaticalized**, i.e. changed lexico-grammatical 'status' from open-class lexical items to discourse-level function words. Some of the most frequent discourse particles used in colloquial Metropolitan French are:

– *disons* 'Let's say'
– *(eh) b(i)en* 'Well . . . , Now . . .'
– *en quelque sorte* 'sort of'
– *en fait* 'actually'
– *enfin* 'finally'
– *hein?* 'right'?
– *j'veux dire* 'I mean'
– *tu sais* 'you know'
– *tu vois* 'you see'
– *quoi* 'anyway . . .'
– *par exemple* 'for instance'

En quelque sorte. Particles like *en quelque sorte* 'sort of' are often called **hedges**, mitigating or weakening the certainty with which speakers mean to convey their message. They typically vehicle a non-committal speaker attitude, and therefore indirectly 'care' for the speaker's positive face in conversation (see section 5.4.3 for more detail).

(eh) b(i)en. The particle *(eh) b(i)en* serves as an opening of a turn in face-to-face conversations, loosely summing up what precedes in the discourse and then presenting the speaker's comments as contrasting with it (Luzzati 1982).

Alors 'so' plays a similar role in initiating a new turn, except that in this case the speakers' comments are intended to be taken as a direct consequence of what had been previously stated. Such expressions are turn-taking devices, signaling to the hearer/addressee that the speaker is positioning him/herself with respect to what precedes, i.e. he/she intends to take into account their jointly elaborated and shared knowledge.

Disons, j'veux dire. The expressions *disons* 'let's say' and *j'veux dire* 'I mean' signal upcoming self-repairs (*marqueur de reformulation*). They both take as their starting point the expression that immediately precedes them, but while *disons* 'let's say' portrays the act of repair as a consensus between the speaker and the hearer/addressee (which is why the *nous* form is used), *j'veux dire* 'I mean' presents the repair as undertaken as the speaker's sole commitment to finding the best expression for his/her thoughts. The self-repair can be genuine, i.e. de facto overwriting what had been said (28), in which case it is called a 'replacement **repair**', or it can be fictitious, serving to further elaborate a thought (29). The egocentric positioning of the speaker towards his/her own statement is obvious in both expressions, however, as the first person in *disons* as well as in *j'veux* carry a 'personalized signature' from the speaker. The only difference is that while the speaker's attitude expressed in *disons* is hearer-oriented, *j'veux dire* attributes a change in orientation towards the meaning of the talk to the speaker alone.

(28)   S1: *Est-ce que tu as vu des résultats probants chez des gens ou des non résultats?*
              'Have you seen promising results with some people or nul results?'

         S2: *Non je vais pas dévoiler . . .*
              'No, I am not going to reveal . . .'

         S1: *Non non mais tout en restant tu n'vas pas parler de ta petite sœur ou d'ta tante mais j'veux dire de de de en restant assez général.*
              'No no but while staying you are not going to talk about your little sister or your aunt but I mean generally speaking.'
              (adapted and translated from Morel and Danon-Boileau 1998:105)

(29)   *Par conséquent ce qui m'intéresse moi ₌c'est qu'en raison qu'il y a une erreur [. . .] qu'on est obligé de faire appel à un autre disons à une autre dimension et cette autre dimension ne peut être donnée que . . .*
              'Consequently what I find interesting is that because of an error [. . .] one has to appeal to another let's say another dimension and this dimension can only be given . . .'
              (adapted and translated from Morel and Danon-Boileau 1998:104)

Tu vois, tu sais. Based on Brown and Levinson's (1986:171) classification, the particles *tu vois* 'you see' and *tu sais* 'you know' would be called 'manner hedges', and therefore be treated as an indirect politeness strategy. It seems, however, that by virtue of their lexical meaning these two particles represent not a covert but a direct effort to involve the hearer/addressee in the process of 'co-enunciation'. Thus *tu vois* and *tu sais* serve more to call on, rather than to actually hedge or scale back, the illocutionary force of the speaker's utterances (see the discussion on *hein?* below).

Both particles focus on some piece of information provided by the speaker. *Tu vois* 'you see' is a direct appeal inviting the other to 'view' or 'perceive' some aspect of what is being said, possibly as an invitation for greater empathy from someone who might not show enough interest or commitment. Utterance-finally, *tu vois* often functions as direct solicitation for back-channel cues, such as *uhm*, *yes*, *right*, as shown in (30).

(30)   S1: *mais j'dis ça veut dire quoi ça brut de pomme elle dit ben ça veut dire vite fait <u>tu vois</u>*
         'But I go what does it mean *brut de pomme* and she goes well that means done fast <u>(you) see</u>'
         S2 *oui mais brut de pomme c'est pas une boisson?*
         'Isn't *brut de pomme* a type of beverage?'
         S1 *si c'est une boisson en plus <u>tu vois</u> j'dis c'est quoi ça et elle m'dit ça veut dire vite fait* [. . .] *<u>tu vois</u> il y a des il y des p'tites expressions comme ça . . .*
         'Yes it is a beverage <u>(you) see</u> I go what is that and she goes that means done fast [. . .] <u>(you) see</u> there are expressions like that . . .'
         (adapted and translated from Fagyal 2004:56)

The meaning of the particle *tu sais?/vous savez?* 'you know?' in interaction is different from *tu vois* 'you see' in that *savoir* 'to know' refers to possessing knowledge rather than being able to perceive the speaker's point of view. The use of this particle can translate a true inquiry into the hearer/addressee's knowledge shared with the speaker, as in (31) where 'you know' (translated as *t(u) sais?*) effectively checks whether the other knows where the town of Monticello is located (from Schiffrin 1987:289):

(31)   Irene: The New Yorkers tend t'go to upstate New York, like to-
         <u>y'know</u> where Monticello is?
         Les New Yorker vont plutôt au Nord de l'Etat de New York, comme à – <u>t'sais</u> où est Monticello?
         Sally: Yeah. The Catskills and all?
         Ouais. Les Catskills et tout?

In other cases, the act of checking on the hearer's shared knowledge is fictitious, because the use of the particle implies that the speaker thinks the hearer/addressee is supposed to have that particular information. In that case, *tu sais?* 'you know' functions as a reminder, such as in (32) where Marie reminds her interlocutor that a diploma is not worth much without work experience (from Morel and Danon-Boileau 1998:97):

(32)   S1:   *Ouais mais t'sais mon diplôme il vaut rien tant qu'j'ai pas travaillé*
                'Yeah but y'know my diploma is not worth anything until I have actually worked'

Par exemple. Interestingly, discourse particles sometimes specialize in certain interactive functions in different varities of the same language. A canonical example of differential grammaticalization of a discourse marker is the case of *par exemple* in Metropolitan vs. Canadian French. In standard usage in both varieties *par exemple* 'for instance' is used as an expression introducing an illustration of a specific point in hand. The example shown in (33), communicated by Dostie (2002:147), shows that the expression introduces a sample of a possibly longer list of 'reasons' why the hearer/addressee might not have called the speaker on the phone for some time.

(33)   *Je voudrais savoir pourquoi tu agis comme ça avec moi? Par exemple, je me demande pourquoi tu ne me téléphones plus?!*
         'I'd like to know why you are acting like this with me? For instance, I am wondering why you don't call me on the phone anymore?!'

Metropolitan varieties of French show similar uses of *par exemple* in the meaning exemplified in (33). In Canadian French, on the other hand, *par exemple* seems to have taken up on the role of an oppositional stance marker in discourse, as the examples in (34) and (35) illustrate (respectively from Dostie 2002:150 and Vincent 1995:59):

(34)   *J'ai une fille de trente-trois ans. Elle dit qu'elle a vingt-cinq par exemple, mais ça change pas grand-chose. Sont-tu pareilles, les filles? Vous aussi vous aimez rajeunir?*
         'I have a thirty-three-year-old daughter. But she says she is twenty-five, however, although it does not change anything. Are you the same you girls? Do you also like to appear younger?

(35)   S1: *Puis Raymond il se promenait en gros: il avait un Cadillac puis . . .*
              'And Raymond showed off a lot: he had a Cadillac, and. . . .'
         S2: *C'était un voleur, par exemple.*
              'He was a thief, nonetheless.'

In its uses as an oppositional discourse marker in Canadian French, *par exemple* demonstrates the properties of what Vincent (1995:61) calls a 'counter-argumentative discourse particle' (*connecteur contre-argumentatif*): it conveys the idea of an opposition between two propositions of the same utterance, e.g.: *il avait un Cadillac* 'he had a Cadillac' and *c'était un voleur* 'he was a thief'. The fact that in its most typical context, the oppositional *par exemple* appears utterance-finally reinforces the interpretation that the particle's meaning spans the entire preceding utterance, and thus can be considered synonymous of other oppositional discourse markers such as *tout de même* and *quand même*.

A similar interactional meaning of *par exemple* can be observed in spoken varieties of Metropolitan French. In these cases, the expression seems to have grammaticalized as an interjection, or what Vincent calls an 'exclamative'. The example in (36) shows a nearly idiomatic context of use of this particle synonymous, and often co-occurring, with fixed expressions such as *ça alors* and other discourse particles as *eh b(i)en*.

(36)   *T'es là, toi? Ça par exemple!*
         'So you are here! Wow!'

Thus in two different, geographically distant varieties of French a somewhat divergent pragmatic change seems to have taken place: "*Tout porte à croire que la valeur non exemplaire de par exemple a surtout évolué dans la direction de l'exclamation en français européen, alors qu'en français québécois, la valeur d'opposition s'est imposée.*" 'Everything seems to indicate that the non-exemplary meaning of *par exemple* has mostly evolved in the direction of exclamations in European French, while in Canadian French the oppositional value took over.' (Vincent 1995:59)

Hein? Quoi? Explicitly involving the hearer/addressee in discourse by seeking his/her agreement vs. excluding him/her from any further discussion is the main divide between the use of two discourse particles: *hein* 'right?' and *quoi* 'anyway'. Although the attitudinal meanings of these two discourse markers (see section 5.4.2.2) are very different, they are both frequently used at the end of turns and both represent 'bald-on-record' communicative strategies. In the first case, a reaction from the hearer/addressee is solicited explicitly, and this meaning is conveyed not only by the particle, but also by its rising intonation. In (37), the teacher who is instructing his students on how to make sound recordings speaks from experience of working with students and makes no secret of his assumption that the students have not yet developed a full understanding of how and why sound recordings are made in fieldwork situations. His insistent use of *hein?* can be paraphrased as a bald-on-record appeal: "guarantee me that you understood what I said, and assure me that you share this opinion, because I am making it clear to you that this is something you haven't understood yet" (from Morel and Danon-Boileau 1998:102). The attitude signalled by *quoi* and its falling or flat intonation is no less 'face off': it conveys that the speaker believes no further discussion is necessary or desirable on what he/she just said. Placed after the particle *enfin* 'anyway', a marker of the end of a list (of examples or illustrations) in (38), *quoi* authoritatively closes the discussion in hand.

(37)   *En tout cas il y a une consigne, c'est ne jamais enregistrer pour rien hein? Parce que après vous vous retrouverez avec des heures d'enregistrement et n'oubliez pas qu'une minute d'enregistrement ça fait déjà une heure de transcription à faire hein? Et c'est fatigant.*
        'At any rate, there is one piece of advice to make, which is never to record for nothing, right? Because then you'll find yourselves with hours of recording and don't forget that one minute of recording amounts to an hour of transcription, right? And that is exhausting.'

(38)   *C'était une émission sur la chirurgie esthétique pour refaire les seins, supprimer mes rides, supprimer la cellulite enfin quoi.*
        'This was a TV show about plastic surgery for breast implants, eliminate my wrinkles, get ride of cellulite and that's it.'
                                (adapted and translated from Morel and Danon-Boileau 1998)

5.4.5   Off-record

A final type of politeness strategy consists of communicating in such a way as to hide one's communicative intents. "In other words, the actor leaves himself an 'out' by providing himself with a number of defensible interpretations [but] he cannot be held to have committed himself to just one particular interpretation of his act" (Brown and Levinson 1986:211). Some of the numerous off-record strategies are: 'hinting', overstating, understating, using self-explanatory statements (called *tautologies*), metaphors, and rhetorical questions. A particular group of such strategies are represented by **euphemisms**, which are often analyzed as a type of metaphorical substitution for 'the real things'.

The idea is that there are referents that speakers prefer not to name or to name indirectly for reasons related to cultural taboo, acceptable behavior in public, and 'politically correct' attitudes towards certain sensitive topics. In certain contexts calling a cleaning lady *technicien de surface* 'surface technician' and suburban ghettos *quartiers* 'districts' in French qualifies as such a strategy.

5.4.6   Politeness: in the eye of the beholder

Address pronouns, hedges, apologies, compliments, mitigation, and indirect speech acts represent a rich arsenal of linguistic means by which conversational attitudes can be expressed. It is important to remember, however, that these means do not 'define' politeness. Speakers' more or less active interest in others' face-wants does not 'reside' in particular linguistic expressions or utterance types: they are expressed by them. This means that politeness and intentions in communication in general, by whatever linguistic or non-linguistic means they are expressed, remain a matter of constant judgment and assessment from both the speaker and the hearer's part. By going beyond Brown and Levinson's model, contemporary research on conversational interactions tries to also understand how factors like race, class, and gender have an impact on interactive language production and interpretation.

A cartoon in the 5 April 2004 issue of the *New Yorker* shows three prehistoric men and women, each sitting on stones disposed in a circle inside a cave. One man standing in front of the group is shown asking: 'Is anyone using this rock?'

Why can this question be interpreted as a 'polite' request? To what extent is it an indirect speech act?

5.5   Exercises

1) How do *ce* 'it', *ça* 'it', and *ils* 'they' refer to their intended referents in the following text? Think in terms of type and directionality of reference.

    Tout semblait s'écrouler. Rien ne marchait. Ce qui était réparé un jour était tombé en panne le jour d'après. Les ingénieurs n'y comprenaient plus rien, donc ça n'allait plus du tout. Ils ont cessé de travaillé aussi. 'Everything seemed to have gone bad. Nothing worked. What had been repaired one day, broke down the day afterwards. The engineers could not understand anything either, so this was bad. They stopped working, too.'

2) What type of reference does the following utterance exemplify? *Julie, c'est une vraie lumière!* 'Julia is a real light!'

3) What illocutionary act is achieved by the utterance: *Voulez-vous que je vous raccompagne, les enfants?* 'Would you like me to take you home, children?' How does this act compare to the illocutionary act conveyed in *Voulez-vous nettoyer votre chambre, les enfants?* 'Would you like to clean up your room, children?'

4) When a French speaker qualifies an excellent theatrical performance *Pas mal!* 'Not bad', he/she is using stylistic means to say less than what the situation would require. What is this 'way of speaking' called, and what Maxim(s) of Grice are specifically violated?

5) Think of at least two real-life situations in which the Code Model of communication provides a sufficient theoretical framework for the aims and goals of communication between two participants.

6) Does the Cooperative Principle apply to communication using sign language? Argue your point of view.

7) Analyze the following exchange using Grice's Cooperative Principle. In what way does S2's utterance represent a felicitous 'answer' to S1's question?

   S1 (to his wife) *Tu as vu mon portefeuille?* 'Have you seen my wallet?'
   S2: *Vide ta poche.* 'Empty your pocket.'

8) A cartoon in Trask's (1996) *Dictionary of Phonetics and Phonology* depicts a car on a road that is heading towards a stretch marked with numerous road signs. The first of these signs says: 'Caution: Meaningless road signs!' How is the Cooperative Principle of linguistic communication violated by this message?

9) How would you characterize the referent of the address pronoun *on* in the following two utterances? (Hint: Consider the English translation of these utterances.) *Allez, on y va, les enfants!* 'Let's go, guys!' *Allez, on (ne) se bat pas, les enfants!* 'Come on, stop fighting, guys.'

10) In some languages, speakers insert the adjective 'little/small' or add a diminutive suffix to nouns they use when they speak to someone whose social-professional position is higher than theirs. Brown and Levinson (1986:178) quote such examples as part of a negative politeness strategy called 'minimize the imposition'. Can you think of such examples in French? (Hint: think in terms of lexical choices.)

11) Explain what might be the reason why the 'polite' suggestion *Si on sortait ce soir?* 'Why don't we go out tonight?' is usually uttered with a final falling intonation.

12) Give an example of a question that is typically <u>not</u> uttered with rising intonation.

13) Imperatives have sometimes been qualified as 'statements with an attitude'. What might this mean in terms of the speech act that is chosen to utter the propositional meaning of the utterance?

14) Why do we say someone has 'passed away' when we mean the person has died? What is the equivalent of this expression in French, and what is the chance of finding equivalent expressions like this in other languages? Explain your answers.

15) According to Ducrot (1980:162), the discourse marker *eh bien!* could be analyzed as follows: « <u>Eh bien</u> *est un connecteur grâce auquel le locuteur introduit un énoncé Q dans une situation S [. . .] dans laquelle Q est présenté comme une suite inattendue [de la situation précédente]* ». '<u>Eh bien</u> is a discourse marker that allows the speaker to introduce an utterance Q in a situation S [. . .] in which Q is presented as an unexpected follow-up [to the previous situation].' Find an adjacency pair to illustrate this use of <u>eh bien</u>. (Hint: Would the marker <u>well</u> in English qualify?)

6   Historical perspectives

6.1   Preliminaries

To study the history of the French language, we must first revert to the questions we asked in the Introduction, concerning the definition of 'French'. Today we think we know what the French language is: the lexicon, morphology, syntax, and phonology of the 'educated native speaker', sometimes supplemented by the geographical designation 'Parisian'. That definition expresses a number of **presuppositions**: (1) the French language is the language of a particular social class in France; (2) some speakers are native and others are not, and the native speakers have special claims on authority; (3) speaking is more important than other language skills (hearing, writing, reading); (4) if 'Parisian' is included, that 'standard' French is indeed of geographical origin.

This definition of the French language has immediate implications for the linguistic analysis of the language. In this section we will consider how such a definition has developed and been supported by institutions of French government and society and how it influences the way the history of the French language has been approached. A history that accepts this definition looks for the changes of cultivated language from its origins, a triumphalist view of the current state of power within the French linguistic community. This approach excludes large amounts of data, and, particularly in the early stages of the language, when texts are few, leads one to view widely disparate texts as part of a single line of linguistic development. In this chapter we will present a broader view of that linguistic history, starting with the prehistory of **Gallo-Romance**.

In this section we will first look at Latin and the development of Gallo-Romance through the first texts that were written deliberately in the vernacular idiom. In a second section we will trace the full flowering of vernacular literature and then the retreat from the diversity of Old French through the sixteenth century. Finally, we will study the shaping of Modern French from the founding of the Académie Française in 1635 to the present.

6.2   Latin and the linguistic prehistory of French

French is a Romance language, which means that the phonology, morphology, syntax, and the majority of its vocabulary can be traced to a common Latin origin with other Romance languages, such as Spanish, Italian, Portuguese, and Romanian. The nature of the Latin taken to these provinces of the Roman Empire, and the languages that were previously used in those provinces, profoundly influenced the development of the Romance language spoken in each region.

A first and necessary distinction is between **Classical Latin** and **Vulgar Latin** (from *vulgus* 'the people', i.e. 'popular Latin'). Classical Latin is a literary language, used by authors such as Cicero and Virgil. Vulgar Latin is the language of the people, of which we get only rare glimpses in the literary record. Between the two lies the *sermo cotidianus*, the everyday speech of educated Romans. The sources for our knowledge of spoken and popular Latin include the *Cena Trimalchionis* ('Trimalchio's feast') by Petronius Arbiter, a literary work recounting a party given by a freed slave; the graffiti found on the walls of buildings in Pompeii, buried by the eruption of Mount Vesuvius in 79 CE; and a collection of corrections to students' errors, known as the *Appendix Probi* (third or fourth century CE). These sources are supplemented by the process of reconstruction, i.e. looking at what is present in the Romance languages and reconstructing what must have been used in spoken Latin, even if we can find no written attestations.

Another variant of Latin is known as Christian Latin or Ecclesiastical Latin. Because the language of the early Church was Greek, the translation of the Bible and the works of the Church fathers into Latin was an important part of the expansion of Christianity into the Western Empire. This act of translation involved the creation of many abstract nouns previously unknown in Classical Latin. The translations made Christian Latin more like Greek, but the target audience of the translations, generally poorer and less educated, led to the use of many features in common with Vulgar Latin, such as the increased use of prepositions instead of case endings. Christian Latin is therefore a combination of more **learned vocabulary** with less learned structures (Nunn 1963).

What ongoing sound changes in Vulgar Latin are pointed to by the following corrections offered by the *Appendix Probi*?

a) 'speculum' non 'speclum'; 'masculus' non 'masclus'; 'calida' non 'calda'.

b) 'pridem' non 'pride'; 'olim' non 'oli'; 'idem' non 'ide'.

c) 'hostia' non 'ostia'; 'adhuc' non 'aduc'.

6.2.1   Phonology from Latin to Early Old French

6.2.1.1   Vowels

The Latin of classical poetry had thirteen vowels, three of which were diphthongs. Each monophthong had a long form and a short form (/a/, /a:/, /e/, /e:/, /i/, /i:/, /o/, /o:/, /u/, /u:/); all diphthongs (/ae/, /au/, /oe/) were inherently long.

Some differences between spoken Latin and written Latin seem widespread across the Roman Empire, while others vary according to regions. In all the Empire the substitution of vowel quality for vowel length occurs. However, the quality chosen varies from region to region. In Gaul, as elsewhere in the western provinces, short /i/ and long /e:/ merge as the closed vowel /e/, while short /e/ becomes /ɛ/. Tombstones often show the mistaken *iacit* 'lies' for the correct *iacet*. Similarly, for back vowels, short /u/ and long /o:/ merge as the closed vowel /o/, while short /o/ becomes open /ɔ/. Vulgar Latin in western provinces therefore had seven vowels, /i/, /e/, /ɛ/, /a/, /ɔ/, /o/, and /u/. The diphthongs /ae/ and /oe/ reduced to /e/, but the diphthong /au/ was simplified only in parts of the Empire, including northern Gaul, but not southern Gaul.

Stress patterns were important in these vowel changes. Unstressed vowels often disappeared altogether, while stressed vowels, especially in open syllables, tended to diphthongize. The loss of unstressed vowels varies by region, with Western Romance languages (Spanish, Portuguese, Catalan, Occitan, and French) more likely to drop unstressed vowels, while Eastern Romance languages (Italian, Romanian) were more likely to keep them. For instance, in Latin *fraxinus* 'ash tree' the stressed syllable is the first syllable, and the second syllable is lost in French (*frêne*), but remains in Romanian (*frasin*) (Herman 2000:35). Stress accent led to the lengthening of stressed vowels, which ultimately resulted in diphthongization in northern Gallo-Romance. The intensification of that stress also led to the weakening, and ultimately the loss, of many unstressed vowels. Once again, this effect is particularly pronounced in northern Gaul, and is usually attributed to the density of the Germanic population.

By the time of the first deliberately vernacular texts, in the ninth century, all tonic, free vowels, except /i/ and /u/, diphthongized. The process began with the low-mid vowels /ɛ/ and /ɔ/, perhaps as early as the third century CE: *petrum* > *pierre* 'stone', *soror* > *sour* 'sister'. These changes are also evident in Spanish and Italian. Later diphthonigizations, of /a/, /e/, and /o/, are limited to northern France, taking place sometime after the sixth century and before the first written texts in the vernacular. In the *Cantilène de Sainte Eulalie* (ca. 880 CE), the oldest French poem to survive, Latin *caput* 'head', is represented as *chief*, presumably pronounced /tʃief/, and *caelum* 'heaven' as *ciel* /tsiel/; *bona* 'good' > /buona/. There is some variation according to region, once again attributed to the strength of the Germanic influence. In Lorraine and other north-eastern dialects, where Germanic presence was concentrated, tonic /e/ and /o/ in closed syllables diphthongized.

The record from the written texts that have survived is always more complicated than these general rules indicate. Furthermore, the written texts must be approached with great caution. The assumption that the written form is a phonetic transcription of how words were pronounced at a given time is foolhardy. The first people to write in the vernacular were strongly influenced by the written Latin norms they had learned (see **learned vocabulary** in section 6.2), as in the use of *anima* 'soul' in *Sainte Eulalie*. Surely the unstressed /i/ is there as a reflection of the writer's or the copyist's knowledge of Latin, rather than as a sign of real pronunciation: the loss of unstressed post-tonic vowels would indicate a pronunciation more like /anmə/. Secondly, we cannot distinguish the language of the author from the language of the copyist. The original writing and the copy might be separated by several centuries, and vast distances. When we look at the examples of vowels and of diphthongs in a given text, we need to be cautious about interpreting actual pronunciation. Our best evidence comes from the study of assonance and rhyming in poetic texts, but even this tells us only that two spellings were pronounced alike, and does not provide us with the phonetic value of those spellings. In the *Cantilène de Sainte Eulalie* vowels and diphthongs are represented as shown in Table 6.1 (probable pronunciation has been inserted when possible, but still must be taken with a grain of salt):

While the intensification of stress led to the loss of some vowels, one vowel was added in Vulgar Latin, which was the **prosthetic vowel** /i/, added before the combination *s* + consonant at the beginning of a word. This affected not only Latin words, such as *scola* 'school', French *école*, but also words borrowed from Germanic, such as *spatha* 'sword', French *épée*. However, the change is not universal, as *Sainte Eulalie* has *spede*, not **espede*, for this word.

What are the differences between the set of vowels and diphthongs in the *Cantilène de Sainte Eulalie* and those of northern Metropolitan French?

6.2.1.2 Consonants

Latin had stops, fricatives, semivowels, liquids and the aspirate /h/, which can be grouped as follows:
– voiced stops: b d g
– voiceless stops: p t k
– fricatives: f s
– nasals: m n
– liquids: l r
– semivowels: w j
– aspirate: h

Table 6.1 *Spelling and pronunciation of vowels in Early Old French based on examples from the* Cantilène de Sainte Eulalie *(ca. 880 CE, cited in Berger and Brasseur 2004: 408–131)*

Letter	Sound	Gallo-Romance		Latin	
a	/a/	*argent*	<	*argentum*	'money'
e	/ɛ/	*bel*	<	*bellum*	'handsome', 'pretty'
	/e/	*honestet*	<	*honestatem*	'honesty'
	/ə/	*adunet*	<	*adunat*	'he states'
i	/i/	*servir*	<	*servire*	'to serve'
o	/o/	*honestet*	<	*honestatem*	'honesty'
	/ɔ/	*mort*	<	*mortem*	'dead'
u	/u/ or /y/*	*figure*	<	*figura*	'form, shape'
ai	/ai/	*faire*	<	*facere*	'to do'
au	/au/	*diaule*	<	*diabolum*	'devil'
ei	/ei/	*veintre*	<	*vincere*	'to conquer', 'to vainquish'
eu	/eu/	*seule*	<	*saeculum*	'century', 'earthly life'
ou	/ou/	*soure*	<	*supra*	'on'
		fou	<	*focum*	'fire'
ie	/ie/	*pagiens*	<	*paganus*	'pagan'
ui	/ui/	*tuit*	<	*totum*	'all'
uo	/uo/	*suon*	<	*suum*	'his'

*whether /u/ had palatalized to /y/ by the ninth century has been a matter of some debate

In spelling, the consonant /k/ was represented by the letter 'c', the semivowel /w/ by the letter 'v', and the semivowel /j/ by the letter 'i'. The letter 'x' represented the combination /ks/. The major changes that take place among the consonants between Latin and Early Old French are:

1) the loss of /h/, later to return with Germanic words, and the loss of final /m/
2) the transformation, under certain circumstances, of the semivowels /j/ and /w/ to the fricatives /zh/ and /β/, respectively
3) the palatalization of stops to produce the affricates /tʃ/ and /dʒ/, /ts/ and /dz/
4) the fricativization and then the disappearance of intervocalic stops, under certain circumstances
5) the simplification of consonant clusters.

Three consonant changes in Vulgar Latin occurred throughout the Empire: the loss of initial /h/, the transformation of the intervocalic semivowel /w/ to the bilabial fricative /β/, and the loss of final /m/. Other consonant changes are more geographically limited. Final 's' was lost in most of Italy and in Romania, but probably after the fall of the Roman Empire; in French it remained until the end of the Old French period, and is still pronounced in some liaison forms, e.g. *vas-y* 'go ahead', 'go there'. Final 't' was more frequently omitted, but remains in the oldest French texts, and in the liaison forms of some French verbs to the present day, as in *vient-il* 'is he coming?', *dit-elle* 'she says', 'she said'.

Palatalization of /k/, /g/, /t/, and /d/ before the semivowel /j/ was general throughout the empire, except in Sardinia and Dalmatia, and dates to the second or third century CE. The combination of /kj/ + vowel became /tj/, then /ts/, and sometimes simply /s/. In an inscription we find the spelling 'consiensia' for *conscientia* /konskientia/ 'conscience', indicating the changes in both the /kj/ and the /tj/ combinations (Herman 2000:43). The sound sequences /gj/ and /dj/ in Gallo-Romance, along with initial /j/, become the affricate /dʒ/ before simplifying to the voiced fricative /ʒ/: e.g. *diurnum* 'day' > French *jour*; *ianuarius* 'January' > French *janvier*. The palatalization of /g/ and /k/ before /a/ was limited to northern Gallo-Romance, and is therefore a later development, perhaps mid-sixth century (Bourciez and Bourciez 1978:134): e.g. *gamba* 'leg' > French *jambe*; *caballus* 'horse' > French *cheval*. This change must have been completed before the complete reduction of the diphthong /au/ to /o/, because 'k' in *causa* 'thing', 'matter' > French *chose* would not have palatalized to /ʃ/ before /o/. This last palatalization did not take place in other parts of the northern Gallo-Romance dialect areas, such as for instance in Normandy and Picardy.

Other phonological differences between Classical and Vulgar Latin that presage the way French developed are the weakening of intervocalic consonants, the simplification of consonant clusters, and the reduction of double consonants (geminates). Intervocalic consonants tended to change in the following sequence: voiceless consonant > voiced consonant > voiced fricative > loss. For instance, the Latin word *mutare* 'to change' became *mudare*, then **muθer*, before ending up as *muer* 'to moult' in Modern French.

Consonant clusters usually assimilated to the second consonant in a group of two, while the middle consonant was generally lost in groups of three. The consonant cluster /ns/ was the first to be simplified, throughout the Empire, to /s/: e.g. *mensis* 'month', French *mois*. Similarly, double consonants were simplified in all regions, a fact already attested in Christian inscriptions in northern Italy from the late Empire, and completed in French by the tenth century. The cluster /kt/ had different outcomes in different regions, indicating a later change. (NB: An earlier change would have similar outcomes throughout the Empire.) In Gaul /k/ palatalized to /j/, eventually forming a diphthong with the preceding vowel: *factum*, 'done' (past participle) > French *fait*. The combination of consonant and semivowel /kw/ simplified to simple /k/: e.g. *quando* /kwando/, 'when' > French *quand* /kã/.

Using *La Cantilène de Sainte Eulalie* as an example, Table 6.2 shows graphic representations of consonants found by Early Old French (based on Berger and Brasseur 2004:108–131). Note that the value of 'g' in *regiel* 'royal' and *pagiens* 'pagan' is not clear, as other texts from the same period omit the 'g' in these intervocalic contexts (as we would expect from the changes affecting

Table 6.2 *Spelling and pronunciation of consonants in Early Old French based on examples from the* Cantilène de Sainte Eulalie *(ca. 880 CE, cited in Berger and Brasseur 2004:108–131)*

Letter	Sound	Vulgar Latin		Old French	Modern French	
b	/b/	bellum	>	bel	bel(le)	'handsome', 'pretty'
c	/ts/ /tʃ/	caelum	>	ciel	ciel	'heaven'
c	/k/	columbum	>	colomb	colombe	'dove'
ch	/tʃ/	caput	>	chief	chef	'head'
ch	/k/	Christus	>	Christ	Christ	'Christ'
cz	/ts/ /tʃ/	ecce hoc	>	czo	ce(ci)	'that'
d	/d/	diabolus	>	diaule	diable	'devil'
d	/th/	presentata	>	presentede	présentée	'presented'
f	/f/	focum	>	fou	feu	'fire'
g	/g/	grandem	>	grand	grand	'tall', 'large'
g	/dʒ/	virginitatem	>	virginit	virginité	'virginity'
gn	/gn/ or /n/	dignat	>	degnet	deigne	'deigns'(3rd subj.pr.)
k	/k/	auscultat	>	eskoltet	écoute	'listens'
l	/l/	bellum	>	bel	bel(le)	'handsome', 'pretty';
m	/m/	malos	>	mals	mal	'evil', 'bad'
n	/n/	numquam	>	nonque	jamais	'never'
p	/p/	paganus	>	pagiens	païen	'pagan'
q	/k/	numquam	>	nonque	jamais	'never'
r	/r/	regalem	>	regiel	royal	'royal'
s	/s/	suum	>	suon	sien	'her'
s	/z/	presentata	>	presentede	présentée	'presented'
t	/t/	totti	>	tuit	tout(e)	'all'
v	/v/	virginitatem	>	virginit	virginité	'virginity'
x	/ks/	rex	>	rex	roi	'king'
z	/dz/	*bellatiorem	>	bellezour	plus bel(le)	'more beautiful'
z	/ts/	intus	>	enz	en	'into'

intervocalic consonants (see above)). The same situation prevails for 'gn', which other Latin and vernacular texts from northern France omit in similar contexts. As for the vocalisation of /l/, Latin texts from northern France were already showing it before a consonant, as in the example *eskoltet* 'listens' > Modern French *écoute* in Table 6.2, but in *Sainte Eulalie* the spelling does not reflect such a change. The letter 'q', as in *numquam* 'never' > Old French *nonque*, always appears in combination with 'u', representing the Latin sound sequence /kw/, but it had probably already reduced to /k/ by the time of the first texts of Old French. And as a final remark, the exact dating of the voicing of the intervocalic /s/ is not certain, but is clearly shown in spellings from the tenth century, such as in the word *Elizabeth* (Berger and Brasseur 2004:125).

> What are the differences between the Old French (shown in Table 6.2) and
> northern Metropolitan French consonantal inventories?

6.2.1.3 Accentuation

The length of the vowel determined the accentuation in longer words. Generally
speaking, the accent fell on the next to last syllable (the penult) if that vowel
was long, or on the **antepenultimate** (second from the last syllable) if the vowel
of the **penultimate** was short. The penult is said to be long 'by position' if it
occurs in a closed syllable. For example, the *a* of *civitatem* 'city' is pronounced
as a long vowel (/a:/), so the accent falls on the penult. The second *i* of the
word *civitas* 'city' is pronounced as a short vowel, so the accent falls on the
antepenult *ci* rather than on the penult *vi*: *cívitas, civitátem*. A word in which
the accent falls on the final syllable is called an **oxytone**; one in which the
accent falls on the next to last syllable is a **paroxytone**; and a word in which
the accent falls on the antepenult is a **proparoxytone**. Accentuation is important
because vowel quality changes differently, according to whether the vowel is
in a stressed or unstressed, open or closed syllable.

Generally speaking the stressed syllable in Classical Latin was also the
stressed syllable in Vulgar Latin and continues to be the stressed syllable in
the modern Romance languages. There are some exceptions to this rule, such
as Classical Latin proparoxytones, in which the next-to-last syllable is followed
by the cluster consonant + *r*. In these words, the accent seems to have shifted
to the penult. For instance, *íntegrum* 'whole, entire' in Classical Latin, became
intégrum in Vulgar Latin (Modern French *entier*).

6.2.2 Morphology and syntax from Latin to Early Old French

6.2.2.1 The morphology of nouns

Nouns, adjectives, and pronouns in Latin have distinctive forms according to
their **case** (see sections 3.2.2 and 3.6.3). Case in Latin is expressed by **inflection**,
typically by adding certain 'endings' to words, much as we express possession
in English by adding *s*. Table 6.3 provides the most common cases of Latin and
the functions they represent. Words that express these functions with the same
endings are said to belong to the same **declension**. Latin has five declensions,
illustrated in Table 6.4, singular and plural.

We can see in these declensions the distinctive nature of vowel length, which
is the only difference between the nominative and the ablative singular in the
first declension, or between the nominative and **genitive** singular in the fourth
declension. There are many forms that are identical, such as the genitive singular, dative singular, and the **nominative** plural in the first declension. In neuter

Table 6.3 *The most common cases of Classical Latin and their grammatical functions*

Case	Primary Function	Examples
Nominative	Subject or predicate nominative	*Petrus natat.* 'Peter swims.' *Petrus poeta est.* 'Peter is a poet.'
Genitive	Possession	*Liber Petri* 'Peter's book'
Dative	Indirect Object	*Marcus librum Petro dedit.* 'Mark gave the book to Peter.'
Accusative	Direct Object	*Lucia Petrum amat.* 'Lucy loves Peter.'
Ablative	Object of a preposition	*Lucia cum Petro egreditur.* 'Lucy left with Peter.'

nouns, the nominative and the accusative case endings are always the same. In all declensions the dative and ablative plural are identical. The loss of word-final /m/, mentioned in the *Appendix Probi*, and the blurring of unstressed vowels wreaked havoc on the declensional system.

In the noun declensions listed in Table 6.4, if the distinction of quantity is lost, as well as word-final /m/, the cases of the first declension are no longer clear. The singular in Vulgar Latin had *rosa* 'rose' for three formerly distinct forms (nominative, accusative, and ablative). The confusion of long /o:/ and short /u/, as well as the loss of final /m/, led to similar confusion in the second declension, where the singular forms for the dative, ablative, and accusative now were identical. In the fourth declension, four of the five cases now had the same ending.

The changes in the ending had important implications for syntax. The lack of differentiation between case forms led to increased use of syntactic means to distinguish the function of a noun in the sentence. In Classical Latin, grammatical function and some aspects of meaning, such as tense and voice, are expressed by synthetic forms through inflection. In Vulgar Latin, these functions and meanings are increasingly expressed by analytic forms, through syntax or paraphrase.

With the demise of distinctive case forms, word order and prepositions became the primary indicators of the function of a noun in the sentence. In Classical Latin most prepositions were followed by the ablative, with some exceptions in which the accusative was used. In Vulgar Latin, the accusative became the dominant form following all prepositions. The use of analytic forms and structures further detracted from the importance of endings as indicators of syntactic function, leading to frequent confusion of usage even among forms that remained distinct, such as the use of the dative for the genitive, and the

Table 6.4 *The five declensions in the singular and plural of Classical Latin*

	First declension Mostly feminine (*rosa* 'rose')	Second declension Masculine (*dominus* 'master')	Second declension Neuter (*templum* 'temple')	Third declension Masculine (*dux* 'leader')	Third declension Neuter (*nomen* 'name')	Fourth declension All genders (*manus* 'hand')	Fifth declension Feminine (*res* 'thing')
SINGULAR							
Nominative	*rosă*	*dominus*	*templum*	*dux*	*nomen*	*manŭs*	*res*
Genitive	*rosae*	*domini*	*templi*	*ducis*	*nominis*	*manūs*	*rei*
Dative	*rosae*	*domino*	*templo*	*duci*	*nomini*	*manui*	*rei*
Accusative	*rosam*	*dominum*	*templum*	*ducem*	*nomen*	*manum*	*rem*
Ablative	*rosā*	*domino*	*templo*	*duce*	*nomine*	*manu*	*re*
PLURAL							
Nominative	*rosae*	*domini*	*templa*	*duces*	*nomina*	*manūs*	*res*
Genitive	*rosarum*	*dominorum*	*templorum*	*ducum*	*nominum*	*manuum*	*rerum*
Dative	*rosis*	*dominis*	*templis*	*ducibus*	*nominibus*	*manibus*	*rebus*
Accusative	*rosas*	*dominos*	*templa*	*duces*	*nomina*	*manūs*	*res*
Ablative	*rosis*	*dominis*	*templis*	*ducibus*	*nominibus*	*manibus*	*rebus*

Table 6.5 *The reduction of the Latin declension system in Old French*

Cases	Singular		Plural	
	Feminine	Masculine	Feminine	Masculine
Nominative	*rose < rosa* 'rose'	*murs < murus* 'wall'	*rose < rosae*	*mur < muri*
Accusative (Oblique)	*rose < rosam*	*mur < murum*	*roses < rosas*	*murs < muros*

accusative for the nominative. As a result of these changes, in Modern French the grammatical function of nouns in sentences is expressed by word order and the use of prepositions:

Nominative: *Paul joue au tennis* 'Paul plays tennis' (word order)

Genitive: *Le livre de Paul* 'Paul's book' (preposition)

Dative: *Agnès a envoyé une lettre à Paul* 'Agnes sent a letter to Paul' (preposition)

Accusative: *Agnès voit Paul* 'Agnes sees Paul' (word order)

Ablative: *Agnès est allée au marché avec Paul* 'Agnes went to the market with Paul' (preposition)

Thus historical changes demonstrate the connection between phonological issues (the distinctions made between certain sounds), morphological issues (the use of inflectional endings to express the function of the noun), and syntactic issues (the use of word order and prepositions to express function).

By the time of the first vernacular texts of northern France, in the ninth century, the case system had been reduced to two cases: nominative/vocative and the so-called **oblique**. The oblique case combined all the functions of the genitive, dative, accusative, and ablative cases. The form was that of the accusative. Thus in the *Serments de Strasbourg* the author/copyist contrasts the nominative *Karlos* with the oblique *Karlon* 'Charles'. The most common feminine declension, based on the first declension (*rosa* 'rose' in Table 6.5) made case distinctions only in the plural, and number distinctions only in the oblique case. The most common masculine declension, based on second declension Latin nouns (*murus* 'in Table 6.5), made case distinctions in both singular and plural.

In addition to the loss of morphological case distinctions between Classical Latin and popular Latin, regularization of the declensional patterns moved nouns from one category to another. Neuter nouns were generally reinterpreted primarily as masculines. The nouns of the fourth and fifth declension moved to the first and second, as did many of the third declension, the most irregular declension of all. For instance, the fourth-declension noun *cornu* 'horn' appears in some texts from the Classical period reinterpreted as a second-declension

Table 6.6 *Irregular forms of adjectives in Classical Latin and Modern French*

Latin	French	
bonus	*bon*	'good'
melior	*meilleur*	'better'
optimus	*le meilleur*	'best'
malus	*mauvais*	'bad'
peior	*pire*	'worse'
pessimus	*le pire*	'worst'
magnus	*grand*	'big'
maior	*plus grand*	'bigger'
maximus	*le plus grand*	'biggest'
parvus	*petit*	'small'
minor	*plus petit/moindre*	'smaller'
minimus	*le plus petit/le moindre*	'smallest'

noun: *cornus*, and the fifth-declension *rabies* 'ferocity', 'madness', as a first-declension *rabia*, which would become in French *rage* 'rabies', 'frenzy'.

Another type of simplification of the system changed **imparisyllabic** declensions of nouns to **parisyllabic** declensions, usually by changing the nominative case form. In imparisyllabic declensions, the nominative singular has fewer syllables than the other forms, for example: *civitas* 'city' (nominative, three syllables) and *civitatis* (genitive, four syllables). In this case a new nominative form, **civitatis* was formed, as we guess from the reconstruction of the origins of the Old French form *citéz*. On rare occasions, the oblique forms were shortened to match the nominative, as *sanguis* 'blood' (nominative, two syllables) and *sanguinem* (accusative, three syllables) was simplified to *sanguis, sanguem* (Zink 1992:25).

6.2.2.2 *The morphology of adjectives*
Latin adjectives fell generally into two groups. In the first, the feminine forms followed the pattern of the first-declension nouns, while the masculine and neuter followed the pattern of the second-declension nouns. In the second group, the forms followed third-declension patterns. Latin adjectives formed their comparative ('stronger') and superlative ('strongest') forms synthetically, i.e. by using an ending: *fortis* 'strong', *fortior* 'stronger', *fortissimus* 'strongest'. As in French and English there were a few irregular forms (see Table 6.6).

In the Romance languages, analytic forms generally replaced the synthetic comparatives and superlatives. The combination of *magis* (Spanish *mas*) or *plus* (French) and the adjective, sometimes redundantly with the comparative form, e.g. *plus fortior* 'more stronger', grew in popularity, except in a few words, such as *pire* 'worse' from Latin *peiorem* and *meilleur* 'better' from Latin *meliorem*. The movement from synthetic forms to analytic forms also occurs in the formation of some verb tenses, as we shall see below.

As was the case for nouns, adjectives changed declensions to simplify the system. For instance, the *Appendix Probi* notes the correction: *tristis non tristus* 'sad', showing that some are replacing the third-declension adjective forms by the second-declension adjective forms.

How are comparatives of adjectives formed in Modern French and Modern English? Give a few examples, and compare with the historical situation in Old French.

6.2.2.3   *Personal, demonstrative, and relative pronouns*

Latin personal pronouns were rarely used in the nominative case, as the subject was usually expressed adequately by the ending of the verb (see below). Furthermore, possession, expressed by the genitive case, would more frequently be expressed by the use of possessive adjectives, the equivalent of English *my* (French *mon, ma, mes*), *your* (French *ton, ta, tes; votre, vos*), *her/his/its* (French *son, sa, ses*), *our* (French *notre, nos*) and *their* (French *leur, leurs*). The possessive of the third person distinguished between a reflexive possessive (*suus, sua, suum*) and a non-reflexive, expressed by the use of the genitive form of the pronoun, typically *eius*. The reflexive/non-reflexive distinction is also present in other forms of the personal pronouns. Thus Latin distinguishes: *se videt* 'he sees himself' from *eum videt* 'he sees him' (someone else) and *Petrus suum librum leget* 'Peter is reading his own book' from *Petruus librum eius leget* 'Peter is reading his book' (someone else's).

The third-person pronouns include the most neutral forms *is* (m.), *ea* (f.) and *id* (n.), as well as three demonstrative pronouns (*hic, haec, hoc; iste, ista, istud; ille, illa, illud*), and two pronouns that express identity (*ipse, ipsa, ipsum* and *idem, eadem, idem*). The demonstratives express three different degrees of distance that correspond roughly to the three persons of the verb. *Hic* relates to objects near the speaker, and thus equates to 'this one here'; *ipse* designates something close to those spoken to, equivalent to the second person, equating roughly to 'that one there near you'; and *ille* points to something further away, translating as the now archaic English form 'that one over yonder'. The demonstrative *ille* would become the third-person pronoun of French and also the definite article, while combinations of the presentative *ecce* 'here is, here are' and the forms *iste* and *ille* would remain, albeit much altered, as the demonstrative forms.

Relative pronouns which link one full clause to another (French *qui, que* 'that', 'who') in Latin are distinguished from the interrogative pronouns in only three forms. The nominative singular forms are *qui, quae*, and *quod* when the pronoun is relative, and *quis, quis*, and *quid* when the pronoun is interrogative. The accusative singular feminine and neuter forms are *quam* and *quod* when the pronoun is relative and *quem* and *quid* when it is interrogative. Thus the relative pronoun, like the third-person pronouns, agreed with its **antecedent** in number (singular or plural), gender (masculine, feminine, or neuter), and case (nominative, genitive, etc.).

What are the agreements required between relative pronouns and their antecedents in Modern French?

6.2.2.4   *The morphology of verbs*

Classical Latin had a rich verbal morphology. Generally speaking, the six persons of the verb are all reflected by the endings of the verb, as illustrated in Table 6.7. It had six distinct oral and written verb forms in the present tense, while Modern French has five distinct written forms, but only three that are pronounced differently. English has only two distinct verb forms, both in writing and in speaking (*call* and *calls*). The loss of distinctive personal verb endings in French has been accompanied by the increased use of personal pronouns (*je, tu, il*, etc.).

The formation of tenses, **moods** and voices in Classical Latin was also accomplished almost entirely by endings. Tenses which in French require a combination of an **auxiliary verb** plus the past participle (*passé composé*: *j'ai dit* 'I said'; *plus-que-parfait*: *j'avais dit* 'I had said'; and the *futur anterieur*: *j'aurai dit* 'I will have said') were all expressed by endings: respectively *dixit, dixeram, dixero*. The transition from the synthetic manner of expressing tense and aspect to the analytic one begins in Vulgar Latin. The combination of an auxiliary verb ('to be' or 'to have') and the past participle might originally have retained the possessive meaning of 'to have', so that *epistolas scriptas habeo* might have meant 'I have written some letters' or 'I have letters that were written' (Classical Latin: *epistolas scripsi*). However, examples from Late Latin seem to leave no doubt that the combination of *habere* 'to have' and the past participle is being considered a single past tense verb form: *episcopum invitatum habes* 'you have invited the bishop' (from Gregory of Tours' *Historia Francorum*, cited in Herman 2000:78).

The movement from possessive to past tense has recently been called into question. Jacob (1998) notes that a non-possessive reading is possible for almost all the common examples of *habeo* + past participle in Classical Latin, and

Table 6.7 *Oral and written verb forms in Classical Latin and Modern French*

	Latin	Modern French		
First-person singular:	*appello*	*appelle*	[apɛl]	'I call'
Second-person singular:	*appellas*	*appelles*	[apɛl]	'you call'
Third-person singular:	*appellat*	*appelle*	[apɛl]	'he/she calls'
First-person plural:	*appellamus*	*appelons*	[aplõ]	'we call'
Second-person plural:	*appellatis*	*appelez*	[aple]	'you call'
Third-person plural:	*appellant*	*appellent*	[apɛl]	'they call'

claims that the first meaning of this construction would be 'to keep something in a particular state'. The subject is not the possessor of the direct object, but rather the one who caused the object to arrive at that state, as in (1). Jacob calls this construction the *copule causative et durative* 'the causative and durative copula', and suggests that such a transition would have occurred most naturally in the legal and religious context, and would express an obligation on the part of the subject, as in (2). In this way *habeo* + past participle is parallel to the construction of the new future (*habeo* + infinitive), the first expressing an obligation proceeding from a completed action, the second an obligation to fulfill an action.

(1)   *Quoius ante aedificium semita in loco erit, is eam semitam lapidibus perpetueis integreis continentem constratam recte habeto.*
    'The person who owns a building with a path alongside is responsible for keeping this adjacent path paved with whole stones over the entire length of the building.' (*Lex Iulia Municipalis*, 53s cited in Jacob 1998:372; text dated from the first century BCE)

(2)   *rogo te, habe me excusatum* 'please excuse me', 'consider me excused' (*Gospel according to Luke* 14: 18, in Jerome's translation (*The Vulgate*), fourth century CE, cited in Jacob 1998:375)

Let us now turn our attention to that periphrase for the future. The future tense in Classical Latin was expressed by the use of endings, either the infix *b* (*do* 'I give', *dabo* 'I shall give'), or by a change of vowels (*agit* 'I act', *aget* 'I will act'). The weakening and ultimate loss of intervocalic /b/, and the lack of distinction between short /i/ and /e/ compromised the distinctiveness of these forms. As a result paraphrases already possible in Classical Latin became more common. Speakers might have used a **modal verb**, such as *volo* 'I want' or *debeo* 'I must' and the infinitive to express a future action: *volo ire* 'I want to go, I will go'; *debeo ire* 'I must go', 'I will go'. Or they might have used the future participle and the verb 'to be': *facturus sum* 'I am about to do',

'I will do'. The combination of the infinitive and the verb 'to have' was initially limited to verbs expressing communication: *quaerere habes* 'you have to (you will) ask', *scribere habeo* 'I have to write', 'I shall write'. Even before the first texts in the Romance languages, the forms of 'to have' seem to have joined the infinitive to form a new inflection for the future. In a seventh-century history of the Franks we find the form *daras* 'you will give' from the combination of the infinitive *dare* 'to give' and the form *habes* 'you have'.

Finally, the Latin passive forms were a mixture of synthetic and analytic forms. In the perfective tenses – perfect, pluperfect, future perfect – Latin used an analytic form similar to English, composed of the verb 'to be' and the past participle: *carmen cantatum est* 'the song was sung'. In other tenses a synthetic form ending in /r/ was used: *carmen cantatur* 'the song is being sung', *carmen cantabatur* 'the song was being sung'. In Vulgar Latin the change to a purely analytic form is hard to pinpoint, as it requires determining at what point *cantatum est* changed its meaning from 'was sung' to 'is being sung'. The changes in meaning are often ambiguous. What is certain is that none of the Romance languages maintained the synthetic passive, which indicates that the transition in the spoken language probably took place before the break-up of the Empire in the fifth century.

Give examples of synthetic and analytic verb forms in Modern English. How do these examples compare to examples of such verb forms in Modern French?

6.2.2.5 *Syntax and word order*

Latin has the same types of agreement between syntactic constituents that we find in Modern French. The verb must agree with the subject in number and person. The adjective must agree with the noun it modifies in number, gender, and case. The pronoun must agree with its antecedent in number, gender, and case. Because of Latin's rich morphology, these agreements generally made it possible to understand which elements went with which others, and therefore the order of words was less important than it is in the modern Romance languages. In Classical Latin two words that agree with each other are frequently separated, as in example (3) where the possessive *mearum* 'my' is separated from the head noun *sororum* 'sister' that it modifies.

(3)   *heus, inquit, iuvenes monstrate, <u>mearum</u> vidistis et quam hic errantem forte <u>sororum</u>*
      'hey', she asked, 'young men, if you have seen one of <u>my sisters</u> wandering about here, point me in the right direction' (Virgil *Aeneid* I, 321–322).

Among the features that distinguish French from its Latin origin are the near obligatory use of a determiner in French, and the relatively fixed order of the constituents of the noun phrase. Classical Latin had no articles, so many noun phrases had no determiner. When there were determiners (demonstratives, possessives, etc.) or modifiers (adjectives), the noun, adjective, and the optional determiner could occur in any sequence. In Vulgar Latin the tendency was for increased use of determiners, though they were still far from obligatory, and for the contiguous placement of the constituents of the noun phrase.

The noun was separated from these other parts of the noun phrase in roughly twenty to thirty percent of the noun phrases of Classical Latin, with much variation from one author to another (Herman 2000:82). In Vulgar Latin, the elements were almost always contiguous, but the order of the elements was not set. The one exception is the relatively fixed order of genitive (possessive) phrases. These almost always follow the noun possessed, as in *partem* (acc.) *praedae* (gen.) 'a part of the booty' (cited in Herman 2000:83). Relative clauses also follow the noun modified in Vulgar Latin (Harris and Vincent 1988:55).

The demonstratives *ille* 'that' and *ipse* 'the same' were used with greater frequency in Vulgar Latin, but still had real anaphoric function, referring back to a noun just mentioned, and therefore they had not yet become standard parts of the noun phrase. In some instances these demonstratives were combined with the interjection *ecce* 'look!'. The melding of these two forms would give rise to the French demonstratives, both pronouns (*celui, celle*, etc.) and determiners (*cet, cette*, etc.).

Although sentential structure was relatively free in Classical Latin, it was not without patterns. Typically, for instance in eighty-five percent of cases in Julius Caesar's prose (Marchello-Nizia 1999:37), the verb appears last in the sentence, following a Subject-Object-Verb (SOV) sentence structure (4), but there are many exceptions, as shown in (5):

(4)   *Hi omnes* [Subject] *lingua, institutis, legibus inter se* [Object]
        differunt [Verb]
        'All of these differ from each other in language, traditions, and law.'
        (*Caesar's Gallic Wars*, I, 1)

(5)   *Apud Helvetios* [Prep. Phrase] *longe* [Adverb] *nobilissimus*
        [Adjective] *fuit* [Verb] *et ditissimus* [Adjective] *Orgetorix* [Subject]
        'Among the Helvetians, Orgetorix was by far the most noble and the
        wealthiest.' (*Caesar's Gallic Wars*, I, 2)

In Vulgar Latin we find more and more often the typical Romance word order SVO. The increased use of this word order can be seen as part of a more general trend towards analytic structure, and part of a typological shift: languages following the head-modifier order will have the order complement

– preposition, verb – object, verb – adverb, auxiliary – verb, all of which are common in the Romance languages. In the earliest Old French texts, both SOV and SVO are found. [S]OV dominates in nine out of ten cases in the *Serments de Strasbourg* (6), with the exception of some cases shown for instance in (7). In the *Cantilène de Sainte Eulalie* the word order is most often SVO (8), but there are exceptions, including both SOV (9) and OVS (10).

(6)   *Ab Ludher* [Prep. Phrase] *nul plaid* [Object] *nunquam* [Adverb]
       prindrai [Verb]
       'I shall never enter into an agreement with Luther.' [Lothair]

(7)   *salvarai* [Verb] *eo cist meon fradre Karlo* [Object]
       'I will help my brother Charles.'

(8)   *Elle* [Subject] *nont eskoltet* [Verb] *les mals conselliers* [Object]
       'She does not listen to the evil counselors.'

(9)   *Elle* [Subject] *colpes* [Object] *non auret* [Verb]
       'She did not have any sins.'

(10)   *A czo* [Ind. Object] *nos* [Dir. Object] *voldret concreidre* [Verb] *li rex
       pagiens* [Subject]
       'This the pagan king did not want to admit.'

COMPOUND SENTENCES in Latin were typically formed by an infinitival construction, in which the subject of the infinitive is in the accusative case, as in (11). Even in early samples of spoken Latin, such as the plays of Plautus (ca. 254 – ca. 184 BCE), a different construction, typical of the Romance languages, appears, albeit rarely. This is the use of a conjunction, most often *quod*, followed by a clause with a finite verb as in (12).

This construction was still relatively uncommon in the written texts of the third and fourth centuries CE, but became more common as the Empire waned, particularly in Christian texts, and especially after verbs expressing communication ('to say', 'to write') and verbs expressing sensory experience ('to feel', 'to hear') (Herman 1989, 2000:88–89). Where the Accusative + Infinitive construction accounted for more than ninety percent of the examples in earlier texts, even those considered representative of Vulgar Latin, in the Christian authors of the fifth century *quod/quia* + finite verb accounts for sixty to seventy percent of the examples, when the structure follows the verb. The use of the Accusative + Infinitive construction was potentially ambiguous, particularly if there was a direct object of the infinitive, and therefore two nouns in the accusative case, and it could be difficult to distinguish which one was the subject of the verb in the infinitive, and which one was the object (11). Such ambiguities were resolved by the use of the *quod* + finite verb construction (12).

(11)   *filiam suam* [acc.] *cecinisse* [infinitive] *dixit*
       'He said that his daughter sang.'

(12)   *dixit quod filia sua cecinit*
       'He said that his daughter sang.'

In the earliest Old French texts, the use of *que* + finite verb are more common than infinitival constructions, which remain in only a few restricted structures, such as the *faire causatif*. There are no constructions of either type in the *Serments de Strasbourg*, but in the *Cantilène de Sainte Eulalie* we find both the *que* + finite verb construction (13) (14), and the causative construction (15). Both structures survive in Modern French.

(13)   *Il li enortet . . . qued elle fuiet lo nom christiien*
       'He exhorts her to give up the name of Christian.'

(14)   *Tuit oram que por nos degnet preier qued auuisset de nos Christus mercit*
       'Let us all pray that she will deign to pray for us, so that Christ will have mercy on us.'

(15)   *Voldrent la faire diaule servir.*
       'They want to make her serve the devil.'

Quod came to be used in a number of other structures as well, such as comparatives (replacing Classical Latin *quam*), or expressing cause (replacing Classical Latin *quia* or *quoniam*). Combinations of prepositions, pronouns, adjectives, or adverbs plus *quod* further enriched the possibilities for subordinating conjunctions, such as *pro* [prep.] *eo* [pro.] *quod* 'for the reason that, because', *post* [prep.] *quod* 'after', *mox* [adv.] *quod* 'as soon as'.

NEGATION in Latin was expressed primarily by a single element, *non*, but other options existed. Negative pronouns (*nullus* 'no one', *nihil* 'nothing') and adverbs (*numquam* 'never') could also convey a sentential negative meaning: e.g. *non te vidi* 'I did not see you', *nullus te vidit* 'no one saw you', *nihil vidi* 'I saw nothing', *eam nunquam vidi* 'I never saw her.' *Ne* was used to introduce negative imperatives and subordinate clauses expressing indirect commands or purpose (16):

(16)   *Cur non mitto meos tibi, Pontiliane, libellos? Ne mihi tu mittas, Pontiliane, tuos.* (Martial, 7.3)
       'Why do I not send you my books, Pontilianus? So that you, Pontilianus, won't send me yours.'

In spoken Latin, from the earliest texts, *non* frequently replaces *ne*. The single negative particle is frequently reinforced, either by another negative (*nullus, nihil*, etc.) or by a word expressing something of little value, such as *neque . . . gutta* 'not a drop' (in Plautus, cited by Väänänen 1981.152). The addition of this second element, after the verb, can be placed within the context of the typological differences between Classical and Vulgar Latin. The preference for the head-modifier word order, consistent with other changes such as the placement of constituents of the noun phrase and the structure of prepositional phrases, predicts that adverbs, including negative adverbs, will be placed after the verb. The use of double negation increased strongly in texts from the fourth century CE, to such an extent that grammarians and other authors of the period, even Saint Augustine, began to complain about this 'erroneous' usage (Molinelli 1989:621–622).

In the *Cantilène de Sainte Eulalie*, negation was expressed via many simple negative expressions (*non, ne, ned, n', nos, nonque*), with the exception of the combination of *niule cose + non*. The simple form *non* is used before both vowels and consonants (17) (18), as are the enclitic form, *no (n')* (19) and (20). The forms seem to be in a state of free variation, which will change later on. The only exception to single negation is found in line 9 of the *Cantilène*. There are three elements in sentence (22): *niule cose* 'nothing', *non* and *omque* 'not . . . ever'. 'Never' could be expressed either by the single element *nonque* < *nunquam / numquam*, or *non . . . onque* < *non . . . umquam*, a continuation of choices available in Classical Latin (sentence (21)).

(17)   *Elle colpes non auret*
         'She had no sins.'

(18)   *La domnizelle celle kose non contredist*
         'The young lady did not object to this thing.'

(19)   *Elle nont eskoltet les mals conseilliers*
         'She did not listen to the evil advisors.'

(20)   *A czo nos voldret concreidre li rex pagiens*
         'This the pagan king did not wish to believe.'

(21)   *Il li enortet, dont lei nonque chielt, que elle fuiet lo nom christiien*
         'He exhorts her to renounce the name of Christian but she pays him no mind.'

(22)   *niule cose non la pouret omque pleier*
         'Nothing could ever make her bend.'

QUESTIONS in Latin could be expressed in one of four ways: (1) syntactically, i.e. by altering the order of elements in the sentence (e.g. inversion); (2) morphologically, by adding the particle *ne* to the end of the verb (see (23)); (3) lexically, by the use of an interrogative pronoun, adverb, or adjective, or

(4) phonetically, by a change in intonation. Partial questions were formed in Latin by the use of interrogative adverbs (*quando* 'when', *quo modo* 'how', *ubi* 'where', *cur* 'why', etc.) and pronouns (*quis* 'who', *quid* 'what'). Total questions were expressed by the use of interrogative particles (*ne, nonne, num*). These interrogative words were usually placed at the beginning of the sentence, either attached to a sentence-initial word (*ne*) or placed before any other word (*nonne, num*). The choice of these particles depended on the type of answer expected. If the answer was unknown, the simple *ne* was used (23). If the speaker expected a positive response, the particle *nonne* would be used (24). If the speaker expected a negative response, however, the particle *num* introduced the sentence (25).

Direct total questions in Vulgar Latin could reportedly be formed by a change in intonation, or by the use of the particle *numquid*, more emphatic than the simple *-ne* of Classical Latin. Another alternative was the use of the conjunction *si* 'if', 'supposing that' (Väänänen 1981:150,164). In the earliest Old French texts there are no examples of questions. In the first texts that do include interrogative constructions, the most common method of indicating a question is the placement of the verb in the initial position. In the eleventh-century *La Vie de Saint Alexis*, the verb precedes the subject in a partial question, as in (26).

(23)   *habesne librum?*
         'Do you have the book?'

(24)   *Nonne habes librum?*
         'Don't you have the book?' 'You have the book, don't you?'

(25)   *Num habes librum?*
         'You don't have the book, do you?'

(26)   *Filz Alexis, por queit portat ta medre?*
         'My son Alexis, why did your mother carry you?'

How does the form of an interrogative often indicate an expected 'yes' or 'no' answer in Modern French? Think in terms of the speaker's presuppositions.

6.2.3   *Vocabulary from Latin to Early Old French*

Much of the vocabulary found in the modern Romance languages is unattested or rarely attested in Classical Latin. Other words are found but are less frequently used in literary texts. Finally, some derivational suffixes and periphrastic constructions are more common in Vulgar Latin than in the Classical language.

In Classical Latin, infixes were used to express differences in aspect, such as *-t-* to express intensity, and *-sc-* to express the beginning of an action. In Vulgar Latin these became the common terms for these actions, and the aspectual differences were lost. For instance, in place of the Classical Latin *iacere* 'to throw', *iactare* 'to hurl' offers both more expressiveness and the simpler morphology of the more regular first conjugation.

Shorter words were frequently replaced by longer words that originally were more limited in scope. *Loqui* 'to speak' was replaced by *fabulare* 'to tell stories' (Spanish *hablar*) and *parabolare* (French *parler*); *os* 'mouth' by *bucca* 'jaw'. These forms also offered the advantage of regularity, changing from a **deponent verb** to a regular first conjugation verb, and from a third declension noun to a first declension noun.

Suffixation was another way that longer, more regular words replaced shorter, irregular words. Sometimes these were diminutives: Vulgar Latin *avicella* for *avis* 'bird' (French *oiseau*), and *auricula* for *auris* 'ear' (French *oreille*). Lengthening suffixes were also common in verbs, particularly *-icare*, *-idiare* in Christian Latin, and the diminutive *-illare*. Modern French *clocher* 'to limp' comes from **cloppicare*, itself based on Vulgar Latin *claudicare* 'to limp', from Classical Latin *claudere*. The *-idiare* suffix of Christian Latin would be transformed into the productive *-iser* suffix of Modern French: *baptidiare* > *baptizare* > *baptiser* 'to baptize'. The diminutive suffix *-iller* of Modern French (e.g. *fusiller* 'to shoot many times', 'to kill by a firing squad') is a continuation of the *-illare* suffix of Vulgar Latin, which indicated repetition of an action.

Word composition was relatively rare in Classical Latin, and condemned by purists such as Cicero and Quintilian (see Väänänen 1981:92). The rejection of *aquiductus* 'aqueduct' in the *Appendix Probi* demonstrates both the purist tradition and the continued generation of such forms. Forms of the verb *facere* 'to do, to make' were frequently used as suffixes in Vulgar Latin to make new nouns, adjectives, and verbs: *beneficium* literally 'did good', 'an act of kindness'; *magnificus* literally 'does great things'; *beatificare* literally 'to make a saint', 'to beatify'. The addition of the prepositional prefix *con* 'fellow', 'with', as in *conservus* 'fellow slave' sometimes added no meaning at all, as in *congentilis* 'relative' (Olcott 1898:xxv).

6.2.3.1   Non-Latin elements in the vocabulary of Latin

Latin borrowed some terms from other inhabitants of the Italian peninsula, both from Indo-Europeans, such as *rufus* 'red' from Oscan, and from non-Indo-Europeans, e.g. *taberna* 'shop' from Etruscan. The largest influence on Latin was Greek. Knowledge of Greek was expected of educated Romans, and facilitated at all levels of society by the high number of Greek slaves in Roman society. Learned words such as *philosophia* 'philosophy' and *grammaticus* 'grammarian, professor of grammar' reflect this, while more numerous are those that suggest a more common origin: *platea* 'place, square', *cincinnus* 'a lock of curly hair', *colaphus* 'a blow with the fist'. Other Greek words came with the spread of Christianity in the Roman Empire: *cathedra* 'chair', *episcopus* 'bishop', *parabolare* 'to speak' (literally 'to make a comparison').

The first invaders of Roman territory were the Celts, sacking Rome in 390 BCE. From contacts with Celts in the Po valley, and later through the Roman conquest of Gaul (121–51 BCE), some Celtic words entered the common Latin language. Some pertained to peculiarities of Celtic culture, such as clothing (*camisia* 'shirt'), while others are more general: *camminus* 'road', *beccus* 'beak'. As the Celts were displaced by the Germans, extensive contact between the Roman Empire and Germanic tribes from the Danube to the North Sea led to the adoption of some Germanic words into Classical Latin, such as *blancus* 'white' *blondus* 'blond', and *sapo* 'hair dye, soap'.

As we have seen, foreign elements in the vocabulary of Vulgar Latin came mostly from Greek. In Vulgar Latin, and later in the Romance languages, these terms replaced the standard terms of Classical Latin. In Classical Latin the term for 'leg' was *crus*, which was replaced in Vulgar Latin by *gamba* (Greek /kampe/ 'knee joint'). The Greek expression *hêpar sukôton* for *foie gras* 'liver of a goose stuffed with figs' translated literally into Latin as *ficatus iecur* and made the Latin term *ficatus* > *foie* 'fig' stand for 'liver', replacing the Classical Latin word *iecur*, even when speaking of the bodily organ of human beings. The Classical Latin term *caecus* 'blind' was replaced by a prepositional structure modeled on the Greek, *ab oculis* 'without eyes', giving Modern French *aveugle*.

What does the following distribution of borrowings from Celtic and Germanic languages tell us about the date of their entry into Latin? *Camisia* is borrowed from Celtic languages, while *blanc* is from Germanic.

Latin	French	Italian	Spanish	Romanian	
camisia	chemise	camicia	camisa	camasa	'shirt'
albus	blanc	bianco	blanco	alb	'white'

6.2.3.2   Adverb formation

Some Latin adverbs were root words, not derived from any others (*saepe* 'often', *paene* 'almost'), but most were derived in one way or another from adjectives. Classical Latin had a bewildering array of means to form adverbs from adjectives. The most common were the use of a long /e:/ or the use of the suffix *-iter*. Latin adjectives fall into two classes, so-called *-is* adjectives of the third declension and the *-us, -a, -um* adjectives of the first and second declensions. Both methods of adverb formation could be used with each type of adjective:

> Long /e:/: *difficilis* 'difficult'; *difficile* 'difficultly, with difficulty';
> *carus* 'dear', *care* 'dearly';
> *-(i)ter*: *brevis* 'brief' – *breviter* 'briefly'; *humanus* 'human' – *humaniter* 'humanly'.

For many adjectives, both forms are attested: alongside *humaniter* we find *humane*, similarly *difficile/difficulter* 'with difficulty'. The only real restriction is that adjectives derived from the present participle use only the *-ter* form.

In Classical Latin, one alternative was to combine the adjective with an abstract noun or a noun indicating a mental state. In the first group Classical Latin used *modo* 'way' and *via* 'way', as in *postmodo* 'afterwards', *qua via* 'how' (literally 'by what way'). The second group included nouns such as *corde* 'heart', *animo* 'soul', giving rise to such adverbial constructions as *ardenti corde* 'ardently' and *toto animo* 'completely, totally'. Sometimes *animo* was combined with the adverbial suffix *-iter*, as in *unanimiter* 'unanimously'. The most common, however, was *-mente* 'mind', as in *mente tranquilla* 'peacefully' (Cicero, *Tusculanarum Disputationum* 4.55, cited in Karlsson 1981:43), which would become generalized in Romance. Karlsson (1981:145–148) lists 178 adjectives that appeared with *-mente* in Classical Latin literature.

The loss of final /m/ and the confusion of unstressed vowels in Vulgar Latin made it difficult to mark as adverbs many forms which in Classical Latin identified an adverb. This had two effects in Vulgar Latin: first it popularized the use of the easily identifiable *-(i)ter* ending already present in Classical Latin, and it also greatly extended the use of the periphrastic construction with *-mente* 'mind'. The *-(i)ter* ending was further reinforced by the addition of *-bil-*, giving such forms as *amabiliter* 'lovingly'. Gregory the Great (ca. 540–604 CE), writing in the late sixth century, invented many new adverbs using the *-ter* suffix (Hauber 1938).

The use of periphrastic constructions with *-mente* was limited in Classical times to first and second declension adjectives (e.g. *tacita mente*, 'silently') and a few fixed constructions such as *qua mente* 'how'. In Late Latin and particularly in Christian Latin the formula enjoyed great popularity, in such phrases as *devota mente* 'devotedly'. One fixed expression from legal practice has come down to us in the vocabulary of wills, *sana mente* 'of sound mind' (Karlsson 1981:46–47), just one example of many found in important legal texts such as the Salic Laws, composed early in the sixth century CE.

Recently Bauer (2003) has called into question this traditional way of viewing the development of *-mente* as an adverbial marker. She points out that many of the cited examples of *-mente* in Christian Latin could be interpreted as lexical rather than adverbial, i.e. they still retain the meaning 'mind', as in an example of the *Vulgate* (Matthew 22:37), shown in (27). In the *Vulgate*, Jerome's translation of the Bible in the fourth century, she found 42 examples of *-mente*, of which 8 instances had *-mente* in combination with an adjective. In none of these is *-mente* clearly adverbial. In the same text there are 69 examples of *animo* (28), of which 23 are in combination with an adjective, and at least 7 of these are clearly adverbial, for instance, connected with another adverb as in:

(27)   *diliges Deum ex toto corde tuo et in tota anima tua et in tota mente tua*
       'Thou shalt love the Lord with all thy heart, with all thy soul and with all thy mind.'

(28)   *prompto animo ac fortiter . . . morte perfungar* (2 Maccabees 6:28)
       'to die willingly and courageously'

If, at this late date, *-mente* is not only not the most common way of expressing an adverb of manner, but is also rarely unambiguously adverbial, how can we account for its presence in all the Romance languages except Romanian? Either it would have to spread extremely rapidly throughout the Empire in the waning days of that Empire, or it would have to spread after the break-up of the Empire, some 150 years after Jerome's translation. Karlsson claims that *-mente* was ultimately preferred over *animo* because *-mente* looked like an adverb, i.e. it ended in *-e*. Bauer suggests that it is rather the multiplicity of uses of *animo* that doomed it as an adverbial marker; the relatively constrained use of *-mente* made it a better, unambiguous marker of the adverbial meaning. The combination of an adjective + *-mente* was always potentially adverbial, while the combination of adjective + *animo* was often clearly not adverbial. Moreover, *animo* could have adverbial value in other contexts, such as after a preposition: *ex animo* 'wholeheartedly'. *Animo* also had more specific meanings, particularly within the context of religious writings ('soul'). The acquisition of such semantic enrichment runs counter to a process of grammaticalization, in which lexical meaning is lost. Therefore, according to Bauer, *-mente* would have been grammaticalized not because of its physical form, but because of its unspecified meaning and more restricted contexts. This still leaves open the question of why *-mente* took different forms in different regions (e.g. *mentre* in Spain, alongside *mente*), and why it grammaticalized differently in different regions, maintaining more independence in the Iberian peninsula than it did in Gaul or Italy. For instance, in Spanish *-mente* can be added only to the last of a series of adverbs, as in (29). Clearly our understanding of the process of grammaticalization of this form, which would become standard in French, still has some important gaps.

(29)   *el autobús avanza segura y lentamente*
       the bus advanced safe and slowly.
       'the bus advanced safely and slowly' (Bauer 2003:441)

6.2.4   *Pragmatic aspects of language use from Latin to Early Old French*

In this section we will consider primarily expressions of politeness and the recognition of class differences in the use of language. The second-person personal pronouns functioned solely to distinguish singular from plural reference. The kinds of social distinctions that would mark their use later were expressed in Classical Latin through the choice of names and other terms of address.

6.2.4.1   *Forms of address*

An important fact in the Modern French pronominal address system is that there are two pronouns available for addressing a single person (see section 5.4.2.1). In Classical Latin, a social distinction between the second-person singular *tu* and the second-person plural *vos* was not observed. The use of *vos* when addressing a single person might be considered parallel to the use of first-person plural forms when the real meaning is 'I', sometimes called the 'royal we', as it is a formula used by monarchs. As in the case of Modern French usage of *tu* and *vous*, the choice of using 'I' or 'we' in Late Latin depended on various social and discourse factors. In his fifth-century correspondence, Pope Leo I uses the 'royal we' when addressing his inferiors (the bishops), but the more modest singular in writing to the emperor (Haverling 1998:340).

Use of plural *vos* 'you' or *vester* 'your' when addressing a single person was virtually unknown in Classical Latin. Examples often cited in the dramatist Plautus and the poet Catullus (84–54 BCE) are subject to other interpretations. In Late Latin, there are some confusing examples in which the author of a letter seems to go back and forth between singular and plural forms when addressing the same person, such as in the Bishop of Carthage Cyprian's letter to fellow-bishop Cornelius (third century CE; cited in Haverling 1998:342). This practice became more and more common in official letters of the fifth and sixth centuries, but we have little evidence of how choices between the two pronouns were made in the spoken language.

The other way to express respect is by the choice of the proper term of address. This depends on a number of social and pragmatic factors as well, including not only the status of the speaker and that of the interlocutor, but also others who might hear the form (on the role of the hearer, see Section 5.2). In private, the same speaker–addressee pair might use different terms than they would in public. A woman addressing her sister who happens to be a medical doctor might use *Dr. Jones* in hospital but *Mary* in the privacy of their home (see 'positive politeness' in section 5.4.2). Similarly, when directly addressing a person, the standard Roman practice was to use the name with no modifier. Roman names were typically composed of three elements, the *praenomen* 'given name', the *nomen gentilicium* 'family name', and the *cognomen* 'nickname': *Gaius Julius Caesar, Marcus Tullius Cicero*. During the period of the Roman Republic

(509–31 BCE), three names were first used by nobility, gradually extending to freeborn Roman citizens. Slaves and foreigners typically had only one name, for instance *Geta*, already branded a slave name in ancient Greece (although it would later be the name of a Roman emperor in the second century CE).

Around the first century CE, both naming practices and ways of addressing people seem to have changed. Roman men had three names whatever their rank in society. As the type of name no longer served to distinguish people, instead of using names, the speaker would address an unrelated adult by terms of politeness, such as *domine* 'master', *magister* 'teacher' (see Dickey 2002). *Domine* was originally considered too strong, but gradually through the Empire it became the standard term of polite address within families and then in all situations (cf. *dans Alexis* 'Lord Alexis', in the eleventh-century French *Life of St. Alexis*, and more recently, the use of *Don* as a Sicilian term of respect due a Mafia boss: *Don Corleone*).

During the Frankish period most people had only one name. Of 411 members of the aristocracy from the fourth to the seventh century, only forty had more than one name (Lefebvre-Teillard 1990:12). Some attributed this to Christian influence, in particular to the practice of taking a new name at baptism, but the dates of the change do not correspond well to the advent of Christianity in Gaul. The choice of name depended on the prestige of that name, and on family tradition. Through the Merovingian and Carolingian period, there is a gradual reduction in the number of different names that are used, until only a few names became dominant. Surprisingly, these are not for the most part the names of Christian saints. In the earliest Old French texts, all those referred to by name are given as a single name: Karles, Ludher, Eulalia, Maximiien. While some names are combined with epithets, such as 'Charles le Chauve' or 'Louis le Débonnaire', these were not hereditary family names.

Historically, English also had two pronominal address forms. What are these, and in what contexts are they still used (if at all)?

6.2.5   *Summary*

As the phonological basis for the elaborate distinctions of the Classical Latin case system weakened, analytic constructions and a more fixed sentence structure increasingly took the place of the synthetic forms of the written literary standard. This made possible a freer sentence structure. In the ninth century several texts appear in the spirit of the Council of Tours (813), in which the clergy was ordered to address the people in the 'rustic Romance language', essentially an effort by learned clergymen to imitate the language of the people. The poem about *Sainte Eulalie* was an ecclesiastical version of this policy, and the *Sermens de Strasbourg* a secular version. The texts are still very Latinate, as we saw from the sentence structure in the *Serments*, sometimes with Latin words inserted among the Romance, for example *anima* 'soul' in the *Cantilène de Sainte Eulalie*. These early texts did not encourage the use of vernacular in writing. In fact, there were almost no other vernacular texts, so far as we know, for two centuries after the composition of these early texts. The only exceptions were a fragment of a sermon, written in a macaronic mixture of Romance and Latin (the so-called *Jonas fragment*), and two poems from the end of the tenth century, included in the same manuscript: one about the life of Saint Léger, the other recounting the Passion, in which northern and southern Gallo-Romance forms are mixed.

6.3   Old and Middle French

This period begins with the literary and cultural flowering of French society in the late eleventh and twelfth centuries, and ends with the reunification of the country after the Wars of Religion at the end of the sixteenth century. Throughout the period, Latin remained the language of education, but by the end French entered into intellectual discourse and had become the primary language of literature and government. At the beginning of the period, regional languages were considered of equal importance; by the end of the period the norm associated with the royal court and the *Parlement de Paris* dominated other regional and social varieties, at least in prestige and written usage.

From the mid-eleventh century on, the status of the vernacular language strengthened. First, it became an ever more common medium for secular as well as religious literature, and then slowly worked its way into official usage, until it was declared the sole official language of the law in 1539. The standardization of the language and the centralization of the state went hand in hand. In the eleventh and twelfth centuries, the literature and the official use of the vernacular was mostly on the periphery of royal power, and the dialect of the Ile de France had no special prominence. With the establishment of a permanent seat of royal power in Paris, and the concomitant royal bureaucracy, as well as the founding of the University of Paris, the use of other dialects became stigmatized, and dialectal features in literature and official business gradually disappeared. This does not mean that the other dialects disappeared; they would persist into the twentieth century, but their prestige and the range of their use, written and oral, diminished over the centuries.

As early as the thirteenth century Louis IX (St Louis) expressed his desire that there be one legal system, one currency, and one language for his entire kingdom. While the unification of these three social institutions would not take place until the Revolution, the first major step in this direction was the requirement

(1454) that all regional laws (the *coutumiers*), until then transmitted orally from generation to generation, be recorded and approved by the Parlement de Paris and the King's Council. This led ultimately to the Ordonnance de Villers-Cotterêts (1539), which required that all legal documents throughout the kingdom be written in *langage maternel françois* 'the maternal French language', an ambiguous phrase that within a few decades had an unambiguous interpretation: the language of the royal court. Not coincidentally, the first grammars of French written in France appeared in the sixteenth century, first the tentative comparison of French and Latin by Jacques Dubois (1531) and then the more thorough treatise of Louis Meigret (1550).

The Wars of Religion in the second half of the sixteenth century led to much regional fighting and a lack of central authority. The reunification of the country under the reign of Henri IV (1594–1610) was the first step towards the creation of stronger central control, and laid the groundwork for real governmental intervention in linguistic issues. It was during the reign of Henri IV that François Malherbe arrived in Paris, and set about creating and imposing a norm for literary language. Thus in terms of the social construct of a linguistic norm and the institutional supports for this norm, the break between Middle French and Modern French occurred during the seventeenth century. Linguistically, the major changes during this period can be summed up as follows:

Phonetic changes significantly altered the pronunciation of lexical items:
– loss of the final consonants, which spelled the end of the declension of nouns and adjectives;
– loss of final schwa, which, combined with the loss of final consonants, changed the way in which masculine and feminine were distinguished;
– simplification of affricates to fricatives;
– reduction of diphthongs and vowels in hiatus to simple vowels (monophthongs).

Changes in the structure of the noun phrase coincided with these word-final phonetic changes:
– increased use of determiners in the noun phrase (e.g. development of the partitive article);
– disappearance of the case system.

Changes in the syntactic structure were also widespread and connected to changes in other parts of the grammar:
– almost obligatory use of double negation;
– increase in the number and variety of subordinating conjunctions;
– increased use of subject pronouns.

The vocabulary was 'relatinized' through the translation of Latin works into French, creating many doublets of learned and popular words; during the sixteenth century many Italian terms were introduced. The distinctions between

Table 6.8 *Spelling and pronunciation of vowels in Old and Middle French*

Letter	Sound	Old/Middle French	Modern French	
o	/ɔ/	*lors*	*lors*	'then'
o	/o/	*dolor*	*douleur*	'sadness'
o	/y/*	*sot*	*sut*	'knew'
e	/ɛ/	*cele*	*celle*	'this one'
e	/e/	*Enide*	*Énide*	'Enid'
e	/ə/	*ne*	*ne*	'not'
a	/a/	*cheval*	*cheval*	'horse'
i	/i/	*li*	*le*	'the'
u	/y/	*aparçut*	*aperçut*	'noticed'
au	/au/	*au*	*au*	'to the'
ai	/ai/	*faillant*	*faillant*	'failing'
ei	/ei/	*leisses*	*laisses*	'[you] leave'
eu	/eu/	*leu*	*lieu*	'place'
ie	/ie/	*chiet*	*choit*[+]	'falls'
oi	/oi/	*poise*	*pèse*	'weighs heavily'
ou	/ou/	*mout*	*moult*[#]	'much'
ue	/ue/	*cuers*	*coeur*	'heart'
ui	/ui/	*vuida*	*(il) vida*	'emptied'
iau	/iau/	*diaus*	*deuil*	'grief'

*uncertain
[+] very rare; usually found only in the infinitive
[#] archaic

tu and *vous* with single reference became more uniform. Hereditary surnames became common, and then legally required.

These changes, however, did not occur uniformly in time or space, but rather gradually, to different extents, and at different times in various regions of the country currently known as France.

6.3.1 Phonology in Old and Middle French

6.3.1.1 Vowels

By the end of the eleventh century, French had expanded upon the vowel inventory of Vulgar Latin. We'll look at this in light of some representative texts. Table 6.8 shows the spelling and possible pronunciation of vowels in lines 4556–4582 of Chrétien de Troye's *Erec et Enide* (edition of Mario Roques, 1970), composed in eastern Champagne in the 1160s. The most noticeable changes are the addition of the front rounded high vowel /y/, and perhaps that of the rounded mid-vowel /œ/. The process of nasalization (see 2.2.2) had by then led to the introduction of at least two fully nasal vowels: /ɑ̃/ and /ɛ̃/. In addition there was a large number of diphthongs and triphthongs.

By the fourteenth century, the vowel inventory increased even further, including three nasal high vowels: /ĩ/, /ỹ/ and /ũ/. The number of diphthongs had dropped. A century later, in the emerging standard language, most of these diphthongs had been reduced to simple vowels; they **monophthongized**. Evidence for this process comes primarily from the rhymes used by poets; for instance, in *Erec et Enide* those words in which the rhyming vowel *é* only rhymes with other words of the same vowel (30). Similarly, if the rhyming vowel sequence is *oi* or *ai(e)*, the second line of the couplet has the same spelling (31)–(32).

(30)   *Cil s'an vont tuit desconforté; le seneschal an ont porté*
         (ll. 3647–3648)
         'They departed disconsolate; they carried the seneschal away.'

(31)   *Li cuens respont: "Je panse et croi*
         qu'il n'est mie plus biax de moi" (ll. 3223–3224)
         'The count responds: "I think and believe that he is not at all
         handsomer than I."'

(32)   *li sans vermauz toz chauz an raie*
         d'anbedeus parz par mi la plaie (ll. 3023–3024)
         'the red blood, still warm, flows from both parts through the wound'

But by the fifteenth century, rhymes could take place between different spellings as well, indicating that diphthongs had further simplified to simple vowels. For instance in Villon's (mid-fifteenth-century) poems, *ré* in *remiré* 'regarded, respected' rhymes with *ray* in *mueray* 'I will change', as do the syllables *moy* 'me' and *mai* 'May'. Yet another century later, at the end of the sixteenth century in Jacques Yver's *Congé à son livre*, *ai* in *aisles* 'wings' rhymes with *e* (*ve*) in *nouvelles* 'new' (cited in Jourda 1965).

The diphthong /oi/ moved to a pronunciation /we/ by the Middle French period, but from that point many differences developed along regional and class lines. Some varieties kept /we/, others reduced it to /e/, while in the Parisian region, except for the Royal Court, it tended to be pronounced /wa/. This variation accounts for the doublets *Français* 'French' /frãsɛ/ and *François* 'Francis' /frãswa/ in Modern French. Regional variation remained strong, however, as exemplified by *La famille ridicule*, an eighteenth-century play from Lorraine, in which *foi* 'faith' is pronounced /fwe/, while /wa/ in *envoyer* 'to send' is simplified /envaje/ and *voici* 'here is' is represented as /vasi/ (Zeliqzon 1916).

Another striking difference between the pronunciation of vowels in Middle French and in Old French is the reduction of vowels in hiatus (for the term, see section 2.4.4.2). The earlier texts abound in forms such as *eage* or *aage* 'age' (Modern French *âge*), *beneoit* 'blessed' (Modern French *benoît*), *leu*

'read' (Modern French *lu*). In *Erec et Enide*, for instance, the word *aage* is
disyllabic, i.e. the *aa* sequence corresponds to two syllable nodes. In Jacques
Yver's poem, from the mid-sixteenth century, the spelling *aage* is also found,
but it corresponds to a monosyllabic word (cited in Jourda 1965). The syllable
count in these cases is determined in light of versification rules: in French
versification each line has to have the same number of syllables. Yver writes in
12-syllable lines, therefore *aage* could only be monosyllabic in (33) to arrive
at the exact syllable count. In Chrétien de Troyes' 8-syllable line shown in
(34), which is from an earlier period, on the other hand, *aa* in *aage* counts as
bisyllabic while the schwa adds an additional syllable to the count.

(33)   *Ou   vas   -tu   pauvre   fol,   ton   aage   te   deffend*
         1   2   3   4   5 6   7   8   9   10 11   12
        'Where are you going poor fool, your age forbids you . . .' (l. 2)

(34)   *onques   nus   hom   de   son   aage*
          1   2 3   4   5   6   78 –
        'never any [no] man of his age . . .' (l. 91)

As mentioned above, an important change through the Old French and Middle
French periods concerns the nasalization of vowels. Although the full nasalization of a vowel massively took place when the vowel was followed by a same-
syllable nasal consonant (see section 2.2.2), in the Old French of eastern France
sometimes the velum remained open long enough for nasalization to affect the
following vowel as well. For instance, *nenil* 'not at all' was transformed into
nanin /nãnĩ/. In Old French, both the nasal vowel and the nasal consonant
were pronounced. Through the Middle French period, in closed syllables, the
nasal consonant ceased to be pronounced, leaving only the nasal vowel *bon*
'good' /bõn/ gradually shifting to /bõ/. In open syllables, the nasal vowel first
denasalised, *bone* /bõnə/, then became open /bɔnə/, finally yielding the Modern
French form *bonne* /bɔn/, with or without word-final schwa depending on the
dialect. These changes would affect the way certain grammatical information
was expressed, such as masculine and feminine, as evidenced by *bon* above.

The first step (nasalization) of this process has been traditionally viewed as
a long process taking from the tenth to the end of the thirteenth century (Pope
1934:169), the second (deletion of /n/) in the fourteenth and fifteenth centuries,
and the last (denasalization) perhaps not being complete until the end of the
seventeenth century. The evidence for the traditional dating is taken from the
types of assonance and rhyme permitted. In *Saint Alexis*, from the mid-eleventh
century, the sequence 'a + nasal consonant' cannot assonate (from the word
assonance) with 'a + oral consonant', indicating that the spelling sequence 'a +
nasal consonant' must represent /ã/, and that the sequence 'a + oral consonant'
must represent /a/. The order of nasalization of vowels can be reconstructed

from the time when poets decided that, in their writings, a 'vowel + nasal consonant' sequence could no longer assonate with a corresponding 'vowel + oral consonant'. The nasalization process gradually moved from low vowels to higher vowels, ending with the nasalization of the highest vowel /i/ in the thirteenth century. This order is not accidental, but rather tied to the articulatory characteristics of vowels: the raising of the tongue necessary to form the high vowel makes it more difficult to lower the soft palate, required to allow air to enter the nasal passage (see also section 2.2.2).

Since the 1980s, another type of evidence has been used for a different dating of the process of nasalization. The study of charters, legal documents from the Middle Ages (e.g. Dees 1980), has the advantage of specific dating and specific location. The study of spelling conventions in these works suggests earlier and simultaneous nasalization of all vowels no later than the twelfth century, and the denasalization of open vowels before the sixteenth century, except perhaps in western dialects (Morin 1994).

The prosthetic vowel /i/ (see section 6.2.1.1) was maintained, and with the loss of preconsonantal /s/ was transformed to /e/: *estendre* /ɛstãndr(ə)/ > *étendre* /etãdr(ə)/. However, through the increasing practice of translation of Latin texts into French, from the late fourteenth century on, new words beginning in 's + consonant' were introduced and retained without the prosthetic /i/, such as *splendeur* 'splendor'.

What is the recommended pronunciation in Modern French of words such as *a<u>o</u>ût* 'August', *alc<u>oo</u>l* 'alcohol', *extra<u>o</u>rdinaire* 'extraordinary', and *paon* 'peacock', spelled with vowel hiatus? Compare with the following comment from Dupleix (1651:143):

"Ce n'est pas seulement le peuple de Paris qui prononce *Aoust* en deux syllables, mais aussi la pluspart des Provinces de France, & mesmes des plus doctes hommes, & le mot *Oust* monosyllable n'est introduit que par ignorance."

'It's not just the common people of Paris who pronounce *Aoust* in two syllables, but also most of the French provinces and even most learned men; only ignorance would introduce *Oust* as a monosyllable.'

6.3.1.2 *Consonants*

The most important changes in the consonantal system during the course of Old and Middle French were the loss of some consonants and the simplification of affricates to fricatives. Consonants might be lost before another consonant, particularly /s/ but also /r/, and in word-final position. The loss of preconsonantal /s/ was usually accompanied by compensatory lengthening of the preceding vowel: *beste* /bɛt(ə)/ > *bête* /bɛːt/. One indication of this is that, for instance, Jean Froissart (fourteenth century) rhymes *blasme* 'blame', a word in which

Table 6.9 *Paths of changes taken by preconsonantal /l/ from Latin to Middle French (NB: Allophones of 'r' varied historically, and are variable today.)*

	Latin	Old French	Middle French		Modern French
/l/ lost					
	filius	/fils/	/fis/	'son'	(*fils* /fis/)
/l/ lost and recovered					
	nullus	/nyls/	/nys/	'none'	(*nul* /nyl/)
	solus	/souls/	/seus/	'only, alone'	(*seul* /sœl/)
	qualis	/kels/	/kes/	'which'	(*quel* /kɛl/)
/l/ vocalized					
	alterum	/altrə/	/autrə/	'other'	(*autre* /otʁ/)
	illos	/ɛls/	/eus/	'them' (acc. masc.)	(*eux* /ø/)
	follis	/fɔls/	/fɔus/	'foolish, mad'	(*fou* /fu/)

s no longer sounded, with *âme* 'soul'. However, several English grammatical texts from the period recognized exceptions, such as *escuser* (*excuser* /ekskyze/ Modern French 'to excuse'). In the fifteenth and sixteenth centuries, borrowings from Italian reintroduced the 's + consonant' sequence, for instance, in the word *bastion* 'fortification'. These borrowings, together with the effect of the Erasmian reform of Latin spelling and pronunciation, encouraged the reintroduction of preconsonantal /s/; some grammarians even attest to the pronunciation /honɛst(ə)/, Modern French *honnête* 'honest' (Thurot 1881–1883, II, 326–329).

The loss of preconsonantal /r/ is first attested in rhymes such as *sage/large* 'wise'/'wide' from the late twelfth century (Marchello-Nizia 1979:83). Because most of these /r/ consonants are not omitted in Modern French, some have preferred to see these as imperfect rhymes rather than lost /r/. Some of the preconsonantal /r/s were lost for good, however, such as in the word *faubourg* < *forsbourg* 'part of the city outside the walls'. This might have been the result of a contamination of meaning between *fors* 'outside' and *faux* 'false'.

A change in the pronunciation of preconsonantal /l/ had already been noted by Late Latin grammarians (Zink 1992:130). By the middle of the twelfth century, preconsonantal /l/ had been lost after the high vowels /i/, /y/, /u/, and sometimes after the high-mid vowel /e/, or it has been vocalized to /u/ in other situations. The paths of change taken by this consonant in different contexts are shown in Table 6.9. There was widespread regional variation on this point, however. In eastern dialects, preconsonantal /l/ was lost after all vowels: *melius* > /miets/, which in central Old French became /mieus/, Modern French *mieux* /mjø/. We can also see from the examples in Table 6.9 that some of the /l/s were reinserted under the influence of Latin late in the Middle French period (*nul* /nyl/, *quel* /kɛl/).

The vocalization of preconsonantal /l/ had an impact on the morphology of nouns and adjectives. In nouns such as *mal* 'evil' and in adjectives such as *royal*, singular and plural were no longer distinguished by the pronunciation of a final /s/, but by the change in the final vowel: *mal* (sing.) /mal/ ∼ *maux* (pl.) /mo/; *royal* (sing.) /rwajal/ *royaux* (pl.) /rwajo/. Other nouns and adjectives do not show this pattern, such as the adjective *bancal* 'lame', which has the plural *bancals*, while yet others, e.g. *banal*, hesitate between the plural forms *banals* and *banaux*. The standard explanation (e.g. Ewert 1933:133–134) attributes the retention of the -*als* plural ending to more recent introduction into the French language, but this is not clear. *Banal* is first attested in the mid-thirteenth century, and fairly recent creations, such as *fédéral*, first attested in the late eighteenth century, frequently exhibit the /al/ ∼ /o/ alternation. Sixteenth-century grammarians admitted no exceptions to the /al/ ∼ /o/ alternation; only in the seventeenth century did lists of exceptions begin to appear (Thurot 1881–1883:73–78), perhaps an indication of the use of the Latinate forms /al/ ∼ /als/ as markers of higher education and social class.

The loss of final consonants had an even more dramatic effect on morphology, and ultimately syntax. The final /t/ of third-person verb forms in the first conjugation was weakly maintained in the earliest Old French texts, both before a consonant and before a vowel, as shown in (35)–(36). The final /t/ and /th/ of such forms had disappeared by the twelfth century, as shown in (37), an excerpt from *Le Couronnement de Louis*, dated around 1130, in which the form *demande* 'asks' no longer contains a final /t/, compared to verb forms like *reguardet* in (35). The final /t/ after a consonant in the other conjugations remained a bit longer, but by the end of the fourteenth century had apparently disappeared, as some poets rhyme *bien* 'good' with *vient* 'he/she comes' (Marchello-Nizia 1979:87).

(35)   *Rodlanz reguardet es monz ed es lariz*
        'Roland looks out on the mountains and the hillsides' (*Chanson de Roland*, l. 1851, cited in Jenkins 1924)

(36)   *Ed il les ploret cum chevaliers gentilz*
        'He weeps for them as noble knights' (*Chanson de Roland*, l. 1853)

(37)   *Il li demande: "Dont venez vos bels nies?"*
        'He asks him: "Where do you come from, handsome nephew?"' (*Le Couronnement de Louis*, l. 116, cited in Langlois 1965)

The loss of final /s/ marked the end of the case declension system, already weak, and the end of the distinction between the first-, second- and third-person singular forms of the verb in most conjugations. The loss of final /s/ occurs first in western dialects and dialects of French in England after the Norman Conquest in the twelfth century and remains stronger in the north, for example in Picard.

The loss of final /s/ was general by the fourteenth century, when the word was at a pause, or when the following word began with a consonant. Other final consonants suffered the same fate, for instance /k/ in *blanc* /blã/ 'white', /f/ in *baillif* /bajif/ > *bailli* /baji/ /'court official', /l/ in *oïl* /oil/ > *oui* /wi/ 'yes', and /p/ in *drap* /dʀa/ 'cloth'.

However, some words retained the pronunciation of these final consonants, and became topics of much discussion by grammarians from the sixteenth century on. Word-final /s/ continued to be pronounced in words such as *fils* /fis/ 'son', and in the numbers *six* /sis/ 'six' and *dix* /dis/ 'ten'. Word-final /t/ was preserved in numbers as well: *sept* /sɛt/ 'seven'. The letters *c* and *q*, representing /k/, continued to be pronounced in a few words, such as *duc* /dyk/ 'duke', and *coq* /cɔk/ 'rooster'. Modern standard French pronunciation was not set until the end of the nineteenth century. In the last quarter of that century, Émile Littré still championed the pronunciation /fi/ for *fils* but accepted /dɔt/ for *dot* 'dowry', although a sixteenth-century text using the spelling 'dos' clearly indicates that questions about this pronunciation had already been raised (*Littré* 1878 II, 1226).

What are the rules, in standard French, for the pronunciation of the final consonants in the following words: *oeuf* 'egg', *moeurs* 'mores', *os* 'bone', *outil* 'tool', *péril* 'peril'?

6.3.2   Morphology and syntax in Old and Middle French

6.3.2.1 Nouns and adjectives

As mentioned in section 6.2.2, Old French nouns and adjectives had a two-case system, but this case system was unstable even before the loss of final /s/ made it disappear. Some classes of words made no distinction between the cases, such as feminine singular nouns of the first declension and most feminine forms of adjectives. Furthermore, the uses of the oblique case far outnumbered those of the nominative case. In texts from the twelfth century on, the oblique case progressively took over several functions of the nominative case: nouns in apposition (38), predicate nominatives (39), and vocatives (40) (see Zink 1992:34–35).

(38)   *si parlent l'un à l'autre*
        'Then they spoke, one to another' [one would expect *li uns*; cited in Zink 1992:34]

(39)   *je ne sui ne duc ne conte*
        'I am neither duke nor count' [one would expect *dus* and *cuens*; *Chastelaine de Vergi*, cited in Zink 1992:34]

(40)   *Senescal, que vous est avis?*
'Seneschal, what is your opinion?' [one would expect *senescaus*; *Jeu de St Nicholas*, cited in Zink 1992:34]

Ultimately, then, the oblique form became the standard form in all functions, including subject. One result of this change was that the marker ±/s/ became solely an indication of number.

A few nominative forms survive in Modern French, particularly for words that were often used as vocatives, such as *copain* 'pal, boyfriend' and *soeur* 'sister'. In some cases both nominative and oblique have survived, sometimes with specialization of function or meaning. *Compagnon* (obl.) 'companion, mate' survives alongside *copain* (nom.), and *garçon* (obl.) 'boy, waiter' alongside *gars* (nom.) 'guy'. The subject pronoun *on* 'one' (< Latin *homo*) is the nominative form of the noun *homme* 'man' (< Latin *hominem*).

Just as /s/ became the marker for plural in nouns and adjectives, the word-final schwa *e* /ə/ became the marker for feminine in adjectives. While this function of *e* was common to first- and second-declension adjectives, third-declension Latin adjectives did not alternate in masculine and feminine, so analogical forms were created. Thus an 'un-etymological' feminine form *grande* 'big' started to appear as early as the eleventh century, although it did not fully supplant the etymological form *grant* until the end of Middle French. More rarely, masculine analogical forms were created based on the feminine forms. In Old French *larc* 'large' was the masculine, and *large* the feminine; today the masculine form, based on analogy with the feminine, is *large*. Today only a few fixed expressions retain the undifferentiated feminine form of Old French, such as *grand-mère* 'grandmother', as well as place names such as *Rochefort*.

> The nominative case of the Latin word *soror* 'sister' has survived in French (*soeur*), although accusative forms are found into the fourteenth century (*serur* from Latin *sororem*). Why has the nominative become generalized for this word, contrary to the much more frequent generalization of the accusative?

6.3.2.2   The syntax of the noun phrase

One of the striking differences between Old French and Modern French is the use of determiners before the noun. In Latin there were no articles and the use of determiners was emphatic (demonstratives) or conveyed certain explicit meaning, such as *idem* 'the same'. In Old French the definite and indefinite articles particularize their referent, and nouns used in a generic sense have no determiner. In (41) and (42) we see that the nouns *chastel, murs, citet, servisies, amistiez, ors, leons,* and *chiens* all appear without determiners. In Late Old

French and in Middle French the use of the article in all situations increased gradually, more quickly in prose than in poetry, more often with concrete nouns than with abstract nouns, and more often in the subject position than as a direct object or object of preposition. Thus as we can see in an excerpt of the XV *Joies de Mariage* written around 1400 (cited in Rychner 1967), shown in (43), an abstract noun such as *nature* as subject lacks a determiner (*nature humaine*), but the more concrete noun *seigneurs* 'lords' has a definite determiner (*les seigneurs*). The direct objects, in this case all abstract nouns, also lack a determiner (*liberté* 'liberty', *franchise* 'freedom').

(41)   *Chastel n'i at ki devant lui remaignet*
         Murs ne citet n'i est remés à fraindre. (Chanson de Roland, ll. 4–5,
         cited in Jenkins 1924*)*
         'There are no castles that remain before him, nor walls nor towns that
         remain to be smashed.'

(42)   *Mandez Charlon, al orgoillos, al fier,*
         Fedeilz servisies et molt granz amistiez.
         Vos li donrez ors e leons e chiens (Chanson de Roland, ll. 28–30*)*
         'Offer Charles, the proud and haughty one,
         Loyal service and great friendship.
         You will give him bears and lions and dogs.'

(43)   *Et pour ce que nature humaine appete de soy liberté et franchise,*
         pluseurs grans seigneuries se sont perdues pour ce que les seigneurs
         d'icelles vouloient tollir franchise a leurs subgitz.
         (Prologue, ll. 18–21*)*
         'And because human nature desires liberty and freedom, several
         large domains have been lost because the lords of those lands wanted
         to take freedom away from their subjects.'

By the mid-sixteenth century, the use of determiners was more widespread, even if still not as frequent as in Modern French. In the *Heptaméron* by Marguérite de Navarre (ca. 1546), almost all nouns had a determiner, as seen in the excerpt in (44).

(44)   *Le premier jour de septembre, que les baings des montz Pyrenées*
         commancent d'entrer en leur vertu, se trouverent à ceulx de
         Cauderetz plusieurs personnes tant de France que d'Espaigne; les
         ungs pour boire de l'eau, les autres pour se baigner, et les autres
         pour prandre de la fange; qui sont <u>choses</u> si myraculeuses que les
         <u>malades</u> habandonnez des <u>medecins</u> s'en retournent tous guariz.
         (Prologue, ll. 1–7)

'The first day of September, when the hot springs of the Pyrenees begin to exert their healing powers, several people, some from France, some from Spain, found themselves at the baths of Cauderetz. Some to drink water, others to bath in it, yet others to take mud baths; which are such miraculous things that sick people whose doctors have given up on them return home completely healed.'

The change from Old French to Middle French usage of determiners is well-illustrated in (44) by *malades* 'sick people' and *medecins* 'doctors', both taken in a generic sense but still preceded by a definite article. In (44), every noun except *choses* 'things', a nominal predicate, and the two names of countries (*France, Espaigne* 'Spain') are preceded by some kind of determiner.

In Modern French a few remnants of the determiner-less structures have survived. Nominal predicates relating to nationality or profession remain without a determiner, such as in *il est médecin* 'he's a doctor', *elle est Pérouvienne* 'she is Peruvian'. Direct objects in fixed expressions such as *avoir faim* 'to be hungry' and *tenir tête* 'to hold one's own against', and prepositional phrases such as *sans aide* 'without help', *avec mépris* 'spitefully', and with feminine names of countries, *en Espagne* 'in Spain'. In addition to the changes in the use of articles, a new determiner, the partitive, developed through the Old and Middle French Periods, as evidenced by the expressions *de l'eau* 'water' and *de la fange* 'bath' in (44).

In Old French, the partitive structure, for example *del vin* 'a certain amount of wine', or *des vins* 'a certain number of the wines' was more definite than in modern usage. In (45) through (47), the definite articles retain some of their demonstrative meaning, for the poet is referring back to the specific wines offered by Charlemagne's host. These examples are most typical of the development of the partitive, as the earlier formations of this type were usually associated with expressions of quantity: *tant* 'so much' as in (45) and *asez* 'enough' as in (46). The plural partitive could be represented by *uns* or *unes* and the plural of the indefinite article 'one', but *des* was more frequent (47). The most common alternative to the plural partitive in Old French was to omit the article altogether, as in (48).

(45)   <u>Del</u> vin e del claret tant eümes beüd (*Voyage de Charlemagne*, l. 665, cited in Aebischer 1965)
        'We had drunk so much of that wine and claret'

(46)   <u>Del</u> vin e del claret asez nus an donastes (*Voyage de Charlemagne*, l. 655)
        'You gave us enough of the wine and claret'

(47)   Franceis furent as cambres si unt beuz <u>des</u> vins (*Voyage de Charlemagne*, l. 457)

'The French were in their rooms and they had drunk some of the wines'

(48)   *Escuz ont genz, espies valentineis,*
         E gonfanons blans et blois e vermeilz (*Chanson de Roland*,
         ll. 998–999)
         'The men have shields and spears from Valencia
         And white, yellow, and red pennants'

When the construction composed of the preposition *de* 'of' + definite article was separated from an expression of quantity, a true partitive was born. In the fifteenth century the form had gained its independence from expressions of quantity (49).

(49)   *Et je m'en voy querir de la farine et du burre* (*Les evangiles des quenouilles*, cited in Gardner and Greene 1958:24)
         'And I am going to look for some flour and some butter'

Gradually, then, a determiner of some sort became a standard part of the noun phrase. With the change in pronunciation of final /s/, the form or choice of the determiner became most often the only indicator of the number of the noun. By the sixteenth century, the use of the article was required in most instances, as indicated in this advice from the poet Pierre de Ronsard: *Tu n'oublieras jamais les articles, & tiendras pour certain que rien ne peut tant défigurer ton vers que les articles délaissés* 'You will never forget articles, and will take as certain the fact that nothing can so disfigure your verse as much as the absence of articles' (1565; cited in Fournier 1998:142).

Another distinctive feature of Old French nominal syntax is a genitive construction without a preposition (50). This construction was common in Old French, but only if the possessor was an animate or personified inanimate noun, in the singular. Most frequently the possessor noun was a proper noun, as in (50), or *Dieu* 'God'. In Middle French, the use of the prepositions *de* 'of' and *à* 'to' became more common, until the absolute genitive construction disappeared, and ultimately *de* replaced *à*. The absolute construction and the use of *à* to express possession remain in place names and fixed phrases, such as *Hôtel-Dieu*, the name of many hospitals in the francophone world, *Dieu merci* 'thanks be to God', and *fils à papa* 'daddy's boy, spoiled young man' (Marchello-Nizia 1979:318–322; Foulet 1968:14–32). The use of *à* to express possession is also current in *français populaire* and in Quebec (Gadet 1997:72; Teibeiriené 2004:3), although condemned by the Académie Française (http://www.academie-francaise.fr/langue/questions.html#a1).

(50)   *Iluec trova Looïs le fill Charle* (*Le couronnement de Louis*, l. 2386)
         'There he found Louis the son of Charles'

> In what situations, not mentioned above, can the determiner be omitted in
> Modern French? How do these contexts compare to English?

6.3.2.3   *Word order*

Word order is usually determined with respect to three elements – Subject, Verb,
and Object – but in Old French the subject pronoun was frequently omitted.
In the *Chanson de Roland* (see Jenkins 1924) the subject pronoun is omitted
in more than 75% of declarative sentences. Only taking into account the three
primary constituents of the sentence, with the subject as optional, Old French
had the following options:

three complements:	SVO	SOV	OVS	OSV	VSO	VOS
two complements:	SV	VS	OV	VO		
single complement:	V					

In declarative sentences the *Chanson de Roland* shows a variety of sentence
structures, but the dominant ones are: VO (46%), OV (21%), and SVO (17%)
(Marchello-Nizia 1999:40–41). In Old French, the VS order is not uncommon
as shown in (51) and (52), but the SV order is more frequent, particularly in
dependent clauses.

(51)   *Ot le Guillelmes, s'en a jeté un ris* (*Le couronnement de Louis*,
        l. 1478)
        'William heard this, he laughed'

(52)   *Vait s'en Guillelmes al Cort Nes le marchis* (*Le couronnement de
        Louis*, l. 1450)
        'William of the short nose, the marquis, goes off'

The expression of the subject pronoun was virtually obligatory by the end of
the Middle French period. By the time of the *Queste del Saint Graal*, a prose
work of the thirteenth century, half the declarative sentences that lack a noun as
subject, use a pronoun. In the XV *Joies de Mariage*, a prose work from the turn
of the fifteenth century (cited in Rychner 1967), the subject pronoun is omitted
only in impersonal constructions, as in (53), but even impersonals sometimes
have subjects, as shown in (54):

(53)   *Si avint une foiz que* . . . (Prologue, l. 30)
        'Thus it once happened that . . .'

(54)   *Mais il n'est pas temps* . . . (Prologue, ll. 65–66)
        'But it is not yet time . . .'

At the same time, the SV(O) order of constituents became dominant, except in so-called disjunct or parenthetical constructions expressing the act of speaking or thinking (55) or in interrogatives (56). These exceptions remain strong today in Modern French.

(55)   *"Amis", dist il, "j'entent bien ta raison"* (*Le couronnement de Louis*, l. 1810)
         '"Friend", said he, "I understand well your reasoning"'

(56)   *Ses tu noveles nules?* (*Le couronnement de Louis*, l. 1460)
         'Do you know any news?'

6.3.2.4 Negation

Negation can occur in several different contexts, and the choice of negative adverb, adjective, pronoun, or prefix depends on those contexts. The following provides a non-exhaustive list of the options:
− negative adverbs, used in responses: *non* 'no', *nenil* 'not at all', *naie* 'no';
− negative adverbs, before the verb: *ne* 'no', *non* 'no';
− negative adverbs, generally after the verb: *ni* 'neither . . . nor', *pas* 'not', *mie* 'not', *goutte* 'not', *point* 'not at all', *guère* 'hardly', *jamais* 'never', *plus* 'no longer', *onque(s)* 'never';
− negative adjective: *nul/nulle, aucun/aucune* 'none';
− negative pronouns: *rien* 'nothing', *personne* 'nobody', *aucun, néant, nul* 'none';
− negative prefixes: *non-, mal-, dé-/dés-, mé-/més-, in-/im-, dis-, sans-, a-*.

As we saw earlier in relation to Modern French (see section 3.8), in Old and Middle French negation can be the sole response to a question (57), it can represent the complete or partial negation of a verb (58) or another part of the sentence (59). Negation could also be part of the lexical structure of the individual word through the use of a negative prefix, such as *mé-* (*mécontent* 'not happy') or *dés-* (*désobéir* 'disobey'). The negative pronoun could occupy the subject position in the sentence (60).

(57)   *. . . ne le feriez vous point? Par mon ame, mon amy, non, je cuide que nanil . . .* (XV *Joies de Mariage, Quinte Joye*, ll. 160–161, cited in Rychner 1967)
         'You would not do it at all? Upon my soul, my friend, no, I think, not at all.'

(58)   *Ne vos salu, n'est pas dreiz que le face* (*Le couronnement de Louis*, l. 2389)
         'I do not greet you; it is not right that I should do so.'

(59)   *Por moi fu dit, <u>non</u> por autrui* (*Érec et Énide*, l. 2518)
        'This was said for me, not for others.'

(60)   *Onques ansanble ne vit <u>nus</u> Tant rois, tant contes, ne tant dus, Ne*
        tant barons a une messe (*Érec et Énide*, ll. 6845–6847)
        'No one ever saw together so many kings, so many counts, so many
        dukes, and so many barons at a single mass.'

In Old French and Middle French, the negative answer to a question or
response to a statement was frequently accompanied by the verbs *avoir* 'to
have', *être* 'to be', or *faire* 'to do', as in (61). The English negative *nay* is a
remnant of this usage, derived from the French *ne* + *ay* (first person of *avoir* 'to
have'). By the sixteenth century, the accompanying verb was usually dropped,
and the simple response of *oui* 'yes' or *non* 'no' sufficed.

(61)   *"C'est la moye" "Par foy, fet le chevaler, noun est"* (Fouke Fitz
        Warin, cited in Gardner and Greene 1958:117)
        'It's mine' 'My faith, says the knight, it's not.'

The negation of the verb in Old French was usually accomplished without
a second element of negation; *non* or *ne* alone were sufficient (62). Even in
the early texts, however, negation is frequently strengthened by the addition of
what had usually been a noun signifying something small: *pas* < Latin *passum*
'a step', *goutte* < Latin *gutta* 'drop', *mie* < Latin *mica* 'crumb', *point* < Latin
punctum 'point' (63).

(62)   *Li reis Marsilies la tient, ki Deu nen aimet* (*Chanson de Roland*, l. 7,
        cited in Jenkins 1924)
        'The king Marsile holds it, he who does not love God'

(63)   *Guenles respont: 'Por mei n'iras tu mie'* (*Chanson de Roland*, l. 296)
        'Ganelon responds: "You will not go in my place."'

The use of a second element of negation slowly increased. In the fifteenth-
century *Jehan de Paris*, *ne* alone was used in about one-third of negations, while
ne + *pas* or *point* was used in about two-thirds. In a selection from Marguerite
de Navarre's *Heptaméron* (ca. 1546), *ne* alone is used only ten times, seven of
those in contexts in which *ne* can be used alone in Modern French (with the
verbs *oser, pouvoir, savoir, cesser* + infinitive), or in some kinds of subordinate
clauses. In the same passage, a second element of negation, usually *pas* or
point, is used twenty-five times. The forms *mie* or *goutte*, already viewed as
archaic, were not used, although they would be maintained in some regional
dialects. For instance *mie*, sometimes reduced to *m* or *me*, has remained the
most common form of negation in the varieties of French spoken in eastern
France and Belgium.

The shift in emphasis from the first (*ne*) to the second (*pas, point,* etc.) element of negation would transform several previously positive nouns and pronouns into negatives. In Old French and Middle French *aucun, rien,* and *personne* were usually used as positives, and only became negative when used in conjunction with *ne*; the grammarian and lexicographer John Palsgrave (1530) listed *aulcunefoys* as meaning 'sometimes'. *Nul* and *nesun* were preferred to *aucun* for the expression of 'none at all' through this period, although *nesun* had become rare by the fifteenth century. In *Bérinus*, composed towards the end of the fourteenth century, the combination *ne . . . nul* is used 262 times, compared to 10 times for *ne . . . aucun* (Marchello-Nizia 1979:143). The use of *pas* or *point*, more rarely *mie*, without *ne* was possible in Old and Middle French, but should not be confused with the omission of *ne* in Modern French (Price 1993). Here again, as in the case of *aucun, rien,* and *personne*, the words *point* in (64) and *mie* in (65) could have a positive or a negative meaning in interrogatives.

(64)   *Et prant l'oignement, si l'en oint*
         Tant com en la boiste en ot point (Chrétien de Troyes, *Chevalier au lion*, ll. 2987–2988, cited in Price 1993:193)
         'And he takes the ointment, and applies it, as long as there is any left in the box at all.'

(65)   *Mais de fromage a il mie?* (*Roman de Renart*, l. 12404, cited in Price 1993:192)
         'But does he have any cheese?' or 'Doesn't he have any cheese?'

By the end of the fifteenth century the negative interpretation of these elements began to dominate, and by then there were already examples in which the only interpretation is negative, as in (66). The change from positive to negative values for the pronouns *aucun, personne,* and *rien,* as well as for the quantifying nouns *pas, point,* and *mie,* occurs in the late fifteenth and sixteenth century, and with that change the omission of *ne* typical of Modern Spoken French became possible.

(66)   *Sont ilz pas douze heures au jour?* (Michel, *Passion*, l. 13454, cited in Price 1993:193)
         'Are there not twelve hours in the day?'

Are there any contexts in which the words *personne, rien,* and *aucun,* can be used positively in Modern French? Give examples.

6.3.2.5   Interrogatives

In Old French, intonation and subject-verb inversion were the primary indicators of an interrogative. Since the subject pronoun was omitted in Old French, as in (67), intonation alone could distinguish interrogatives from declarative sentences:

(67)   *"Oncles", fait-il, "estes sains et haitiez?" (Le couronnement de Louis*, l. 1157)
        "'Uncle', said he, 'are you safe and sound?'"

An important change from Old to Middle French was that the inventory of interrogative structures came to include so-called complex or 'subject-clitic inversion' (68). As mentioned earlier (see section 3.10.1), this meant inserting a clitic subject pronoun as the placeholder of the full subject noun after the inflected verb, and leaving the full noun in sentence-initial subject position, e.g. *Paul vient-il?* In Old French inversion could take place with a full noun subject of virtually any length and type (69), which is not the case in Modern French. In later Middle French, subject-clitic inversion appears among the many means of asking a question, although it is sometimes difficult to tell whether, structurally, we are dealing with a dislocated sentence or subject-clitic inversion, as evidenced by (70), where the pronoun *elle* 'it' (fem. sing.) anaphorically refers to the full noun phrase *de l'eau* 'water'.

(68)   *Claimes tu Rome com ton dreit eritage? (Le couronnement de Louis*, l. 881)
        'Do you claim Rome as your lawful heritage?'

(69)   *Don n'est biax et riches cist dons? (Erec et Enide*, l. 1268)
        'For what reason is this gift not beautiful and dear?'

(70)   *Or ça, de l'eau, comment s'appelle elle en latin? (Récréations et joyeux devis*, nouvelle 21, published in 1558)
        'But that, water, how is that said in Latin?'

Subject-verb inversion involving a pronominal subject only could take place after various interrogative pronouns and adjectives (71) (72), referred to earlier as 'wh-words'(see section 3.10).

(71)   *Que fais tu or, sainz Pere? (Le couronnement de Louis*, l. 1086)
        'What are you doing now, Saint Peter?'

(72)   *Dont ies tu, frere? (Le couronnement de Louis*, l. 1458)
        'Where are you from, brother?'

The use of *est-ce que* originally had an emphatic meaning, and was used in combination with the interrogative pronouns *que* 'what' and *qui* 'who' (73). This emphatic meaning is demonstrated by the frequent use of *est-ce que* with the conjunction *si* 'thus', *si est-ce que* 'so it is that'. The change in the semantics of *est-ce que*, from a meaningful element to a simple marker of interrogation, was slow, but recent evidence (Rouquier 2003) suggests that it might have started earlier, in the Old French period. By the fifteenth and sixteenth century, *est-ce que* could appear alone, as an indication of a question in total interrogation, but such examples were still rare (74). This usage was more common in comic dramatic texts than in other types, which might reflect a difference between common spoken and more prestigious forms, although such interpretations must be taken with a grain of salt, since this evidence comes from stylized literary discourse.

(73)   *qu'est ce que vous avez dit?* (*Jehan de Paris*, cited in Gardner and
        Greene 1958:127)
        'And what is it that you said?'

(74)   *Est-ce que je dois prandre un autre lavement?* (*La farce de maître
        Pierre Pathelin*, written ca. 1470)
        'Should I get another cleansing?'

In the sixteenth century, inversion with singular third-person pronouns (*il* 'he, *elle* 'her', *on* 'one/they/we') could be made with a *-t-* inserted to avoid hiatus (75). The relative rarity of the *-t-* in literary texts (76) is not necessarily an indication of pronunciation, as several sixteenth-century grammarians, starting with Jacques Peletier du Mans in the 1550s, note that a /t/ was often pronounced, even though it was not written (Thurot 1881–1883, II, 240–243).

(75)   *a-t-elle fait chose indigne de soy?* (Robert Garnier, *La Troade*, p. 99,
        FRANTEXT)
        'Did she do something unworthy of herself?'

(76)   *n'y en a il poinct d'autre en la compaignye mariez que Hircan et
        moy?* (Marguerite de Navarre (ca. 1546) *Heptaméron, première
        journée, huitième nouvelle*)
        'Are there no others in the group who are married besides Hircan and
        myself?'

In various regional and social varieties, the reduced form of the construction *t-il* (arising from *-t-* + *il* 'he'), *ti*, became an interrogative marker on its own, as shown in (77), and remains a feature that distinguishes 'standard' French from many other varieties (see also section 3.10.3).

(77)   *t'es-ti point grosse?* (Guy de Maupassant, *Contes et nouvelles*,
        1883:93; cited in FRANTEXT)
        'You ain't pregnant, are you?'

6.3.3   Vocabulary in Old and Middle French

Translation and other cultural contacts had an important impact on the vocabulary of Old and Middle French. In the eleventh and twelfth centuries, the Crusades and the translation of Arabic scientific texts introduced many Arabic terms, some of which passed through Spanish or Italian before being incorporated into French. Translation led to an infusion of words from Classical Latin in the fourteenth century, while wars in northern Italy and subsequent royal marriages brought a wave of Italian words into French in the sixteenth century.

In the twelfth century, the wars in the Holy Land led to contact with the material and cultural riches of Arabic countries. On the material side, French borrowed such terms as *coton* 'cotton', and *jupe* 'skirt'. The translation of Arabic science introduced *alchimie* 'alchemy' and *algèbre* 'algebra'. The effects of war are shown in borrowings like *amiral* 'admiral' (originally 'general' of the army).

In the last quarter of the fourteenth century, King Charles V (1338–1380; reigned 1364–1380) promoted the translation of Latin scientific and philosophical works into French. He founded the Bibliothèque du Louvre, a manuscript collection that presaged the creation of a national library. The collection focused on the subjects taught in the University of Paris, such as astronomy, theology, mathematics, and philosophy, including the works of Aristotle, Cicero, and Seneca. As a result of these efforts, a number of doublets were formed, between words that had undergone the phonetic changes through the centuries, and those that in the Middle Ages were reintroduced into French in their Classical Latin form: learned *cause* 'trial' and popular *chose* 'thing' < Latin *causa*; learned *direct* 'direct' and popular *droit* 'straight', 'right' < Latin *directum*.

The translators felt the necessity of recreating the technical terms of Latin philosophy, as well as the rich synonymy of Latin vocabulary. As a result, the suffixes *-tion, -tude,* and *-ité* were reintroduced into French, to reproduce the abstract terms of Latin: *démonstration* 'demonstration', *aptitude* 'aptitude', *probabilité* 'probability', to name but a few. In addition, Greek words and endings, entering French through Latin, were borrowed into French at this time: *aristocratie* 'aristocracy', *étymologie* 'etymology', *pédagogue* 'teacher'.

Italian culture became the vogue in sixteenth-century France, leading to a mania for Italian words that has been compared with the borrowings from English in the twentieth century. Commercial contacts between northern Italy and Lyons in the fifteenth century were followed by a series of French invasions into northern Italy (1494–1516). The bankers brought with them Italian financial terms, such as *banque* 'bank', *banqueroute* 'bankruptcy', and *crédit* 'credit'. In 1516, François I brought Leonardo da Vinci to France to spend his last years there. The influence of Italian artists and architects is felt in such words as *balcon* 'balcony' and *façade* 'façade'. The marriage of Catherine de Médici to the future Henri II in 1533 brought a new wave of Italian courtiers, and Italian terms related to the courtly life: *courtisan* 'courtier', *mascarade* 'masquerade', and *pantalon* 'pants'. The superlative suffix *-issime* (e.g. *richissime* 'extremely wealthy') became part of French derivational morphology at that time.

The overuse of Italian and 'Italianate' words soon led to a backlash. In 1560, Grévin's play *Les Esbahis* 'The Astounded Ones' includes a scene mocking Italians. The leader of the backlash was Henri Estienne, the son of the famous printer Robert Estienne and a distinguished scholar of Greek in his own right. His *Traicte de la conformité du langage françois avec le grec* 'The Conformity of the French language with Greek' (1565) claimed superiority for French over Italian because French was closer to Greek, while Italian was more like Latin. In 1578 he wrote *Deux dialogues du nouveau langage francois italianizé et autrement desguizé* 'Two dialogues about the new French language, Italianized and otherwise deformed', a savage satire of courtiers' Italianate language. Many words that entered French from Italian at this period have since disappeared, but there was still a lasting effect in certain domains, especially the arts.

In what ways is the mania for Italianisms in the sixteenth century comparable to or different from the use of Anglicisms in the twentieth century?

6.3.4   Pragmatic aspects of language use in Old and Middle French

In Old French, the address pronouns *tu* and *vous* seemed to alternate with no apparent logic. Even within the same sentence both singular and plural forms can be used with the same reference (78). The first two verbs, *soiés* 'be' and *mangiés* 'eat' are second-person plural, while the third verb, *lai* 'leave', and the possessive determiner *ta* 'your' are both second-person singular; all referring to the same person. This has led many early commentators to throw up their hands and give up on trying to explain *tutoiement* and *vouvoiement* in Old French.

(78)   *soiés chois, si mangiés del pain et des pois, si lai ester ta fole entente*
         (*Courtois d'Arras* cited in Foulet 1968:199)
         'Be quiet, eat some bread and peas, and leave aside your wild
         imagination.'

Others, however, have persevered (Kennedy 1972; Maley 1974, Price 1998). The prose *Lancelot* was originally composed in the late twelfth century, but the manuscripts that include it range from the early thirteenth to the late fifteenth century. A study of usage over the course of these texts has provided some logic to the seemingly illogical usage of some poetic works (Kennedy 1972). In this work, *vous* with singular reference is definitely the norm, particularly between equals in age and social rank. However, *tu* is sometimes used to remind a lower-ranking man of his youth, a way of putting him in his place. The choice of *tu* is therefore not strictly a matter of social rank, but rather of emotion at a given time, thus explaining the variation one can find between the same characters. When a character is angry at another he might use *tu*, then revert to *vous* once the situation has calmed (Kennedy 1972:138–139). Similar arguments relating to pronoun choice according to emotional state are found in Bakos (1955), concerning the *Chanson de Roland*. In a study of the thirteenth-century play *Le miracle de Théophile*, Faral (1951:193) also suggests a difference between Parisian and regional usage, but the evidence is so scanty, and the counter-examples so numerous for both regional and Parisian usage that it is risky to make any firm conclusions.

In Middle French, the trend is for people of the bourgeoisie and the nobility to use *vous* among themselves, and for people of the lower classes to use *tu* among themselves. People of the upper classes might use *vous* or *tu* when addressing people of the lower classes. People of the lower classes almost always use *vous* when addressing people of the higher classes (Schliebitz 1886). Every case, however, admits a number of exceptions, and towards the end of the sixteenth century Pasquier sums up the confusion in his *Les Recherches de la France* (1596):

[. . .] *combien que ce mot de* Vous *fust anciennement destiné pour ceux qui nous estoient seulement superieurs, si ne laisse-l'on de le pratiquer non seulement à nos égaux, mais aussi quelquesfois à nos inférieurs, selon la facilité de nos naturels.*

'[. . .] although this word *vous* was formerly used in addressing only those who were superior to us, we continue to use it not only with our equals but also sometimes with our inferiors, according to our natural tendencies.' (Book VIII, ch. 4, p. 1530 in the 1596 edition; the book was begun in 1565; this chapter was added in the 1596 edition)

In poetry, *tu* was frequently used even when addressing kings, varying according to the type of poem (Maley 1974: 23–24).

The other pragmatics issue we are following through the history of the language is the practice of personal names. At the beginning of the Old French period, people were given single names, and the variety of those names was diminishing. At the end of the eleventh century, perhaps instigated by the reforms of Pope Gregory VI, the cult of martyrs and saints changed the naming patterns. The name *Jean*, previously little used, now became the most popular boy's name in France, followed by *Pierre*. As this change established itself, the French names used to represent anyone/everyone, equivalent to English *every Tom, Dick, and Harry*, switched from the Germanic *Gautier et Guillaume* 'Walter and William' to the more saintly *Pierre et Paul* 'Peter and Paul' (Peterson 1929:20–22). The popularity of these saints led to a new problem with homonymy, and soon after the use of surnames grew more common. This was a primary reason for the development of hereditary surnames, but not the only one. The connection of this custom to the clearing of new farmland might also have contributed, along with changes in legal process.

The practice started among the nobility, and gradually spread to include all the population. The names might be based on a personal characteristic, such as *Legrand* 'the tall'. The names of nobles were most frequently based on their seigneurial holding, the so-called *noms à particule*, in which the preposition *de* 'of' was combined with the name of the holding, e.g. *d'Aubigné*. The names of commoners might also have a geographic source, such as a distinctive topographic feature, e.g. *Dubois* 'of the woods' or *Dumoulin* 'of the mill'. Others might note a place of origin for families that had migrated from one region to another, such as *Picard* and *Normand*. Another naming practice indicated parentage, 'son of', although this is less widespread in French surnames than in English. In this case the *fils de* 'son of' has been dropped, and only the first name of the father remains, thus reducing *fils de Bertrand* to *Bertrand*. Finally, the names might represent a profession or social status, such as *Lebouteillier* 'the bottler' (Lefebvre-Teillard 1990:28–29).

While these names were passed from father to first, inheriting, son, the transformation of surnames to family names occurred when the other members of the family – subsequent sons, daughters and wives – took the name. This happened in the late thirteenth and fourteenth century, and gained legal recognition in the fifteenth century. Once legal records were kept of births, deaths, and marriages, the use of a first and last name became the norm.

> A recent change in French law (1 January 2005) permitted parents to choose to give either the father or the mother's surname to a newborn. What are the implications of this change for state and private records?

6.4 French in the modern world

At the beginning of the seventeenth century, French was still a language that admitted much variation, even at the highest levels of literary and legal usage. While the monarchy had intervened to require the use of French in legal activity throughout the kingdom, 'proper usage' had not been defined, and certainly not established through state power. Over the following centuries, to the present day, the state has intervened more and more to establish a standard and to spread the use of that standard. At the same time, the territory under the control of the state expanded, first along the borders and then increasingly overseas as the French empire grew. Paradoxically, just as the power of the state and other social forces within France imposed a single standard form of the language, the expansion of the empire would lead to new diversity in the French spoken around the world.

The first grammars of French composed for French speakers appeared in the sixteenth century, starting in 1531 with the *In linguam gallicam IsagΩge* by

Jacques Dubois (Sylvius). Other grammars followed but none was authoritative. Early in the seventeenth century François de Malherbe critiqued the poetry of Philippe Desportes, condemning the choice of vocabulary, stylistic excesses, and illogical or inconsistent grammatical structures (see Brunot 1891).

Malherbe's severe limitations on poetic language were not without critics, but his group of admirers were well connected. They began meeting weekly at the home of the Parisian nobleman Valentin Conrart (1603–1675). Louis XIII's secretary, Cardinal Richelieu, took note of these meetings, and proposed that the group take on an official role within the state, so that language might be governed by the state as all other matters. Thus the Académie Française came into being in 1635.

The Académie Française originally had one goal: to make French "pure, eloquent, and capable of being a medium for discussion of the Arts and Sciences" (Article 24 of the Académie's bylaws). It would accomplish this task through two means: the composition of four types of reference works on language (a grammar, a dictionary, a guide to rhetoric, and a guide to poetics) and the correction of literary works that would be submitted to the Académie.

The first official activity of the Académie related to the second type of activity. In 1638 the Académie was called on to discuss the qualities of a play, *Le Cid*, by Pierre Corneille (1606–1684). Much like the commentaries of Malherbe on Desportes, the *Sentimens de l'Académie concernant la tragicomédie du Cid* provided a detailed commentary on the choice of words, the construction of the play, and the grammatical features used by Corneille. This was the first and last publication of the Académie criticizing a specific literary work.

The Académie felt more comfortable in pursuing the other charge it was given: to provide a series of reference works relating to the French language. The Académie produced the first of these, a dictionary, in 1694. The editors chose to exclude words that a noble person should not use, such as words relating to technical work or the sciences, or words deemed too base. This decision made it a less than complete dictionary of the French language, even though subsequent editions have been more open.

The Académie did not produce a grammar until 1932, but this does not mean that the Académie was silent on grammatical matters for the first 300 years of its existence. The first secretary of the Académie, Claude Favre de Vaugelas (1585–1650), produced a series of commentaries on the French language in 1647, and these were themselves the object of revisions by the Académie later in the seventeenth century. At the request of the Académie, Regnier Desmarais (1632–1713) wrote a traditional grammar of French early in the eighteenth century. The Académie, in a work composed by Mézeray, also commented on spelling reform in the second half of the seventeenth century. However, the other two reference works promised in the charter of the Académie, the guides to rhetoric and to poetics, have never appeared.

The work of the Académie today includes the preparation of the ninth edition of the dictionary, and the approval of technical terms created by the terminological commissions created in the 1970s. These terminological commissions were formed as a reaction to the dominance of English in scientific and technical fields.

The standardization of French through the activities of the Académie affected the usage of the nobility and the bourgeoisie, but had little impact on the majority of French speakers. The educational system of the *Ancien Régime* was in the hands of the Church and focused on the learning of Latin. Although educational reformers such as Charles Rollin (1661–1714) recommended increased attention to learning the native language, this change in the educational system would only take place after the French Revolution (1789). The ideal education of the good citizen was different from that of the good subject. Good citizens were expected to participate in government, and to do this they needed to know the national language.

Two surveys, one conducted by the Abbé Grégoire in 1790 and the other launched in 1807 by Coquebert de Montbret, confirmed the fact that a large majority of the population did not speak a French recognizable by the educated. They might speak a regional, rural variety of French (the so-called *patois*), or the related but distinct languages of southern France, today grouped under the term Occitan, or they might speak a completely different language: Flemish, German, Breton, Basque, Corsican, or Catalan. What both surveys confirmed was the urgent necessity of instituting an educational system focused on the teaching of the national language.

Teaching a subject that had not been part of the curriculum before was quite a challenge. A contest was held in 1795 to select the national school grammar, and in 1798 Lhomond's *Elemens de la grammaire francaise* 'Elements of French Grammar' was declared the winner. Teachers could look for guidance to Urbain Domergue's (1745–1810) *Journal de la langue française*, a periodical devoted to questions of grammar and style, which started in 1785 and continued, under various titles and editors, until 1840. National inspection of schools began in the 1830s. Throughout the nineteenth century inspectors were dismayed at the quality of French of the students, and of the teachers. In the 1880s the institution of free, mandatory education, under the control of the state rather than of the church, further advanced the spread of the national language. So did military conscription, as soldiers were threatened with extended tours of duty if they had not learned to speak French during their first tour. By the early twentieth century, all of these factors had the cumulative effect of making virtually all French people capable of speaking French, although they might still prefer to express themselves in their local language.

Throughout this period of the standardization of French usage in France, other varieties of French were being created in the far-flung territories of the

French Empire. From the early seventeenth century until 1763 France controlled Canada and the Ohio and Mississippi valleys of North America. The combination of dialects primarily from western France and the separation of these regions from Parisian influence led to the creation of different forms of French in Quebec, Acadia, and Louisiana. The interaction between French dialectal speakers and the African languages of the slaves brought to the Caribbean islands, French Guiana, and Louisiana formed new creole languages in those regions. French colonies were established in North Africa, West and Central Africa, and in the South Pacific in the nineteenth century. Each expansion of territory resulted in the creation of new varieties of French, and in the borrowing into Metropolitan French of terms used in the local languages of the conquered people: *bled* 'isolated town' from Arabic, *banane* from the Bantu languages of West Africa, and *tomate* from the Indian languages of Central America.

Even with the loss of much of that Empire in the second half of the twentieth century, French is today an official language in more than thirty countries. One of the enduring legacies of the French Empire is the conflict between the Metropolitan French standard and local varieties in official and educational settings. As early as the 1840s a debate arose in Quebec over the relationship between Quebecois French and the language of the mother country (see Dionne 1912). Similarly, in the twentieth century, the relative status of French and French Creoles in the Caribbean has been the subject of much discussion.

6.4.1   Phonology in Classical and Modern French

Languages never stop changing, but it seems to be the case that the rapidity of change has slowed since the beginning of the eighteenth century. This could be the result of institutional changes; the founding of a uniform nationwide educational system in France, universal military conscription for men, and later the development of radio and television have all contributed to strengthen the notion of a single standard, and to spread that notion throughout the country. Nonetheless Brunot's statement about eighteenth-century French, that "*les sons se modifient; ils ne se transforment plus*" 'sounds are modified but they no longer change' is at the least an exaggeration (Brunot 1966: VI, 973); as the previous chapters demonstrated, there is widespread ongoing variation in all varieties of French.

An advantage we have in studying the pronunciation of the Classical and Modern periods is the abundance of grammatical commentary on the subject, combined with attempts at phonetic transcription. From the early seventeenth century we have the remarkable attempt by the royal physician Jean Héroard to note down the speech of the young Louis XIII. At the beginning of the eighteenth century Gile Vaudelin (fl. 1692–1715) attempted to transcribe French as it was spoken (*Nouvelle manière d'écrire comme on parle en France*, 1713).

At the end of the eighteenth century the Abbé Féraud (1725–1807) was the first French lexicographer to add systematically the pronunciation of each word, in his *Dictionnaire critique* (1787). In the early nineteenth century Coquebert de Montbret (1755–1831) collected versions of the parable of the prodigal son in the speech of many regions of France. The establishment of linguistics as a scientific discipline in the nineteenth century included much work on dialectology. Ultimately the needs of dialectologists and of modern language teachers led to the creation of a more scientific phonetic transcription, the International Phonetic Alphabet, by Paul Passy (1859–1940; see Ladefoged 1999) and his colleagues at the end of the century.

Much of the commentary on pronunciation throughout the Classical and Modern period has focused on the question of reforming French spelling. Gile Vaudelin created his transcription in an effort to make it easier for people to read religious materials. The Académie Française reformed spelling in its dictionaries of 1740 and 1835. The French philosopher Voltaire (1694–1778) contributed to the orthographic debates through the middle of the eighteenth century. Once the state school system and the national exams were established in the nineteenth century, spelling (*dictée* 'dictation') became a favorite teaching technique, an exercise that emphasized spelling accuracy. Late in the nineteenth century reforms were proposed, leading to the *tolérances officielles*, excusable variation of spelling in state examinations. In 1990 another attempt at spelling reform had very limited results, primarily concerning the circumflex accent and hyphenated words. Each of these spelling reform movements was inspired by a recognition that the pronunciation of French had changed, while the spelling of French had remained virtually unchanged.

6.4.1.1 Vowels

The most important changes in the vowel system during the Classical Period include:

- the variation between /o/ and /u/; a lively debate in the sixteenth and seventeenth centuries;
- the pronunciation of the letter sequence *oi*;
- the number and nature of the nasal vowels.

In the sixteenth century, commentators attributed the pronunciation of /u/ for /o/ to regions south of Paris, but spanning the country from Angers to Lyon. They condemned such pronunciations as /ʃuz/ for *chose* and /purtrɛ/ for *portrait*. In the last quarter of the sixteenth century and in some seventeenth-century commentaries, the use of /u/ was perceived as an affectation of courtiers. By the end of the seventeenth century such a pronunciation was simply viewed as archaic, and then as typical of illiterates (see Ayres-Bennett 2004:191–201 for full discussion). Today a few remnants of this pronunciation remain, in words like *tourment* 'torment' and *fourmi* 'ant'. It also remains a common feature in regional literature, as exemplified by the spellings *coûté* (Standard French *côté* 'side') and *la voutre* (Standard French *la vôtre* 'yours') in some stories written in the 1970s in the dialect of the department of Maine in Western France (Déan-Laporte 1975:27, 37).

The grapheme or spelling sequence *oi* could be interpreted as /ε/, as /wε/, or as /wa/ in the seventeenth and eighteenth centuries. The alternation between /ε/, /wε/, and /wa/ is noted as early as the thirteenth century, usually indicated through rhymes such as *toiles~telles* signifying the pronunciation /wε/ in Villon (cited in Nyrop 1914: I, 177), or by distinctive spellings, such as *oe* for /wε/, in *aperçoeve* 'appears' (first- or third-person singular subjunctive; cited in Nyrop 1914: I, 177) and *e* for /ε/ in *avet*, found in the late thirteenth-century *Élégie hébraïque* (cited in Nyrop 1914: I, 178). The pronunciation /wa/ was much more rare in Old French, although not impossible, as the example in (79) from Nyrop suggests:

(79)   *puet on bien voar?* (= Modern French *voir*; cited in Nyrop 1914: I, 180)
        'Can one see well?'

In 1530, the English grammarian John Palsgrave recommended the pronunciation /wa/ for *bois* 'woods', *voix* 'voice', and even for the imperfect endings *-ois* and *-oit* (*disoat*, 'said', as Palsgrave wrote it), and /oj/ for words such as *roy* 'king'. However, other grammarians condemned both /ε/ and /wa/, finding the first a 'lazy' pronunciation, and the latter 'vulgar'. The social interpretation of the varying pronunciations is unclear. Before the French Revolution, Urbain Domergue found acceptable both /wa/ and /wε/, but after the Revolution he condemned /wε/ as a remnant of aristocratic pronunciation. On the other hand, the Abbé Féraud, writing in 1787, claimed that /wa/ was of a higher register, and /ε/ was more ordinary (Séguin 1972:43).

In Modern French the pronunciation /wε/ is present in regional French, both in France and overseas. In the early 1840s in Quebec, the Grand Vicar Thomas Maguire advised grade school teachers to correct their students of a common 'mistake' in Quebecois French, the pronunciation /wε/ for /wa/, judging such correction "an immense responsibility to the students and to society" (Dionne 1912:105). Another Grand Vicar, Jérôme Demers, responded with a long examination of the opinions of the major grammarians and lexicographers of the late eighteenth and early nineteenth century (Féraud, Boiste, Landais, Lévizac, Noël et Chapsal, Catineau, Rolland, Gattel) and concluded that usage in France was too undecided to give a model to young Quebecois.

In northern Metropolitan French, /ε/ remains in certain words, such as adjectives denoting nationality (*français* 'French', *polonais* 'Polish', but note *hongrois* /õgrwa/ 'Hungarian'), and in the endings of the imperfect tense. The change in spelling of the imperfect from *-ois* to *-ais* was first recommended in the seventeenth century, promoted by Voltaire in the eighteenth century, and finally adopted by the Académie Française in the sixth edition of their dictionary, in 1835. Elsewhere /wa/ has come to be the dominant pronunciation.

Nasal vowels were another area of widespread divergence among speakers of French (see also section 2.2.2). In a study of 111 native speakers of French within continental France and Corsica, Walter (1994) found that a significant majority, seventy-seven percent, still distinguished four or more nasal vowels, typically /õ/, /ã/, /œ̃/, and /ɛ̃/. Some reportedly made up to six nasal vowel distinctions. Her informants from the Ile-de-France, Champagne, and Bretagne frequently had only three, having lost the opposition /ɛ̃/~/œ̃/. Although Walter's fine-grade, auditory categorization of vowel quality should be taken with a grain of salt, as it is well known that the perceptual categorization of vowels is continuous (gradient) rather than discrete (categorical), especially if it relies on a single speaker's perception (however accurate it may be), she nonetheless provides strong indication of different tendencies in different dialects. Walter's conclusions are not surprising in light of the historical development of French, as the distinction between /ɛ̃/ and /œ̃/ was already weakening in the seventeenth century, but is still strong in southern and eastern France, as well as in Quebec.

The nasal vowels have been shifting for some time (see also section 2.2.2). In the 1920s several observers noted that /ɛ̃/ was shifting towards /ã/, and that this change was being used to distinguish *pain* 'bread', pronounced closer to /pã/ or perhaps /paɛ̃/, from *pin* 'pine tree', pronounced /pɛ̃/ (Carton 1995:33). At the same time confusions arose between distinctions based on /ã/ and /õ/, such as between *blond* 'blond' and *blanc* 'white', noted by the phonetician Paul Passy in 1917 (cited in Carton 1995:33).

The following words were all spelled by the sequence *oi* in the seventeenth century. How are they spelled and pronounced now? *Danois* 'Danish', *Polonois* 'Polish', *pommeroie* 'apple orchard', *foible* 'weak', *poire* 'pear', *moi* 'me', *disoit* 's/he said'.

6.4.1.2   Consonants

In this section we will look at two changes that have taken place since 1600 in French: the change in the point of articulation of the consonant /r/, and the varying practices concerning the so-called 'aspirate' h. The /r/ of seventeenth- and eighteenth-century French was most typically an apical trill, and this pronunciation has been preserved in some regional dialects until today (see also section 2.2.2). Starting in the mid-eighteenth century, the fashion among the Parisian nobility and bourgeoisie moved towards a dorsal pronunciation. Pierre Léon studied the transformation of the pronunciation of /r/ in his native village in the

Touraine, where the apical /r/ was replaced by the dorsal /ʀ/ over the course of three generations from the late nineteenth century through the first half of the twentieth century (Léon 1973:785). Nonetheless, in musical performance the trill remained the standard until the mid-twentieth century (Carton 1995:36).

As mentioned earlier (see section 2.4.4.2) the *h-aspiré* 'aspirate h' label in Modern French applies to a specific list of words that are spelled with *h*, but are phonologically vowel-initial. Their peculiarity is that they block liaison and prevent the elision of the vowel preceding the word, e.g. *les haricots* is pronounced /leariko/ instead of /lezariko/ 'the beans', and *la haine* is uttered /laɛn/ instead of /lɛn/ 'hatred'. Most but not all of these words are derived from Germanic words. The 'aspirate h' stopped being pronounced in the sixteenth or seventeenth century, although some grammarians kept insisting that it be pronounced into the early twentieth century. Some words displaying phonological characteristics similar to *h-aspiré* 'aspirate h' words are not spelled with a word-initial *h*: e.g. *onze* 'eleven' and *ouate* 'cotton stuffing'. Others are spelled with a non-etymological initial *h*, such as *huit* 'eight' from Latin *octem*. The word *héros* 'hero' is an 'aspirate h' word, but its derivatives are not: *héroïne* 'heroine', *héroïque* 'heroic'. According to the purist tradition, some words do not follow typical liaison and elision when preceded by an article, but do when preceded by a preposition: *la Hongrie* 'Hungary', *la reine d'Hongrie* 'the queen of Hungary'.

Because the phonological behavior of 'aspirate h' words can no longer be predicted from spelling, and they require memorization of many irregularities such as the ones exemplified above, they are ideal for making social distinctions and demonstrating one's schooling. As early as the seventeenth century, Vaugelas had described the incorrect pronunciation of these words as typical of French spoken on the other side (south) of the Loire (1647:196). Fifty years later the commentaries of the Académie Française on Vaugelas' remarks include an indication of the hesitation felt even among those at the Court, noting that some find it less grating to say *l'hideuse image* 'the hideous image' although saying *la hideuse image* is 'safer' in polite company (cited in Streicher 1936: I, 409). Further discussion of 'aspirate h' is found in virtually every collection of remarks on French through to the present day, with mistakes being ascribed to social class differences (e.g. Sauger-Préneuf 1843, condemning *l'Hollande* 'Holland') and to the inattention of 'good authors' (e.g. Le Gal 1932), citing literary works that include the expression *par un bel hasard* 'by a stroke of good luck', and claiming that an 'aspirate h' would require *beau hasard* 'good luck').

In modern usage, the blocking of liaison and elision seems to be gaining ground in formal French, while losing ground in everyday conversation. Carton (1995:41) cites the preference for *le un* for *l'as* 'the ace' in a game of cards, and the extension of the phenomena to proper nouns and acronyms which are not spelled with *h*: *le S.T.O.* /ləɛsteo/ *le Service du Travail Obligatoire*

'Forced Labor Requirement' (in occupied France during World War II). At the same time, Moisset (1996) also shows that in less guarded speech 'aspirate h' phenomena seem to be on the decline.

List as many words as you can that are not spelled with an initial *h* but which behave like 'aspirate h' words, i.e. they block liaison and elision (for these notions, see section 2.4.4.2).

6.4.2 Morphology and syntax in Classical and Modern French

The composition of the first grammars in the sixteenth century, often accompanied by long lists of noun and especially verb forms, have been instrumental in regularizing the morphology of standard French in the formal uses and registers of the language, even as other dialects continued to use other forms. In the second half of the sixteenth century and the seventeenth century, the variety of forms used in official and literary French diminished markedly. In syntax, the acceptance of more 'popular' forms (i.e. initiated by less educated speakers) has brought into written French forms that previously would have been excluded, such as interrogative and negative structures abundant in less educated speakers' spoken language (see sections 6.3.2.3 and 6.3.2.4). The most obvious change is in the forms of negation, which took place in two steps: first a 'learned' change, brought by the spread of the standard and written forms of expression, contributed to the reduction of the number of second elements (e.g. *mie, point,* etc.), then a 'popular' change, typical of less educated speakers, led to the progressive loss of *ne,* the first element.

6.4.2.1 Future stems and auxiliary selection: être ou avoir?

The forms of the future stems competed through Old and Middle French and then, rather abruptly in the mid-seventeenth century, many irregular forms disappeared (Fennell 1975). The 'regular', synthetic formation inherited from Latin adds future endings to an infinitival base form: *donner* 'to give' + the *-ai* ending marking the first-person singular of the future tense of the verb: *je donnerai* 'I shall give'. In Middle French many alternative forms existed, such as *assaudray* 'I shall attack' (Modern French *assaillirai*), and *buvray* 'I shall drink' (Modern French *boirai*). In the case of *laisser* 'to leave', it was a case of competing infinitives (*laire/laiss(i)er*). The FRANTEXT database has no examples of *lairray* or *lairrai* 'I shall leave' after 1659, although the forms were about equally distributed with *laisseray* and *laisserai* before the seventeenth century. The last attestation in that database of *aray* 'I shall have' (Modern French *aurai*) is from 1646. In 1647, Vaugelas called forms like *donray "monstres"* 'monsters' (1647 [1934]:119). The cumulative effect of a centralized court culture and institutions like the Académie Française was the rejection of variation in favor of a single norm.

In a process that stretched longer into the Modern French period, many verbs that could be conjugated with either *être* or *avoir* were reduced to a single option, usually *avoir*. In both in (80) and (81), the author is referring to the act of disappearing, but in the sentence in (80) he is using *être*, while in (81) he is using *avoir* to depict the same movement.

(80)   *comme en un instant le monstre est disparu* (1631, J de Gombauld, *L'amaranthe*, cited in FRANTEXT)
    'in a flash of an eye the monster disappeared'

(81)   *le songe fugitif qui a disparu à son réveil* (1699, Fénelon, *Les Aventures de Télémaque*, cited in FRANTEXT)
    'the fleeting dream that disappeared upon his waking'

In the eighteenth century, Condillac makes a semantic distinction in auxiliary selection, suggesting that the freedom of choice for expressing the action has disappeared:

on ne peut pas choisir indifféremment entre les deux auxiliaires, quoique les participes puissent se construire également avec l'un et avec l'autre. Il faut toujours considérer si on veut exprimer un état, ou si on veut exprimer une action; et c'est d'après cette règle qu'on doit choisir entre il est accouru, il a accouru, il est disparu, il a disparu. (1775, Abbé de Condillac, *Cours Instruction du Prince*, cited in FRANTEXT)

'You cannot choose the auxiliary verb indifferently, although the participles can be added to either of them. You must always ask yourself if you wish to express a state, or if you wish to express an action; it is according to this rule that you must choose between *il est accouru, il a accouru, il est disparu, il a disparu.*'

The same distinction between result and action continued in the nineteenth century. In 1835 Platt de Concarneau argued that one could use the auxiliary *avoir* with the verb *tomber* 'to fall', when the item falling changed its nature upon reaching its destination. According to him one could say *la pluie a tombé* 'the rain fell', because the water ceases to be rain when it hits the ground. Similarly, for him, if one said *l'enfant est tombé* 'the child fell' it means that the child is still on the ground, but if one were to describe later what happened, one could say *il a tombé* 'he fell'.

An extension of that explanation was offered in 1823 by Blondin, in his *Manuel de la pureté du langage*. According to him, intransitive verbs such as *tomber* select *être* because its past participle *tombé* could be used as an adjective: *un homme tombé, une femme tombée*. Other intransitive verbs such as *dormir*, 'to sleep' were conjugated with *avoir* because one could not say *un homme dormi, une femme dormie*. These explanations were not supported by usage, though. The rare examples of *avoir tombé* in twentieth-century literature are either impersonals (82) or representations of lower-class speech (83). In the twentieth-century texts included in the FRANTEXT database, there are 510 instances of *est tombé* as opposed to 8 of *a tombé*, all of which fall into the two categories represented in the examples in (82) and (83).

(82)   *elle [la neige] a tombé pendant treize heures toute la journée de dimanche* (Julien Green, *Journal*, T. 3, 1943, cited in FRANTEXT)
        'it fell thirteen hours, throughout the day on Sunday'

(83)   *d'un coup tout en bas qu'elle a tombé!* (Céline, *Voyage au bout de la nuit*, 1932, cited in FRANTEXT)
        'in an instant she fell all the way down!'

What non-pronominal verbs can be conjugated with both *être* and *avoir* in the compound past tenses? What are the differences between the two forms?

6.4.2.2   *Types of interrogative and* ne *deletion*

Social factors play a significant role in the distribution of the two syntactic features we shall consider here. The change in interrogative types and the changes in the deletion of the negative particle *ne* are tied in modern usage to factors of class and age. A burning question in historical sociolinguistics is how to interpret this data. Does it mean that there was stability over the past 300 years, and the only difference now is our ability to record and our interest in recording the usage of the working classes? Or does it mean that French is shifting towards an SVO word order in interrogation and the deletion of *ne* in negation? There is plenty of room for further research into this new area, considering many variables that have social significance.

Interrogation in Old and Middle French was largely though not exclusively expressed by a change in word order. As we have seen above, SV(O) was typical of declarative sentences, and VS(O) or (O)VS of interrogative sentences. In the last century of the Middle French period the construction *est-ce que* + SV(O) became more common, although even in the seventeenth century *est-ce que* often retained its semantic force, 'is it that . . .?', indicating that the entire proposition was in question (84), as opposed to inversion in which the relationship between the subject and the verb is in question (85). The difference can be demonstrated syntactically by the possibility of separating *est-ce* from *que*, as in (86):

(84)   *est-ce que vous êtes malade?* (1673, Molière, *Le malade imaginaire*, Act I, Scene 5; cited in Fournier 1998:122)
        'is it that you are sick?'

(85)   *Êtes-vous malade?*
        'Are you sick?'

(86)   *Et comment est-ce, dit Phillis, que vous avez pris garde à luy?* (1610;
        Honoré d'Urfé, *L'Astrée*, cited in FRANTEXT)
        'And how is it, said Phillis, that you were watching over him?'
        (= how did it happen that)

Therefore in Classical Literary French the use of *est-ce que* is not a sign of a lack of sophistication, the inability to master complex inversion of the type *Pierre dit-il* 'Pierre, does he say', but rather serves a different pragmatic function (Fournier 1998:122). Vaugelas acknowledges a controversy between the two types of question formation, but rather likes *est-ce que* (1934 [1647]:458). But by the end of the seventeenth century, forming questions with *est-ce que* is considered to be of a "very familiar style", and not appropriate for written French (Académie Française 1704:488).

The condescension towards the *est-ce que* form in literary usage continued into the twentieth century. In particular, the use of *est-ce que* with an interrogative adverb (*pourquoi* 'why', *où* 'where') is considered superfluous, a kind of double interrogative (Joran 1928:155–156). Martinon (1927:243) finds it "absolutely correct" but unwelcome in written language. However, inversion is not possible with many first-person forms, although the list of those condemned forms changes during the Classical and Modern French periods. In Modern French, such inversion is limited to a very few verbs, all monosyllables, and generally to a literary style: *suis-je* 'am I', *dois-je* 'may I', *puis-je* 'can I', *ai-je* 'have I', *dis-je* 'say I'. Even more literary and rare is the use of a form ending in *-é* for inversions with the subject pronoun *je*: *aimé-je* 'do I love', as in (87):

(87)   Phylis: [. . .] *ne vous aimé-je point?* (1637, Pierre Corneille, *La Place royale*, Act II, Scene 7, cited in FRANTEXT)
        'Do I not love you?'

In Classical French the list of verbs admitting inversion with *je* was longer than it is today. Vaugelas complains that even at the royal court some people invented forms like *menté-je* 'am I lying' and *perdé-je* 'am I losing', but he accepts *mens-je* and *perds-je*, which are not used today. In 1676 the Académie Française decided, on the contrary, that *dorme-je* was preferable to *dors-je* 'am I sleeping' (Streicher 1936: II, 1021). Grevisse cites a few modern examples of first-person present tense forms ending in *-é* in inversion questions (1969:665). In the FRANTEXT database, there are no examples of *perds-je* after the mid-seventeenth century, and none of *sens-je* 'am I feeling' after the early nineteenth century, and even that late only in archaizing texts (Baour-Lormian's poems of Ossian, 1827).

In twentieth-century French, the controversy moved to another type of interrogative, the use of *c'est que* + SVO order, as shown in (88). Even more roundly condemned by purists is the construction that puts the interrogative ('wh') word in sentence-final position, as in (89).

(88)   *quand c'est que tu viens?*
        'When is it that you are coming?'

(89)   *Tu viens quand?*
        'You are coming when?'

These forms, practiced in informal spoken French throughout the centuries, and described as childish by the grammarians, are now penetrating into the spoken language of educated speakers, and even into literary usage, albeit usually in imitations of children's or uneducated people's usage (90). The use of this structure is perceived as growing (Fuchs 1997:19; Marchello-Nizia 1999:65–66), but we still await precise sociolinguistic data.

(90)   *tu vas où? demanda le père.* (1931, Jean Giono, *Le grand troupeau*, cited in FRANTEXT)
        'You are going where? Asked the father.'

The loss of *ne* is also perceived as growing, but in this case we have firmer data and an ongoing debate about the interpretation of that data. In section 6.3.2.4 we noted that *ne* could be omitted in interrogative structures through Middle French, and in fact through the mid-seventeenth century. Vaugelas defended the omission of *ne* in questions, but stated that *ne* is obligatory in declarative sentences (1934 [1647]:210). The Académie Française, commenting on Vaugelas almost sixty years later, rejected the omission of *ne* in either structure (1704:232). Martineau and Mougeon (2003) trace the pre-twentieth-century history of *ne* deletion and conclude that the feature is connected to other processes, such as the transformation of subject pronouns into affixes, all progressing rapidly in central and western France as well as in Quebec during the nineteenth and twentieth centuries.

Although the use of *ne* in written French continues to be the norm, in spoken French it has all but disappeared in Canadian French, and its use among speakers from the Hexagon (continental France) seems to be diminishing. Scholars agree that it is less used by younger speakers than by older speakers (Ashby 1981, 1991), but the significance of that fact is still in question. Does this mean that younger speakers will continue to omit *ne* in the future, eventually leading to the complete loss of *ne* in French? Or will those speakers change their behavior and "talk like adults", with greater use of *ne* (Blanche-Benveniste and Jeanjean 1987)? Is this usage changing or is it stable? More recent data by Ashby (2001) suggests that a change is indeed in progress, as the percentage of *ne* deletion in older speakers is rising rapidly.

Sankoff and Vincent in 1977 indicated that in spoken Canadian French *ne* has disappeared almost completely, and yet the use of *ne* remains an important factor in demonstrating that one is educated. In the French language examination for entrance into the Université du Québec en Outaouais, retention of *ne* is listed as one of the criteria to judge if a student has an adequate command of French syntax (Web-based publication, January 2005). In Belgium teachers are adamant about the use of *ne* (Lafontaine 1986, cited in Coveney 1998:161–162), which may reflect dialectal preference as well as level of education, since eastern dialects of French have tended to retain *ne* in a double negation structure.

Nonetheless, use of *ne* in surveys taken in Metropolitan France from 1960 to 1997 varies from a high of 92% in 1960–1961 (Ägren 1973) to a low or very low of 7% and 1% in 1983 (Pooley 1996). These studies were done in different parts of the country: Ashby's in Paris and Tours (west central France), Coveney's in the department of the Somme (north-eastern France), Pooley's in the Nord. Moreau's (1986) survey covered a wider geographic range, but a single professional category (cultural celebrities interviewed on the radio). Geographic factors do not seem to be decisive within Metropolitan France.

One important conclusion of these surveys was that what is important is the subject of the sentence: *ne* is retained frequently by all users, when the subject is the pronoun *nous* 'we' or a noun, but is dropped frequently when the subject is the pronoun *ce* 'it', *je* 'I', or *tu* 'you' (Coveney 1998:163). Equally important is the second element of negation. If the second element is the exceptive *que* (*ne . . . que* 'only'), *ne* is retained more frequently, while if it is *pas* it is less likely to be retained (Coveney 1998:165). The percentages vary from one study to another, but the hierarchy remains the same. Both of these might relate to the factor proposed by Moreau (1986): frequent collocations would tend to omit *ne*, while less frequent collocations would retain *ne*. In this way she explains fairly accurately the almost universal omission of *ne* in phrases such as *je (ne) sais pas* 'I don't know' or *ça (ne) marche pas* 'that doesn't work', along with the hierarchy determined by Coveney both in his field samples and in his Intuitions Elicitation Test. Similarly Armstrong and Smith's (2002) comparison of corpora drawn from radio samples in the early 1960s and the 1990s shows a consistent reduction of the use of *ne*, but a retention of the hierarchy according to the preceding element.

In both of these areas, the formation of questions and the use of *ne*, French syntax is changing slowly, or else we are simply studying a broader segment of the population and seeing patterns that were not readily apparent when studies were limited to written texts. Sound recording techniques have been available for roughly a century now, allowing the incorporation of spoken evidence and expanding the range of social contexts observed. The understanding of syntactic change over time will be strengthened by continued broad-based research, including both spoken and written data.

When does *ne* alone have negative meaning? When does *ne* not have a negative meaning? What are the stylistic and social meanings of such usage?

6.4.3   Vocabulary in Classical and Modern French

In the seventeenth and eighteenth centuries the creation of new words and phrases generated a major controversy, as the doctrines of *clarté* 'clarity' clashed with the inventiveness of court usage. In the nineteenth and twentieth centuries, it was not so much the creation of new words, as the borrowing of words, especially from English, that had the attention of the public, of language scholars, and of the governments of French-speaking countries.

La préciosité 'preciousness' is a term used in the seventeenth century to describe certain lexical fads, attributed primarily to women of the court, such as:

- the invention of periphrases: *fauteuil* 'chair' becomes *commodité de la conversation* 'a facilitator of conversation', a book is *un maistre muet* 'a silent master';
- the use of intensifying adverbs such as *furieusement* 'furiously' in place of *très* 'very';
- the use of adjectives as nouns, e.g. *du sérieux, mon fier*.

Some limit *la préciosité* to a specific group of women in the 1650s, but these linguistic patterns existed to some extent before that (see Brunot 1966: III, 68–70), and continued afterwards, even though they were widely mocked, for instance in Molière's *Les précieuses ridicules*, first performed in 1659. It is not clear how widespread the practice was, and how much it was limited to women's language (see Ayres-Bennett 2004:133–143).

From *préciosité* the concerns of the protectors of the French language turned to neologism, the creation of new words. The *précieux* did not so much invent new words as use common words in unexpected combinations. In the eighteenth century, as experimental science began to take hold, as well as new philosophical and political ideas, new terms were needed. Without such inventions the expressivity of the language would be reduced. Although the eighteenth-century creations were equally mocked, for instance in Guyot-Desfontaines' *Dictionnaire néologique*, first published in 1726, many terms that he ridiculed have become unobjectionable members of French vocabulary, such as *impressionner* 'to impress' and the use of the suffixes *-isme* and *-iser*.

The debate over neologisms concerned the necessity of alternative terms. Were existent terms sufficient to express the ideas one wanted to express? The rejection of synonymy that marked Malherbe's 'doctrine' in the seventeenth century gradually shifted to an appreciation of the ability of synonyms to express different facets of the same notion, so-called *nuances* 'nuances', comparable to the shades of color (Nye 2000). This led to the production of dictionaries of synonyms, such as the Abbé Girard's *Synonymes françois, leurs significations, et le choix qu'il en faut faire pour parler avec justesse* (1736). For Girard, the use of synonyms made language clearer, because the multiple perspectives synonyms provided gave a more complete image of the object described than any one word could.

The Académie Française and the *philosophes* of the eighteenth century would therefore make a distinction between *néologie* 'neology' and *néologisme* 'neologism'. The former described the necessary creation of new words to express new ideas. This was a scientific process, such as the creation of new chemical terminology by Lavoisier. The latter, though, was condemned, as it implied random word creation, frequently when a perfectly adequate word seemingly already existed. In the article from the *Encyclopédie* on *néologisme*, the practice is described as *l'affectation de certaines personnes à se servir d'expressions nouvelles & éloignées de celles que l'usage autorise* 'some people's affectation of using new expressions completely unauthorized by usage'. In the nineteenth century Victor Hugo perceived neologisms as destroying the tissue of the language (Alaoui 2003:173). The attitude towards neologic activity gradually shifted, so that by the twentieth century it was generally perceived as a sign of scientific progress (Pruvost 2003).

Neologic invention was only justified by necessity, in which case the art of neology, what we might call today 'terminology', would be brought to bear to determine how best to express a new idea. Thus it was that Rousseau (1750) and the Abbé Féraud (1787) justified the creation of the term *investigation*, in the sense of 'extended research into a subject', a word each of them thought he had invented, although the word had been used with a different meaning since the fifteenth century.

The French Revolution would be a period of massive neologic activity, consecrated by the supplement added to the fifth edition of the *Dictionnaire de l'Académie Française* in 1798, and by Louis-Sébastien Mercier's *Néologie: ou Vocabulaire de mots nouveaux, à renouveler, ou pris dans des acceptions nouvelles* (1801). The prefix *démo-* (Greek 'people') and the suffix *-cratie*, from the Greek verb 'to rule', would be the source for many new words, such as *démagogue* 'leader of a popular faction' (according to the fifth edition of the *Dictionnaire*) and *gynécocratie* 'state where women can rule'.

Aside from the creation of new words, another way to expand the vocabulary of the language was to borrow from other languages. This process was encouraged in the sixteenth century, from both regional languages of France and from Italian, condemned in the seventeenth century, and then revived in the eighteenth century. Since the eighteenth century, the primary source of borrowings has been English. This raised few eyebrows in the eighteenth century, as the borrowings were limited in number and in semantic scope. The fifth edition of the *Dictionnaire de l'Académie Française* acknowledges an English source for some 60 words, most of them political terms such as *alderman* 'alderman', *communes* 'House of Commons', and *législature* 'legislature', although there are terms from everyday life such as *flanelle* 'flannel' and *aile* 'ale'. In addition to vocabulary, the rise in popularity of the English ending *-ing* has led to a class of nouns that the French are not quite sure how to pronounce, as illustrated by the debate over alternate spellings and pronunciations: *meeting/mitine* (/mitiŋ/, /mitin/), and the complete **assimilation** of *shampooing* 'shampoo' /shɑ̄pwɛ̄/ (on borrowings with a velar nasal consonant, see also 2.3.2).

With the increase of Anglicisms and wars with England during the Revolutionary and Napoleonic period came antagonism towards such borrowings. In 1791 the *Assemblée Législative* voted to ban the term 'honourable member' from the floor (Mackenzie 1939:I, 117). The first conference to discuss the 'problem' of Anglicisms in French was held in Liège, Belgium in 1905. By the 1930s French associations began to study ways of creating and promoting technical terms in French, to supplant borrowings from English.

After World War II, the pace of borrowing accelerated substantially, partly the result of American political and economic power, and partly because of the advances in technology in the unoccupied English-speaking countries during the war. The number of committees and societies devoted to the issue grew accordingly: the Conseil du langage scientifique (1952), the Cercle de Presse Richelieu (which would become Défense de la Langue Française; 1953), the Association Française de Normalisation (1954), etc. The creation of official agencies to combat the penetration of Anglicisms in other francophone countries (Fichier français, in Switzerland, 1959; Office du bon langage in Belgium, 1961; Office de la langue française in Canada, 1961), combined with the publication of *Parlez-vous franglais?* by René Étiemble in 1964, increased pressure on the French government.

Shortly thereafter, in 1966, Prime Minister Georges Pompidou launched the Haut comité pour la défense et l'expansion de la langue française. In 1970, once Pompidou had become President, he started a number of terminological commissions, which were given the charge of developing technical terms that would permit each ministry to perform all of its work without recourse to terms borrowed from other languages, primarily English. There is now such a terminological commission in every ministry, and a general terminological commission that reviews their decisions, before forwarding them to the Académie Française for approval. In addition, two laws have been passed that require government officials, and encourage others, to use French terms, and limit the use of foreign words in public advertising and signs (Loi Bas-Lauriol, 1975; Loi Toubon, 1994). Much stricter laws with the same purpose have been passed in Quebec.

Such laws are presented as consumer protection laws: a French person should be able to conduct business entirely in French in a French-speaking country.

These initiatives have had limited success in French-speaking Europe, and rather more success in French-speaking Canada. The Laws can only succeed if the people are willing to follow them, and the will of francophone Canadians has been substantially stronger than that of their European counterparts, who generally feel less threatened by the phenomenon (Flaitz 1988; Truchot 1990). In France the use of English in advertising shows no signs of abating (Martin, 2006), but in more militant francophone Canada the laws have been more successful.

While some suggestions from the terminological commissions have stuck, most notably *ordinateur* 'computer' and *logiciel* 'software', many more have struggled to gain popularity. The French government issued a *Dictionnaire des termes officiels* (1994), along with many supplements and guides to the vocabulary in specific areas (e.g. *Vocabulaire de la chimie et des matériaux* 2004), in an effort to encourage specialists and the general public to accept the French substitutes suggested. An ongoing problem for francophone countries is the failure to achieve unity in the words proposed to replace English terms. Thus while the French government has proposed *bois un* 'one wood' (golf), the Canadians have opted for *décocheur* 'driver'. Efforts to unify usage have met resistance primarily in France, and particularly in the Académie Française, which since 1996 has had veto power over suggestions from the terminological commissions. While the French terminological commissions have worked in cooperation with their counterparts in Canada, Switzerland, and Belgium, their best efforts have sometimes been thwarted by the Académie Française.

The rapidity of technological and social change combined with ever easier contact between cultures requires new vocabulary to represent new realities or perceptions of reality. The shift from agricultural to industrial society and the democratization of that society are reflected in the attitudes towards the creation of new words, and the borrowing of words from other languages. The euphemisms of the *précieux*, the inventions of the Revolutionary period, and the Anglicisms of contemporary French, as well as the terminological reactions to them, are reactions to cultural pressures. As those factors change, some of the new words remain, while many disappear. We do not yet have the ability to predict scientifically the fate of new words (Mamavi, Depecker, and Chansou 1997).

A burning issue for terminological commissions in the past thirty years has been the creation of feminine forms for nouns denoting professions that previously were limited to men. What are the feminine equivalents proposed for the following masculine nouns? (NB: different countries have suggested different solutions!) *vendeur* 'salesman', *auteur* 'author', *acheteur* 'buyer', *chauffeur* 'driver', *procureur* 'prosecuting attorney', *rapporteur* 'official reporter', *sculpteur* 'sculptor'.

6.4.4 Pragmatic aspects of language use in Classical and Modern French

In attitudes towards the loss of *ne* (see section 6.4.2.2) and towards new vocabulary (see 6.4.3), we have noted a progressive movement, or at least an openness, towards features once disparaged as 'lower class' or 'familiar'. The same is true of the aspects of pragmatics that we have been following: the use of *tu* and *vous* with singular reference and the practices of naming.

The use of *vous* with singular reference was the norm in seventeenth-century French court society, but even this mark of respect was not considered adequate. Vaugelas states that *vous* at the end of a phrase must be followed by another form of respectful address, such as *monseigneur* 'my lord', *monsieur* 'sir', *madame* 'ma'am', or *mademoiselle* 'miss' as in his example: *il n'appartient qu'à vous de faire . . .* 'it is your duty alone to do . . .'. This formulation would be disrespectful, and should be corrected as *il n'appartient qu'à vous Monseigneur de faire . . .* (1934 [1647]:545–546). Richelet's dictionary (1680) introduces the term *tutoyer* and specifies that it is used when speaking to children or close friends, or when lower-class people argue. *Tu* is more likely to be used when addressing female servants than male servants. Usage in Molière's plays is even more restricted, with *vous* appearing almost exclusively, except when parents are expressing anger or authority over their children. A more curious exception is between young nobles (Fay 1920), a practice that some blamed on the *précieuses* (Maley 1974:28). Although the general rule is for exclusive use of *vous* with singular reference, class and gender play a role in usage during the *ancien régime*.

When class and gender differences were challenged at the beginning of the French Revolution, the use of *vous* with singular reference was too. In 1792 the sentiment grew through the *sociétés populaires* 'societies of the people', local revolutionary organizations, and in masonic lodges. This led to a proposal by Claude Basire, a lawyer from Dijon, that *tutoiement* be made obligatory, as he found the use of *vous* in single reference "ridiculous and servile". The motion was passed by the Convention on 1 November 1793 over protests that using *tu* might cause riots in the streets. Six months later, though, Basire was executed during the mad bloodletting of the Terror. In the calm that followed the overthrow of the leaders of the Terror, practice returned to more habitual forms.

However, the spirit of that revolutionary period was not without effect in the nineteenth century. By mid-century, parents regularly used *tu* with their children, and by the end of the century children would respond in kind. Husbands and wives started to use *tu* among themselves in the wave of republican egalitarianism after 1871 (Maley 1974:34–35). In twentieth-century France the gradual trend towards the use of *tu* continued, with some acceleration after the events of May 1968. Studies in the immediate post-1968 period confirmed that *tu* was then the rule among students and within families, and was more common when teachers addressed students, though generally unacceptable when students addressed teachers (Bryan 1972, Bustin-Lekeu 1973). The prohibition against using *tu* when speaking to a teacher is still found in some school by-laws, but other schools, particularly alternative schools for children in difficulty, promote the reciprocal use of *tu* between faculty and students as a way of lowering barriers. The choices among colleagues in the workplace are still quite varied, and can be a source of tension.

In francophone Canada, the use of *tu* has undergone more rapid change. A study of male college-age students in 1967 found widespread use of *vous* with single reference within families and with people of authority (Lambert 1967). Contrary to findings in Metropolitan French, *vouvoiement* towards parents and other adult family members was more common among working-class children than among those from the bourgeoisie. Since then the use of *tu* has greatly increased, with the switch to *tu* taking place very rapidly among people meeting for the first time (Peeters 2004:12, citing Vincent 2001). In Louisiana Cajun French *tu* is almost universal with singular reference. *Vous* is limited to singular reference in the most formal contexts. *Vous-autres* is used for plural reference, typically joined to a third-person singular verb.

The practices of naming have also been a matter for legal intervention in Modern French, with, once again, a tendency towards greater liberty. During the French Revolution two dramatic changes took place. First, concerning place names, revolutionary fervor led to the renaming of towns and cities whose names reflected the monarchy or the Church. Thus it was that Marly le Roi was renamed Marly la Machine, and Saint-Denis became Franciade.

The Revolution was also concerned about personal names, both family names and given (first) names. The *noms à particules* 'names with prepositions' (indicating family landholdings) were forbidden, as signs of the old aristocracy. As for first names, the Convention debated whether a child could be named *Liberté* 'liberty' (14 November 1793). Gilbert Romme, the same politician who, with Fabre d'Églantine, invented the Revolutionary calendar, argued for complete freedom in naming, and his arguments carried the day. In August 1794 (6 Fructidor An II) a law on names required that the baptismal names correspond to the names on the governmental birth certificate, nor could people change their family names. Starting 1 January 2005 the French government permitted parents to choose which surname the child would receive, the mother's, the father's, or both.

In 1802, the law of 11 Germinal An X limited the possible first names to those found on calendars, generally saints' names, and names from classical antiquity. Public officials were forbidden to accept birth certificates with other names. In particular this was aimed at stopping people from using family names as first names. Unofficial lists of permissible names were drawn up by various jurists during the nineteenth century (Dupont 1865, Béquet 1883, both cited in Lefebvre-Teillard 1990:141), but these had no legal standing. The liberalization promised by the reinstitution of republican government in 1871 was reflected by the names *Lucifer Vercingétorix Blanqui* proposed for one Parisian child in 1887.

Regional names posed another threat to this system, particularly as regionalism was viewed with some suspicion. This issue would explode in the 1960s, as Breton nationalists tried to give their children names reflecting their cultural heritage. In June of 1962 a court in Rennes refused to accept the name of *Maïwenn* which the Manrot family wished to give their daughter. Because six of his twelve children had names the courts would not recognize, Mr. Manrot was refused *allocations familiales* (subsidies for large families) for them. It took until 1979 for his children to be duly recorded on the official rolls. In 1965 the court in Caen refused to recognize the names *Kelig* and *Kaelaïg*, but did accept *Mikealaïg*. These challenges led to a ministerial decree on 12 April 1966, which gave the courts more leeway to determine if the name proposed was likely to be harmful for the child. Still, officials were authorized to refuse "fantastical" names, or other names that "cannot normally serve as first names", such as family names, names of things, animals, and political events.

The challenge that finally broke this system was the case of *Fleur de Marie Armine Angèle Guillot*, which started in 1983 and finally ended in 1996. *Fleur de Marie* is the name of a character in *Mystères de Paris*, a novel by Eugène Sue (1804–1857). The courts argued that a name had to be limited to two names, and would have accepted *Fleur-Marie*, but the family insisted. The case went all the way to the European Court of Human Rights, which ruled in favor of the French government. Although the government had won, it had lost its taste for these legal battles, and all limitations on the choice of names, except for those that might be harmful to the child, have been abandoned.

What are the situations in which *tutoiement* and *vouvoiement* are not reciprocal? What social and regional variation is there in the non-reciprocal use of pronouns of address?

6.5   Conclusions

One might view the history of French as a pendulum swinging between relative control and relative freedom. The Gallo-Romance vernaculars were born from the relative freedom of Latin dialects to differentiate themselves, following the demise of the Roman Empire. What we know as French was developed through the ever-increasing controls exemplified by the unification of French law, the founding of the Académie Française, and the institution of the *école républicaine* 'the school of the Republic'. The regional movements starting in the nineteenth century (Thiesse 1991), the democratization of French life in the twentieth century, the dissolution of the French colonial empire, and new waves of migration have moved the pendulum back somewhat in the other direction. At every period there are partisans for each side.

6.6   Exercises

1) Establish, based on the following examples, how the use of demonstrative determiners and pronouns has changed since Old French.

La domnizelle celle kose non contredist (Sainte Eulalie, l. 23)

'The young lady did not oppose this action' [cutting off her head]

. . . Maximien chi rex eret a cels dis soure pagiens (Sainte Eulalie, ll. 11–12)

'Maximien who was king over the pagans in those days'

En tant dementres le saint cors conreerent tuit cil seinur (Saint Alexis, ll. 498–499)

'In the meantime, all those lords prepared the holy man's body'

Si grant ledece nus est apareude, d'icest saint cors, que avum am bailide (Saint Alexis, ll. 533–534)

'Thus great joy has come to us, from this holy body that we have in our possession'

2) In the following examples, how are the singular and plural of masculine and feminine distinguished? How has this changed since Latin? Consider both spelling and pronunciation.

	Latin	Old French	Modern French	
Singular	hominem	om	homme	
				'man'
Plural	homines	oms	hommes	
Singular	caballum	cheval	cheval	
				'horse'
Plural	caballos	chevals	chevaux	
Masculine	falsum	fals	faux	
				'false'
Feminine	falsam	false	fausse	
Masculine	grandem	grant	grand	
				'big, tall'
Feminine			grande	

3) How do we know that the place of the stressed syllable changed between Latin and French in the following words: *filíolum > filleul, tónitrum > tonnerre*?

4) Place of object pronouns: Look at the frequency table and the nature of the infinitival verb for the construction *je le veux* + infinitive 'I want to X it' (examples from ARTFL). What patterns do you see?

	+ *faire*	+ *être*	+ *croire*	Total
1600–1650	8	9	11	100
1650–1700	2	1	7	48
1700–1750	1	0	6	11
1750–1800	0	0	5	9
1800–1960	3	1	3	19

5) Adverb formation:
   a) Why do the following adverbs seem to be exceptions to the rule that adverbs are formed with the feminine form of the adjective + *ment*: *constamment* 'constantly', *savamment* 'knowingly', *vraiment* 'truly', *récemment* 'recently'?
   b Why is *présentement* 'at present' (Quebec French) an exception rather than the rule?

6) Strong stems and weak stems: In Old French, strong stems of the verb had the accent on the stem, while weak stems had the accent on the ending. From the following examples, how does this affect the pronunciation of verbs? How has this changed since Old French? List five verbs in Modern French that have kept traces of a strong/weak stem alternation in the present tense.

| *il aime* | *nous amons* |
| *elle trueve* | *nous trovons* |

7) What do the following nouns have in common, with respect to their origin: *silhouette, poubelle, calepin*?

8) a) What patterns do you discern in the popularity of first names given to children in France in the following years based on the two tables below (1 – most popular, 10 – least popular)?
   b) How many names continue from one period to the next? What is the relationship between girls' names and boys' names? What is the origin of the names?

	1901	1948	2002
Girls			
1	Marie	Marie	Léa
2	Jeanne	Monique	Manon
3	Marguerite	Nicole	Emma
4	Germaine	Françoise	Chloe
5	Louise	Danielle	Camille
6	Yvonne	Christiane	Océane
7	Madeleine	Jacqueline	Clara
8	Suzanne	Annie	Marie
9	Marthe	Michelle	Sarah
10	Marcelle	Chantal	Ines
Boys			
1	Jean	Jean	Lucas
2	Louis	Michel	Théo
3	Pierre	Alain	Thomas
4	Joseph	Daniel	Hugo
5	Henri	Bernard	Maxime
6	Marcel	Gérard	Enzo
7	Georges	Christian	Antoine
8	André	Jacques	Clément
9	Paul	Claude	Alexandre
10	René	Pierre	Quentin

9) a) In the sentence *ce livre est à moi*, literally 'this book is to me', the preposition *à* 'to' is used to express possession. Typically, with nouns, *de* is used to express possession (*le livre de Marie* 'Mary's book'). In what circumstances can *à* be used to express possession?

b) How is possession expressed in the following place names, and what is this structure a remnant of: *Bourg-la-Reine*, *Pont l'Évêque?*

10) a) How is the pronoun *soi* used today? Consider the following examples from the past (taken from the ARTFL database):

> *Veez ci le marquis revenir*, [. . .] *soy et sa gent* (Philippe de Mezières, *L'estoire de Griseldis*, 1395)
> 'Here comes the marquis, he and his people'
> *c'estoit passetemps celeste les veoir ainsi soy rigouller* (Rabelais, *Gargantua*, 1534)
> 'it was a heavenly way to pass the time, watching them amuse themselves'

b) How is the expression *soi-disant* 'so-called', 'self-styled' a reflection of archaic usage?

Glossary

NB: The swing dash '~' is used to show identical French and English terminology. The dash '–' is used to show that there is no French equivalent to the English term.

ablative (case), *ablatif* (n.m.): Type of case that marks a noun or pronoun as signifying circumstances, e.g. location, instrumentality, source, time.

accent, accented, *accent, -ué* (n.m., adj.): Physical manifestation of (metrical) stress*.

accusative case, *accusatif* (n.m.): Type of case* that marks the use of a noun or pronoun as the direct object of a sentence.

acronym, *acronyme* (n.m.): Word formed from the first letters of a name, or from a combination of first letters and parts of words, e.g. *SMIC* from *Salaire Minimum Interprofessionnel de Croissance*.

addressee, *destinataire ou récépteur* (n.m.): Any of the immediate intended recipients of the speaker's communication, as grammaticalized in second-person morphemes.

adjacency pair, *paire adjacente* (n.f.): Unit of conversation that contains an exchange of one turn* by two speakers.

affix, affixation, *affixe, -ation* (n.m./n.f.): Bound morpheme* added to a base form to create a new word; they can be of three types: prefixes*, infixes*, and suffixes*.

affricate, *affriquée* (n.f.): Stop consonant whose release contains a prolonged period of friction.

allomorph, *allomorphe* (n.m.): Alternate form or variant of a morpheme, e.g. *ven-* and *viendr-* for *venir*; also known as *variante combinatoire* (n.f.).

allophone, ~ (n.m.): Sound that is not lexically distinctive in the language but alternates with (represents a contextual variant of) another sound.

analytic, *analytique* (adj.): Type of linguistic structure in which different grammatical functions are predominantly expressed by independent words, e.g. past tense is expressed analytically (*il/elle **a aimé** *'he/she loved') in Modern French, while it is expressed synthetically* in Latin (*amavit*).

anaphora, anaphoric, *anaphore, -ique* (n.m., adj.): Reference of an expression to its antecedent which provides its intended referent in the context, e.g. '*A well-dressed man* was speaking; *he* had a foreign accent'; see also cataphora*.

antecedent, *antécédent* (n.m.): Leftmost element of a referential link or word to which a pronoun refers anaphorically, e.g. *Nous avons vu la femme que vous avez décrite* 'We saw the woman you described.'

antepenultimate, *antépénultième* (n.f.): The second from last syllable of a word, e.g. *in* in the Latin word *integrum*; also called 'antepenult'.

antonym, *antonyme* (n.m.): Word having a meaning opposite to that of another word, e.g. 'wet' is an antonym of 'dry'.

apheresis, *aphérèse* (n.f.): Suppression of the first part of a word, e.g. *autocar* > *car* 'coach/bus'.

apocope, *apocope* (n.f.): Loss of the last part of a word, e.g. *cinéma* > *ciné* 'movie'.

approximant, *approximant* (n.m.): Type of consonant and mode of articulation arising through the open approximation (vs. narrow closure or stricture) of the articulators, e.g. glide* and tap*.

argument, *argument* (n.m.): Piece of information represented by one or more lexical items (words and phrases) that must be syntactically expressed for the sentence to be semantically complete.

aspect, aspectual, *aspect, -uel* (n.m., adj.): Grammatical category associated with verbs that expresses a temporal view of the event or state expressed by the verb.

aspiration, *aspiration* (n.f.): Puff of outward air that accompanies the release of voiceless stop consonants, e.g. in 'key' and 'tea' in English.

assibilation, *assibilation* (n.f.): Process during which a stop consonant acquires a friction-like noise in its release; manner of articulation intermediate between a stop* and a sequence of a stop followed by a fricative*.

assimilation, *assimilation* (n.f.): Umbrella term for linguistic processes by which a sound becomes similar to an adjacent sound, sharing some or all of its features; see e.g. vowel harmony*.

assonance, *assonance* (n f.): Poetic device and type of rhyme, in which the vowels of the rhyming syllables must be the same, but not the final (coda) consonants, e.g. in Old French 'iers' in *conseilliers* 'consulters' could rhyme with 'iel' in *ciel*.

auxiliary verb, *verbe auxiliaire* (n.m.): Type of verb that, when combined with a lexical verb expresses grammatical information such as person, number, aspect, or voice, e.g. *être* 'to be' and *partir* 'to leave' in *il est parti*, 'he left'.

back formation, *dérivation regressive* (n.f.): Creation of a new word by the removal of an affix, e.g. *géographie* 'geography' > *géographe* 'geographer'.

base, *base* (n.f.): Principal morpheme* of a word after all affixes are removed; see also stem*.

borrowing, *emprunt* (n.m.): Word or expression taken from another language, but not necessarily having the same meaning in the new language as in the original language, e.g. *pressing* 'dry cleaner' from English into French.

boundary tone, *ton de frontière* (n.m.): In autosegmental-metrical approaches to intonation, the tonal target aligned at the right or left boundary of a prosodic domain.

bound morpheme, *morphème lié* (n.m.): Morpheme that cannot be used alone as an utterance or sentence, see affix*.

calque, *calque* (n.m.): Nativization of borrowings by direct translation from the donor language, e.g. *gratte-ciel* from *skyscraper*, *lune de miel* from *honeymoon*; also known as **loan translation**.

case, *cas* (n.m.): grammatical category determined by the syntactic or semantic function of a noun or pronoun; see nominative*, ablative*.

cataphora, *cataphore* (n.m.): Expression referring forward to another expression that constitutes its intended reference in the context, e.g. 'If you need *one*, there's *a towel* in the top drawer'; see also anaphora*.

chain shift, *changement en chaîne* (n.m.): Type of change in the articulation of several vowels when vowels moving from one position to another within the vowel space 'push' (push shift) or 'pull' (pull shift) other vowels to move into the newly available positions.

Christian Latin, *latin écclésiastique* (n.m.): The Latin of the Christian Church in the period of the late Roman empire (third to fifth centuries) marked by extensive use of borrowings and calques from Greek and Hebrew, and grammatical structures similar to Vulgar Latin*; also known as **Ecclesiastical Latin**.

chuintante, – (n.f): Impressionistic term (French phonological tradition) referring to the palato-alveolar sibilants* ʃ/ and /ʒ/.

Classical Latin, *latin classique* (n.m.): The Latin of the 'Golden Age' of the Roman Empire from about the first century BCE to the first century CE. Also refers to a highly stylized written literary variant of the language.

cleft sentence, *phrase clivée* (n.f.): Complex sentence in which a simple sentence (*il ne peut pas venir*) is embedded using a subordinate clause (*c'est . . . que*), e.g. *c'est dommage qu'il ne puisse pas venir*.

clipping, *troncation* (n.f.): see truncation*.

clitic, *clitique* (n.m.): A morpheme that has the syntactic characteristics of a word, but shows evidence of being phonologically bound to another word.

clitic climbing, *la montée des clitiques*: Specific behavior of clitics in some languages, where they move before the inflected modal auxiliary. E.g. in Spanish 'Lo voy a ver', 'Him I go to see', but not in French *Le je vais voir* (instead of *Je vais le voir*).

closed syllable, *syllabe fermée* (n.f.): Syllable ending with one or several consonants.

closed vowel, *voyelle fermée* (n.f.): Any one of the oral vowels /i/, /y/, /u/ and /ɪ/, /ʏ/ and /ʊ/ in French, characterized by the most elevated tongue position or tongue 'height' (*aperture* in French terminology); also known as **high vowel**.

coarticulation, *coarticulation* (n.f.): Influence of adjacent speech sounds on one another within a given prosodic domain (syllable, word, phrase).

coda, *coda* (n.m.): The rightmost part of a syllable, following the nucleus; when it is filled, it includes one or more consonants.

collocation, *collocation* (n.f.): Words that appear together, e.g. *feu* with the verbs *prendre* and *faire*: *prendre feu, faire feu*.

community of practice, *communauté de pratique* (n.f.): Community of people who are informally bound by what they do together in what is understood as a joint enterprise. It binds members together into a social entity, and produces a shared repertoire of resources, such as routines, artifacts, vocabulary, style, etc.

complement, *complément* (n.m.): Syntactic expression showing one of the arguments of the verb, e.g. direct and indirect object, etc.

componential analysis, *analyse componentielle* (n.f.): Analysis of words in terms of their semantic components, which usually come in pairs called semantic oppositions, e.g. 'up/down', back/ forth', etc.; also known as **semic analysis**.

composition, *composition* (n.f.): Word formation process that consists of joining two free morphemes to obtain a new word, e.g. *clairvoyant* 'clairvoyant' (able to see the future).

compound, compounding *(nom) composé* (n.m.): Word containing a stem* that is made up of more than one base.

connotation, *connotation* (n.f.): The affective part of a word's meaning expressing speakers' attitude, e.g. *vieillard* 'old' (pejorative) from *vieux* 'old'.

constituent, *constituant* (n.m.): One of two or more grammatical units that enter syntactically or morphologically into a construction, i.e. an arrangement of hierarchically organized grammatical units, at any level, e.g. determiner + noun to form a noun phrase*.

contextual nasalization, *nasalisation contextuelle* (n.f.): Widespread coarticulatory phenomenon in languages by which oral vowels become nasalized in contact with nasal consonants.

contextual style, *style contextuel* (n.m.): Formal properties (words, sounds, sentence types, etc.) of language thought to emerge in speech situations defined on a continuum between *careful* and *casual* speech, e.g. in formal interviews vs. phone conversations between friends, depending on the amount of attention paid to speech.

contextual variant, *variante contextuelle* (n.f.): see allophone*.

continuant, *continuant* (n.m.): see liquid*.

conventional implicature, *implication conventionnelle* (n.f.):   implicature* that arises from the particular choice of words or syntax rather than from conversational maxims, e.g. *moreover* conventionalized as a synonym of *on top of this*.

conversational implicature, *implication conversationnelle* (n.f.): Implicature* that is not conventional, and that is based on an addressee's assumption that the speaker is following the Cooperative Principle*.

conversational move, *tactique conversationnelle* (n.f.): Stretch of talk that forms a unit, and that has a functional relation to the conversation of which it is a part, e.g. the back-channel cues *uh huh* and *yeah* are moves that return speakership to another participant.

conversion, *conversion* (n.f.): Change of grammatical category without any change in the form of the word; e.g. the use of an adjective as a noun: *français* 'French' > *un Français* (French person), *le français* 'French language'.

Cooperative Principle, *Principe de Coopération* (n.m.): 'Make your contribution such as it is required, at the stage which it occurs, by the accepted purpose or direction of the talk exchange in which you are engaged.' (Grice 1975:45)

copula/copular verb, *verbe copule* (n.m.): Verb that connects the subject to its predicate, and that usually does not describe an action being performed e.g. *être*.

co-reference, *coréférence* (n.f.): Reference in one expression to the same referent* of another expression, e.g. the address pronouns *tu* 'you' in *Tu as dit que tu viendrais* 'You said you would come.'

count noun, *nom à quantité dénombrable* (n.m.): Type of noun that denotes an entity that can be counted. It can have plural forms, and can be modified by numerals and quantifiers like 'one', 'two', 'every', 'most', etc; see also mass noun*.

creole, *créole* (n.m.): Outcome variety of the blending of two or more languages, usually coming in contact through colonization, and forming a distinct new variety that becomes the native language of subsequent generations.

dative case, *datif* (n.m.): Case that marks the use of a noun or pronoun as the indirect object of the sentence; see also accusative case*, and oblique case*.

deadjectival noun, *nom adjectival* (n.m.): Noun formed from an adjective, e.g. *délicat* 'delicate' > *delicatesse* 'delicacy'.

declension, *déclinaison* (n.f.): Feature of languages that use inflection* to form words that express grammatical information with 'endings', or inflectional morphemes*.

deictic, deixis, *déictic, deixis* (adj., n.m.): Expression whose interpretation is relative to the (usually) extralinguistic context of the utterance, e.g. who is speaking, the time of speaking, gestures, and the location of the exchange.

denominal noun, *nom dénominal* (n.m.): Noun created from another noun, e.g. *cuisine* 'kitchen' > *cuisinier* 'cook'.

denotation, *denotation* (n.f.): The referential* meaning of a word; what it denotes.

deponent verb, *verbe déponent* (n.m): Type of verb that has active meaning but a passive form, e.g. Latin *loquor* 'I speak' replaced in French by *parler* (< Latin *parabolare*, a regular verb).

derivation, *dérivation* (n.f.): Word formation process that consists of changing the meaning and/or the lexical class of a word by adding another morpheme, e.g. by suffixation*; see also affixation*.

determiner, *déterminatif* (n.m.): Umbrella term for traditional lexical categories of articles, e.g. definite, indefinite and partitive, possessive, and demonstrative adjectives.

deverbal noun, *nom déverbal* (n.m.): Noun created from a verb, e.g. *nager* 'to swim' > *nageur* 'swimmer'.

devoiced, devoicing, *dévoisé, -ment* (adj., n.m.): Sound that is otherwise voiced*, but with no vibrations of the vocal folds; partial synonym of **sourd**; see also voiceless*.

dialect, *dialecte* (n.m.): A variant of a language spoken in a certain, usually large, geographic location, usually further divided into sub-dialects.

diglossia, *diglossie* (n.f.): A situation in which one form of a language (so-called H(igh) variety) is used for formal purposes (writing, speeches) and another (the so-called L(ow) variety) is used for conversation (and is rarely if ever written down); a typical example is Arabic.

diphthong, *diphthongue* (n.f.): Vowel reaching two different articulatory targets in the nucleus of the same syllable.

discourse particle/marker, *mot/particle du discours* (n.m.): Segmentation marker and interjection such as 'ah', 'yes', 'well', 'now', as well as hesitation markers like 'er' and 'um' that segment and connect utterances in spoken language and support the turn-taking system, or mark salient information in discourse.

dislocation, dislocated (construction), *dislocation, (phrase) disloquée* (n.f., adj.): Detachment of a constituent from a syntactic phrase and replacement of it by a pronoun with which the constituent becomes coreferential. Left dislocation*: e.g. ***La petite fille***, le chien l'a mordue 'The little girl, the dog bit her.' Right dislocation: *Ton vélo, il l'a acheté,* **ton père**, *en fin de compte?* 'Your bike, has your father bought it, finally?'

distinctive, *distinctif* (adj.): Involved in differentiating the meanings of words; see phoneme*, minimal pair*.

doublet, *doublet* (n.m.): Words having the same origin, but differing in form and meaning, i.e. *fragile* and *frêle*, from the Latin *fragilis*.

echo-word, *mots-échos* (n.m.): Compound resulting, through partial reduplication, in a form in which the second element differs from the first by only one sound, e.g. *clic-clac* 'folding sofa-bed'.

elision, *élision* (n.m.): In general, the omission of a segment. In particular, the omission of a vowel at the end of one word when the next word begins with a vowel; avoidance of hiatus*.

elliptic, ellipsis, *elliptique, ellipse* (adj., n.m.): Describes a syntactic construction that lacks an element that is recoverable or inferable from the context.

enchaînement (n.m.): see linking*.

endangered language, *langue en voie de disparition* (n.f.). Language with only a few or without monolingual speakers. The language is not passed on to children because of its low prestige, explicit discriminatory policies, or a relatively small number of people using it in the community (or all the above).

enunciation, *énonciation* (n.f.): Act of speaking producing *(des) énoncés* 'utterances'. Term encompassing locutionary*, illocutionary*, and perlocutionary* components of a speech act* in the French pragmatic tradition.

epistemic modality, *modalité épistémologique* (n.f.): The status (veracity, falsity, etc.) of a proposition in terms of speaker commitment, i.e. the attitude shown by the speaker through the use of certain linguistic means towards his/her own role of declaring something.

etymon, *etymon* (n.m.): Word from which another word is derived, e.g. *fragilis* for the words *frêle* and *fragile* 'fragile'.

euphemism, *euphémisme* (n.m.): A euphemism is a metaphorical or metonymic use of an expression in place of another expression that is disagreeable or offensive; see also metaphor* and metonymy*.

evidential, evidentiality, *évidentiel, -alité* (n.m.): Epistemic modality* that connotes the speaker's assessment of the evidence for his or her statement.

face, *face* (n.f.): Symbolic notion that refers to an image or a view of one's self that is emotionally invested and that can be lost, maintained, or enhanced through interactions with others.

final lengthening, *allongement final* (n.m.): Lengthening of the final syllable(s) of a prosodic constituent in a give prosodic domain.

forward syllabification, – see linking*.

free morpheme, *morphème non-lié* ou *libre* (n.m.): Morpheme unattached to a bound morpheme that can be used in isolation, i.e. open-class lexical items, such as nouns, verbs, adjectives, adverbs, etc.

French-based Creole, *créole de base française* (n.m.): Mother tongue originating from extensive contact between French and an indigenous language, with the latter borrowing much of the lexicon of the former.

fricative, *fricative* (n.f.): Type of consonant and mode of articulation formed through a partial closure of the oral cavity, enabling the articulators to produce audible friction, with the air still escaping orally.

Gallo-Romance, *gallo-roman* (n.m.): Gallo-Romance is the collection of dialects derived from Latin and spoken in Gaul (modern-day France).

geminate, *géminée* (n.f.): Consonant pronounced with a longer duration but not necessarily spelled as a double consonant.

genitive case, *génitif* (n.m.): Case that marks primarily the possessive use of a noun or pronoun, e.g. *liber Petri* 'Peter's book'.

genre, *genre* (n.m.): Category used to classify discourse and literary works usually by form, technique, or content; types of utterances or speech situations characterized by recognizable conventions, e.g. greetings, speeches, proposals of marriage, etc.

glide, *semi-voyelle/semi-consonne* (n.f.): Vowel-like segment showing the linguistic properties of a consonant; also known as **semi-vowel** and **semi-consonant**.

gliding, *synérèse* (n.f.): Phonological process by which a closed vowel preceded by a single consonant or a consonant cluster with no liquid*, and followed by another vowel in the same word, becomes a glide*.

grammaticalization, ~ (n.f.): A subset of linguistic changes that make a lexical item or construction in certain uses take on grammatical characteristics, e.g. *avoir* 'to have' becoming an auxiliary*.

grammatical morpheme, *morphème grammatical* (n.m.): Articles, pronouns, prepositions and conjunctions, which constitute a fixed inventory of forms in the language and function as links between lexical morphemes*.

***h-aspiré* (word)**, *(mot en) h-aspiré* (n.m.): Word of Latin or Germanic origin spelled with the letter 'h' but pronounced with an empty onset* in initial position, thus blocking elision* (*la haine* 'hatred') and *liaison** (*des hauteurs* 'heights').

head, *tête* (n.f.): A constituent in a syntactic construction that governs the agreement of grammatical categories, such as person and number, as well as the occurrence of other constituents.

hearer, *auditeur* (n.m.): Ratified participant of an exchange or discourse who is part of the intended audience; often the same as the addressee*.

hedge, *adoucisseur* (n.m.): Linguistic (syntactic, lexical, prosodic, etc.) means by which the illocutionary force of the utterance can be mitigated.

heritage language, *langue d'origine* (n.f.): Any ancestral, i.e. indigenous, colonial, or immigrant, language that is regularly used in the home and the community.

hiatus, *diérèse* (n.f.): The separation of adjacent vowels into independent syllable nuclei in the same prosodic domain due to absence of gliding* (*truand* 'crook') or an *h-aspiré** word (*le héro* 'the hero').

high vowel, *voyelle fermée* (n.m.): see closed vowel*.

holonym, *holonyme* (n.m.): 'The whole' in a relation of the 'part' and the 'whole', e.g. *voiture* 'car' to *volant* 'wheel'; see also meronym*.

homonym, *homonyme* (n.m.): Words that are pronounced the same but have different meanings, while the spelling can be different or identical, e.g. *paire* 'pair' and *père* 'father', *louer* 'to rent' and *louer* 'to praise'.

homophone, *homophone* (n.m.): Words pronounced in the same way but differing in meaning, spelling, or both (*tante* 'aunt', *tente* 'tent').

homorganic, *homorganique* (adj.): 'Same place', e.g. consonants having the same place of articulation.

hypercorrection, ~ (n.f.): Overcompensation used by a speaker to avoid a form which is mistakenly assumed to be incorrect, e.g. 'He wrote to Sally and I' instead of 'Sally and me'.

hyperonym, *hypéronyme* (n.m.): A representative of a lexical class, also known as **superordinate**, see also hyponym*.

hyponym, *hyponyme* (n.m.): Member of the lexical class represented by a hyperonym*, e.g. *chien* 'dog' for *animal* 'animal'; also known as **subordinate**.

iamb, *ïamb* (n.m.): Type of metrical foot resulting from the association of a weak and a strong syllable.

illocutionary act, *acte illocutionnel* (n.m.): A complete speech act made in a typical utterance that consists of delivering the propositional content of the utterance with a particular illocutionary force by which the speaker asserts, suggests, promises, etc.

imparisyllabic, *imparisyllabique* (adj.): Words that have forms with differing numbers of syllables, e.g. Old French *gars* 'boy' (nominative case, one syllable) and Modern French *garçon* (oblique case, two syllables).

implicature, *implication* (n.f.): Information that is inferred from an utterance but that is not a condition for the truth of the utterance, e.g. *Some of the boys were at the party* implicates in most contexts *Not all of the boys were at the party*. Implicature can be conversational* or conventional*.

inference, *inférence* (n.f.): Drawing a conclusion as a logical consequence of what precedes; conclusion established on the 'unsaid'.

infix, *infixe* (n.m.): Affix* inserted in the middle of a word to create a new word, e.g. *-sc-* yielding *finire* 'to finish' > *finiscere* 'to begin to finish' in Latin and *-ir/-iss* verb conjugations in Modern French.

inflection, *flexion* (n.f.): Modification or change in the form of a word to mark case, gender, number, comparison, tense, person, mood, voice; e.g. *Venez!* 'Come here' from *venir* 'to come'.

intransitive (verb), *verb intransitif* (n.m.): Verb that cannot take an object as its complement*. In syntactic terms a verb that can only has one argument*, e.g. 'The boy sleeps/runs' etc.; see also intransitive*.

inversion, *inversion* (n.f.): Placing of the subject after a finite verb in a sentence normally showing an SVO (subject-verb-object) word order: e.g. *Viendras-tu ce soir?* 'Will you come tonight?'

isogloss, *isoglosse* (n.m.): Dialect boundary delimiting localities where certain features of vocabulary and pronunciation are used.

koiné, *koiné* (n.m.): 'Common' in Greek; in modern linguistics it is a local language that becomes commonly used in a area, after it has lost its specific local characteristics while keeping features common to most contact varieties.

lax, laxing, *relâché, -ment* (n.m.): Pronouncing a sound with relatively relaxed muscle tension; vowels with shorter duration and a more central articulation than cardinal vowels; see also tense*.

learned vocabulary, *vocabulaire savant* (adj.): Words that have been borrowed directly from Latin rather than passing through patterns of regular sound change, e.g. *fragile* 'fragile' is a learned word, while *frêle* is the popular form.

lengthening consonant, *consonne allongeante* (n.f.): The consonants /v/, /z/, /ʒ/, or /ʁ/ that, in the primary stressed syllable of a lexical word and a prosodic phrase, are perceived as lengthening the duration of the preceding non-schwa vowel.

lexeme, *lexème* (n.m.): Lexical item considered apart from its inflected forms, e.g. *chien* 'dog' is a lexeme that includes the inflected forms *chiens, chienne, chiennes*.

lexical hierarchy, *hiérarchie lexicale* (n.f.): Levels of relations between superordinates* and hyponyms*, e.g. *chien, chat*, and *éléphant* are all hyponyms of the superordinate *animal*, and are at the same level of the lexical hierarchy. *Animal* is at the same level of the lexical hierarchy as *plante*.

lexical morpheme, *morphème lexical* (n.m.): Nouns, adjectives, verbs, and adverbs carrying the principal ideas within a sentence or utterance, and forming open-ended categories that can be added to or subtracted from our mental lexicon.

lexicon, *lexique* (n.m.): The entire stock of free morphemes of a language; synonym of 'dictionary' as it is traditionally defined; the mental representation of words and expressions.

lexifier language, *langue lexifiante* (n.m.): Mostly, but not always, a main European language of which the vocabulary of a newly created Creole language is derived, e.g. French to Haitian Creole, English to Tok Pisin.

liaison, ~: Resyllabification of an otherwise silent word-final consonant to the first vowel of the next word.

lingua franca, ~ (n.f.): Language used for the purposes of international commerce and cultural communication beyond the boundaries of the countries or regions of their native speakers; also known as **vehicular language**.

linking, *enchaînement* (n.m.): Linking of intervocalic consonants to the onset of the following syllable within and across word boundaries.

liquid, *liquide* (n.f.): Type of consonant, typically /l/ and /r/, articulated by letting the outgoing air pass through or around the obstruction created in the oral cavity; also known as **continuant**.

loan translation, *calque* (n.m.): see calque*.

locutionary act, *acte locutionnel* (n.m.): The physical act of uttering words; part of illocutionary* and perlocutionary* acts.

loi de position (la) (n.f.), 'Open/closed syllable adjustment': phonological constraint specifying that mid vowels in open (CV) syllables should be closed, and that those in closed (CVC) syllables should be open.

mass noun, *nom de quantité* (n.m.): Type of noun that cannot be modified by a number without specifying a unit of measurement; therefore mass nouns have singular but no plural forms, e.g. *furniture*; see also count noun*.

Maximal Onset Principle, *principe de l'attaque maximale* (n.m.): Principle partly determining underlying syllable division by stating that intervocalic consonants are maximally assigned to the onsets of syllables in conformity with universal and language-specific conditions; see also sonority hierarchy*.

merger, *neutralisation* (n.f.): Loss of distinction between two sounds, resulting in a single sound and a number of homophones, formerly distinguished by the two sounds.

meronym, *méronyme* (n.m.): In a part-whole relationship, part of the whole, e.g. *volant* 'wheel' for *voiture* 'car'; see also holonym*.

metaphor, *métaphore* (n.f.): A word usually designating one thing used to designate another because of shared properties between them, e.g. *soie* 'silk' > *jours tissés de soie* 'happy days' (luxury associated with silk).

metonymy, *métonymie* (n.f.): Rhetorical process consisting of using one word to stand for another without a necessary relationship between the two, e.g. *Le Quai d'Orsay se mit en grève* 'The Ministry of Foreign Affairs went on strike' (Quai d'Orsay = the Ministry of Foreign Affairs located at this address in Paris).

mid vowel, *voyelle moyenne* (n.m.): Vowels in between the closed and open vowel series: i.e., /e/, /ɛ/, /ɸ/, /œ/, /o/ and /ɔ/. The two series are sometimes referred to as tense* and lax*, respectively.

minimal pair, *paire minimale* (n.f.): Two words whose meanings are distinguished by a single phoneme, thus exemplifying a lexical contrast in the language, e.g. *faire* 'to do' vs. *fort* 'strong'.

modal verb, *verbe à modalité* (n.m.): Verb expressing whether a proposition is considered obligatory, possible, or desirable, e.g. *pouvoir* 'can', *vouloir* 'want to', *devoir* 'should, ought to'.

modifier, *modifiant* (n.m.): Syntactic construction that conveys optional information about the circumstances in which the action depicted by the verb is performed.

monophthong, monophthongization, *monophtongue, -isation* (n.m., n.f.): Vowel whose articulation is steady throughout its phonation, i.e., without gliding* towards a new position of articulation; reduction of diphthongs* to simple vowels.

mood, *mode* (n.m): Grammatical expression of the way(s) in which a sentence is used, e.g. stating (indicative) *je viens* 'I am coming', giving a command (imperative) *Viens!* 'Come!', expressing reservation in dependent clauses (subjunctive) *il faut que tu viennes* 'you must come'.

morpheme, *morpheme* (n.m.) or *monème* (n.m.): Minimal unit of meaning in the spoken language or its equivalent in the written language.

nasal, nasalized, nasalization, *nasal(isé)(isation)* (adj., n.f.): Sound produced via the flow of air entering the nasal cavity and leaving the vocal tract through the mouth or both the nose and the mouth.

nasal appendix, *appendice nasal* (n.m.): Sequence of a partially nasalized vowel followed by an audible consonantal element, e.g. *pain* 'bread' in dialects of southern French.

neologism, *néologisme* (n.m.): A newly-created word, e.g. *mégaoctet* 'megabyte'.

nominative (case), *nominatif* (n.m.): Type of case* expressing the syntactic function of subject. In Latin this is expressed morphologically (synthetically); in French usually syntactically (analytically), e.g. *Puella librum leget* vs. *la fille lit le livre* 'the girl is reading the book'.

noun phrase (or **NP**), *syntagme nominal* (n.m.): Syntactic phrase centered around a noun, e.g. *les trois autres jeunes filles* 'the three other young girls' in which the head word is *filles* 'girls'.

nucleus, *noyau* (n.m.): The loudest part or center of a syllable.

oblique (case), *oblique* (n.m): In Old French, a type of case* usually based on the form derived from the Latin accusative that subsumed all the other Latin cases except the nominative*.

obstruent, *obstruent* (n.m.): Collective term for stops and fricatives formed through a relatively tight closure of the oral cavity (in opposition to liquids*).

OL cluster, *groupe liquide* (n.m.): Groups of consonants whose first element is either a stop or a fricative (obstruent*), and whose second is either /l/ or /ʁ/ (liquid*).

onomatopoeia, *onomatopée* (n.f.): A word imitating the sound it represents, e.g. *cocorico* 'cock-a-doodle-do'.

onset, *attaque* (n.f.): Leftmost part of a syllable, preceding the nucleus; if it is filled, it can be occupied by a consonant, a glide or a glottal stop.

open/closed syllable adjustment, *loi de position* (n.f.): See *loi de position**.

opening, *ouverture* (n.f.): First few sequences or adjacency pairs* of a conversational exchange.

open syllable, *syllabe ouverte* (n.f.): Syllable ending with a vowel.

open vowel, *voyelle ouverte* (n.f.): Among the oral vowels, /a/ and /ɑ/, characterized by the least raising of the tongue or tongue 'height' (*aperture* in French terminology).

oxytone, oxytonic, *oxytone, -ique* (n.m., adj.): Word with stress on the last syllable, e.g. *correct, delete* in English.

palatal, palatalized, palatalization, *palatal(isé)(isation)* (n.f., adj.): Raising the tongue body towards the front-central part of the hard palate during the articulation of a consonant in anticipation of an upcoming front vowel.

parasynthetic, parasynthesis, *parasynthétique* (adj., n.f.): Word formed by the simultaneous addition of a prefix (*em-*) and a suffix (*-ment*), e.g. *empiècement* 'yoke' (of a dress).

parisyllabic, *parisyllabique* (adj.): Words that have the same number of syllables in all their forms. Many Latin words that were imparisyllabic* were altered to become parisyllabic in the Romance languages, e.g. Latin *flos* (nominative, one syllable), *florem* (accusative, two syllables) 'flower' simplified in Old French to *flors* (nominative), *flor* (accusative).

paroxytone, paroxytonic, *paroxytone, -ique* (n.m., adj.): Word with stress on the penultimate* (the last but one) syllable, e.g. *mangare*, 'to eat' in Italian.

partial (wh) question, *question partielle*, (n.f.): Question that contains an interrogative pro-form, such as *why, what, when*, etc. in English, and *qui, quoi, quand* in French. These forms stand for, and therefore elicit answers for, an item that is being questioned.

particle, *particule* (n.f.): Word that is neither a lexical nor a grammatical morpheme, is invariable in form, and typically has grammatical or pragmatic meaning, e.g. English *to, not*, French *ne, ah*; see also discourse particle*.

passive, *passif* (n.m., adj.): Form of verb (called 'voice' in traditional grammar) indicating that the agent and grammatical subject of the sentence becomes the object, i.e. is affected by or undergoes the action of the verb.

patois (n.m.): Derogatory label for local spoken dialect thought to lack historical authenticity and homogeneity.

penultimate, *pénultième* (adj.): The next to last unit in a structure, e.g. the syllable /ta/ in the Latin word *civitatem* 'city'; also called **penult**.

perlocutionary act, *acte perlocutionnel* (n.m.): Speech act expressed in the speaker's utterance that produces an effect, intended or not, on the addressee*, e.g. scaring, getting someone to do something in the physical world.

phoneme, *phonème* (n.m.): The simplest lexically distinctive* unit of sound.

pitch, *fréquence fondamentale* (n.f.): Rate of vibration of the vocal folds; also referred to as the **melody** of the language.

pitch accent, *accent intonatif* (n.m.): Specific, lexically distinctive* tonal 'melody' applied to words, e.g. final prominence in standard French.

plosive, *plosive* (n.f.): Mode of articulation characterizing the majority of stop consonants formed by pushing lung air through the vocal tract.

polysemy, *polysémie* (n.f.): Capacity of every sign to have multiple meanings; e.g. *bank* in English.

PP-island constraint, – (n.): Constraint that states that no single item (word or syntactic phrase) can be extracted from a prepositional phrase.

predicate, *prédicat* (n.m.): Portion of a syntactic clause, excluding the subject*, that expresses something about the subject, e.g. '(being) sick' in *Peter is sick*.

prefix, *préfixe* (n.m.): Affix* added to the beginning of a word to create a new word, e.g. *re + vendre* 'to sell' > *revendre* 'to sell again'.

prescriptivism, *prescriptivisme* (n.m.): Laying down authoritatively as a guide for others how a language should be spoken and/or written; often opposed to the 'descriptivism' advocated by most modern linguistic analyses.

presumption, *présupposition* (n.f.): Assumption made by speakers that will stand as a fact and serve for further shared background* in conversation, unless contested or proven otherwise.

presupposition, *presupposition* (n.f.): Background belief, relating to an utterance that must be mutually known or assumed by the speaker and the addressee* for the utterance to be considered appropriate in context.

pretonic lengthening, *allongement de la pénultième* (n.m.): Lengthening of the syllable preceding the stressed, i.e. tonic, syllable in the phrase. In Canadian French, the penultimate syllable of a larger prosodic phrase.

productive (affixes), *(affixes) productifs* (adj.): Affixes that are still being used to create new words, e.g. the suffix *-ble* used to create new adjectives (*risible*, etc.). The suffix -*resse*, although used to create new words in the past (*doctoresse, vengeuresse*), is no longer productive.

proparoxytone, proparoxytonic, *proparoxytone, -ique* (n.m., adj.): Word with stress on the antepenultimate* (the last but two) syllable, e.g. *operational* in English.

prosodic hierarchy, *hiérarchie des constituants prosodiques* (n.f.): Universal ranking of prosodic constituents consisting of: syllable, foot, prosodic word, phonological phrase, intonational phrase, and utterance.

prosthetic vowel, *voyelle prostétique* (n.f.): A non-etymological vowel added to the beginning of a word, e.g. Latin *scriptum* 'written', in Old French became *escrit* (Modern French *écrit*).

protrusion, *protrusion* (n.f.): Projection of the upper and lower lips forward to form an additional resonance cavity, thus lengthening the vocal tract, e.g. in /y/ in French.

push shift, *changement en chaîne poussée* (n.m.): Change in the articulation of several vowels triggered by a vowel impeding on the space of another vowel, and causing others to be 'pushed' in a certain direction of the vowel space.

quantifier, *quantificateur* (n.m.): Pre-head modifier in an NP that expresses 'quantity'.

quantifier floating, *flottement du quantificateur* (n.m.): The plural forms *tous* and *toutes* (and perhaps *seul(e)s*) quantifying a subject can be floated to a position after the verb, e.g. *Les garçons sont tous venus* 'The boys have all come' vs. *Tous les garcons sont venus* 'All the boys have come.'

reduplication, *redoublement* (n.m.): Word formation process in which the root, stem, or part of a word is repeated in the form of an identical or partial copy, e.g. *tic tac* 'clock noise'.

referent, referential (meaning), *(sens) referent(ial)* (n.m.): Concrete object or concept that is designated by a word or expression; object, action, state, relationship, or attribute in the speaker's real or imaginary world.

register, *registre* (n.m.): Contextually appropriate subset of a language's lexicon and/or grammar, e.g. *agent de police* 'police officer' in a more formal setting, *flic* 'cop' in a familiar conversation.

repair, *réparation* (n.f.): Alteration that is suggested or made by a speaker, the addressee, or audience in order to correct or clarify a previous conversational contribution.

rhotic, *(?)*: Umbrella term for allophones of 'r' or 'r'-like sounds (trills* and taps*).

rhyme, *rime* (n.f.): A poetic device (and part of the internal structure of a syllable) in which, at a minimum, the final vowel and final consonant of two lines are identical, e.g. *Li uns a l'autre granz cos done, des tierce* *jusque pres de none* 'The one gave the other mighty blows from 3 a.m. to 9 p.m.' (Chrétien de Troyes' *Erec et Enide* ll. 3795–3796)

schwa, *schwa* (n.m.): Reduced vowel typical in unstressed positions within and at the end of words, i.e. final vowel in *porte* 'door' in French.

scope, *envergure, portée* (n.f.): Part or parts of a sentence/utterance which is subjected to an overarching syntactic process, e.g. negation.

seme, *sème* (n.m.): The smallest unit of meaning in the analysis of the meaning of words, e.g. [+human] is a seme of *femme* 'woman'.

sememe, *sémème* (n.m.): Bundle of semes* that combine to form the meaning of a word, e.g. [+human], [+female], [+adult] constitutes the sememe of *femme* 'woman'.

semic analysis, *analyse sémique* (n.f.): see componential analysis*.

semi-consonant, *semi-consonne* (n.f.): see glide*.

semi-vowel, *semi-voyelle* (n.f.): see glide*.

shared knowledge (convention/background), *base commune* (n.f.): Minimally, speakers' and addressees' mutually agreed background belief upon which a conversational exchange is built.

sibilant, *assibilées* (n.f.): Type of fricative* formed by the outward air striking a constriction set against a particular place of articulation.

sifflante (n.f.): Impressionistic term (French phonological tradition) referring to the alveolar fricatives* /s/ and /z/.

simile, *comparaison* (n.f.): Overt comparison of one thing with another, e.g. *pleurer comme un bébé* 'cry like a baby'.

sociolect, *sociolecte* (n.m.): Language varieties spoken and/or written by a certain social stratum, i.e. a social group, a social class, or a subculture*.

soft palate, *palais mou* (n.m.): see velum*.

sonorant, *sonorant* (n.m.): Umbrella term for the most sonorous sounds of human languages, such as liquids*, glides* and nasals*.

Sonority Hierarchy, *hiérarchie de sonorité* (n.f.): Relative scale of sounds based on their inherent loudness.

speech act, *acte de parole* (n.m.): An essentially social act that a speaker performs when uttering words, and that are further decomposed into locutionary*, illocutionary*, and perlocutionary* acts.

spelling pronunciation, *pronunciation orthographique* (n.f.): Pronunciation pattern based on spelling.

stance, *attitude* (n.f.): Attitude or mood about the likelihood of an action that is being expressed, the speaker's or addressee's own stance, and the way in which a conversational exchange is progressing.

stem, *base, racine* (n.f.): The base or principal morpheme of a word to which affixes are added, e.g. stem *chant-* + inflection *-ons* > *chantons* 'we sing'; the base of a word plus an affix, to which a further affix can be added, e.g. *musical* + *-ity* > *musicality*. The base can be a stem, but not all stems are bases. In our example, *music* is both a base and a stem, but *musical* is only a stem.

stop, *occlusive* (n.f.): Type of consonant and mode of articulation of consonants involving closure of the oral cavity, holding of the closure, and sudden release of the closure.

stress, stressed (syllable), *(syllable) accentuée*: Abstract metrical category referring to a syllable that is perceptually more prominent (longer, louder, and/or higher in pitch) than the syllables that surround it.

strict layer hypothesis, *alignement des constituants prosodiques* (n.m.): Hierarchical organization of speech units exhaustively contained in the next largest constituent of which they are a part.

structuralism, *structuralisme* (n.m.): A theory of humankind and human thought according to which all elements of human culture, including language, literature, clothing, etc. are thought to be parts of a system of signs.

style, ~ (n.m.): In classical sociolinguistic theory, a continuum of speech situations depending on the amount of attention paid to speech; accommodation to a speaker's audience.

subculture, *culture alternative* (n.f.): A set of people having distinct behavior and beliefs within a larger culture, and being aware of their singularity (differences in style, clothing, music, etc.).

subject, *sujet* (n.m.): Grammatical relation exhibiting independent syntactic properties, such as being the agent of transitive verbs, the single complement of intransitive verbs, the conditioning factor of agreement (e.g. in number) on the verb, etc.

substratum, *substrat* (n.m.): Linguistic background upon which another language is built, i.e. a local language variety that influences a language brought into the community through migration or conquest.

suffix, suffixation, *suffix(e)(ation)* (n.m./n.f.): Affix* added to the end of a word to create a new word, e.g. *vendre* 'to sell' > *vendeur* 'seller'.

superordinate, *superordonnée* (adj., n.f.): see hyponym*, hyperonym*.

superstratum, *superstrat* (n.m.): Language built upon a preexisting linguistic background, i.e. language variety brought into the community through migration or conquest, influencing a local language.

suppletion, *supplétion* (n.f.): Replacement of a regular form by an unrelated form, e.g. *(il) ira* as future of *aller* 'to go'.

syllabic, *syllabique* (adj.): Sounds that cannot form the center or 'nucleus' of a syllable, e.g. consonants other than liquids* (in some languages), and glides*.

synecdoche, *synecdoque* (n.f.): Type of metonymy* in which one object is part of the other, e.g. *un village à 400 feux* in which *feux* 'hearths' stands for 'households'.

synthetic, synthetically *synthétique* (n.f., adv.): Type of linguistic structure in which different grammatical functions are expressed predominantly by assembling different elements into one element, e.g. past tense is expressed synthetically (*amavit* 's/he loved') in Latin, while it is expressed analytically* (*il/elle **a aimé***) in Modern French.

tap, *battue* (n.f.): One-time contact between an active and a passive articulator in producing a rhotic*.

tense, tensing: 1. *tendu, renforcement* (n.m.): Pronunciation of sounds with relatively tight muscle tension; vowels with longer duration and more peripheral articulation than their lax* counterparts, e.g. one series of high vowels in Canadian French. 2. *temps* (n.m.): Expression of the time of the action of the verb, e.g. past, present, future.

theta-roles, *rôles théta* (n.m.): semantic, i.e. meaning-related, relation between the verb and its arguments, e.g. Agent, Theme, Goal, etc.

topic, topicalization, *topic, -alisation* (n.f.): A noun phrase that expresses what a sentence is about, and to which the rest of the sentence is related as a comment. In English and other languages: the initial position in the word order in an utterance.

total (yes-no) question, *question totale* (n.f.): Question type for which an answer of *yes* or *no* is expected. In French, it is formally distinguished by rising final intonation.

transitive (verb), *verbe transitif* (n.m.): Verb that takes a direct object, e.g. *Dog bit men*; see also intransitive*.

trill, *trille* (n.f.): Multiple taps of the active articulator against the passive articulator resulting in repetitive cycles of vibration.

trochee, *trochée* (n.f.): Type of metrical foot resulting from the association of a strong and a weak syllable.

truncation, *troncation* (n.f.): The use of a part of the word for the whole word, e.g. *métropolitain* > *metro*; also known as **clipping**.

turn (taking), *tour (de parole)* (n.m.): A turn is a time during which a single participant speaks, within a typical, orderly arrangement in which participants speak with minimal overlap and gaps between them.

uvula, *luette* (n.f.): small cone-shaped mass of tissue hanging down from the soft palate (also known as velum*). It is essential in the formation of uvular consonants.

vehicular language, *langue véhiculaire* (n.f.): see *lingua franca**.

velar, velarization, *velaire, vélarisation* (n.f.): The movement of the point of articulation of a consonant towards the velum, i.e. one intermediate step in the loss of the intervocalic /k/ of Latin from *locare* 'to place' /lokare/ > /loɣare/ to the French *louer* 'to rent' /lue/.

velum, *luette* (n.f.): Muscular flap closing off the nasopharynx during swallowing and speaking (except for nasal vowels and consonants), also known as **soft palate**.

verb phrase (or **VP**), *syntagme verbal* (n.m.): Syntactic phrase centered around the verb, e.g. *elle **nous** regarde* 'she is watching us' in which the head of the phrase is *regarde* 'is watching'.

vernacular, *vernaculaire* (n.m.): Everyday language spoken by a people, as distinguished from the literary language; a variety of everyday language specific to a social group or region.

voiced, **voicing**, *voisé, voisement* (n.m.): Sound produced with the vibrations of the vocal folds.

voiceless, *non voisé* (*sourd*) (adj.): Sound produced with no vibrations of the vocal folds (not synonym of devoiced*).

voice onset time (VOT), *début du voisement* (n.m.): Time interval between the stop release and the onset of voicing as discerned on the waveform in terms of periodic (repeating) cycles of laryngeal pulses.

vowel harmony, *harmonie vocalique* (n.f.): Vowel-to-vowel assimilation* which, in French, makes all non word-final mid vowels in open syllables assimilate in height to the final, primary stressed vowel of the word.

vowel quadrilateral, *quadrilatère vocalique* (n.m.): Diagram of a schematized vowel space on which the vertical axis shows the tongue 'height', while the horizontal axis depicts tongue 'fronting'.

Vulgar Latin, *latin vulgaire* (n.m.): Vernacular* (spoken) varieties of Latin used mostly in reference to the western provinces of the Roman Empire.

wh-question, *question partielle* (n.f.): see partial question*.

word-compounding, *composition* (n.f.): Formation of new words by combining two or more existing words, e.g. *gratte-ciel* 'skyscraper'.

yes-no question, *question totale* (n.f.): see total question*.

References

Académie Française (1704) *Observations de l'Académie Françoise sur les remarques de M. de Vaugelas*, Paris: Jean-Baptiste Coignard.

Aebischer, Paul (ed.) (1965) *Le Voyage de Charlemagne à Jérusalem et à Constantinople*, Genève: Droz.

Ägren, John (1973) *Étude sur quelques liaisons facultatives dans le français de la conversation radiophonique: fréquences et facteurs*, Uppsala: Uppsala University Press.

Akmajian, Adrian, Demers, Richard A., Farmer, Ann K., and Harnish, Robert M. (1997) 'Pragmatics: The Study of Language Use and Communication', in *Linguistics: An Introduction to Language and Communication*. London, Cambridge (MA): MIT Press, pp. 343–393.

Alaoui, Khalid (2003) 'Petite histoire de la néologie: approche conceptuelle et idéologique (XVIe–XIXe siècle)', in Jean-François Sablayrolles (ed.) *L'innovation lexicale*, Paris: Honoré Champion, pp. 149–180.

Aleong, S. (1984) 'Naissance et diffusion du suffixe (o)thon dans le lexique québécois', *Cahiers de Lexicologie* 45: pp. 130–138.

Anzorge, Isabelle (1995) 'La variante topolectale. Problèmes posés dans le cadre exolingue du Togo', in Michel Francard and Danièle Latin (eds.), *Le régionalisme lexical*, Louvain-la-Neuve: Duculot, pp. 101–109.

Armstrong, Nigel (2001) *Social and Stylistic Variation in Spoken French*, Amsterdam, Philadelphia: John Benjamins.

Armstrong, Nigel and Jamin, Michael (2002) 'Le français des banlieues: uniformity and discontinuity in the French of the Hexagon', in K. Salhi (ed.), *French in and out of France: Language Policies, Intercultural Antagonisms and Dialogues*, Bern: Peter Lang, pp. 107–136.

Armstrong, Nigel and Smith, Alan (2002) 'The Influence of Linguistic and Social Factors on the Recent Decline of French *ne*', *Journal of French Language Studies* 12(1): pp. 23–41.

Ashby, William J. (1981) 'The Loss of the Negative Particle *ne* in French: a Syntactic Change in Progress', *Language* 57: pp. 674–687.

Ashby, William J. (1991) 'When Does Variation Indicate Linguistic Change in Progress?', *Journal of French Language Studies* 1(1): pp. 1–19.

Ashby, William J. (1992) 'The Variable Use of *on* versus *tu/vous* for Indefinite Reference in Spoken French', *Journal of French Language Studies*, 2(2): pp. 135–157.

Ashby, William J. (2001) 'Un nouveau regard sur la chute du *ne* en français parlé tourangeau: s'agit-il d'un changement en cours?', *Journal of French Language Studies* 11(1): pp. 1–22.

ATILF: 'Analyse et Traitement Informatique de la Langue Française', on-line dictionary at http://atilf.atilf.fr/tlf.htm

Austin, John L. (1962) *How to Do Things with Words*, Oxford: Oxford University Press.

Ayres-Bennett, Wendy (2004) *Sociolinguistic Variation in Seventeenth-Century France. Methodology and Case Studies*, Cambridge: Cambridge University Press.

Azra, Jean-Luc and Cheneau, Véronique (1994) 'Language Games and Phonological Theory: Verlan and the Syllabic Structure of French', *Journal of French Language Studies*, 4(2): pp. 147–170.

Bach, Kent and Harnish, Robert M. (1979) Linguistic Communication and Speech Acts, Cambridge (MA): MIT Press.

Bakos, Ferenc (1955) 'Contributions à l'étude des formules de politesse en ancien français', *Acta Linguistica Hungarica* 5: pp. 296–367.

Bar-Hillel, Yehoshua (1954) 'Indexical Expressions', *Mind* 63: pp. 359–379.

Baudino, Claudie (2001) *Politique de la langue et différence sexuelle. La politisation du genre des noms de métier*, Paris: L'Harmattan.

Bauer, Brigitte L. M. (2003) 'The Adverbial Formation in *-mente* in Vulgar and Late Latin. A Problem in Grammaticalization', in Heikki Solin, Martti Leiwo, and Hilla Halla-aho (eds.) *Latin vulgaire – Latin Tardif VI. Actes du VIe colloque international sur le latin vulgaire et tardif*, Hildesheim, Zurich, New York: Olms-Weidmann, pp. 439–457.

Bauer, Laurie (2001) *Morphological Productivity*, Cambridge: Cambridge University Press.

Beard, Robert (1995) *Lexeme-Morpheme Base Morphology: A General Theory of Inflection and Word Formation*, Albany, NY: SUNY Press.

Beeching, Kate (2002) *Gender, Politeness and Pragmatic Particles in French*, Amsterdam: John Benjamins.

Benguerel, A.-P. and Cowan, Helen A. (1974) 'Coarticulation of Upper Lip Protrusion in French', *Phonetica* 30: pp. 41–55.

Benveniste, Emile (1966) *Problèmes de linguistique générale*, vol. 1, Paris: Gallimard.

Berger, Roger and Brasseur, Annette (eds.) (2004) *Les séquences de Sainte Eulalie*, Genève: Droz.

Blampain, Daniel (ed.) (1997) *Le français en Belgique: une langue, une communauté*, Louvain-la-Neuve: Duculot.

Blanche-Benveniste, Claire and Jeanjean, Colette (1987) *Le français parlé: Transcription et édition*, Paris: Didier érudition.

Blanchet, Philippe (1995) *La Pragmatique: d'Austin à Goffman*, Paris: Bertrand-Lacoste.

Blondeau, Hélène (2001) 'Real-Time Changes in the Paradigm of Personal Pronouns in Montreal French', *Journal of Sociolinguistics*, 5(4): pp. 453–474.

Blondin, Jean-Noël (1823) *Manuel de la pureté du langage*, Paris: Chez l'auteur.

Boë, Louis-Jean, Heim, Jean-Louis, Honda, Kiyoshi, and Maeda, Shinji (2002) 'The Potential Neanderthal Vowel Space was as Large as that of Modern Humans' *Journal of Phonetics* 30: pp. 465–484.

Bothorel, André, Simon, P., Wioland, F., and Zerling, J.-P. (1986) *Cinéradiographie des voyelles et consonnes du français*, Strasbourg: Institut de Phonétique de Strasbourg.

Bourciez, E. J. and Bourciez, Jean (1978) *Phonétique Française, étude historique*, Paris: Klincksieck.

Boysson-Bardies, Bénédicte de (1999) *How Language Comes to Children: From Birth to Two Years*, Cambridge (MA): MIT Press.

Brault, Grégoire (2004) 'Pour une typologie des emplois de *là-bas*', *Lingvisticæ Investigationes,* 27(1): pp. 25–45.

Browman, P. Catherine and Goldstein, Louis (1986) 'Towards an Articulatory Phonology', *Phonology Yearbook* 3: pp. 219–252.

Brown, Penelope and Levinson, Stephen C. (1986) *Politeness: Some Universals in Language Use*, Cambridge: Cambridge University Press.

Brown, Rebecca and Jun, Sun-Ah (2002) 'Intonational Phonology and the Domain of French Liaison', *Paper presented at the First Joint Meeting of the ASA and IFA*, Cancun (Mexico): Mexican Institute of Acoustics, manuscript.

Brown, Roger and Gilman, Albert (1960) 'The Pronouns of Power and Solidarity', in Thomas A. Sebeok (ed.), *Style in Language*, Cambridge, (MA): MIT Press, pp. 253–276.

Brunet, Etienne (2003) http://www.eduscol.education.fr/DO102/liste-mots-frequents. htm

Brunot, Ferdinand (1891) *La doctrine de Malherbe d'après son commentaire sur Desportes*, Paris: G. Masson.

Brunot, Ferdinand (1966) *Histoire de la langue française*, Paris: Armand Colin.

Bryan, Anne-Marie (1972) 'Le "*tu*" et le "*vous*"', *The French Review* 45: pp. 1007–1010.

Bustin-Lekeu, Francine (1973) 'Tutoiement et vouvoiement chez les lycéens français', *The French Review* 46: pp. 773–782.

Bybee, Joan (2001) *Phonology and Language Use*, Cambridge: Cambridge University Press.

Byrne, Catherine and Foulkes, Paul (2004) 'The "Mobile Phone" Effect on Vowel Formants' *The International Journal of Speech, Language and the Law*, 11(1): pp. 83–102.

CALLIOPE (1989) *La parole et son traitement automatique*, Paris: Masson.

Carroll, Raymonde (1987) *Cultural Misunderstandings: The French–American Experience*, Chicago: The University of Chicago Press.

Carton, Fernand (1995) 'La prononciation du français', in Gérald Antoine and Robert Martin (eds.) *Histoire de la langue française 1914–1945*, Paris: CNRS-Éditions, pp. 27–59.

Carton, Fernand (1999) 'L'épithèse vocalique en français contemporain: étude phonétique', *Faits de langue* 13: pp. 35–45.

Casagrande, Jean (1984) *The Sound System of French*, Washington D. C: Georgetown University Press.

Catach, Nina (2001) *Histoire de l'orthographe française*, Paris: Slatkine-Honoré Champion.

Cervoni, Jean (1992) *L'énonciation*, Paris: Presses Universitaires de France.

Chansou, Michel (2003) *L'aménagement lexical en France pendant la période contemporaine (1950–1994). Étude de sociolexicologie*, Paris: Honoré Champion.

Charette, Monik (1991) *Conditions on Phonological Government*, Cambridge: Cambridge University Press.

Clark, Eve V. (1986) *The Acquisition of Romance with Special Reference to French*, Stanford: Stanford University Press.

Clark, Herbert H. and Carlson, T. B. (1982) 'Hearers and Speech Acts', *Language* 58: pp. 332–373.

Cohn, Abigail (1990) 'Phonetic and Phonological Rules of Nasalization', Ph.D. dissertation, UCLA.

Commission générale de terminologie et de néologie (2000) *Répertoire terminologique*, Paris: Éditions des journaux officiels.

Coquillon, A., Di Cristo, A., and Piterman, M. (2000) 'Marseillais et Toulousains gèrent-ils différemment leurs pieds? Caractéristiques prosodiques du schwa dans les parlers méridionaux', *Actes des XIIIèmes Journées d'Etudes sur la Parole*, Aussois, pp. 89–92.

Corbin, Danielle (1987) *Morphologie dérivationnelle et structuration du lexique*, Tübingen: Max Neimeyer.

Corneau, Caroline (2000) 'An EPG Study of Palatalization in French: Cross-dialect and Inter-subject Variation', *Language Variation and Change* 12(1): pp. 25–49.

Coveney, Aidan (1996) *Variability in Spoken French. A Sociological Study of Interrogation and Negation*, Exeter: Elm Bank Publications.

Coveney, Aidan (1998) 'Awareness of Linguistic Constraints on Variable *ne* Omission', *Journal of French Language Studies* 8(2): pp. 159–187.

Coveney, Aidan (2001) *The Sounds of Contemporary French. Articulation and Diversity*, Exeter: Elm Bank Publications.

Coveney, Aidan (2003) 'Anything *you* Can Do, *tu* Can Do Better: *tu* and *vous* as Substitutes for Indefinite *on* in French', *Journal of Sociolinguistics* 7: pp. 164–191.

Coveney, Aidan (2004) 'The Alternation Between *l'on* and *on* in Spoken French', *Journal of French Language Studies* 14(2): pp. 91–112.

Cruse, D. Alan (1986) *Lexical Semantics*, Cambridge: Cambridge University Press.

Crysmann, Berthold (2003) 'Clitic Climbing Revisited', in Y.-B. Kim and S. Wechsler (eds.), *Proceedings of the 9th International Conference on HPSG*, Stanford: CSLI, pp. 67–89.

Culioli, Antoine (1995) *Cognition and Representation in Linguistic Theory. Texts selected, edited, and introduced by Michel Liddle; translated with the assistance of John T. Stonham, Current issues in linguistic theory*, 112, Amsterdam, Philadelphia: John Benjamins.

Dal, Georgette (ed.) (2003) 'La productivité morphologique en questions et en expérimentations', *Langue Française* 140.

Déan-Laporte (1975) *Les contes manceaux. Récits et monologues en patois du Maine*, Le Mans: Éditions de la Société Littéraire du Maine.

De Cat, Cécile (2000) 'Towards a Unified Analysis of French Floating Quantifiers', *Journal of French Language Studies* 10(1): pp. 1–25.

Dees, Anthonij (1980) *Atlas des formes et des constructions des chartes françaises du 13e siècle*, Tübingen: Niemeyer.

Delais-Roussarie, Elizabeth (2000) 'Vers une nouvelle approche de la structure prosodique', *Langue Française* 126: pp. 92–112.

Delais-Roussarie, Elizabeth (2001) 'Prosodie des clitiques en français', in Claude Muller, Paulo de Carvalho, L. Labrune, F. Lambert, and K. Ploog (eds.) *Clitiques et cliticisation, Actes du colloque de Bordeaux, octobre 1998*, Paris: Honoré Champion, pp. 227–249.

Délégation générale à la langue française (1994) *Dictionnaire des termes officiels*, Paris: Direction des journaux officiels.

Dell, François (1973) *Les règles et les sons: Introduction à la phonologie générative*, Paris: Hermann.

Demolin, Didier (2001) 'Some Phonetic and Phonological Observations Concerning /ʀ/ in Belgian French', *Etudes and Travaux*, Université Libre de Bruxelles, 4: pp. 63–73.

Deshaies, Denise (1985) 'Références personnelles et types de discours en situation d'entrevue', in P. R. Léon and P. Perron. (eds.), *Le Dialogue*, Ottawa: Didier, pp. 77–91.

Dickey, Elizabeth (2002) *Latin Forms of Address: from Plautus to Apuleius*, Oxford: Oxford University Press.

Di Cristo, Albert (1999) 'Vers une modélisation de l'accentuation du français: première partie', *Journal of French Language Studies* 9(2): pp. 143–179.

Di Cristo, Albert (2000) 'Vers une modélisation de l'accentuation du français: deuxième partie', *Journal of French Language Studies* 10(1): pp. 27–44.

Di Cristo, Albert and Hirst, Daniel (1998) *Intonation Systems: A Survey of Twenty Languages*, Cambridge: Cambridge University Press.

Dionne, Narcisse-Eutrope (1912) *Une dispute grammaticale en 1842. Le G.-V. Demers vs. le G.-V. Maguire*, Québec: Laflamme and Proulx.

Di Vito, Nadine (1997) *Patterns Across Spoken and Written French*, Boston-New York: Houghton-Mifflin.

Dostie, Gaétane (2002) 'L'exemplarité de "par exemple". Un cas de pragmaticalisation en français québécois', *Journal of French Language Studies* 12: pp. 149–167.

Dubois, Jacques [Sylvius] (1531) *In linguam gallicam IsagΩge*, Paris: Robert Estienne.

Dubois, Jean (1962) *Étude sur la dérivation suffixale en français moderne et contemporain*, Paris: Larousse.

Dubois, Jean (1971) *Dictionnaire du français contemporain*, Paris: Larousse.

Dubois, Jean and Dubois-Charlier, Françoise (1999) *La derivation suffixale en français*, Paris: Nathan.

Ducrot, Oswald (1980) *Les mots du discours*, Paris: Les éditions du Minuit.

Dupleix, Scipion (1651) *Liberté de la langue françoise dans se pureté*, Paris: Denys Becnet.

Eckert, Penelope and McConnell-Ginet, Sally (1998) 'Communities of Practice: Where Language, Gender and Power All Live', in J. Coates (ed.), *Language and Gender: A Reader*, Oxford: Blackwell, pp. 448–494.

Eelen, Gino (2001) *Critique of Politeness Theories*, Manchester: St Jerome's Press.

Encrevé, Pierre (1988) *La Liaison avec et sans enchaînement*, Paris: Editions du Seuil.

Espinal, Teresa M. (1991) 'The Representation of Disjunct Constituents', *Language* 67(4): pp. 726–762.

Estienne, Henri (1565) *Traicte de la conformité du langage françois avec le grec*, Genève: H. Estienne.

Étiemble, René (1964) *Parlez-vous franglais?* Paris: Gallimard.

Ewert, Alfred (1933) *The French Language*, London: Faber and Faber.

Fagyal, Zsuzsanna (1998) 'Le retour du e final en français parisien: changement phonétique conditionné par la prosodie', in A. Englebert, M. Pierrard, L. Rosier, and D. Van Raemdonck (eds.) (2000) *Vivacité et diversité de la variation linguistique*, Vol. III, Tübigen: Max Niemeyer Verlag, pp. 151–160.

Fagyal, Zsuzsanna (2002) 'Prosodic Boundaries in the Vicinity of Utterance-medial Parentheticals in French, *Probus* 14(1): pp. 93–111.

Fagyal, Zsuzsanna (2004) 'Action des médias et interactions entre jeunes dans une banlieue ouvrière de Paris: Remarques sur l'innovation lexicale', in Thierry Bulot (ed.) *Les Parlers jeunes, le parler des jeunes*, Paris: L'Harmattan, pp. 41–60.

Fagyal, Zsuzsanna and Moisset, Christine (1999) 'Sound Change and Articulatory Release: Where and Why are High Vowels Devoiced in Parisian French?', *Proceedings of the XIVth International Congress of Phonetic Science*, San Francisco, vol. 1, pp. 309–312.

Fagyal, Zsuzsanna, Nguyen, Noël, and Boula de Mareüil, Philippe (2002) 'From *dilation* to Coarticulation: Is There Vowel Harmony in French?', *Studies in the Linguistic Sciences* 32(1): pp. 1–21.

Falkin, April (1988) 'Dialogue Analysis Beyond the Sentence Unit: A Comparison of *Huis Clos* and Spontaneous Conversation', *Language and Style* 21(2): pp. 203–255.

Faral, Edmond (1951) 'Quelques remarques sur le *Miracle de Théophile* de Rutebeuf', *Romania* 52: pp. 191–192.

Fay, Percival B. (1920) *The Use of tu and vous in Molière*, Berkeley: University of California Press.

Fennell, T. G. (1975) *La morphologie du futur en moyen français*, Genève: Droz.

Féraud, Jean-François (1787) *Dictionnaire critique de la langue française*, Marseille: Jean Mossy.

Flaitz, Jeffra (1988) *The Ideology of English: French Perceptions of English as a World Language*, Berlin, NewYork: Mouton de Gruyter.

Fónagy, Iván (1989) 'Le français change de visage', *Revue Romane* 24(2): pp. 225–254.

Fougeron, Cécile and Delais-Roussarie, Elisabeth (2004) '"Fais_en à Fez_en avril": étude comparative de la liaison et de l'enchaînement', XXVe *Journées d'Etude sur la Parole*, Fes (Maroc), pp. 221–224.

Foulet, Lucien (1919 [1968]) *Petite syntaxe de l'ancien français*, Paris: Champion.

Fournier, Nathalie (1998) *Grammaire du français classique*, Paris: Belin.

Fuchs, Catherine (ed.) (1997) *La place du sujet en français contemporain*, Louvain: Duculot.

Gadet, Françoise (1992) *Le français populaire*, Deuxième édition corrigée, Paris: Presses Universitaires de France.

Gadet, Francoise (1997) *Le français ordinaire*, Paris: Armand Colin.

Gardner, Rosalyn and Greene, Marion A. (1958) *A Brief Description of Middle French Syntax*, Chapel Hill: University of North Carolina Press.

Gardner-Chloros, Penelope (1991) 'Ni *tu* ni *vous*: principes et paradoxes dans l'emploi des pronoms d'allocution en français contemporain', *Journal of French Language Studies*, 1(2): pp. 139–155.

Garmadi, Juliette (1981) *La sociolinguistique*, Paris: Presses Universitaires de France.

Gilliéron, Jules and Edmont, Edouard (1902–1920) *Atlas: linguistique de la France*, Paris: Honoré Champion.

Girard, Gabriel (1736) *Synonymes françois, leurs significations et le choix quil en faut faire pour parler avec justesse*, Paris: Laurent d'Houry.

Goffman, Erving (1967) *Interaction Ritual*, Pantheon: New York.

Gordon, Mathew (2003) 'Collecting Phonetic Data on Endangered Languages', *Proceedings of the 15th International Congress of Phonetic Sciences*, Barcelona, pp. 207–210.

Goudailler, Jean-Pierre (1997) *Comment tu tchatches!* Paris: Maisonneuve et Larose.

Grammont, Maurice (1939) *Traité de phonétique*, Paris: Delagrave.

Green, Georgia (1996) *Pragmatics and Natural Language Understanding*, Philadelphia: Laurence Erlbaum.

Grevisse, Maurice (1968) *Précis de grammaire française*, Gembloux: Duculot.

Grevisse, Maurice (1969) *Le bon usage. Grammaire française avec des remarques sur la langue française d'aujourd'hui*, 9th ed., Gembloux: Duculot.

Grevisse, Maurice (1980) *Le bon usage,* 11th ed., Gembloux: Duculot.

Grice, Paul, H. (1957) 'Meaning', *The Philosophical Review* 66: pp. 667–688.

Grice, Paul, H. (1975) 'Logic and Conversation', in Peter Cole and Jerry Morgan (eds.), *Syntax and semantics. Speech Acts, Vol. III*, New York: Academic Press, pp. 41–58.

Grimes, Barbara F. and Pittman, Richard S. (ed.) (1996) *Ethnologue: Languages of the World*, 13th edition, Dallas (TX): Summer Institute of Linguistics.

Halle, P. A., de Boysson-Bardies, B. and Vihman, Marylin M. (1991) 'Beginnings of Prosodic Organization: Intonation and Duration Patterns of Disyllables Produced by Japanese and French Infants', *Language and Speech* 34(4): pp. 299–318.

Hambye, Philippe and Michel Francard (2004). 'Le français dans la Communauté Wallonie-Bruxelles. Une variété en voie d'autonomisation?', *Journal of French Language Studies* 14(1): pp. 41–59.

Hansen, Anita (1994) 'Etude du E caduc-stabilisation en cours et variations lexicales' *Journal of French Language Studies* 4(1): pp. 25–54.

Hansen, Anita (2001) 'Lexical Diffusion as a Factor of Phonetic Change: The Case of Modern French Nasal Vowels', *Language Variation and Change* 13(2): pp. 209–252.

Hansen, Anita and Mosegaard, H. Maj-Britt (2003) 'Le schwa prépausal et l'interaction', in Anita Hansen and H. M.-B. Mosegaard (eds.), *Structures linguistiques et interactionnelles dans le français parlé*, Copenhagen: Museum Tusculanum Press, pp. 89–109.

Harris, Martin and Vincent, Nigel (1988) *The Romance Languages*, New York: Oxford University Press.

Hauber, Rose Marie (Sister) (1938) *The Late Latin Vocabulary of the Moralia of Saint Gregory the Great: A Morphological and Semasiological Study*, Washington DC: Catholic University of America Press.

Haverling, Gerd (1998) 'On the 'illogical' *vos* in Late Latin Epistolography', in Louis Callebat (ed.) *Latin vulgaire, latin tardif* IV. *Actes du 4e colloque international sur le latin vulgaire et tardif. Caen, 2–5 septembre 1994*, Hildesheim, Zürich, New York: Olms-Weidmann, pp. 337–353.

Herman, József (1989) 'Accusativus cum infinitivo et subordonnée à *quod, quia* en latin tardif – nouvelles remarques sur un vieux problème', in Gualtiero Calboli (ed.) *Subordination and Other Topics in Latin. Proceedings of the Third Colloquium on Latin Linguistics, Bologna, 1–5 April 1985*, Amsterdam, Philadelphia: John Benjamins, pp. 33–153.

Herman, József (2000) *Vulgar Latin*, translated by Roger Wright, University Park (PA): Pennsylvania State University Press.

Hollerbach, Wolf (1994) *The Syntax of Contemporary French*, Lanham (MD): University Press of America.

Jacob, Daniel (1998) 'À propos de la périphrase *habeo* + participe parfait passif', in Louis Callebat (ed.) *Latin vulgaire, latin tardif IV. Actes du 4e colloque international sur le latin vulgaire et tardif. Caen, 2–5 septembre 1994*, Hildesheim, Zürich, New York: Olms-Weidmann, pp. 367–381.

Jeanneret, Thérèse (1999) *La coénonciation en français: Approches discursive, conversationnelle et syntaxique*, Bern, Berlin, Frankfurt: Peter Lang.

Jenkins, T. Atkinson (ed.) (1924) *La Chanson de Roland*, Boston: D. C. Heath.

Jones, Michael A. (1996) *Foundations of French Syntax*, Cambridge: Cambridge University Press.

Joran, Théodore (1928) *Les manquements à la langue française. Tournures et locutions vicieuses méthodiquement classées et redressées*. 3e édition. Paris: Gabriel Beauchesne.

Jourda, Pierre (ed.) (1965) *Conteurs français du XVIe siècle*, Paris: Bibliothèque de la Pléaide.

Jun, Sun-Ah and Fougeron, Cécile (1995) 'The Accentual Phrase and the Prosodic Structure of French', *Proceedings of the ICPhS of Stockholm*, vol. 2, pp. 722–725.

Jun, Sun-Ah and Fougeron, Cécile (2000) 'A Phonological Model of French Intonation', in A. Botinis (ed.) *Intonation: Analysis, Modeling and Technology*, Amsterdam: Kluwer, pp. 209–242.

Jun, Sun-Ah and Fougeron, Cécile (2002) 'Realizations of Accentual Phrase in French Intonation', *Probus* 14(1): pp. 147–172.

Karlsson, Keith E. (1981) *Syntax and Affixation. The Evolution of MENTE in Latin and Romance*, Tübingen: Max Niemeyer.

Kassai, Ilona (2001) 'Fiziológiai ritmus a fonológiában?' [Physiological rhythm in phonology?] in M. Bakró-Nagy, E. K. Kiss, and Z. Bánréti (eds.), *Ujabb tanulmányok a strukturális magyar nyelvtan és a nyelvtörténet köréból*, Budapest: Osiris, pp. 344–354.

Keane, Mark T. and Costello, Fintan J. (1997) 'Where do "Soccer Moms" Come From?: Cognitive Constraints on Noun–Noun Compounding in English', in Tony Veale (ed.), *Proceedings of MIND II*, http://www.cs.ucd.ie/staff/fcostello/home/papers/CostelloKeane97b.pdf

Kennedy, Elspeth (1972) 'The use of *Tu* and *Vous* in the First Part of the Old French Prose *Lancelot*', in F. J. Barnett, A. D. Crow, C. A. Robson, W. Rothwell, and S. Ullmann (eds.), *History and Structure of French. Essays in Honour of Professor T. B. W. Reid*, Totowa (NJ): Rowman and Littlefield, pp. 135–149.

Kibbee, Douglas (1995) 'Assertion/atténuation, subjectivité/objectivité en anglais et en français: 'seem'/'sembler'', in Michel Ballard (ed.), *Relations discursives et traduction*, Lille: Presses Universitaires de Lille, pp. 73–87.

King, Ruth and Nadasdy, Terry (1999) 'The Expression of Evidentiality in French–English Bilingual Discourse' *Language in Society* 28(3): pp. 355–365.

Kleiber, Georges (1990) *La sémantique du prototype. Catégories et sens lexical*, Paris: Presses Universitaires de France.

Knecht, Paul and Rubattel, Christophe (1984) 'A propos de la dimension sociolinguistique du français en Suisse romande', *Le Français moderne*, 52(2): pp. 138–150.

Laberge, Suzanne and Sankoff, Gillian (1979) 'Anything *you* can do', in G. Sankoff (ed.) *The Social Life of Language*, Philadelphia: University of Pennsylvania Press, pp. 271–293.

Labov, William (2001) *Principles of Linguistic Change: Social Factors*, Oxford: Blackwell.

Lacheret-Dujour, Anne and Beaugendre, Frédérique (1999) *La Prosodie du français*, Paris: CNRS Editions.

Ladefoged, Peter (ed.) (1999) *The Handbook of the International Phonetic Association*, Cambridge: Cambridge University Press.

Ladefoged, Peter and Maddieson, Ian (1996) *The Sounds of the World's Languages*, Oxford: Blackwell.

Lakoff, George and Johnson, Mark (2003) *Metaphors We Live By*, Chicago: University of Chicago Press.

Lambert, Wallace E. (1967) 'The Use of *tu* and *vous* as Forms of Address in French Canada, a Pilot Study', *Journal of Verbal Learning and Verbal Behavior* 6: pp. 614–617.

Landick, Marie (1995) 'The Mid-Vowels in Figures: Hard Facts', *The French Review* 69(1): pp. 88–102.

Landick, Marie (2004) *Enquête sur la prononciation du français de référence*, Collection Espaces Discursifs, Paris: L'Harmattan.

Langlois, Ernest (ed.) (1965) *Le couronnement de Louis, Chanson de geste du XII siècle*, Paris: H. Champion.

Leech, Geoff, N. (1983) *Principles of Pragmatics*, London: Longman.

Lefebvre-Teillard, Anne (1990) *Le nom: droit et histoire*, Paris: Presses Universitaires de France.

Le Gal, Étienne (1932) *Cent manières d'accommoder le français*, Paris: Nouvelle librairie française.

Lehmann, Alise and Martin-Berthet, Françoise (2000) *Introduction à la lexicologie. Sémantique et morphologie*, Paris: Nathan.

Lehmann, Gun (1959) 'L'emploi moderne de l'adverbe français *tellement*, comparé à celui du *si* et du *tant* d'intensité', Lund: CWK Gleerup.

Lennig, Matthew (1978) 'Acoustic Measurement of Linguistic Change: the Modern Paris Vowel System', Ph.D. dissertation, University of Pennsylvania.

Léon, Pierre (1973) 'Réflexions idiomatologiques sur l'accent en tant que métaphore sociolinguistique', *The French Review* 46, pp. 783–789.

Léon, Pierre (1992) *Phonétisme et prononciation du français*, Paris: Nathan Université.

Léon, Pierre (1993) *Précis de phonostylistique: parole et expressivité*, Paris: Nathan Université.

Léon, Pierre and Carton, Fernand (1983) *Les accents des français*, Paris: Hachette. http://accentsdefrance.free.fr/

Lepoutre, David (1997) *Coeur de banlieue: codes, rites, et langages*, Paris: Odile Jacob.

Lieberman, Philip and Crelin, E. S. (1971) 'On the Speech of Neanderthal Man', *Linguistic Inquiry* 2: pp. 203–222.

Littré, Émile (1878) *Dictionnaire de la langue française*, Paris: Hachette.

Lodge, R. Anthony (2004) *A Sociolinguistic History of Parisian French*, Cambridge: Cambridge University Press.

Ludwig, Pascal (1997) *Le Langage: textes choisis et présentés*, Paris: GF Flammarion.

Luzzati, Daniel (1982) '*Ben* appui du discours', *Le Français Moderne* 50: pp. 193–207.

Mackenzie, Fraser (1939) *Les relations de l'Angleterre et de la France d'après le vocabulaire*, Paris: E. Droz.

Maddieson, Ian (1984) *Patterns of Sounds*, Cambridge: Cambridge University Press.

Malderez, Isabelle (1991) 'Tendance de neutralisation des oppositions entre voyelles nasales dans la parole des jeunes gens d'Ile-de-France', in *Actes du XIIème Congrès international des sciences phonétiques: 19–24 août 1991 Aix-en-Provence, France*, Aix-en-Provence: Université de Provence, vol. 2, pp. 174–177.

Malécot, André and Paul Lindsay (1976) 'The Neutralization of /æ/ – ɛ̃/ in French', *Phonetica* 33(1): pp. 45–61.

Maley, Catherine A. (1974) *The Pronouns of Address in Modern Standard French*, University (MS): Romance Monographs, Inc.

Mamavi, Gina, Depecker, Loïc, and Chansou, Michel (1997) *La mesure des mots: cinq études d'implantation terminologique*, Rouen: Publications de l'Université de Rouen.

Marchello-Nizia, Christiane (1979) *Histoire de la langue française aux XIVe et XVe siècles*, Paris: Bordas.

Marchello-Nizia, Christiane (1999) *Le français en diachronie*, Gap: Ophrys.

Marguérite de Navarre (ca.1546 [1999]) *Heptaméron*, Édition critique par Renja Salminen, Genève: Droz.

Martin, Elizabeth (2006) *Marketing Identities Through Language: English and Global Imagery in French Advertising*, New York: Palgrave Macmillan.

Martin, James, G. and Bunnell, Timothy H. (1981) 'Perception of Anticipatory Coarticulation Effects', *Journal of Acoustical Society of America* 69: pp. 559–567.

Martin, Pierre (2002) 'Le système vocalique du français du Québec: de l'acoustique à la phonologie', *La Linguistique* 38(2): pp. 71–88.

Martineau, France and Mougeon, Raymond (2003) 'A sociolinguistic study of the Origins of *ne* Deletion in European and Quebec French'. *Language* 79(1): pp. 118–152.

Martinet, André (1969) 'De l'économie des formes du verbe en français parlé', in *Le français sans fard*, Paris: Presses Universitaires de France, pp. 91–120.

Martinon, Philippe (1927) *Comment on parle en français, La langue parlée correcte comparée avec la langue littéraire et la langue familière*, Paris: Larousse.

Marty, Fernand (1975) *Elements for Self-Instruction in French*, Champaign (IL): Audio-Visual Publications.

Marty, Fernand (2001) 'Les signaux morphologiques du français parlé', *Le Français Moderne* 69(2): pp. 211–240.

McCool, George J. (1994) 'Teaching the Formation of Questions: Lessons from New French', *Modern Language Journal* 78: pp. 56–60.

Meigret, Louis (1550) *Tretté de la grammère françoeze*, Paris: Chrestien Wechel.

Merle, Pierre (2000) *Argot, verlan et tchatches*, Paris: Les Essentiels de Milan.

Mettas, Odette (1979) *La prononciation parisienne: Aspects phonique d'un sociolecte parisien (du Faubourg Saint-Germain à la Muette)*, Paris: Conseil International de la Langue Française et Laboratoire des Langues et Civilisations à Tradition Orale du CNRS.

Miller, Jessica S. and Fagyal, Zsuzsanna (2005) 'Phonetic Cues to Common and Special Cases of Liaison: Looking for a Prosodic Domain', in Gess, Randall S. and Rubin, Edward J. (eds.) (2005) *Theoretical and Experimental Approaches to Romance Linguistics (LSRL)* Salt Lake City, Utah, Amsterdam, Philadelphia: John Benjamins, pp. 179–196.

Miller, Philippe, A. and Sag, Ivan A. (1997) 'French Clitic Movement without Clitics or Movement', *Natural Language and Linguistic Theory* 15(5): pp. 573–639.

Mills, Sarah (2003) *Gender and Politeness*, Cambridge: Cambridge University Press.

Milroy, James and Milroy, Leslie (1985) *Authority in Language. Investigating standard English*, London: Routledge.

Moisset, Christine (1996) 'The Status of h-aspiré in French Today', in *University of Pennsylvania Working Papers in Linguistics*, 3(1): pp. 223–236.

Moisset, Christine (2000) 'Variable Liaison in Parisian French', Ph.D. Dissertation, University of Pennsylvania.

Molinelli, Piera (1989) 'Double Negation from Latin to Italian', in Gualtiero Balboli (ed.) *Subordination and Other Topics in Latin. Proceedings of the Third Colloquium on Latin Linguistics, Bologna, 1–5 April 1985*, Amsterdam, Philadelphia: John Benjamins, pp. 611–633.

Molinier, Christian and Françoise Levrier (2000) *Grammaire des adverbes, Description des formes en -ment*, Genève-Paris: Droz.

Montagu, Julie (2004) 'Les sons sous-jacents aux voyelles nasales en français parisien', in *Actes des XXVe Journées d'Etudes sur la Parole*, Fes (Maroc), Aix-en-Provence: Université de Provence, pp. 385–388.

Montreuil, Jean-Pierre (2002) 'Vestigial Feet in French', in *Proceedings of the 2002 Texas Linguistic Society Conference on Stress in Optimality Theory*, The University of Texas at Austin, http://uts.cc.utexas.edu/~tls/2002tls/Jean-Pierre_Montreuil.pdf

Moreau, Marie-Louise (1986) 'Les séquences préformées: entre les combinaisons libres et les idiomatismes. Le cas de la négation avec ou sans *ne*', *Le Français Moderne* 54: pp. 137–160.

Morel, Mary-Annick and Danon-Boileau, Laurent (1998) *Grammaire de l'intonation: L'exemple du français*, Paris: Ophrys.

Morford, Janet (1997) 'Social Indexicality in French Pronominal Address', *Journal of Linguistic Anthropology*, 7(1): pp. 3–37.

Morin, Yves-Charles (1994) 'Quelques réflexions sur la formation des voyelles nasales en français', *Communication and Cognition* 27: pp. 27–110.

Mufwene, Salikoko (2001) *The Ecology of Language Evolution*, Cambridge: Cambridge University Press.

Muller, Claude (1984) 'L'association négative', *Langue française* 62: pp. 59–94.

Nespor, Marina and Vogel, Irene (1986) *Prosodic Phonology*, Dordrecht: Foris.

Nguyen, Noël and Fagyal, Zsuzsanna (in press) 'Acoustic aspects of vowel harmony in French', *Journal of Phonetics*.

Noailly, Michèle (1990) *Le substantif épithète*, Paris: Presses Universitaires de France.

Nunn, H. P. V. (1963) *An Introduction to the Study of Ecclesiastical Latin*, third edition, Oxford: Basil Blackwell.

Nye, Edward (2000) *Literary and Linguistic Theories in Eighteenth-Century France. From Nuances to Impertinence*, Oxford: Oxford University Press.

Nyembwe, Ntita (1995) *Le français au Zaïre ou le français zaïrois. Considérations lexicales*, in M. Francard and D. Latin (eds.) *Le régionalisme lexical*, Louvain-la-Neuve: Duculot, pp. 111–118.

Nyrop, Kristoffer (1914) *Grammaire historique de la langue française*, Copenhague: Gyldendalske Boghandel Nordisk Forlag.

Office de la langue française (1986) *Titres et fonctions au féminin: essai d'orientation de l'usage*, Quebec: Office de la langue française.

Olcott, George N. (1898) *Studies in the Word Formation of the Latin Inscriptions. Substantives and Adjectives. With Special Reference to the Latin Sermo Vulgaris*, Rome: Sallustian Typography.

Oukada, Larbi (1982) 'On *On*', *The French Review*, 56(1): pp. 93–105.

Palsgrave, Jehan (1530) *Lesclarcissment de la langue Francoyse*, London: R. Pynson.

Papen, Robert and Rottet, Kevin (1997) 'A Structural Sketch of the Cajun French Spoken in Lafourche and Terrebonne Parishes', in Albert Valdman (ed.) *French and Creole in Louisiana*, New York: Plenum, pp. 71–108.

Paradis, Carole and Prunet, Jean-François (2000) 'Nasal Vowels as Two Segments: Evidence from Borrowings', *Language* 76(2): pp. 324–357.

Pasquier, Estienne (1596) *Les recherches de la France*, Paris: G. de Luyne.

Peeters, Bert (2004) '*Tu* ou *vous?*', *Zeitschrift für französische Sprache und Literatur* 114: pp. 1–17.

Peterson, Axel (1929) *Le passage populaire des noms de personne à l'état de noms communs dans les langues romanes et particulièrement en français. Étude de sémantique*, Uppsala: Appelbergs Boktryckereri Aktiebolag.

PHONO (1998). 'Principales caractéristiques phonétiques du français québécois', web page maintained by the Phonetics Laboratory of Laval University, Québec: http://www.ciral.ulaval.ca/phonetique/phono/

Picone, Michael D. (1996) *Anglicisms, Neologisms and Dynamic French*, Amsterdam, Philadelphia: John Benjamins.

Platt de Concarneau (1835) *Dictionnaire critique et raisonné du langage vicieux ou réputé vicieux*, Paris: A. André.

Plénat, Marc (1985) 'Morphologie du largonji des loucherbem', *Langages* 78: pp. 73–95.

Poirier, Claude (1995) 'Les variantes topolectales du lexique français: Propositions de classement à partir d'exemples québécois', in M. Francard and D. Latin (eds.) *Le régionalisme lexical*, Louvain-la-Neuve: Duculot, pp. 13–56.

Pöll, Bernhard (2001) 'Français de référence et pluralité identitaire: un antagonisme inconciliable?', in M. Francard, G. Géron, and R. Wilmet (eds.) *Le français de référence. Constructions et appropriations d'un concept*, Louvain:VALIBEL, Vol. 2, pp. 141–151.

Pooley, Timothy (1996) *Chtimi: The Urban Vernaculars of Northern France*, Clevedon, Philadelphia: Multilingual Matters.

Pope, Mildred K. (1934) *From Latin to Modern French with Especial Consideration of Anglo-Norman. Phonology and Morphology*, Manchester: Manchester University Press.

Posner, Rebecca (1997) *Linguistic Change in French*, Oxford: Clarendon Press.

Post, Brechtje (2000) 'Pitch accents, Liaison and the Phonological Phrase in French', *Probus* 12: pp. 127–164.

Price, Glanville (1993) '*Pas (point)* Without *ne* in Interrogative Clauses', *Journal of French Language Studies* 3: pp. 191–195.

Price, Joseph Edward (1998) 'Motivations for Pronominal *alteros*-affixation in Proto-Romance and the Development of *vous autres* in French', unpublished MA thesis, University of South Carolina.

Priss, Uta (1996) 'Classification of Meronymy by Methods of Relational Concept Analysis', *Online Proceedings of the 1996 Midwest Artificial Intelligence Conference*, Bloomington (IN): Indiana University.

Pruvost, Jean (2003) 'La traque des mots "néologisme" et "néologie" dans les dictionnaires monolingues monovolumaires français de la fin du XVIIIe s. jusqu'au début du XXIe s.', in Jean-François Sablayrolles (ed.) *L'innovation lexicale*, Paris: Honoré Champion, pp. 181–205.

Rézeav, Pierre (2001) *Dictionnaire des régionalismes de France: géographie et histoire d'un patrimoine linguistique*, Bruxelles: De Boeck/Duculot.

Riallanu, Annie (1988) 'Review of Encrevé, Pierre, "Liaison avec et sans enchaînement: Phonologie multidimensionelle et usage du français"'. *Language* 66: pp. 134–138.

Rialland, Annie (1994) 'The Phonology and Phonetics of Extrasyllabicity in French', in Patricia A. Keating (ed.) *Phonological Structure and Phonetic Form: Papers in Laboratory Phonology III*, Cambridge: Cambridge University Press, Vol.3, pp.136–159.

Richelet, Pierre (1680) *Dictionnaire françois: contenant les mots et les choses, plusieurs nouvelles remarques sur la langue françoise: ses expressions propres, figurées & burlesques, la prononciation des mots difficiles, le genre de noms, le régime des verbes, avec les termes les plus connus des arts & des sciences: le tout tiré de l'usage et des bons auteurs de la langue françoise*, Genève: J.-H. Widerhold.

Rigault, André (1971) *La grammaire du français parlé*, Paris: Hachette.

Rigault, Lucien (1888) *Dictionnaire d'argot moderne*, Paris: P. Ollendorff.

Roques, Mario (ed.) (1970) *Les Romans de Chrétien de Troyes, édités d'après la copie de Guiot (Bibl. Nat., fr. 794), I Érec et Énide*, Paris: H. Champion.

Roulet, Eddy (1995) 'Geneva School', in Jef Ver schuren, Jan-Ola Ostman, Jan Blommaert, and Chris Bulcaen (eds.), *Handbook of Pragmatics*, Amsterdam, Philadelphia: John Benjamins, pp. 319–323.

Roulet, Eddy, Auchlin, Antoine, Rubattel, Christian, and Schelling, Marianne (1985) *L'articulation du discours en français contemporain*, Berne: Peter Lang.

Rouquier, Magali (2003) 'La sequence *est-ce* dans les interrogatives en *qui/que* en ancien et en moyen français', *Journal of French Language Studies* 13: pp. 339–362.

Rychner, Jean (ed.) (1967) *Les XV. Joies de Mariage*, Genève: Droz.

Sacks, Harvey (1992) *Lectures on Conversation*, Oxford: Blackwell.

Sankoff, Gillian, Blondeau, Hélène, and Charity, Anne (2001) 'Individual Roles in a Real-time Change: Montreal (r→R) 1947–1995', *Etudes and Travaux, Université Libre de Bruxelles* 4: pp. 141–157.

Sankoff, Gillian and Vincent, Dianne (1977) 'L'emploi productif du *ne* dans le français parlé à Montréal', *Le Français Moderne* 45: pp. 243–256.

Sauger-Préneuf, François (1843) *Des locutions vicieuses, les plus répandues dans la société, considérées sous le rapport de la Syntaxe et de la Prononciation, avec leur correction, d'après le Dictionnaire de l'Academie*, 3e édition, Limoges: Martial Ardant frères.

Saussure, Ferdinand de (1916) *Cours de linguistique générale*, Paris: Payot.

Schiffrin, Deborah (1987) *Discourse Markers*, Cambridge: Cambridge University Press.

Schliebitz, Victor (1886) *Die Person der Anrede in der französischen Sprache*, Breslau: Jungfer.

Scollon, Ronald, and Scollon, Suzanne W. (1995) *Intercultural Communication: A Discourse Approach*, Oxford: Blackwell.

Scullen, Mary Ellen (1997) *French Prosodic Morphology: A Unified Account*, Bloomington (IN): Indiana University Linguistics Club.

Searle, John (1969) *Speech Acts: An Essay in the Philosophy of Language*, Cambridge: Cambridge University Press.

Searle, John (1975) 'Indirect Speech Acts', in Peter Cole and Jerry Morgan (eds.) *Syntax and Semantics, Vol. 3, Speech Acts*, New York: Academic Press, pp. 59–82.

Seguin, Jean-Pierre (1972) *La langue française au XVIIIe siècle*, Paris, Bruxelles, Montréal: Bordas.

Seguin, Jean-Pierre, Bouverot, D., Caron, Philippe, Fournier, Nathalie, and Landy-Houillon, Isabelle (1990) 'Les marqueurs du mauvais usage dans le *Dictionaire critique de la langue française* de l'abbé Jean-François Féraud', *Lexique*, 9: pp. 129–151.

Selkirk, Elizabeth (1978) 'The French Foot: On the Status of French Mute e', *Studies in French Linguistics* 1: pp. 141–150.

Selkirk, Elizabeth (1986) 'On Derived Domains in Sentence Phonology', *Phonology Yearbook*, 3: pp. 371–405.

Sifianou, Maria (1992) *Politeness Phenomena in England and Greece*, Oxford: Clarendon.

Signol, Christian (1984) *Les cailloux bleus*, Paris: Robert Laffont.

Silverman, David and Sacks, Harvey (1998) *Social Science and Conversation Analysis*, Cambridge: Polity Press.

Singy, Pascal (1996) *L'Image du français en Suisse Romande: Une enquête sociolinguistique en Pays de Vaud*, Paris: L'Harmattan.

Smedley-Weill, Anette and Geoffroy-Poisson, Simone (2001). 'Les assemblées d'états et la mise en forme du droit. Comparaisons et analyses formelles des coutumes rédigées et réformées d'Auxerre, de Sens et de Touraine', *Cahiers du Centre de Recherches Historiques* 26 pp. 13–92.

Smith, Caroline (2003) 'Vowel Devoicing in Contemporary French', *Journal of French Linguistic Studies* 13(2): pp. 177–194.

Spencer-Oatey, H. (2000) *Culturally Speaking: Managing Rapport Through Talk Across Cultures*, London: Continuum.

Sperber, Dan and Wilson, Deidre (1986) 'Précis of Relevance: Communication and Cognition', *Behavioral and Brain Sciences* 10: pp. 697–699.

Steriade, Donca (1999) 'Lexical Conservatism in French Adjectival Liaison', *Formal Perspectives in Romance Linguistics: Selected Papers from the 28th LSRL*, University Park: Pennsylvania State University, pp. 243–270.

Streicher, Jeanne (1936) *Commentaires sur les remarques de Vaugelas par La Mothe le Vayer, Scipion Dupleix, Ménage, Bouhours, Conrart, Chapeliain, Patru, Thomas Corneille, Cassagne, Andry de Boisregard et l'Académie Française*. Paris: E. Droz.

Stenström, Anna-Brita, Andersen, Gisle, and Hasund, Kristine I. (2002) *Trends in Teenage Talk: Corpus Compilation, Analysis and Findings*, Amsterdam, Philadelphia: John Benjamins.

Tannen, Deborah (1990) *You Just Don't Understand: Women and Men in Conversation*, New York: William Morrow.

Teibeiriené, Nijole R. (2004) 'Les particularités morphosyntaxiques du français québécois', *Kalbotyra* 54(3): pp. 1–8.

Temple, Martine (1996) *Pour une sémantique des mots construits*, Villeneuve d'Ascq: Les Presses Universitaires du Septentrion.

Thibault, Linda and Ouellet, Marise (1996) 'Tonal Distinctions Between Emphatic Stress and Pretonic Lengthening in Quebec French', *4th International Conference of Spoken Language Processing (ICSLP)*, vol. 2, pp. 638–641.

Thiele, Johannes (1987). *La formation des mots en français moderne*, translated by André Clas, Montréal: Presses de l'Université de Montréal.

Thiesse, Anne-Marie (1991) *Écrire la France. Le mouvement littéraire régionaliste de langue française entre la Belle Époque et la Libération*, Paris: Presses Universitaires de France.

Thurot, Charles (1881–1883) *De la prononciation française depuis le commencement du XVIe siècle, d'après les témoignages des grammairiens*, Paris: Imprimerie Nationale.

Toolan, Michael, J. (1996) *Total Speech: An Integrational Linguistic Approach to Language*, Durham, London: Duke University Press.

Touratier, Christian (1998) 'Le mot, unité linguistique?' *Langues et Langage* 7: pp. 41–53.

Tranel, Bernard (1987) *The Sounds of French*, Cambridge: Cambridge University Press.

Tranel, Bernard (1996) 'French Liaison and Elision Revisited: A Unified Account within Optimality Theory', in Claudia Parodi, Carlos Quicoli, Mario Saltarelli, and Maria-Louisa Zubizarreta (eds.) *Aspects of Romance Linguistics*. Washington, D.C.: Georgetown University Press, pp. 433–455.

Trask, R. L. (1996) *A Dictionary of Phonetics and Phonology*, London, New York: Routledge.

Trubetzkoy, Nicholas (1939[1969]). *Principles of Phonology*, translated by Christiane Baltaxe, Berkeley: University of California Press.

Truchot, Claude (1990) *L'anglais dans le monde contemporain*, Paris: Le Robert.

Université du Québec *French language examination criteria* for entrance into the Université du Québec en Outaouais (http://www.uqo.ca//etudiants-actuels/guichet-etudiant/guide-francais.asp).

Väänänen, Veikko (1981) *Introduction au latin vulgaire. Troisième edition revue et augmentée*, Paris: Éditions Klincksieck.

Valdman, Albert (1993) *Bien entendu! Introduction à la prononciation française*, Englewood Cliffs (NJ): Prentice Hall.

Valdman, Albert and Iskrova, Iskra (2003) 'A New Look at Nasalization in Haitian Creole', in Ingo Plag (ed.) *The Phonology and Morphology of Creole Languages*, Tübigen: Max Niemeyer, pp. 25–41.

Van den Berghe, Christian L. (1976) *La phonostylistique du français*, The Hague, Paris: Mouton.

Vaudelin, Giles (1713) *Nouvelle Manière d'écrire comme on parle en France*, Paris: Veuve Jean Cot.

Vaugelas, Claude Favre de (1647 [1934]) *Remarques sur la langue françoise. Introduction, bibliographie, index par Jeanne Streicher*, Paris: Droz.

Vincent, Diane (1995) 'Remarques sur *par exemple* en français québécois', *Le Français Moderne* 63: pp. 55–71.

Vincent, Diane (2001) 'Remarques sur le tutoiement et le vouvoiement en français parlé au Québec', in *Actes du colloque "La journée du Québec"*, Copenhague: Institut d'études romanes, Université de Copenhague, pp. 11–22.

Walker, Douglas C. (1984) *The Pronunciation of Canadian French*, Ottawa: University of Ottawa Press.

Walker, Douglas C. (2001) *French Sound Structure*, Calgary: University of Calgary Press.

Walter, Henriette (1977) *La phonologie du français*, Paris: Presses Universitaires de France.

Walter, Henriette (1983) 'La nasal vélaire /ŋ/: un phonème du français?', *Langue française* 60: pp. 14–29.

Walter, Henriette (1994) 'Variétés actuelles des voyelles nasales du français', *Communication and Cognition* 27: pp. 223–235.

Walter, Henriette (2002) 'La dynamique phonologique peut-elle dépendre de la dynamique lexicale?', *La Linguistique*, 38(2): pp. 133–137.

Watson, Keith (1997) 'French Complement Clitic Sequences: A Template Approach', *Journal of French Language Studies* 7(1): pp. 69–89.

Wierzbicka, Anna (1980) *Lingua Mentalis: The Semantics of Natural Language*, Sydney: Academic Press.

Wierzbicka, Anna (1996) *Semantics, Primes and Universals*, Oxford: Oxford University Press.

Wionet, Chantal (2004) 'Les marques d'usage dans la première édition du *Dictionnaire de l'Académie Française* (1694)', contribution à une histoire des marques d'usage, *Cahiers de Lexicologie*, 84(1): 55–67.

Wisniewski, Edward (1995) 'Prior knowledge and functionally relevant features in concept learning', *Journal of Experimental Psychology: Learning, Memory, and Cognition* 21: pp. 449–468.

Yaeger-Dror, Malcah (2002) 'Register and Prosodic Variation, a Cross Language Comparison', *Journal of Pragmatics* 34: pp. 1495–1536.

Yaguello, Marina (1991) 'Les géminées de M. Rocard', in *En écoutant parler la langue*, Paris: Seuil, pp. 64–70.

Zeliqzon, L. (ed.) (1986) *La famille ridicule, Comédie messine en vers patois*, Metz: Verlag der Gesellschaft.

Zink, Gaston (1986 [1991]) *Phonétique historique du français* (3rd edn.), Paris: Presses Universitaires de France.

Zink, Gaston (1992) *Morphologie du français médiéval*, 2e édition mise a jour, Paris: Presses Universitaires de France.

Name index

Subject index